THE ROUTLEDGE HANDBOOK OF INFRASTRUCTURE DESIGN

The Routledge Handbook of Infrastructure Design explores the multifaceted nature of infrastructure through the global lens of architectural history. Infrastructure holds the world together. Yet even as it connects some people, it divides others, sorting access and connectivity through varied social categories such as class, race, gender, and citizenship. This collection examines themes across broad spans of time, raises questions of linkage and scale, investigates infrastructure as phenomenon and affect, and traces the interrelation of aesthetics, technology, and power.

With a diverse range of contributions from 33 scholars, this volume presents new research from regions including South and East Asia, Sub-Saharan Africa, South America, North America, Western Europe, the Middle East, and the former Soviet Union. This extraordinary group of authors bring close attention to the materials, functions, and aesthetics of infrastructure systems as these unfold within their cultural and political contexts. They provide not only new knowledge of specific artifacts, such as the Valens Aqueduct, the Hong Kong waterfront, and the Pan-American Highway, but also new ways of conceptualizing, studying, and understanding infrastructure as a worlding process.

The Routledge Handbook of Infrastructure Design provides richly textured, thoroughly evidenced, and imaginatively drawn arguments that deepen our understanding of the role of infrastructure in creating the world in which we live. It is a must-read for academics and students.

Joseph Heathcott is Chair of Urban and Environmental Studies at The New School in New York. He has held visiting positions at Princeton University School of Architecture, the London School of Economics, the University of Vienna, and Sciences Po, Paris. His most recent book is *Capturing the City: Photographs from the Streets of St. Louis* (2016).

THE ROUTLEDGE HANDBOOK OF INFRASTRUCTURE DESIGN

Global Perspectives from Architectural History

Edited by Joseph Heathcott

NEW YORK AND LONDON

Cover image: Galata Bridge, Istanbul, ca. 1900. Photochrome print courtesy of the Library of Congress, LC-DIG-ppmsc-06061

First published 2022
by Routledge
605 Third Avenue, New York, NY 10158

and by Routledge
4 Park Square, Milton Park, Abingdon, Oxon, OX14 4RN

Routledge is an imprint of the Taylor & Francis Group, an informa business

© 2022 selection and editorial matter, Joseph Heathcott; individual chapters, the contributors

The right of Joseph Heathcott to be identified as the author of the editorial material, and of the authors for their individual chapters, has been asserted in accordance with sections 77 and 78 of the Copyright, Designs and Patents Act 1988.

All rights reserved. No part of this book may be reprinted or reproduced or utilized in any form or by any electronic, mechanical, or other means, now known or hereafter invented, including photocopying and recording, or in any information storage or retrieval system, without permission in writing from the publishers.

Trademark notice: Product or corporate names may be trademarks or registered trademarks, and are used only for identification and explanation without intent to infringe.

Library of Congress Cataloging-in-Publication Data
Names: Heathcott, Joseph, 1968- editor.
Title: The Routledge handbook of infrastructure design: global perspectives from architectural history edited by Joseph Heathcott.
Description: New York, NY: Routledge, 2022. | Includes bibliographical references and index. | Identifiers: LCCN 2021036903 (print) | LCCN 2021036904 (ebook) | ISBN 9780367554910 (hardback) | ISBN 9781032188393 (paperback) | ISBN 9781003093756 (ebook)
Subjects: LCSH: Public works. | Architecture and society.
Classification: LCC TA145 .R756 2022 (print) | LCC TA145 (ebook) | DDC 624–dc23

LC record available at https://lccn.loc.gov/2021036903
LC ebook record available at https://lccn.loc.gov/2021036904

ISBN: 9780367554910 (hbk)
ISBN: 9781032188393 (pbk)
ISBN: 9781003093756 (ebk)

DOI: 10.4324/9781003093756

Typeset in Bembo Std
by KnowledgeWorks Global Ltd.

CONTENTS

List of Contributors   ix
Acknowledgments   xv

    Infrastructure Designs: Dreaming and Building Worlds   1
    Joseph Heathcott

PART I
Materialities   17

1   Kingship and the Rocks: Infrastructure and the Materiality of Empire   19
    Braden Lee Scott

2   In Between Technology and Architecture: Claude-Nicolas Ledoux and the French Royal *Saline*   30
    Carmelina Martinez

3   Cement as Weapon: Meta-Infrastructure in the "World's Last Cement Frontier"   40
    Robby Fivez and Monika Motylińska

4   Notes from the Underworld: Excavation as Architectural Counter-History   51
    Stefano Corbo

PART II
Embodiments   61

5   Virtual Gardens: Gendered Space in the History of Afghanistan's Telecommunications   63
    Hannah Ahlblad

6 Mobilizing Labor for Infrastructure in Northeast Brazil, 1915–1932 76
Laura Belik

7 Everyday Living in Cairo's City of the Dead 85
Reem Saad Sardina, Sherif Elfiki, and Ahmed El Antably

PART III
Natures **95**

8 Dams, Lakes, and Water Sports: Building a Hybrid Landscape in Belgium's Eau d'Heure Valley, 1933–1987 97
Marie Pirard

9 Pedagogic Landscapes: Recreation, Play, and Danish Infrastructure Design 108
Margaret Birney Vickery

10 A Vast Demographic Void: Infrastructure, Ecology, and the Amazon 118
Catherine Seavitt Nordenson

PART IV
Flows **129**

11 Visualizing the Valens Aqueduct in Early Modern Istanbul 131
Fatma Sarıkaya Işık and Pelin Yoncacı Arslan

12 The Airport Terminal: Circulation and Soft Power 142
Menno Hubregtse

13 The Porous Infrastructures of Somali Malls in Cape Town 153
Huda Tayob

PART V
City Making **163**

14 Bridging the Bosporus: Mobility, Geopolitics, and Urban Imaginary in Istanbul, 1933–1973 165
Sibel Bozdoğan

15 Brasilia, a Story Seen from the Roadside: Narratives of Landscape Transformation and the Technological Sublime 176
Sued Ferreira da Silva

16 More than a "Circulation Machine": Recasting the Geographies of
    Infrastructure in Modernist Urbanism   187
    Mejrema Zatrić

17 Infrastructure as a Political Tool of Regime Legitimization in Doha, Qatar 198
    Peter Chomowicz

PART VI
The Long Road   **209**

18 The Global Spread of Street Pavement Materials and Technology, 1820–1920 211
    Robin B. Williams

19 Parallel Lines: Urban Expressways in the United States   222
    Romina Canna

20 Good Neighbors and *Automovilistas*: Imaginaries of Hemispheric Travel along
    the Pan-American Highway, 1936–1942   234
    Dicle Taskin

PART VII
Power Fields   **245**

21 Nuclear Power Stations in Post-War Britain: Picturesque Landscapes for
    the Masses   247
    Laura Coucill and Luca Csepely-Knorr

22 TVA in the Desert: U.S. Development Projects in the Hashemite Kingdom
    of Jordan, 1951–1961   258
    Dalal Musaed Alsayer

23 Shaped from Above: Cartographic Domination and U.S. Military Infrastructure
    in 1950s Spain   269
    José Vela Castillo

PART VIII
Liquid Worlds   **281**

24 Water and Infrastructure in Late Colonial Guanajuato   283
    Luis Gordo Peláez

25 Land Reclamation in the Making of Hong Kong   294
    Charlie Qiuli Xue and Cong Sun

26 Bombay/Mumbai Waterfronts in the Hindi Film *Deewaar* [*The Wall*] (1975)   306
    Vandana Baweja

Index   318

CONTRIBUTORS

Hannah Ahlblad, Adjunct Professor of Architecture at University of San Francisco, holds an M.Arch from the University of Texas at Austin where her research on cognitive mapping was funded by the School of Architecture and the Teresa Lozano Long Institute of Latin American Studies (LLILAS). Her work explores the transformation of architectural symbolism and geopolitics in the age of social media. She is a project designer at Ann Beha Architects.

Dalal Musaed Alsayer is an Assistant Professor of Architecture at Kuwait University. Her research lies at the intersection of architecture, environment, and development in the context of Arabia during the twentieth century. She holds a Bachelor of Architecture from Kuwait University, postgraduate degrees from Columbia and Harvard, and a PhD from the University of Pennsylvania. She is the co-author of *Pan-Arab Modernism: History of Architectural Practice in The Middle East* (2021) and is the co-founding editor of *Current: Collective for Architecture History and Environment* (www.current-collective.org).

Ahmed El Antably is an Associate Professor in the Department of Architecture at the Arab Academy for Science, Technology, and Maritime Transport. His research interest is in the juncture of history, theory, and technology in architecture. He has published *Experiencing the Past: The Virtual (Re)Construction of Places* (2013), and many articles in international peer-reviewed journals and conferences.

Pelin Yoncacı Arslan is an Assistant Professor of Architecture at the Middle East Technical University Department of Architecture, Turkey. In 2015, she obtained her PhD in Architecture and Urban Design from UCLA. As an architect and an architectural historian, her research interests include historical topography of late antique and Byzantine cities, and 3D visualization and mapping tools applied in architectural history writing.

Vandana Baweja is an Associate Professor in the School of Architecture and the Sustainability Program at the University of Florida, Gainesville. She obtained her PhD in architecture from the University of Michigan, Ann Arbor. She was trained as an architect in New Delhi, India, and obtained a Master's in Architecture at the Architectural Association (AA) School of Architecture in London, UK. She is the co-editor of *Arris: The Journal of The Southeast Chapter of The Society of Architectural Historians*.

Laura Belik is a PhD candidate in architecture at University of California, Berkeley. Other publications by Belik include "Spatial Transformation and Debates on Urban Democracy: The Case of Minhocão Elevated Highway, São Paulo" in *The Routledge Handbook of Planning Megacities in the*

Global South (2020). Her current doctoral research focuses on the histories and dimensions of socio-spatial inequalities in the Brazilian Northeast region and how to interpret multiple memories of the built environment.

Sibel Bozdoğan is Visiting Professor of Modern Architecture and Urbanism at Boston University and has also taught history-theory courses at Rensselaer Polytechnic Institute, MIT and GSD/Harvard University. Interested in global histories of modern architecture, she is the author of *Modernism and Nation Building: Turkish Architectural Culture in the Early Republic* (the recipient of the 2002 Alice Davis Hitchcock Award of the Society of Architectural Historians) and *Turkey: Modern Architectures in History* (2012, co-authored with Esra Akcan).

Romina Canna is Assistant Professor and d-Lab Director at the School of Architecture and Design at IE University. She is also a Visiting Professor at the Technical School of Architecture in Valencia (ETSAV) and previously has taught at the Illinois Institute of Technology and in the National University of Rosario. Her research focuses on the relationship between infrastructure and urbanism in American cities.

Peter Chomowicz is an architect with a firm specializing in the architectural and spatial possibilities of institutional and cultural transformation. His academic appointments include Dean of Academic Affairs and Research at Virginia Commonwealth University in Qatar, Chair of the Environmental Design Department at the Maryland Institute, College of Art, and visiting professor at Brown University's Watson Institute. His work focuses on the origins of architecture and urban planning in the Middle East and its relationship to current building schemes.

Stefano Corbo is a practicing architect and Associate Professor at the Rhode Island School of Design. Before joining RISD, he taught at several academic institutions in Europe, the Middle East, and China. Corbo has contributed to many international journals and has published three books: *From Formalism to Weak Form: The Architecture and Philosophy of Peter Eisenman* (Ashgate/Routledge, 2014), *Interior Landscapes: A Visual Atlas* (2016) and, more recently, *Notes from the Underworld* (2019).

Laura Coucill is a Senior Lecturer in Architecture at Queen's University Belfast with practice expertise on large industrial and complex heritage sites. Her interest is in the spatial manifestation of culture, policy and technology. Laura's work adopts cross-thematic spatial analysis techniques, which combine historical and theoretical methods with contemporary data mapping to capture spatial capacity, operation, performance, and experience. She works closely with architectural practices, technology experts, local authorities, and government organizations.

Luca Csepely-Knorr is a chartered landscape architect and art historian working as Reader at the Manchester School of Architecture (MSA), where she co-directs the Architecture Research Hub and is Joint Programme Leader of the Master of Landscape Architecture. Her research and writing center on the histories of landscape architecture, architecture and urban design from the late nineteenth century to the 1970s, with a particular emphasis on the development of design theories of public spaces, international knowledge transfer and the role of women in the profession.

Sherif Elfiki, Professor of Architecture, is the Head of the Department of Architectural Engineering and Environmental Design in the Arab Academy for Science, Technology, and Maritime Transport, Cairo. In 2003, he obtained his PhD in Architecture from Edinburgh College of Art, UK. His research interests are mainly in design process, environmental behavior and architectural education. His research-work is published in reputable journals and international conferences around the world. He is also a licenced practicing architect.

Contributors

Sued Ferreira da Silva is a PhD candidate in landscape planning at the Swedish University of Agricultural Sciences, Uppsala. She is an architect and urban planner with a double Master's in Urbanism Studies at KTH Royal Institute of Technology, and History, Theory and Criticism of Architecture and Urbanism at the University of Brasilia. Her studies dwell upon the intersections between landscape, power, and infrastructure, departing from roads to the concept of green structure and derivate planning paradigms, while holding a keen interest in the ontologies and epistemologies of landscape, history, and cultural studies more broadly.

Robby Fivez is a PhD candidate and Teaching Assistant at Ghent University in Belgium. He is currently writing his PhD dissertation, under the working title "A Concrete State. Building Ambitions in the (Belgian) Congo, 1908-1964." So far, his PhD research resulted in a number of participations in international conferences and workshops and in published research papers and articles, among others in *ABE Journal* and the *Journal of Landscape Architecture*.

Luis Gordo Peláez is an Assistant Professor of Art History at California State University, Fresno. He has previously taught at Southern Methodist University in Dallas, The College of William & Mary in Virginia, and University of Tennessee. The history of the built environment in the early modern Hispanic world is his primary research interest. His most recent work examines the urban reform projects and public works agenda of Bourbon Mexico, particularly in the region of El Bajío.

Joseph Heathcott is Chair of Urban and Environmental Studies at The New School in New York. He has served as the U.S. Fulbright Distinguished Chair for the United Kingdom and as the Mellon Distinguished Fellow in Architecture, Urbanism, and the Humanities at Princeton University. Additionally, he has taught at the University of the Arts London, the London School of Economics, and the University of Vienna. Most recently he was a Visiting Scholar at L'École Urbaine de Sciences Po in Paris. His work crosses between comparative urbanism, history and theory of the built environment, and the visual and material cultures of cities.

Menno Hubregtse is a Sessional Lecturer at the University of Victoria. His book, *Wayfinding, Consumption, and Air Terminal Design* (Routledge, 2020), examines how architects design contemporary airport interiors in order to guide people through the space and to encourage spending. His publications also include journal articles and book chapters on Marcel Duchamp's *Fountain*, Eero Saarinen's TWA terminal, digital design, and Gilles Deleuze's influence on architectural theory.

Carmelina Martínez is a Tenured Professor at Universidad Anáhuac México since 2008. Her research areas are Theory and History of Architecture, focused on architectural utopic visions. She participated in the winning project for the international competition "Chambord Inachevé," selected to be part of the 500th anniversary exhibit at Chambord Castle (2019).

Monika Motylińska is principal investigator and head of the interdisciplinary research group Conquering (with) Concrete. German Construction Companies as Global Players in Local Contexts at the Leibniz Institute for Research on Society and Space (IRS) in Erkner, Germany. In her ongoing project she investigates entrepreneurial agendas of the builders and material histories and of construction projects in the "Global South." She has published in refereed journals such as *ABE Journal* and *Comparativ*.

Marie Pirard is a part-time PhD candidate and Teaching Assistant at the University of Louvain in Belgium. Her research focuses on the interplay between architecture, nature, and leisure in the context of welfare and proto-welfare policies. Alongside her research and educational practice, she works at AgwA, a Brussels-based architecture office.

Contributors

Charlie Qiuli Xue has taught architecture at Shanghai Jiaotong University and City University of Hong Kong. An award-winning architect and writer, he has published more than 100 articles as well as 14 books, including *Building a Revolution: Chinese Architecture since 1980* (2006), *Hong Kong Architecture 1945–2015: From Colonial to Global* (2016), and *Grand Theater Urbanism: Chinese Cities in the 21st Century* (2019). His book on Hong Kong was awarded by the International Committee of Architectural Critics in 2017.

Reem Saad Sardina is currently a PhD candidate in the Faculty of Architecture and Urbanism at the Bauhaus University in Weimar. She received her Master of Science in Architecture and Engineering from the Arab Academy for Science, Technology, and Maritime Transport, where she served as a teaching assistant.

Fatma Sarıkaya Işık is a PhD student at Boğaziçi University, Department of History. She obtained her MA in Architectural History from Middle East Technical University in 2019. Her studies focus on the interface between Byzantine and Ottoman urban topography of Istanbul, early modern urban depictions, and the historical water distribution systems of Ottoman cities.

Braden Lee Scott is a PhD candidate in art history at McGill University. In his dissertation project, he argues that fifteenth- and sixteenth-century artists and architects assembled the earliest pictures of ancient Egypt and West Asia that unfolded modern archaeological imagination.

Catherine Seavitt Nordenson is a Professor and Director of the graduate landscape architecture program at the Spitzer School of Architecture, City College of New York. Her work examines the intersections of political power, environmental activism, and public health, particularly as seen through the design of equitable public space and policy. Recent books include *Depositions: Roberto Burle Marx and Public Landscapes under Dictatorship* (2018) and *Structures of Coastal Resilience* (2018).

Cong Sun is a Ph.D. candidate and a Research Assistant at the City University of Hong Kong. She is interested in the research on urban cultural architecture and high-density environments. She has published papers in many refereed journals such as *Urban Design International, Frontiers of Architectural Research*. She had worked in a global architecture firm for more than three years and had been involved in many large projects such as West Kowloon Terminus.

Dicle Taskin is a PhD candidate at the Taubman College of Architecture and Urban Planning, University of Michigan. She holds a B.Arch from the Middle East Technical University in Turkey, and an M.Arch from Politècnica de Catalunya in Spain. Her ongoing dissertation research focuses on the Pan-American Highway and questions how this infrastructure project shaped the imaginary of hemispheric integration.

Huda Tayob is a Senior Lecturer at the School of Architect, Planning, and Geomatics at the University of Cape Town. Her research focuses on migrant, minor, and subaltern architectures with a particular interest in trans-national networks on the African continent. She holds a PhD from the Bartlett School of Architecture, UCL and is co-curator of Racespacearchitecture.org, an open-access curriculum project and the online pan-African exhibition, *Archive of Forgetfulness*.

José Vela Castillo is Associate Professor at the School of Architecture and Design, IE University (Segovia and Madrid, Spain), where he teaches Architectural History and Theory and Design Studio. He regularly publishes, in Spanish and in English, in architecture journals. Vela Castillo is author of the books *De la deconstrucción, la fotografía, Mies van der Rohe y el Pabellón de Barcelona* (2010) and *Richard Neutra. Un lugar para el orden* (2003).

Contributors

Margaret Birney Vickery is a Lecturer and Undergraduate Program Director at the University of Massachusetts. She has twice been a visiting lecturer at Amherst College. Her most recent book is *Landscape and Infrastructure: Re-Imagining the Pastoral Paradigm for the 21st Century* (2019). She also has a chapter, "Collaborations: The Architecture and Art of Sigrid Miller Pollin" in *The Routledge Companion to Women in Architecture* (2021).

Robin B. Williams chairs Architectural History at the Savannah College of Art and Design and specializes in the history of modern architecture and cities. He obtained his PhD in Art History from the University of Pennsylvania with a dissertation on the urban transformation of nineteenth-century Rome. Since joining SCAD in 1993, Williams has focused on Savannah, authoring *Buildings of Savannah* (2016). His current research analyzes the evolution of street and sidewalk pavement across North America.

Mejrema Zatrić is an architect, historian, and independent researcher, focusing on the history of architectural environmentalism and contemporary territorial transformations in the light of critical urban theory and environmental justice. She holds a doctoral degree from ETH Zürich, where she has been a doctoral fellow at the Institute for the History and Theory of Architecture. She has been a curatorial advisory board member for the Museum of Modern Art's exhibition *Toward a Concrete Utopia: Architecture in Yugoslavia, 1948–1980*.

ACKNOWLEDGMENTS

Any large-scale project like this can only emerge out of networks of care, collegiality, and camaraderie. This is all the more so in a world beset by the catastrophe of a global pandemic, which not only resulted in the death of millions of people, but also exposed massive inequalities built in to our various infrastructure systems. Who has the luxury and freedom to use a private automobile, while others crowd onto buses and trains? Who can protect themselves from Covid-19 by working from home, and who must expose themselves continuously in order to pay the rent? What are the extents and limits of access to health care infrastructure? I am, therefore, profoundly indebted to the people who have been delivering food to my door, repairing and maintaining the electric grid that powers this computer, hauling supplies across continents and oceans, filling my prescriptions at the local pharmacy, and attending to the health of my family, friends, and neighbors. If nothing else, I hope that this book helps to illuminate the contingency and fragility, the unevenness and inequality, of the worlds in which we are enmeshed.

The genesis of this volume can be traced to the 2016 annual meeting of the International Planning History Society in Delft. That year, Carola Hein and Paul Meurs organized the best infrastructure tour I have ever experienced—a remarkable and absorbing eight-hour circuit around the polders, berms, locks, dams, and storm barriers of the Dutch Deltaworks. Subsequently, the Society for Architectural Historians provided the opportunity to hold a session on infrastructure at the 2019 annual meeting in Providence, with superb presentations by Sibel Bozdoğan, Alex Bremner, Kenny Cupers, Prita Meier, Dalal Musaed Alsayer, and Iulia Stătică. The overwhelming interest in the session convinced me that it was time to capture the state of the art of scholarship on infrastructure design. To this end, I am grateful to Christine Bondira and Krystal Racaniello at Routledge for their patience, hard work, and knowledgeable guidance in bringing this volume to completion. I also owe thanks to The New School for providing excellent graduate assistants Emily Bowe, Daniel Chu, and Paola Sastre Garcia, who helped organize various stages of the project.

As editor of this volume, my views on infrastructure have inevitably shaped how I have read, commented on, challenged, and arranged the work of the contributors. It is only fitting, then, that I acknowledge and give thanks to the many people whose ideas have influenced my own, though they should not be held accountable for any errors in my thinking. Above all, conversations with and writings by Keller Easterling, AbdouMaliq Simone, Fran Tonkiss, and Larry Vale have proven formative in my approach to the topic; together they have been my intellectual lodestar. I also owe a debt to the crucial work of scholars of infrastructure such as Nikhil Anand, Matt Gandy, Stephen Graham, Maria Kaika, Brian Larkin, David Nye, Ann Spirn, and Eric Swygedouw.

Acknowledgments

Since this is a book about design and its (dis)contents, it is important to recognize the many people who have challenged and improved my understanding of this fundamental human capacity. In this respect, I am fortunate to teach at The New School, where I have access to colleagues at the forefront of design studies and related fields, including Clive Dilnot, Mindy Fullilove, Shannon Mattern, Brian McGrath, Miodrag Mitrasinovic, William Morrish, Radhika Subramaniam, Jilly Traganou, McKenzie Wark, and Mia White. They are all far ahead of me, so I am constantly trying to keep up with them and to learn what I can along the way. I have also gained immeasurably from conversations on design, space, and human creativity with brilliant scholars and practitioners such as Paul Goodwin, Orit Halprin, Jeff Hou, Aseem Inam, Alan Plattus, Vyjayanthi Rao, Damon Rich, Brian Rosa, Rebecca Ross, Ananya Roy, and Steve Rugare.

Social researchers and historians of planning, technology, and urbanization have produced scholarship essential to understanding both the political and economic frameworks of infrastructure development, but also the cultural and ideological worlds in which such development unfolds. My mentors in this arena have included Robert Fishman, Kenneth Jackson, Raymond Mohl, Mark Rose, and Eric Sandweiss, all of whom I have been fortunate to call friend. Ongoing conversations with great scholars such as Nicholas Bloom, Ann Forsyth, Kanishka Goonewardena, Suzi Hall, Amy Howard, Nancy Kwak, Christoph Lindner, Steve Moga, Andrew Sandoval-Strausz, Peter Soppelsa, Jonathan Soffer, and Rae Zimmerman have proven highly influential and engaging over the years. And I continue to find inspiration and insight for my work on built environments from Nathan Connolly, Yasser El-Shastaway, Ann Forsyth, Walter Greason, Owen Gutfreund, Mona Harb, Maria Kaika, Hesam Kamalipour, Elizabeth MacDonald, Hassan Radoine, Andrea Roberts, and Jennifer Robinson.

At its core, this is a book devoted to views of infrastructure design from within and around architectural history. I am therefore indebted to a group of scholars who are pushing the boundaries of architectural history—not just in terms of objects of study, but in the very way that we frame questions about the designed and built world. Whether or not they identify strictly as architectural historians, their work has proven catalytic. Those of us who work in this field have felt the profound influence of Margaret Crawford, Dolores Hayden, Mark Jarazombek, Reinhold Martin, Mary Ryan, Dell Upton, and Gwendolyn Wright. Similarly, many architectural historians continue to push (or perhaps pull) the field into new registers, including Daniel Barber, James Buckley, Swati Chattopadhyay, Marta Gutman, Diane Harris, Zeynep Kezer, Fernando Lara, Ana Maria León, Sara López, Paula Lupkin, Patricia Morton, David Rifkind, Susanne Schindler, Arjit Sen, Jessica Sewell, Andrew Shanken, Anooradha Siddiqi, and Carla Yanni.

Finally, it is family and friends that sustain one in a project of this scale, particularly under the sign of pandemic. For over a year I have not been able to hug my parents, Dave and Jackie Heathcott, my sister Penny Heathcott, or my in-laws Tom and Sharyn Cruce. Nevertheless, they have all been a continual source of strength and support, and I cannot wait to be present with them again. Above all, my partner in life Ashley Cruce has had the greatest influence on how I see, think about, and experience the world. Together we have journeyed across thousands of miles of roads, rivers, and runways, and tooled around uncountable dams, reservoirs, ports, docks, power stations, and other infrastructure. It is to her that I dedicate this volume.

Joseph Heathcott

INFRASTRUCTURE DESIGNS
Dreaming and Building Worlds
Joseph Heathcott

Infrastructure emerges from deep within our dreams. It takes form through designed artifacts that in turn give rise to new dreams. It is at once an object and an ideal, a technique and a fable, a prosthesis and a prophecy. It reflects a continual quest for the facilities of movement and exchange, sociality and togetherness, power and control. Infrastructure is simultaneously an affect of the fervent human desire for connection and a reflection of our failures to forge such connections on the basis of equality and justice. It is, to paraphrase philosopher Michel Serres, the flawed angel that heralds the unevenly connected world.

This book considers infrastructure across a wide variety of forms, locations, and temporalities. The extraordinary group of authors gathered here provides not only new knowledge of specific infrastructure artifacts, such as the Valens aqueduct, the Hong Kong waterfront, and the Pan-American highway. They also provide new ways of conceptualizing, studying, and understanding infrastructure as a worlding process. Their chapters connect disparate regions, explore themes across broad spans of time, examine questions of linkage and scale, investigate materiality and affect, and trace the interrelation of aesthetics, technology, and power. Some focus on singular infrastructural elements, others on whole systems or interrelated networks; together, they provide a rich and multiform account of how we build and connect the world.

Beneath and Between

The term *infrastructure* is an ambiguous and drifting signifier. This ambiguity has led to several key challenges for scholars of the built environment. The first challenge has to do with the ambit of the word itself. Nineteenth-century French engineers coined the term to refer to the substrate of support for rail lines—the structure beneath the structure.[1] The term spread through transatlantic and colonizing networks, particularly among civil engineers engaged in road building and water projects, as well as military officers concerned with defense works and territorial control. Gradually it came to refer not only to structures below, but also between—physical networks connecting one node or place to another in a system. Today, we regard infrastructure as both visible and invisible, below and between, material and immaterial. It is no longer just the packed gravel substrate under the train tracks, it is also the train tracks themselves, and it is the switches, signals, chronometers, sheds, rotundas, terminals, and operational standards that comprise the system of rail transit, and it is the bodies, social relations, and visions of the world remade by high velocity travel.[2]

Another challenge has to do with the application of the term. Even as the concept of infrastructure expanded to include more artifacts, it also came to be used retrospectively to account for structures built long before the advent of the term. Thus, the term is freighted with assumptions built into the modern Enlightenment project in which it was born—assumptions such as progress through technology and the superiority of scientific reason over other knowledge forms. Scholars have too often read these assumptions backward into accounts of infrastructure in ways that justify Eurocentric notions of civilization, development, and empire. The expansion of European and U.S. hegemony over the last five centuries has been embedded in and accompanied by self-justifying narratives that view power as the inevitable outcome of technological superiority. Even as this so-called modern world became fractured by successive world wars, faith in progress and the embrace of the "technological sublime" survived and spread globally.[3] And while the term infrastructure has been applied retrospectively, it has also become a standard element in projections of the future. U.S. Presidential advisor and economist Walter Rostow's "stages of growth" encapsulates this vision of a world "modernized" and "improved" through the adoption of Western technology and infrastructure.[4]

Finally, researchers must contend with the reality that while the term refers to connecting affordances, those very affordances often become resonant places in their own right, thickened with significance and leavened over time through countless repeated uses.[5] The oldest known bridge in the world at Argolis was constructed by a Bronze Age Mycenaean Greek community to span a stream and carry chariots along the highway connecting Tiryns and Epidauros. It remains in use today, its irregular corbel arch settled comfortably into the Peloponnesian landscape. The two cities that it connected and helped to grow, however, lay in deposition, long since abandoned. But the bridge stands as a beloved local site and tourist attraction. Similarly, the Galata Bridge (now in its fifth iteration, see Figure 0.1)

Figure 0.1 Strolling and fishing on the Galata Bridge in Istanbul. Galata Bridge is a prime example of infrastructure both as a connector of places and a place in its own right.

Source: Photograph by Joseph Heathcott.

facilitates the flow of people and vehicles across the Golden Horn, connecting Sultanahmet and Beyoğlu. But the bridge itself is a lively destination, a platform for strolling, fishing, and taking in the breeze off the Bosporus.

Despite these challenges, or perhaps because of them, the term has opened up felicitous ways of describing the designed and built world. While it may be overdoing it to declare an "infrastructure turn" in scholarship, infrastructure nevertheless presents a critically important field for investigation as a key affordance in the production of both space and mobility over time.[6] A focus on infrastructure allows us to attend to the details of complex socio-technical systems and built environments—the connectors, the interstitial networks, the nodes that amplify, compress, and switch the flows. And not just material objects, but the invisible pathways, lines of force, and radiant fields that they produce, and the varied relations that emerge through the interconnected web of locations, practices, and things. By centering infrastructure we open ourselves to new stories, new ways of looking at the world.

Design Stories

The core purpose of this volume is to tell new stories about the design of infrastructure. And we tell these stories from an intellectual space animated but not confined by architectural history. What can the perspective of architectural history provide in the way of deeper understandings of infrastructure design? What might a sustained study of infrastructure contribute to architectural history, and how might architectural history provide us with new insights and ways of apprehending infrastructure? To answer these questions, we have to think through what we mean by architectural history as an intellectual project and design as a human endeavor.

In this volume, we take a broad view of design as a neurocognitive capacity shared by all humans. Engagement in design tasks activates particular neuropathways associated with ideation, trial and error learning, task set configuration, and visual-spatial information processing.[7] Through design, we amplify our ability to connect our imagination with action in the world in order to transform that world to suit a desired outcome. In this sense, design is related but not reducible to "problem-solving," a closed loop activity where the variables in a situation are known, as when we find a rock and use it to break open a nut. Rather, design is an open process characterized by an ability to identify and discern between changing variables, as when we hold the same rock and see something different in our mind's eye embedded within the it—the arrowhead, the axe blade, the adornment. In practice, it is a form of abductive reasoning based on iteration, prototyping, and movement between general and specific propositions. It is an inherently futuring cognitive affordance. Like language or perception, design may be more or less advanced from one individual to the next, more or less facilitated by neurophysiology, but every person has the capacity to design.[8]

Given that design is a fundamental human capacity, architecture, as the design of built form, is a practice broadly shared within and across cultures. In popular lexicon, architecture is often used to refer to unique, geospatially fixed buildings designed by professionally credentialed architects—the grand edifice, the monument, the iconographic structure. Likewise, definitions of architecture by architects tend to re-enforce their status as creative geniuses responsible for transcendent works of art. As Jay Pritzker famously declared, "architecture is intended to transcend the simple need for shelter and security by becoming an expression of artistry."[9] Such a definition implies that shelter and security are "simple needs," rather than immensely complex and creative human endeavors, and that the development of human habitat is devoid of artistry unless it involves the work of an architect. While great monuments and edifices certainly count as expressions of architecture, architecture itself is not reducible to such objects; rather, it instantiates through generative practices of form making, temporal marking, and aesthetic expression grounded in human social relations. These practices unfold along continuum from professional to untrained, fixed to mobile, unique to repetitive, integral to modular and permanent to momentary. Architecture emerges from and reflects constant negotiation among people over the production of space, the terms of exchange, the vectors of mobility, and the making of lived worlds.[10] The task of architectural history is to account for these negotiations over time, and the artifacts, spatial forms, and social relations that they engender.

Nevertheless, as Stephen Parcell has ably demonstrated, while architecture changes over time, so do our definitions of what constitutes architecture.[11] In the mid-nineteenth century a powerful discourse took hold around the notion that the locus of authority to design inheres in the credentialed professional. This conceptualization of design as specialized knowledge acquired through the rigors of training parallels the broader emergence of institutional and discursive practices that codified expertise in fields from medicine to public health, social welfare, education, civil engineering, and planning. The professions gained organizational strength as gatekeepers in the production of scarcity around knowledge, and as managers of the complexity of a rapidly urbanizing and industrializing society.[12] As such, they not only served the interests of powerful state and market actors, but also their own interests as a middling class, with narratives constructed to justify their existence. And indeed, who does not want to traverse a bridge designed by an engineer, or send their children to learn from a qualified teacher?

The question for architectural historians, then, is how do we tell stories about the history of the designed and built world in ways that do not read backward through or reify nineteenth-century notions of design as the delivery of progress and modernity by the credentialed professional? After all, no singular act of genius created the canals of Suzhou or Xochimilco (Figure 0.2), the rail networks of

Figure 0.2 Xochimilco in Mexico City, a listed World Heritage site, comprises a remnant of the Aztec *chinampas*, a unique form of land reclamation with an infrastructure of canals and irrigation channels still in use today.

Source: Photograph by Joseph Heathcott.

colonial India or the Soviet trans-Siberian east, the Mughal port of Surat or vast expanses of modular warehouses surrounding airports across the globe. These infrastructures take form through processes that are highly contingent, spatially and temporally uneven, and seldom predictable. They might have a leader to guide their development, as Mimar Sinan oversaw the creation of the Kırkçeşme water system or as Robert Moses envisioned the transformation of New York City for the automobile age. But most often the design of infrastructure is a multi-authorial process, the result of countless actors toiling in obscurity with varied capacities and skills: carpenters, masons, wheelwrights, founders, haulers, accountants, bureaucrats, laborers. Thus, infrastructure elements might unfold through a directing plan, or they might reflect the work of many hands. They might rise up in great nervous eruptions of energy and investment, or take form gradually across manifold instances of trial and error, addition and subtraction, accretion and obsolescence.

In all cases, our histories of infrastructure design have to be delinked from discourses that frame technological affordances as the inevitable result of the march of civilization. Reading infrastructure back through the lens of modernity and progress reinforces the developmentalist logics that have been central both to nation-building projects as well as to European and U.S. hegemony.[13] Nineteenth-century chroniclers of national growth and development often used infrastructure as a proxy for measuring success in the expansion of settlement, the control over territory, the movement of people and goods, and the formation of citizen-subjects. Infrastructure, like so many other facets of technology, is tightly wound into circular and self-justifying narratives from which it can be difficult to escape. Essays in this volume counter these narratives by reminding us that infrastructure emerges out of processes that are temporally ad-hoc and contingent, spatially rough and uneven, rather than a smooth or continuous flow of things.

Instead of describing an inexorable arc of progress, then, infrastructure ramifies in manifold ways: when the Spanish conquerors drained the lakes of the Valley of Mexico in the seventeenth and eighteenth centuries, they created new land for rapid construction of urban fabric; but in the process, they destroyed the lacustrine habitat so carefully engineered by the Aztecs over several centuries (refer to Figure 0.2), which has led to unending problems of flooding, subsidence, and increased risk from earthquakes.[14] The emergence of discourses on sanitation and hygiene in the nineteenth century led to crucial improvements in water and waste management. However, it also led middle-class reformers from Brazil to India to the U.S. to associate Black, migrant, and poor populations with filth and disease burdensome to the body politic, in turn justifying efforts of isolation or removal.[15] The extension of the Tennessee Valley Authority electric grid provided more access for more people in one region, but at the same time the uneven enrollment and "last mile" challenges lead to a reorganization, rather than elimination, of socio-spatial inequalities.[16] Communities in the South Bronx rose up in opposition to the construction of the Cross Bronx Expressway. The new road destroyed intact urban neighborhoods, but greatly improved the flow of traffic into and out of the city—that is, until it didn't. Like so many expressways, its status as a common pool rival good led not only to frequent traffic gridlock, but also to a public health crisis: an alarming increase in asthma rates among children in the South Bronx.[17] Infrastructure never submits to a simple account.

Infrastructure in an Expanded Field

In order to tell new stories about the design of infrastructure over time, the authors in this volume consider infrastructure beyond its object state into an expanded field. After all, infrastructure unfolds in excess of itself, congeries of always-incomplete social relations, human desires, material resonances, and stories that simultaneously focus and amplify, compress and expand the world. The Silk Road, for example, never existed as one coherent artifact; instead, it comes to us as a compression of many stories that we have forged into a singular narrative. It was at once a collection of spatial and architectural forms that emerged, accumulated, and faded over time—routes, markers, caravanserai, fortifications, ports, custom houses, water wells—and at the same time a space of world-making across geography

Figure 0.3 Caravanserai-i-Shah at Qazvin, Persia (Iran), from Eugène Flandin, *Voyage en Perse* (Paris: Gide et Baudry, 1851). The caravanserai were crucial features of overland trade routes through Central Asia, as well as elements in Orientalist constructions of the world.

Source: Courtesy of Wikimedia Commons.

and culture (Figure 0.3). The nilometers of ancient Egypt not only enabled the practical exercise of recording the annual flood, they provided data for the calculation of hydrological cycles that undergirded the mysteries of priestly power. The U.S. Interstate is both a slab of asphalt with supremely engineered fault tolerances, and a space for projecting freedom, mobility, and American power. And while it ramifies spatially, it is never experienced in totality by any one person, but rather in fragments, ideated through countless maps and atlases. Every airport terminal is a more or less humdrum feature of long-distance travel, and at the same time a tightly wound nodal point in the networked shrinkage of the globe. But we do not know that network as a whole; we know the check-in counter, the security cordon, the departure gate. Wires and switches dumbly send us electricity, but also envelop us in the hypnotic spell of the technological sublime.

The present volume examines infrastructure within an expanded field. This expanded field includes not only the immediate artifacts of infrastructure—the dams, bridges, water pipes, fiber optic cables—but also the materials of which they are composed, the processes that produce them, the labor that animates them, the human affects that they reflect and engender, the landscapes and ecologies that they transform, and the stories within which they are enmeshed. These stories are not only about the construction of structures and systems, but also about the desires behind these constructions, the forms of life that they make possible, and the path dependencies that organize their emergence into the world. Rather than view infrastructure as a taken-for-granted element of modernity, this volume approaches infrastructure through Bruno Latour's assertion that modernity is itself a multiform narrative. Infrastructure, then, constitutes a historically contingent element in the construction and dissemination not of modernity, but of the *story of modernity*—that contradictory knot of dreams, aspirations, and values that shape how we narrate the world.[18]

Moreover, the chapters in this volume explore the political, economic, and social alignments through which infrastructure unfolds. As Fran Tonkiss demonstrates, infrastructure has developed within a wide range of political economies over time, with greatly varied systems of production, use, maintenance, dissembly, and reconstruction.[19] These include absolutist states such as Pharaonic Egypt and contemporary North Korea; localized tributary and reciprocal forms as in Medieval Europe and Dravidian India; extractive imperial systems of Mughals, Ottomans, and British; laissez-faire economies such as those found in Latin America in the long nineteenth century; command socialist governments such as the Soviet Union and China; monarchic regimes with immense sovereign wealth funds, such as Bahrain and the Emirates; and the constitutional liberal democracies of contemporary Europe and North America, characterized by corporate rent-seeking and mixed public/private investment. It also includes emerging transnational forms, as in the decades following World War II, when infrastructure development in Global South countries relied increasingly on World Bank loans for privatized construction subject to the imposition of austerity measures and the lowering of trade barriers.[20]

Infrastructure always reflects, often re-enforces, and sometimes transforms these political alignments. Moreover, once created, infrastructure networks and systems often generate outcomes that are difficult to control over the long term. The great network of Roman roads enabled the movement of garrisons to far-flung precincts of the empire, but also facilitated the movement of dangerous rival ideas such as Christianity as well as existential threats from warring armies from the north. Native American trails became colonial market roads, which became turnpikes and highways, which expanded settler colonial habitat and projected the terrain of empire into continental space through bloody paroxysms of violence against Native American people. When we examine infrastructure in an expanded field, we see not only the objects themselves, the path dependencies they follow, and the newly forged networks they create, but also the political, social, and ecological ramifications of these entangled systems.[21]

Take communication infrastructure, for example. The root level of communication is the singular event punctuated by visual or auditory exchange where a signal encoded with meaning is transmitted from one person and received by another who decodes or interprets that meaning. This is the province of the knowing look, the verbal repartee, the hand sign, the semaphore flag. Every form of communication that exceeds this spatial co-presence is based on signal relay. Chasqui runners on the great Inca road network carried messages between settlements along mountain spines, creeks, and stony trails. The towers of the Great Wall of China served as relay beacons, employing serial fires to warn of enemy attack. Kikuyu villages in East Africa used drum combinations and rhythmic compositions to send nuanced messages from one village to the next through a chain of settlements. The overland stagecoaches of North America carried newspapers, mail, and passengers in twenty-mile segments across mountains, rivers, and plains, until the transcontinental railroad cast them into obsolescence.

The advent of the telegraph did not obviate the relay principal, but it did speed up transmission considerably. While messages sent through the first transatlantic cables in the mid-nineteenth century took hours to transmit, that was still far more rapid than the month required for sending a message on a sailing ship. By the end of the nineteenth century, a thicket of transatlantic cable meant that news could travel from New York to London to Paris in a matter of minutes. With the 1911 completion of the last leg of the "All Red Line" between Brisbane and the booster station at Tabuaeran Island in the mid-Pacific, a message could flow around the world through 28,000 miles of cable in 16.5 minutes. To underscore the line's status as a consummate British imperial project, operators boasted that it would require 42 cuts to overcome the redundancies built into the system.[22] Indeed, by the twentieth century, routes of communication had emerged as central features in the expansion of colonial power across the globe (Figure 0.4).

The compression of signals into electrical impulses created a new system of communication based on ancient principles. But the infrastructure that made such a system possible far exceeded the wires

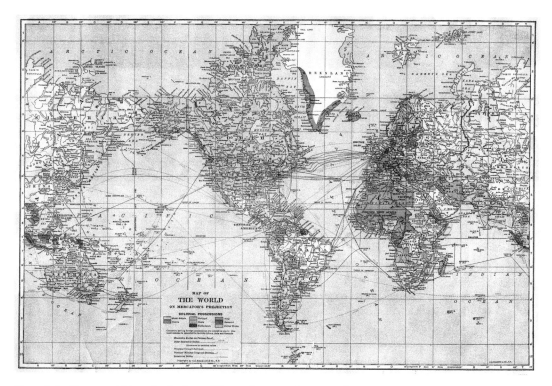

Figure 0.4 Hammond Map of colonies and lines of communication and travel, ca. 1930. This map indexes infrastructure as a feature of high imperialism.

Source: Courtesy of the British Studies Institute, University of Toronto Libraries.

through which the signals traveled, or the poles that held those wires aloft, or the cables that carried them along the ocean bed. The copper and steel had to mined, refined, and extruded through a series of industrial processes. The vast "negative spaces" left behind—the yawning pits in the ground—were just as much a part of the infrastructure. Gutta purcha, the latex substance used for wire insulation, had to be tapped from a Malaysian evergreen; as with so many economically catalytic plants, it was enveloped in a web of botanical imperialism, monopolized by the British through their control over plantation agriculture, coercive labor recruitment, and the export platform.[23] All of these materials had to be sourced, aggregated, shipped, disaggregated, shipped again, collected and installed. Tall straight timbers felled by the thousands formed the overland vertebrae, while ships lay spool after spool of finished cable, complete with end-coupling devices, across vast bodies of water. An ensemble of equipment such as transmitters, receivers, and eventually printers filled telegraph offices around the world. And of course, human labor animated the entire system.

Today our seemingly instantaneous forms of communication continue to operate on relays, now through modulated carrier waves travelling at nearly the speed of light. The armature of the system takes shape around the unfathomable web of fiber optic cables, diodes, semiconductors, amplifiers, routers, satellite arrays, and sprawling server facilities with massive cooling equipment and electricity demands. All of this allows for the rapid transmission, retrieval, processing, storage, switching, and control of the binary signals that comprise data. Manufacturers funnel millions of tons of materials into the system, including selenium, tin, arsenic, indium, gallium, zinc, and silicon, laid down on boron-doped substrates or extruded into elegant glass strands.[24] As with telegraphy and telephony, our current system of fiber-optic and satellite communication is animated by armies of engineers, chemists, technicians, contractors, installers, street crews, and sales personnel.

All of these communicative practices are at once constitutive of infrastructure, and at the same time more than infrastructure. Infrastructure in an expanded field is always an assemblage of materials and ideologies, but these assemblages create wholes greater than the sum of its parts. Infrastructure is the space between things, but it is also those things remade by their very connection to infrastructure. It is the telephone wire and the water pipe, but it is also the body remade through entangled relations with socio-technical systems that augment, extend, and transform the human—the prosthesis, the cyborg.[25] It is the drum, the fire tower, the cable, the geosynchronous orbital satellite, but it is also the kinship network, the conception of territory, the longing for connection, the sublimity of transcending gravity. Infrastructure is never apart from the swirling eddies of desires, visions, and meanings through which it takes form. It is never innocent or neutral, but always/already entangled in social, political, and economic processes across space and time. However fixed to landscape, it is never fixed in its meaning. Infrastructure builds worlds that far exceed it.

New Vantages

Reading infrastructure in an expanded field brings to the fore many features of its design over time. If we perhaps push the boundaries of what counts as infrastructure a bit far at times, it is a small price to pay for the intellectual ground we gain. Not everything is infrastructure, of course; but few features of the contemporary world remain outside or untouched by the spaces of flows constituted through infrastructure. Thus, the authors in this volume take a broad and inclusive view of infrastructure as the entangled ensembles of nodes, networks, and processes that facilitate the movement of people, ideas, and things from one place to another. Such a framework, in turn, provides new avenues of approach, new vantages from which to recast the stories we tell about the design of infrastructure. I will review five of these vantages and their implications here.

Infrastructure beyond the Teleological Narratives that Constrain It

Far from a uniform and straightforward expansion over time, infrastructure projects tend to be unleashed in nervous eruptions at key historical moments, often as exercises in war, nation-building, or imperial control. At other times they accrue slowly, even imperceptibly, as separate projects knitted together over time, like the Indian Ocean trade network of the thirteenth century. At other times infrastructure erodes or disappears, like so many Mayan temples and processional streets entwined by jungle, or the Late Dynastic Port of Thonis slowly eroding below the azure waters of the Mediterranean. Such contingent and uneven histories remove infrastructure from its overdetermined role as a herald of progress, rung on the ladder of development, or step in the march of improvement. Moreover, infrastructure from one era can be repurposed for another, as with the recent trend of converting decommissioned train lines into linear parks. Despite these temporal complexities, we tend to collapse our accounts of infrastructure into a suite of tropes and narrative conventions that recruit roads, bridges, utility networks, and communication lines into unilinear stories of progress (Figure 0.5). Such stories, in turn, become justification for further infrastructure building.

Infrastructure as a System that both Reveals and Conceals Itself

Infrastructure tends to obscure the forces of its own production as well as the materials that flow through it. Immense expenditures of capital and labor shape networked materialities and spaces of flows, even while those expenditures recede into the overdetermined symbolism of the forms themselves. If we are fortunate, infrastructure brings water and gas to our homes, but those substances have been dramatically transformed from their source origins, and our relationship to them is attenuated by distance and the black box of technology.[26] Meanwhile, dams, docks, pipes, rail lines, and other artifacts seldom reveal their political and economic affordances. When we cross the

Figure 0.5 Cover of the *Municipal Journal and Engineer* Vol. 17, No. 6, 1904. The *MJ&E* was the leading periodical for planners, civil engineers, and city officials in the U.S. during the late nineteenth and early twentieth centuries.

Source: Courtesy of the Library of the University of Michigan.

Akashi Kaikyō Bridge to Kobe, we are mesmerized by its exquisite span, but we do not see the mass dampers that stabilize the bridge's resonance frequencies against strong winds, or the political, environmental, and contracting controversies that have plagued the bridge since its inception. The beautifully designed Bangalore-Mysore cloverleaf interchange obscures the legislative appropriations, land acquisitions, construction contracts, and hard labor that made such a piece of kit possible. Moreover, these infrastructures become such routine features of life that they tend to disappear or sublimate into our unconscious, only to be revealed in moments of crisis, as when the Tangshan Earthquake of 1976 destroyed many of the streets needed for rescue access, or when the blackout of 2003 blanketed the Northeastern United States and Southeastern Canada in darkness.

Infrastructure as Fragmentary and Uneven

This approach reflects what Stephen Graham and Simon Marvin have so aptly described as the "splintering" quality of infrastructure.[27] In their formulation, infrastructure is an always incomplete, spatially uneven set of bundling and unbundling processes that forge the distribution of flows, the forms and limits of territories, and the conditions of inclusion and exclusion. While the sheer extensivity of infrastructure lends it an air of totality and smoothness, close observation and local experience always reveal it to be rough, anisomorphic, and discontinuous. Even as it connects, it disconnects; as it assembles, it dissembles; as it brings some people together, it keeps others apart. At the same time, the contingent and incomplete nature of infrastructure opens up a great variety of uses and tactics among marginalized and disempowered people. In his now classic essay "People as Infrastructure," AbdouMaliq Simone forwards the crucial insight that subaltern groups compensate for the lack of physical infrastructure by establishing embodied routines, substituting labor for capital, and forming "interconnected socialities."[28] And as Swati Chattopadhyay demonstrates, Indian rickshaw drivers, vendors, hawkers, even children playing cricket in the streets have "appropriated and gnawed" at infrastructure to generate linkages, exchange, and tactics of engagement that "are not just unnoticed by the state, but beneath its register."[29]

Infrastructure as Nested in and Connecting across Scale

Following from the notion of infrastructure as fragmented and multiform, this approach allows us to trace its connections across scale. Sometimes infrastructure networks squeeze into the tight precincts of cities and urbanized regions, bundled in overlapping spatial envelopes of collective consumption. Streetcar tracks run atop roadways, which are bracketed by telephone and electric poles. Sewers provide tubing for the extension of wires, fiber optic cables, and other filaments of communication. Dammed and channeled waterways provide navigable routes for shipping, drainage of waste and industrial runoff, and hydroelectric power. Intermodal linkages between networks amplify their respective capacities and provide opportunities for architectural production, as with the grain silos of Buffalo, New York that afford efficient transfer between barges on the Erie Canal and freight train lines. In other cases, infrastructure spreads across space and territory to cover entire regions of the world. Long roads, transcontinental train lines, oceanic shipping lanes, canalized rivers all produce territories far in excess of their physical dimensions. Meanwhile, the globe is enmeshed in planetary surveillance technologies, locational grids, satellite networks, sensors arrays, microwaves, and all manner of manifold overlapping invisible systems. But we experience these globally dispersed technologies in moments and increments, through haptic contact with cell phones, computer and television screens, and dashboard GPS.[30]

Infrastructure as Deeply Implicated in Spatial Inequality and Violence

Infrastructure has always been a factor in the exertion of violence in the world, sometimes in ways that are highly visible, and at other times occulted and obscure. The European network of rail lines and terminals that signified the continent's modernity also served the deportation, movement, and murder of Jewish people during the Shoah. Haussmann's grand boulevards were as much about beauty and order as they were avenues for Second Empire military mobilization against an unruly populace. Chicago's Dan Ryan Expressway facilitated the north-south flow of traffic through a growing city, while re-enforcing the barrier against Black people's westward movement into White neighborhoods. French colonial officials planned *cordons sanitaires* in cities from Casablanca to Saigon in order to establish zones of separation between "native" and European populations (Figure 0.6). The extents and limits of piped water, electricity, transit, and other affordances are major factors in the production of socio-spatial inequalities. At the same time, as Fran Tonkiss reminds us, infrastructure produces forms of citizenship and belonging not dependent on official documents or membership in an electoral roll. "The pipe that runs below my building and connects to the sewer main," she notes, "is a line of civic membership activated far more frequently than my intermittent trips to the voting booth."[31] Such physical networks bind people into polities in ways that are often unpredictable, unintended, even invisible.

In sum, the examination of infrastructure designs in an expanded field presents a range of possibilities for new ways of understanding our interactions with the built world. This is more than simply adding

Figure 0.6 Aerial view of the Place de France, Casablanca, ca. 1920. French colonial officials constructed the space as part of the *cordon sanitaire* separating the walled old city from the *ville nouvelle*.

Source: Photograph courtesy of the Alamy Banque d'Images.

typologies and artifacts to the roster of infrastructure, though that alone would be a valuable outcome. Rather, it opens up a view of infrastructure as an ever-changing assemblage of socio-technical objects, networks, and processes mutually constituted and continuously iterated through spatial imaginaries and material flows. It also opens up considerations of affect, of what infrastructure makes possible in our emotional, spiritual, and material lives. The drone of the subway and the heat of the packed subway car after work. The *eruv*, comprising fishing line connected to lampposts and telephone poles and elevated train tracks, enclosing the Jewish faithful in a protected wall wherein they can perform tasks otherwise forbidden on Sabbath. The stunning views of mountains, valleys, and streams from the Tribhuvan Highway between Chitwan and Katmandu. The dark water of a canal in Xochimilco, gently rippling with the movement of a canoe paddle. The bridge where we last saw a friend, the street corner where we fell in love.

Structure of the Volume

This book considers infrastructure across a wide variety of forms, locations, and temporalities. The authors take us to disparate world regions, explore themes across broad spans of time, examine questions of linkage and scale, investigate infrastructure as phenomenon and affect, and trace the interrelation of aesthetics, technology, and power. Some focus on singular infrastructural elements, others on whole systems or interrelated networks; together, they provide a rich and multiform account of how we build and connect the world. The chapters themselves are organized into eight sections. The first four sections emphasize broad thematic approaches, while the second four sections emphasize typological approaches. This is by no means meant to be a discrete division; indeed, each chapter in the thematic sections deals with specific types and examples of infrastructure, and each chapter in the typological section illuminates critical themes in infrastructure design. Moreover, chapters interrelate across the divisions into which they have been placed, some tied together by geography, others by time period, still others through a focus on political, economic, or cultural dimensions of infrastructure. In all cases, authors bring highly developed conceptual frameworks and thoroughly empirical studies to the table.

The first section investigates material forms, compositions, and installments of infrastructure. Braden Lee Scott's chapter takes us to Imperial Rome, where successive rulers sought to legitimize their power through the quarrying, transport, and installation of Egyptian stone. Carmelina Martinez considers the work of eighteenth-century French architect Claude-Nicolas Ledoux, who regarded the creation of infrastructure around salt production as an opportunity to propose ideal relations between architecture, technology, and nature. Robby Fivez and Monika Motylińska bring us to twentieth-century cement production in Sub-Saharan Africa, using a novel genealogical approach to trace the ruptures and continuities in infrastructure building between colonial and post-independence Nigeria, Tanzania, and the Republic of Congo. Finally, Stefano Corbo's chapter presents an intriguing architectural inversion, where excavated, hidden, and concealed spaces comprise the "underworld" of infrastructure under late capitalism.

In the second section, authors consider infrastructure in terms of embodied subjects in formation. Hannah Ahblad opens a view onto how Pashtun women have adopted and used communication infrastructure in Afghanistan in order to construct gendered spaces for expression and exchange, particularly in the post-Soviet period. In the context of drought-stricken Northeast Brazil in the early twentieth century, Laura Belik traces the spatial containment of migrant families, which in turn facilitated their recruitment into a regime of coerced labor for infrastructure projects. And Reem Sardina, Sherif Elfiki, and Ahmed El Antably present a novel account of Cairene cemeteries as an infrastructure both for the transportation of souls to the beyond and the habitation of squatters in a city rapidly running out of space for the living.

Visions of the natural world and its relationship to infrastructure form the basis of chapters in section three. Marie Pirard examines the transformation of the Eau d'Heure Valley in Belgium, where for fifty years planners, architects, and engineers constructed a series of dams and reservoirs that resulted in the formation of a hybrid "machine in the garden" landscape. Margaret Vickery's chapter provides a critical evaluation of contemporary Danish approaches to infrastructure design, where architects and engineers seek to incorporate such elements as wastewater treatment and power generation plants into spaces for recreation, education, and play. And Catherine Seavitt Nordenson traces the long durée of the expansion of infrastructure into the Amazon as a project of resource exploitation and territorial control, from early colonial mapping efforts to the rise of the environmental conservation movement in the 1970.

The fourth section presents chapters that frame infrastructure in terms of the spaces of flows. Fatma Sarıkaya Işık and Pelin Yoncacı Arslan show how artists and cartographers from the fifteenth through the eighteenth centuries came to include and render the great bridge of the Valens Aqueduct—a classic space of flows—in their representations of the Ottoman capital. Menno Hubregtse takes on the airport terminal, arguing that since its inception in the early twentieth century it has constituted a highly charged site in terms of its design and technical organization, its growing importance in the self-image of nations, and its more recent role as a site of protest by various social movements. And Huda Tayob follows the flows of people and goods through the space of "Somali Malls," ordinary office blocks modified to perform vital nodes of cultural and economic exchange for the migrant communities of Cape Town.

With section five we shift the organizational emphasis from conceptual rubrics to genres and types of infrastructure. The authors in section five examine infrastructure as imbricated in urban form and city making. Sibel Bozdoğan's chapter explores the long drawn out effort to construct the first bridge over the Bosporus as part of a broader story about changing political alignments, governmental priorities, and dreams of mobility and expansion. Sued Ferreira da Silva tells a new story of

Brasilia that takes us beyond the standard focus on the Modernist city itself, but as the catalyst for the development of a national road network to link the new capital and transform the "wilderness" landscape. Mejrema Zatrić examines emerging ideas of mobility in the context of interwar Belgium and post-war Yugoslavia, where architects and planners reconceptualized cities as "circulation machines" tied in to broader infrastructure systems that could unite territories into political and economic wholes. Peter Chomowicz takes us to Doha, where successive Qatari Emirs have used road building, electrification, and other infrastructure projects as a way to legitimize their rule both at home and internationally.

In the sixth section, authors examine the specific qualities of roads and highways as a type of infrastructure replete with multiple significations and meanings. Robin Williams reveals a growing international exchange in the nineteenth and twentieth centuries among designers, planners, and engineers with regard to street paving methods—debates that were as much about optimal technologies as they were about the political economies of resources. Romina Canna provides a new look at the development of the U.S. interstate highway system, arguing that the aims shifted from the production of an abstract grid laid over national territory to a network explicitly linking together cities, culminating in the construction of urban expressways. And Dicle Taskin explores long-distance travel on the Pan-American Highway in the 1930s and 1940s, arguing that the road reflected and catalyzed dreams of hemispheric cooperation and freedom of mobility.

Section seven considers the construction of fields of power in the flow of resources, technologies, and political control. Luca Csepely-Knorr and Laura Coucill examine the rapid expansion of power production and transmission in postwar Britain, and the search among the varied design disciplines for an aesthetic language suitable to such a large-scale nation-building project. Dalal Musaed Alsayer provides novel insight into the Cold War era efforts by the United States to expand political, economic, and cultural influence in Hashemite Kingdom of Jordan through the extension of large-scale water damning and distribution projects. Keeping with the theme of U.S. Cold War power brokering, José Vela Castillo's chapter takes a close look at the development and use of aerial photography and cartography in the expansion of American military infrastructure in Spain during the 1950s.

Finally, the eighth section of the volume explores water and the infrastructure surrounding it as a major feature of human life across space and time. Luis Gordo Peláez takes us to late eighteenth-century Guanajuato and the long struggles by local officials, residents, and landowners to exert control over the flood prone river in this mountainous landscape. Charlie Qiuli Xue and Cong Sun delve into the great Hong Kong estuary to examine the history of land reclamation efforts from the colonial era to the present, with a focus on the architectural expressions, land use variations, and place-making endeavors that characterize these hard-won urban spaces. And in the final chapter of the volume, Vandana Baweja brings us into the cinematic realm with a close study the 1975 Hindi film *Deewaar* (*The Wall*), tracing its representation of docks, avenues, industrial zones, and other infrastructure spaces of the Mumbai Waterfront.

All told, the authors gathered into this volume cover a broad swath of time periods, geographies, scalar registers, materialities, political and economic forms, and human social relations in the study of infrastructure design. Moreover, while they are all experts on their topics, they come to the volume from varied locations, fields, and career stages, from doctoral students to emerging field leaders to seasoned senior scholars. This variation provides an invaluable range of perspectives in the composition of the chapters. At the same time, the work presented here reveals an emerging consensus around infrastructure design as more than an aesthetic or technical pursuit, important as these are, encompassing in addition matters of territorial expansion, power and control, accommodation and resistance, cultural meaning and modes of human togetherness. Most importantly, the authors introduce us to an incredibly wide range of opportunities, and a suite of novel and engaging approaches, for rethinking infrastructure design as a foundational feature in the dreaming and building of worlds.

Notes

1 Philippe Diest, *Le poids des infrastructures militaires 1871–1914: Nord-Pas-de-Calais* (Villeneuve d'Ascq, France: Septentrion, 2019).
2 Keller Easterling, *Extrastatecraft: The Power of Infrastructure Space* (New York: Verso, 2014); Nikhil Anand, Akhil Gupta, and Hannah Appel, eds, *The Promise of Infrastructure* (Durham, NC: Duke University Press Books, 2018); Maria Kaika, *City of Flows: Modernity, Nature, and the City* (New York: Routledge, 2004).
3 David E. Nye, *American Technological Sublime* (Cambridge, MA: MIT Press, 1996).
4 W.W. Rostow, *The Stages of Economic Growth: A Non-Communist Manifesto* (Cambridge, UK: Cambridge University Press, 1960).
5 Yi-Fu Tuan, *Space and Place: The Perspective of Experience* (Minneapolis, MN: University of Minnesota Press, 1977); Tim Cresswell, *Place: An Introduction* (Chichester, UK: Wiley-Blackwell, 2014), 15–18.
6 See, for example, recent important publications such as: Penelope Harvey, Casper Jensen, and Atsuro Morita, eds, *Infrastructures and Social Complexity: A Companion* (New York: Routledge, 2019); Kregg Hetherington, ed., *Infrastructure, Environment, and Life in the Anthropocene* (Durham, NC: Duke University Press Books, 2019); Rahul Mukherjee, *Radiant Infrastructures: Media, Environment, and Cultures of Uncertainty* (Durham, NC: Duke University Press Books, 2020).
7 Sonia Vieira and others, "The Neurophysiological Activations of Mechanical Engineers and Industrial Designers While Designing and Problem-Solving," *Design Science* 6 (2020): 1–35; Katerina Alexiou, Theodore Zamenopoulos, and Sam Gilbert, "Imaging the Designing Brain: A Neurocognitive Exploration of Design Thinking," in *Proceedings of the Design Computing and Cognition Annual Meeting 2010*, ed. John S. Gero (Dordrecht: Springer Netherlands, 2011), 489–504; L. Hay and others, "The Neural Correlates of Ideation in Product Design Engineering Practitioners," *Design Science* 5 (2019): 1–14.
8 Jan Auernhammer, Neeraj Sonalkar, and Manish Saggar, "NeuroDesign: From Neuroscience Research to Design Thinking Practice," in *Design Thinking Research: Interrogating the Doing*, ed. Christoph Meinel and Larry Leifer, Understanding Innovation (Cham, Switzerland: Springer International Publishing, 2021), 347–355.
9 Jay Pritzker, "Presentation Speech for the Award to Hans Hollein" (The Pritzker Prize Ceremony, The Huntington Library, San Marino, CA, 1985).
10 Mark M. Jarzombek, Vikramaditya Prakash, and Francis D.K. Ching, *A Global History of Architecture* (Hoboken, NJ: Wiley, 2010); Mark Gelernter, *A History of American Architecture: Buildings in Their Cultural and Technological Context* (Hanover, NH: University Press of New England, 2001); Spiro Kostof, *A History of Architecture: Settings and Rituals*, ed. Gregory Castillo, 2nd edn (New York: Oxford University Press, 1995).
11 Stephen Parcell, *Four Historical Definitions of Architecture* (Montreal: McGill-Queen's Press, 2012).
12 Daniel T. Rodgers, *Atlantic Crossings: Social Politics in a Progressive Age* (Cambridge, MA: Belknap Press, 2000); Alan Trachtenberg, *The Incorporation of America: Culture and Society in the Gilded Age* (New York: Hill and Wang, 2007).
13 Partha Chatterjee, *The Nation and Its Fragments: Colonial and Postcolonial Histories* (Princeton, NJ: Princeton University Press, 1993), 95–112.
14 Vera Candiani, *Dreaming of Dry Land: Environmental Transformation in Colonial Mexico City* (Stanford, CA: Stanford University Press, 2014); Matthew Vitz, *City on a Lake: Urban Political Ecology and the Growth of Mexico City* (Durham, NC: Duke University Press, 2018).
15 Samuel Kelton Roberts, *Infectious Fear: Politics, Disease, and the Health Effects of Segregation*, Studies in Social Medicine (Chapel Hill, NC: The University of North Carolina Press, 2009); Gilberto Hochman and Diane Grosklaus Whitty, *The Sanitation of Brazil: Nation, State, and Public Health, 1889-1930* (Urbana-Champaign, IL: University of Illinois Press, 2016); Nikhil Anand, *Hydraulic City: Water and the Infrastructures of Citizenship in Mumbai* (Durham, NC: Duke University Press, 2017).
16 Christine Macy and others, *The Tennessee Valley Authority: Design and Persuasion* (New York: Princeton Architectural Press, 2007); Michael J. McDonald and John Muldowny, *TVA and the Dispossessed: The Resettlement of Population in the Norris Dam Area* (Knoxville, TN: University of Tennessee Press, 1981).
17 Evelyn Gonzalez, *The Bronx* (New York: Columbia University Press, 2006), 135–137; Owen D. Gutfreund, "Rebuilding New York in the Auto Age: Robert Moses and His Highways," in *Robert Moses and the Modern City: The Transformation of New York*, ed. Hillary Ballon and Kenneth Jackson (New York: W.W. Norton, 2007), 86–93.
18 Bruno Latour, *We Have Never Been Modern* (Cambridge, MA: Harvard University Press, 1993); Tilo Schabert, *The Figure of Modernity* (Boston, MA: De Gruyter, 2020).
19 Fran Tonkiss, *Cities by Design: The Social Life of Urban Form* (Cambridge: Polity, 2014), 139–140.
20 Ngaire Woods, *The Globalizers: The IMF, the World Bank, and Their Borrowers* (Ithaca, NY: Cornell University Press, 2007); Michael A. Cohen, "Macroeconomic Adjustment and the City," *Cities*, Special Issue: Urban Innovation for the 21st Century, 7, no. 1 (February 1, 1990): 49–59.

21 Tonkiss, *Cities by Design*, 142.
22 Robert W.D. Boyce, "Imperial Dreams and National Realities: Britain, Canada and the Struggle for a Pacific Telegraph Cable, 1879-1902," *The English Historical Review* 115, no. 460 (2000): 39–70.
23 John Tully, "A Victorian Ecological Disaster: Imperialism, the Telegraph, and Gutta-Percha," *Journal of World History* 20, no. 4 (2009): 559–579.
24 Tatiana Schlossberg, *Inconspicuous Consumption: The Environmental Impact You Don't Know You Have* (New York: Grand Central Publishing, 2019); Eric Williams, "Environmental Impacts in the Production of Personal Computers," in *Computers and the Environment: Understanding and Managing Their Impacts*, Eco-Efficiency in Industry and Science, ed. Ruediger Kuehr and Eric Williams (Dordrecht: Springer Netherlands, 2003), 41–72.
25 William J. Mitchell, *Me++: The Cyborg Self and the Networked City* (Cambridge, MA: MIT Press, 2003); Matthew Gandy, "Cyborg Urbanization: Complexity and Monstrosity in the Contemporary City," *International Journal of Urban and Regional Research* 29, no. 1 (2005): 26–49.
26 Kaika, *City of Flows*, 62–66.
27 Stephen Graham and Simon Marvin, *Splintering Urbanism: Networked Infrastructure, Technological Mobilities, and the Urban Condition* (New York: Routledge, 2001).
28 AbdouMaliq Simone, "People as Infrastructure: Intersecting Fragments in Johannesburg," *Public Culture* 16, no. 3 (2004): 407–429.
29 Swati Chattopadhyay, *Unlearning the City: Infrastructure in a New Optical Field* (Minneapolis, MN: University of Minnesota Press, 2012), 248.
30 Charles R. Acland and others, *Signal Traffic: Critical Studies of Media Infrastructures*, ed. Lisa Parks and Nicole Starosielski, 1st edn (Urbana: University of Illinois Press, 2015); Orit Halpern and others, "Test-Bed Urbanism," *Public Culture* 25, no. 2 (March 1, 2013): 272–306.
31 Tonkiss, *Cities by Design*, 143.

PART I
Materialities

1
KINGSHIP AND THE ROCKS
Infrastructure and the Materiality of Empire
Braden Lee Scott

The Pantheon in Rome continues to stand as an architectural attestation of what was once a networked ancient empire. The superstructure that one encounters today is an updated version of its predecessors, and it is Hadrian's reconstructed portico that is at the center of my chapter. Here, I focus specifically on the Pantheon's column shafts that are carved from single blocks of stone that were extracted from two different quarries in Egypt: red granite from Aswan, and grey granite from Mons Claudianus. First, we must answer questions around acquisition and mobility: just how did the ancient Romans cut these fifty-foot monoliths, carry them across the desert, haul them onto ships, transport them to Rome, and then drag them up to the city center where they would be installed in the temple that was awaiting their arrival? Each piece of the process left behind traces of an ancient infrastructure, and tells us a story of Rome's technics of resource extraction. Technology and systems in place during the second century CE afforded Roman emperors the ability to convey columns from the deserts of Egypt to Rome. But this chapter is also concerned with what this kind of infrastructure means. In the case of rose granite columns, this material had already been used for millennia as the intimate casing of inner tomb chambers for Egyptian rulers. By transporting red granite to Rome for the columns of the Pantheon's portico, Hadrian positioned himself as a dynastic ruler of a vast and polychronic Mediterranean world.

Presenting the Pantheon's massive columns for a BBC camera, historian Mary Beard quips that, for Imperial Rome, "the stone *is* the message."[1] Along with the red granite obelisks in Rome, the Pantheon's columns ostentatiously display the control that emperors exercised over the movement of material resources. The large granite monoliths were quarried in Egypt: the twelve grey exterior columns from the eastern Sahara, and the four red interior columns from Aswan (Figure 1.1).[2] While a strong infrastructure of resource extraction and transportation is implied, it is the symbolic quality of Egyptian granite that rhetorically displays cosmological command and dynastic success.[3]

This chapter examines the movement of granite, as both material substance and symbol of power, through imperial networks instantiated by infrastructure. After first analyzing Roman networks of material transport, I move back into Pharaonic Egypt to unveil how granite accumulated symbolic meaning of cosmology and dynasty, and how this lithic message was processed across the millennia to include Rome. I show that material histories of granite enable "grounded interpretations of complex phenomena" that "cut across the cultural sky like fiery comets."[4] Situating the Pantheon among other Egyptianized architectural programs in Rome, it is evident that not only the columns of the portico, but the entire building itself is in dialogue with the Pharaonic Egyptian world view. A complex infrastructure that entangled land, sea, and spaces of ritual processed the Pantheon's monumental presence.

DOI: 10.4324/9781003093756-3

Figure 1.1 The porch of the Pantheon, Rome.

Source: Photograph courtesy of Joseph Heathcott.

Of Empire and Infrastructure

The arrival of monolithic Egyptian granite in Rome begins with the first emperor. After Julius Caesar's heir Octavian defeated the Ptolemaic Pharaoh Cleopatra and her consort, Marc Antony, at the Battle of Actium in 31 BCE, Egypt was annexed as a Roman province. Within a year, and after the suicide of Cleopatra and Antony, Octavian became the sole ruler of Egypt—an act of unification of the Northern and Southern Mediterranean that Livy claimed "brought about peace on land and sea."[5] As the Macedonian kings of Egypt had done since the late fourth century BCE, Octavian immediately crowned himself Pharaoh in Egypt and began temple-building projects and sculptural programs that included his own image in the Pharaonic style (Figure 1.2). In 27 BCE, he was the first Roman ruler to be given the divine title Augustus.

Octavian, now Augustus, exercised command over an expanding empire and began developing a complex infrastructural network for the transport of building materials. Writing in the second and third centuries, Suetonius and Dio declared that Augustus found Rome made of brick and clay, but left it a city of marble.[6] Despite Dio's disclaimer that Augustus "did not thereby refer literally to the appearance of its buildings, but rather to the strength of the empire," there was actually a considerable amount of truth to the lithic metaphor: it was because of Augustus that Rome began to import and display Egyptian obelisks after 10 BCE—the first two being the Montecitorio and Flaminian obelisks—and it was also because of Augustus that marble, "both coloured and white," became integral to Roman architectural projects that were "on a scale hitherto unknown."[7]

Augustus inherited a Mediterranean world in which architectural marble and granite were already in use. He also inherited an established network of grain transport, a resource that Vitruvius

Figure 1.2 Relief of Augustus offering Ma'at, Kalabsha.
Source: Photograph by Braden Lee Scott.

claimed was behind the establishment of Alexandria as a major port city.[8] In a move that emulated Alexander, Augustus amplified military presence in Egypt to secure these resource networks.[9] The empire controlled Ptolemaic mines and quarries after annexation, and as the relevance of stone materials increased in Rome, emperors pushed towards the "nationalization" of lithics.[10] While there is evidence of Pharaonic mining in the eastern Sahara, it was the Romans who developed a massive network of new roads and settlements devoted to quarrying. Pharaonic Red Sea ports connected Egypt to Arabia, southern Africa, and India.[11] Whole ships were assembled on the Nile, disassembled inland, and carried across the desert in "ship kits" to the Red Sea, where they were reassembled.[12] These routes required roads in the eastern desert. With Pharaonic networks already established, Augustus simply had to update and expand the infrastructure to accommodate a new demand for Egyptian shafts.

The *granito del foro*—grey granite—shafts of the pantheon were quarried at Gebel Fatireh, or Mons Claudianus.[13] Building a site in the desert mountains 120 km east of the Nile required a new infrastructure of transportation. The Roman military built new roads to serve only the quarries and the *hydreumata*, the garrison outposts along the way. The population that ranged between 700 and 900 laborers was a community of mixed professions, including skilled architects who selected which sections of the mountain to cut into columns for the Roman Empire (Figure 1.3).[14] While Josephus claimed that captives from Jerusalem after 72 CE were enslaved and put to work in Egypt, only free skilled workers appear in the archaeological record at Mons Claudianus.[15] After laborers cut and shaped the monoliths

Figure 1.3 Traces of extraction at Mons Claudianus, Egypt.

Source: Photograph by Braden Lee Scott.

on site (Figure 1.4), the columns were hauled to Caenopolis (modern Quena) where they were placed on Nile barges to be brought downstream to Alexandria.

While roads are the manufactured artifacts of infrastructure, currents in rivers and seas are part of the topography of mobility and globalization. Coining the method "network archaeology," Nicole Starosielski argues that, too often, scholarship on networks tends to focus on the abstract visualization of connections.[16] With such an emphasis on flow and continuity, scholars often neglect the affordances and frictions of the political borders and environments in which these movements take place. Monoliths that weigh anywhere between 50 and 400 tons do not simply *flow* from Egypt, and yet, they appear *as if* they had. Commanding a difficult medium with ease, and at the expenditure of massive amounts of human energy, is what boasts a ruler's power in the production of monumental architecture.[17]

While tracking the departure and arrival of materials is crucial to the global turn in architectural history, a deeper meaning is mined when we process the nodes and links that determine mobility. A topographical consideration of mobility must take into account the ways that infrastructures are already "embedded into existing natural and cultural environments."[18] These infrastructures extend beyond trails, rivers, and seas to include the laboring bodies involved, both human and animal.

Camels and donkeys were the beasts of burden in northeastern Africa, and their infrastructural role is evidenced on one of the few primary written sources that directly mentions the movement of columns in Egypt.[19] The Greek message on papyrus from December 29, 118 CE is a desperate request:

Figure 1.4 Abandoned column at Mons Claudianus.

Source: Photograph by Braden Lee Scott.

> … we have a great number of animals for the purpose of bringing down a fifty-foot column, and already we are nearly out of barley. You would render me a very great favour in this, brother, if the barley … were to arrive swiftly.[20]

Although we will never know if the camels and donkeys received their barley, the papyrus reveals that a monolith was on its way to the Nile when Hadrian commissioned the Temple of Trajan and the Pantheon.[21] Egyptians from the previous millennia harnessed animal labor in their infrastructures of transport, but they rarely strayed far from the Nile.[22] Quarrying the eastern Sahara required an expansive update to the minimal infrastructure and yoked animal bodies in the process.

Once the shafts had been brought to Caenopolis, they would be loaded onto ships to sail 800 km down the Nile. In Alexandria, they would be reloaded onto larger ships that harnessed exterior ballasts, and were filled with lentils to float and stabilize the monoliths during their journey across the sea. On the ship made of fir that transported the Vatican obelisk, Pliny writes: "it is certain that nothing more wonderful than this ship has ever been seen on the sea."[23] Pliny's praise of the role of ships documents the transport of the Vatican obelisk and provides clever rhetoric. Without directly referencing Plato's metaphor of a ship's captain as a nation's ruler, Pliny reminds his reader that through successful transport and erection of the obelisk, the emperor was in command of Roman society and could bring order to the unruly sea.[24] The monoliths were unloaded at Ostia and either stored in coastal magazines or dragged up to the Roman hilltops. The entire process, especially the spectacle of monoliths dragged through the streets of Rome, displayed the emperors' command over nature. If "a medium reveals a medium—as a medium," and "infrastructure begets infrastructure," then Egyptian granite monoliths in Rome boasted and sustained a thalassocratic message.[25] Nautical transport was both a practical use of waterways and a symbol of a king's command over society and nature.

Since granite is not exclusive to Egypt, and other valuable stones were available throughout the Mediterranean, why was Egyptian granite a standard for monolithic columns in the Roman Empire? The answer lies in the symbolic association of Aswan granite with a king's divine and eternal command over the world, a meaning that was alive in Egypt 3,000 years before Rome appropriated Egyptian materials and rituals. This meaning proved so powerful that the might of the Roman imperium shaped and bent infrastructure around the procurement of this highly symbolic material.

The Symbolic Power of Granite

Rome's embrace of granite as a sign of power emerges from a series of events that began with the formation of the prehistoric Egyptian state. Before the fourth millennium BCE, agrarian societies developed along the fertile banks and floodplains of the Nile river. With localized stability came the development of centers of production, marketable goods, and trade with West Asia.[26] Art from the fourth millennium evidences cross-cultural transmission, which has led to the conclusion that Egypt and Mesopotamia were developing trade networks, most likely through intermediaries in Canaan and Palestine. With access to the delta and the sea, Lower Egyptian traders directed these emerging *entrepôts*, which solicited attention from the powerful Upper Egyptian kings to the south, who took control over both regions and moved the capital north to Memphis. In Egyptian religion, this moment of unification at the end of the fourth millennium BCE was cast as a cosmological event: a world-view wherein *ma'at*—order—was established.

Upon unification, kings used granite from Upper Egypt as the intimate lining of inner tomb chambers to ensure an eternal afterlife. First Dynasty King Den's tomb in Abydos (ca. 2950 BCE) is the earliest extant use of Aswan granite in Egyptian architecture, and was a model for successors, whose architects took advantage of the Nile's embedded infrastructure to transport granite blocks 1,000 km to mortuary complexes in Saqqara and Dahshur.[27] Future memory of a unified kingdom demanded eternal presence for deceased nobles, and Aswan granite supplied the durable material to inscribe this message in architecture. The conspicuous consumption of energy rhetorized the ruler as Pharaoh, a more than human king with divine command over society and nature.

Fourth Dynasty rulers imported massive shipments of Aswan granite to build the pyramids on the Giza plateau (ca. 2500 BCE). While architects used nearby limestone for the fabric of the mortuary complex, they used granite as structural adornment in the lining of the interior chambers and the sarcophagus itself. The durability of granite was likely considered, as it was also used to encapsulate the pyramids below the final casing of polished limestone.[28] Ritual function is also clear: the movement of stone from Upper to Lower Egypt was infrastructural performance of unification. The scale of transport ended after the third largest pyramid was built, and by the decline of the Old Kingdom around 2150 BCE, the pyramids at Giza had been left to stand unattended and were raided. Political dissent effected the downfall of the Sixth Dynasty, and the once-unified Egyptian state fragmented into discrete *nomes* (provinces) ruled by princes.

Later Egyptians knew that Aswan granite had been the choice medium for the massive tombs of the Old Kingdom; its cosmological significance amplified through architecture.[29] Around 2040 BCE, Theban kings reconquered Lower Egypt and reunified the state under a single Egyptian ruler. Early dynastic uses of granite rhetorically boasted unification, and granite in Middle Kingdom architectural programs "indicated the importance of the building."[30] Centuries later, the state was divided after the invasion and establishment of a Hyksos ruler in Lower Egypt. A Theban king directed his armies north, reconquered Lower Egypt, and the state was unified, once again. New Kingdom Pharaohs resubstantiated the rhetoric of unification through monumentality and sculptural styles from both the

Old and the Middle Kingdoms; this included the quarrying and transport of granite at a magnitude that had not been seen for centuries.[31] These repetitive stages—series of events that Whitney Davis calls "chains of replication"—continually processed Egyptian kingship through events that linked governance over society with infrastructural command over nature.[32]

During the first millennium BCE, Egypt struggled to remain unified. Resubstantiating dynastic iconography and materials sustained the Egyptian world-view during these periods of crisis, and Aswan granite conveyed the currency of this message.[33] In 332, Alexander III of Macedon took control of Egypt from the Persians and was embraced as a divine savior. Upon his death in 323, his empire was divided up by his generals, and Ptolemy I Soter took Egypt. Ptolemy did not just rule as a Macedonian king—he took on the role of Pharaoh, had his image carved in Egyptian style, and continued the worship of Egyptian gods in temples from the previous millennia. The durability of this religious devotion as well as the materials that secured it in architecture would prove irresistible to the expanding Roman Empire.

Solar Power and Performative Infrastructure

When Augustus arrived in 30 BCE, it was not Hellenistic Egypt that fascinated him; like Alexander, it was the religion, ritual, and architecture of Egypt's mightiest empire, the New Kingdom. Among the many trappings of Pharaonic power, Egyptian granite proved highly alluring to Roman leaders.

The significance of Egyptian granite had increased with the rise of New-Kingdom solar cults, where the ruddy stone indicated the rising and the setting of the sun. Temple roofs were opened so that the sun god—not a sculpted effigy—could be worshipped directly. Solar worship carried an erotic charge. In the temple at Heliopolis—city of the sun—a pyramidion referred to as *benben* is the origin of the shape of the pyramids at Giza, and of all obelisks. In Egyptian religion, after the sun god self-engendered and rose from the primeval sea, the first thing he did was masturbate. Ejaculating into the frothy water, his semen hardened and formed the first solid matter in the universe. This was the birth of the earliest landmass, the Primeval Hill. The *benben* was covered in gold foil so that the creamy iridescence of semen would be broadcast, and the stone was held on top of a long granite shaft to monumentalize the sun god's penis mid-ejaculation.[34] The erotic act determines formative power: it is from the sun god that the divine and human worlds were created.

Temple architecture—microcosms of the Primeval Sea and Hill—functioned as environmental analogues where mythology of cosmic origins married divine rituals of Pharaonic unification. The *sed* festival, held around the thirty-year mark of a king's coronation, was a territorial performance that displayed the body of the king as the single nexus of unification as he moved between ritual architecture—once enthroned as the king of Upper Egypt, and then as king of Lower Egypt.[35] Since the king's body also represents the natural world, granite was freshly cut in Aswan and shipped up the Nile as ecological accompaniment to the performance. Beyond the ephemeral event, temple statues of the king were sculpted to perform eternal unification, a concept "expressed in the materials": stones from the north such as brown quartzite would be used to sculpt the king of Lower Egypt, wearing a red crown (*deshret*), and granite from the south was used to sculpt the king of Upper Egypt, wearing the white crown (*hedjet*).[36] The king's body performed the infrastructural machinations of the ongoing unification of the Egyptian state.

While the *sed* festival spanned the dynasties, the *opet* festival was practiced during and after the New Kingdom in Thebes. The temples at Karnak and Luxor face each other on a north–south axis, connected by a sphinx-lined path. The king and his entourage would assemble at Karnak with an array of ritual regalia, including a barque that contained a concealed sculpture of Amun-Ra—Karnak's combined deity, both sun god and creator of the universe. The boisterous, celebratory procession made its way to Luxor where, upon entering the temple, the generative life-force—*ka*—of all deceased kings would rejuvenate divine kingship.[37] Ithyphallic—erect—deities were depicted as part of the transmission of *ka*, as rejuvenation ensured with each rising sun the king's bull-like virility and fertile potential to create.[38]

From Luxor, the procession walked to the Nile and sailed on boats back to Karnak. During the entire procession, zealous throngs circulated through chapels at Karnak and shrines along the route to Luxor.

Augustus continued these ritual processions between Karnak and Luxor as Egypt's Pharaoh. As Alexander had done, Augustus continued to preserve and build at Karnak, and he erected chapels to house eternal sculpted images of himself for cult worship.[39] After Augustus, Luxor was an important temple in the province where Roman emperors were worshipped as dynastic successors of the Egyptian pantheon until the fourth century CE.

Building the Pantheon

Considering Rome's active presence in Egyptian religion, it is no surprise that Egyptian architectural programs appear in Rome. The Ara Pacis provides a case in point. The Roman Senate commissioned the Ara Pacis following Augustus' victories in Spain and Gaul in 13 BCE, and dedicated it four years later on the Campus Martius. Combining sculpted panels of mythology and family history, the altar is as much a monument of peace as it is a display of dynastic origins.[40] While the sculpted ornament is appropriately Hellenistic in the early imperial style, the architectural iconography is identical to the New Kingdom chapels that were still used at Karnak during Augustus' time in Egypt.[41] When considered as part of the urban organization of the Campus Martius, particularly the Mausoleum of Augustus, the Montecitorio Obelisk, and the Pantheon, the Egyptian origin of the Ara Pacis is further solidified.

It is within this larger spatial program of the Campus Martius that the Pantheon most clearly evinces the architectural substantiation of the Egyptian world view. This is present in iconographic transference, orientation, and material. To design and supervise the construction of the Pantheon, Augustus tapped his son-in-law and trusted counsel Marcus Vipsanius Agrippa. Agrippa likely drew on the Alexandrian temple devoted to Macedonian and Egyptian gods as a prototype for his design.[42] The Tychaion was circular with twelve sculptural niches and a colossal statue of a Ptolemaic Pharaoh was lauded. The Pantheon is alike in structural form, has eight niches in similar distribution, and inside stood a colossal statue of Julius Caesar. Further, the iconographic source of Augustus' Mausoleum is most likely Alexander's rotunda tomb in Alexandria, which means that both the Mausoleum and the Pantheon have probable iconographic sources in Egypt.

The orientation of the Pantheon places it in dialogue with the Mausoleum and the Ara Pacis. The Pantheon veers slightly northwest so that the entrance of the pantheon can form a perfect axial line with the mausoleum's entrance. Since both buildings were constructed at the same time, and the urban space between them was open, their axial coincidence is unlikely.[43] The Ara Pacis, while slightly east of the axial line, received ceremonial processions that traversed the distance between the mausoleum and Pantheon. In other words, processions used the Ara Pacis the same way in Rome as they did in Egypt, suggesting that the mausoleum and Pantheon could represent Lower and Upper Egypt, or perhaps in a broader sense the ideal of imperial unity.

The orientation also reveals a crossover of solar worship, present in the installation of the Montecitorio obelisk as the gnomon for Augustus's sundial. Diane Favro argues "each day, the sun god Apollo brought the Horologium Augusti to life."[44] Every morning the sun cast its shadow east toward the Ara Pacis, then in the afternoon, south toward the Pantheon, finally reaching north to the Mausoleum Augusti. The solar narrative illuminates Augustus' origins, then the conquest of Egypt that defined Rome as a newly formed Empire, and ends in the final resting place of the Julii. Roman carryover of Egyptian erotics in solar religion is also evident. John Pollini argues that the Egyptian word for obelisk *thn* (to pierce) and the Greek word *obeliskos* (small spit, or skewer) are sexual when considering the origin of the *benben* in solar religion, from which the phallic form of the obelisk derives, and the procreative language used in Augustus' own expressions of bringing forth peace.[45] On September 23, Augustus' birthday, the shadow of the obelisk penetrated the doorway of the Ara Pacis: a symbol of generative cosmic birth and erective power appropriated from Egyptian ritual.

This brings us back to the material that boasts the Pantheon's message: Egyptian granite. Agrippa built the Pantheon in the first decade of Augustus's reign, but it burned down, was repaired by Domitian, and when lightning struck during the reign of Trajan, it burned again. Most scholars agree that around 113 CE, Hadrian rebuilt the Pantheon that we see today. As was customary of Roman emperors before him, he also crowned himself Pharaoh in Egypt and continued to transport granite monoliths around the Mediterranean.

Hadrian's design for the porch leaves us with one final thought. Until the Roman Empire, the grey granite used for the exterior file had never been quarried. While red granite was used throughout global building projects, grey stones were reserved for architecture in Rome. Grey granite was not a rare or expensive stone, but it provided something exceptional: new architectural media for the Roman Empire.[46] Because it "had no established associations," J. Clayton Fant argues, grey granite "was free to be identified as closely with the new rulers in Rome as Aswan had been with the Egyptian kings."[47] If, as has been argued, every detail in the Pantheon's design rhetorically conveys the building as the nexus of the unification of the world, then the colors of the columns were not haphazardly selected.[48] The encasing of four red columns with twelve grey columns reanimates the material symbolism of Pharaonic tomb and temple architecture, but it does so with a reminder that Rome is Egypt's successor. Just as Egypt, through chains of replications, continuously processed its unification of two realms along a body of water, so too did Rome: the Pantheon extends the rhetoric of unification to the north and south of the Mediterranean.

Embedded with what Swetnam-Burland calls a "charge"—a storage of meaning that conveys a message—Egyptian granite in Rome transmitted a loud signal. This signal is a message of empire: distant provinces controlled by a single ruler, infrastructural networks, spectacular technics of resource extraction, and monumental links to ancient dynasties. Of course, the columns should not be read on their own, nor the Pantheon. However, when considered within the broader material histories of imperial expansion, the granite columns of the Pantheon's porch illuminate both the cosmological assertion of Roman power as well as the infrastructures that made it possible.

Notes

1 *Mary Beard's Ultimate Rome: Empire Without Limit*, season 1, episode 2, directed by Chris Mitchell, written by Mary Beard, aired May 4, 2016, on BBC.
2 Seventeenth-century popes replaced the dilapidated eastern file with three red granite shafts. Kjeld de Fine Licht, *The Rotunda in Rome: A Study of Hadrian's Pantheon* (Copenhagen: Gyldendal, 1968), 20, 241.
3 Diane Favro, "Reading Augustan Rome: Materiality as Rhetoric *In Situ*," *Advances in the History of Rhetoric* 20, no. 2 (2017): 180.
4 Alan Mikhail, ed., *Water on Sand: Environmental Histories of the Middle East and North Africa* (Oxford: Oxford University Press, 2012), 2; Alina Payne, "The Portability of Art: Prolegomena to Art and Architecture on the Move," in *Territories and Trajectories: Cultures in Circulation*, ed. Diana Sorensen (Durham: Duke University Press, 2018), 104.
5 Livy, 1.19.
6 Suetonius, 2.28.3; Dio 56.30.3–4.
7 Hazel Dodge, "Decorative Stones for Architecture in the Roman Empire," *Oxford Journal of Archaeology* 7, no. 1 (1988): 66.
8 Vitruvius, 2.0.4.
9 Colin Adams, *Land Transport in Roman Egypt: A Study of Economics and Administration in a Roman Province* (Oxford: Oxford University Press, 2007), 159.
10 Pliny *NH* 36.11; J.B. Ward-Perkins, "Quarrying in Antiquity: Technology, Tradition and Social Change," *Proceedings of the British Academy* 57 (1973): 144–145.
11 Strabo, 2.5.12.
12 Kathryn A. Bard and Rodolfo Fattovich, *Seafaring Expeditions to Punt in the Middle Kingdom: Excavations at Mersa/Wadi Gawasis, Egypt* (Leiden: Brill, 2018), 15–17, 60.
13 David P.S. Peacock and Valerie A. Maxfield, eds, *Survey and Excavation at Mons Claudianus, 1987–1993* (Cairo: Institut Français d'Archéologie Orientale, 1997–2006).
14 Ward-Perkins, "Quarrying in Antiquity," 139.

15 Valerie A. Maxfield, "Stone Quarrying in the Eastern Desert with Particular Reference to Mons Claudianus and Mons Porphyrites," in *Economies Beyond Agriculture in the Classical World*, eds David J. Mattingly and John Salmon (London: Routledge, 2001), 157.
16 Nicole Starosielski, *The Undersea Network* (Durham: Duke University Press, 2015), 15.
17 Bruce G. Trigger, "Monumental Architecture: A Thermodynamic Explanation of Symbolic Behaviour," *World Archaeology* 22, no. 2 (1990): 125.
18 Starosielski, 28.
19 Richard W. Bulliet, *The Camel and the Wheel* (New York: Columbia University Press, 1990), 111–119.
20 J. Theodore Peña, "*P.Giss.69*: evidence for the supplying of stone transport operations in Roman Egypt and the Production of Fifty-Foot Monolithic Column Shafts," *Journal of Roman Archaeology* 2 (1989): 127.
21 Paul Davies, David Hemsoll, and Mark Wilson Jones, "The Pantheon: Triumph of Rome or Triumph of Compromise?" *Art History* 10, no. 2 (1987): 146.
22 Roger S. Bagnall, *Egypt in Late Antiquity* (Princeton: Princeton University Press, 1993), 34–40.
23 Pliny, *HN* 16.76.
24 Plato, *Republic*, 6.488.d–e.
25 John Durham Peters, *The Marvelous Clouds: Toward a Philosophy of Elemental Media* (Chicago: The University of Chicago Press, 2015), 111; Shannon Mattern, *Code+Clay, Data+Dirt: Five Thousand Years of Urban Media* (Minneapolis: The University of Minnesota Press, 2017), vii.
26 Kathryn A. Bard, "Political Economies of Predynastic Egypt and the Formation of the Early State," *Journal of Archaeological Research* 25, no. 1 (2017): 1–36.
27 Kathryn A. Bard, "The Emergence of the Egyptian State (c.3200-2686 BC)," in *Oxford History of Ancient Egypt*, ed. Ian Shaw (Oxford: Oxford University Press, 2000), 68; W.M. Flinders Petrie, *The Royal Tombs of the First Dynasty* (London: Egypt Exploration Fund, 1900), 1:4.
28 Mark Lehner and Zahi Hawass, *Giza and the Pyramids: The Definitive History* (Chicago: Chicago University Press, 2017), 48–50, 152, 153; Dieter Arnold, *Building in Egypt: Pharaonic Stone Masonry* (Oxford: Oxford University Press, 1991), 164–176.
29 A Middle Kingdom text reads "they who built in granite and constructed halls in goodly pyramids with fine work," in R.O. Faulkner, "The Man Who Was Tired of Life," *Journal of Egyptian Archaeology* 42, no. 1 (1956): 27.
30 Alexander Badawy, *A History of Egyptian Architecture* (Berkeley: University of California Press, 1966), 1:1, 64.
31 Badawy, 2:84, 195–197; Arnold, 41. Also see Michael J. Waters, "Reviving Antiquity with Granite: Spolia and the Development of Roman Renaissance Architecture," *Architectural History* 59 (2016): 149–179.
32 Whitney Davis, *Masking the Blow: The Scene of Representation in Late Prehistoric Egyptian Art* (Berkeley: University of California Press, 1992), 9.
33 Molly Swetnam-Burland, *Egypt in Italy: Visions of Egypt in Roman Imperial Culture* (Cambridge: Cambridge University Press, 2015), 71.
34 Henri Frankfort, *Kingship and the Gods: A Study of Ancient Near Eastern Religion as the Integration of Society & Nature* (Chicago: The University of Chicago Press, [1948] 1978), 20–25, 153–154, 380–381.
35 John Baines, "Public Ceremonial Performance in Ancient Egypt: Exclusion and Integration," in *Archaeology of Performance: Theaters of Power, Community, and Politics*, eds Takeshi Inomata and Lawrence S. Cohen (Lanham: AltaMira Press, 2006), 261–302.
36 Arielle P. Kozloff, *Amenhotep III: Egypt's Radiant Pharaoh* (Cambridge: Cambridge University Press, 2012), 123–124.
37 Lanny Bell, "Luxor Temple and the Cult of the Royal *Ka*," *Journal of Near Eastern Studies* 44 (1985): 258–260.
38 Gay Robins, "Male Bodies and the Construction of Masculinity in New Kingdom Egyptian Art," in *Servant of Mut*, ed. Sue D'Auria (Leiden: Brill, 2014), 208–209.
39 Erin A. Peters, "Octavian Transformed as Pharaoh and as Emperor Augustus," in *The Ancient Art of Transformation: Case Studies from Mediterranean Contexts*, eds Renee M. Gondek and Carrie L. Sulosky Weaver (Oxford: Oxbow, 2019), 116–126.
40 Peter J. Holliday, "Time, History, and Ritual on the Ara Pacis Augustae," *Art Bulletin* 72, no. 4 (1990): 544–548.
41 Jennifer Trimble, "Appropriating Egypt for the Ara Pacis Augustae," in *Rome, Empire of Plunder: The Dynamics of Cultural Appropriation*, eds Matthew P. Loar, Carolyn MacDonald, and Dan-el Padilla Peralta (Cambridge: Cambridge University Press, 2017), 111.
42 Judith S. Mckenzie and Andres T. Reyes, "The Alexandrian Tychaion: A Pantheon?" *Journal of Roman Archaeology* 26 (2013): 39–52.
43 Eugenio la Rocca, "Agrippa's Pantheon and Its Origin," in *The Pantheon: From Antiquity to the Present*, eds Tod Marder and Mark Wilson Jones (Cambridge: Cambridge University Press, 2015), 51–52, 73–75.
44 Diane Favro, *The Urban Image of Augustan Rome* (Cambridge: Cambridge University Press, 1996), 130.
45 John Pollini, *From Republic to Empire: Rhetoric, Religion, and Power in the Visual Culture of Ancient Rome* (Norman: University of Oklahoma Press, 2012), 215–216. Also see Bernard Frischer and others, "New Light on the

Relationship of the Montecitorio Obelisk and the Ara Pacis of Augustus," *Studies in Digital Heritage* 1, no. 1 (2017): 18–119.
46 Leah E. Long, "Extracting Economies from Roman Marble Quarries," *Economic History Review* 70, no. 1 (2017): 61–62.
47 J. Clayton Fant, "Ideology, Gift, and Trade: A Distribution Model for the Roman Imperial Marbles," in *The Inscribed Economy: Production and Distribution in the Roman Empire in the Light of* instrumentum domesticum, ed. W.V. Harris, Supplement, *Journal of Roman Archaeology* 6 (1993): 150.
48 Indra Kagis McEwen, "Hadrian's Rhetoric I: The Pantheon," *RES* 24 (1993): 63.

2
IN BETWEEN TECHNOLOGY AND ARCHITECTURE

Claude-Nicolas Ledoux and the French Royal *Saline*

Carmelina Martinez

The employment of infrastructure on the Royal Saline at Arc-et-Senans built during the last quarter of the eighteenth century, near the forest of Chaux, and the plan for the Ideal City of Chaux described by Claude-Nicolas Ledoux in his treatise "Architecture Considered in Relation to Art, Mores, and Legislation" (1804), is the main input of this chapter. The Royal Saline at Arc-et-Senans designed by Ledoux for the French monarchy, with the purpose of standardizing the production of salt, incorporates industry as a mechanical process. His proposal includes not just the exploitation of resources, but also the wellbeing of society using infrastructure. In the Ideal City of Chaux, Ledoux draws and characterizes a city with the visionary thought of planning for an "economic utopia" at the end of the eighteenth century. In these projects, Ledoux shows us the use of infrastructure as a tool for the mediation between architecture and technology. Ledoux drew on the visual language of the picturesque in his descriptions and in his own drawings. His writings are a fusion of the physiocratic thinking, with the inclusion of the culture related to the woods, fields, and gardens, where the infrastructure plays an important role as a bond between them. Ledoux's architecture and his contributions on social reform established a relation with nature through infrastructure. Ultimately, he considers nature as a "remedy to Modernity" within a context where industrialization seemed to be erasing the natural world.

The royal *saline* at Arc-et-Senans was built near the forest of Chaux during the last quarter of the eighteenth century. Designed by Claude-Nicolas Ledoux at the request of the French monarch Louis XV, the works were part of an effort to standardize the production of salt. However, Ledoux's design incorporated not only an industrial plant for the exploitation of resources, but also an "ideal city" for the wellbeing of those who would use the facilities. In the Ideal City of Chaux, Ledoux envisioned the creation of a well-ordered, rationally planned "economic utopia." Together, these projects displayed Ledoux's commitment to using infrastructure as a tool for mediation between architecture, technology, and civic order.

Claude-Nicolas Ledoux (1736–1806) was born in Dormans, Marne, France. He studied classics at College de Beauvais, and architecture with Jacques Francois Blondel, one of the most recognized teachers, theorists, and writers of his time. He worked with Louis-François Trouard, who had a large knowledge of antique and classical architecture. Ledoux earned a reputation for his projects of neo-classical chateaux and pavilions, and laid out his approach to design in his 1804 treatise, "Architecture Considered in Relation to Art, Morals, and Legislation."

In his descriptions and drawings, he employed the language of the "picturesque" aesthetic ideal. His writings fused physiocratic thinking with tradition related to the woods, fields and gardens. Infrastructure played an important role as a bond between them. Ledoux's architecture and his contributions to social reform established a relationship with nature by using infrastructural design.

Like many of his contemporaries, he considered environment to be a "remedy to Modernity" during a time and place where urbanization and industrialization seemed to be transforming the natural world.[1]

Early Industrialization and its Impact on Architecture

Ledoux's proposals were conceived in the dawn of Industrial Revolution, when architecture had to address the needs of new forms of production and social organization. These were not, however, sudden changes; the expanding political power of the monarchy was entwined with state investment in building and manufacturing projects. Thus, at the end of the seventeenth century, the French state intensified efforts to demonstrate the absolute power of the monarch through a transformation in the working environments of industrial production. Jean-Baptiste Colbert (1619–1683), powerful minister to Louis XIV, promoted this "the spirit of progress," first as the Superintendent of Buildings, then Secretary of the Navy, and finally in a consolidated position as Controller-General of Finance. Particularly in this latter capacity, he encouraged the development of private manufacturing that would advance the interest of the state. This resulted in the rapid expansion of many manufactures: Saint-Gobain, a producer of mirrors and glass; Saint-Étienne, a producer of armaments; and Morlaix, a producer of tobacco.

In the early to mid-eighteenth century, under the reign of Louis XV, the state continued the policies of economic development through industrialization, promoting the development of a new workspace for Sèvres, a porcelain manufacture, and the construction of the Royal Saline at Arc-et-Senans. Such royal largesse elevated the stature of the monarch, but also encouraged the expansion of art, crafts, science, and culture around the entire nation. The Morlaix Tobacco Factory (1740) provides a case in point. Designed by Jean-François Blondel (1683–1756), the Morlaix plant was one of the first facilities built under this promotional effort. Blondel's design for the Morlaix plant, included integrated spaces for production, warehousing, and worker lodgings, each with its own specifications for light, air, ceiling clearance, circulation, machine load, and other considerations.

Until then, most of the buildings that the French government (with the support of private investors) endorsed to house production processes were adaptations to preexisting edifices. Galleries used to house the workshops of a variety of craftsmen, as indicated in the definition published by the Encyclopedia of Diderot and D'Alembert: "By the word manufactory, we commonly mean a considerable number of workers, gathered in the same place to do a sort of work under the eyes of an entrepreneur."[2] The representation of these buildings, featured in the Encyclopedia, shows a large roof that covered the space of production. These structures were merely utilitarian.

Another Venue for Change: Physiocracy

Ledoux's approach to infrastructure planning took shape amid the intellectual movement of physiocracy, an economic theory that attributed the origin of a nation's wealth to nature. Its chief exponents included François Quesnay (1694–1774), Quesnay's disciple Victor Riquetti, Marquis de Mirabeau, and Anne Robert Jacques Turgot (1727–1781). The movement upheld ideas that clashed with royal prerogatives. Charles-Alexandre de Calonne (1734–1802), for example, proposed a series of tax reforms that prompted Louis XVI to exile him to the Lorraine region in northeastern France.

Since the administration of Jean Baptiste Colbert, the commercial sector of France had expanded dramatically. Industrial activity was buoyant, communication routes improved, and the different regions of France had become more economically interdependent.[3] However, progressive landowners and rural nobles saw in the English mercantile system more freedom than they themselves had. Well in advance of the revolution, the emerging bourgeoisie began to view the tax and customs systems that governed them as a hindrance to their endeavors.

Many of them turned to physiocracy as an explanatory framework and justification for liberal economic, political, and social reform. Adherents grew within the ranks of government officials as well as among the commercial bourgeoisie and a sector of the intelligentsia. By the middle of the eighteenth century, these burgeoning classes had become the social ground for physiocratic philosophy. The physiocrats became a type of "social court" whose task it was "to directly influence the king or, in some instances, his mistress."[4] Throughout the following decades, physiocrats deftly infiltrated key posts in the government from where they intended to achieve "laisser-faire."[5] In contrast, other social strata—even those wanting tax reform—continued to favor state protectionism. Among these groups were "the guild craft and a large part of the tenant tax collectors, the financiers."[6]

Ledoux's Approach to Physiocracy

Amid these debates over the role of various actors in economic development, Ledoux was much influenced by Quesnay's "Tableau Économique" (1758), which promoted the free interaction and interdependence of the different sectors as a way to level the field against accumulation. Quesnay's denouncement was portrayed in his *Fermiers*' definition in the *Encyclopedia*:

> It is the riches of the fermiers (farmers) who fertilize their land, who multiply their beasts, who cause the inhabitants to stay and who bring about the strength and prosperity of the nation. Industry and commerce within the disorder of luxury and amassed riches in the cities, go against the improvement of goods, cause the devastation of the fields and inspire contempt for agriculture. It increases costs, harms the family, oppose the development of men and debilitates the state.[7]

Ledoux's architectural designs for the city of Chaux reflect Quesnay's arguments for the integration of nature and industry and envisioned the automation of production. These plans also included the construction of various buildings that reflected the character of their purpose. The inclusion of gardens to the workers' homes would enable the working community to be a self-sufficient one.

In developing his proposal, Ledoux drew on the knowledge of Charles Philibert Trudaine de Montigny (1733–1777), director of the Department of Water and Forests. A noted chemist, Trudaine de Montigny had conducted experiments seeking improvement in the conditions of salt exploitation in the Franche-Comté and the villas located along the saline banks. Trudaine de Montigny conceived the idea to build a modern *saline* within the proximity of a forest—a concept which Ledoux would realize at the Saline at Arc-et-Senans. It was Trudaine de Montigny who recommended Ledoux for other projects in Besançon and Aix.

In 1771, the engineer and architect Jean-Rodolphe Perronet, director of the École des Ponts et Chaussées (School of Bridges and Roads) and inspector general of the *salines*, appointed Ledoux as his Deputy Commissar of the *salines* at the Franche-Comté, Lorraine, and the three bishoprics of Verdum, Metz, and Toul. Little has been recorded about what Ledoux learned during his time working with Perronet; however, Ledoux's design for the Loüe river bridge, a project included in his treatise, deployed structural solutions used by Perronet, which made it possible to reduce the thickness of the columns (pillars) and create a greater gap between them so as to facilitate barge traffic. Ledoux's design incorporated the use of four pillars that resembled ships and had three rectilinear vaults. The Loüe river bridge was itself part of the infrastructure for the region of the Franche-Comté.

Water and Progress

Eighteenth-century philosophers established the powerful notion that reason provided the only viable path to human progress and prosperity. For them, whether or not mother nature was the product of divine design, it was certainly a terrain that could be conquered, refined, and improved through human ingenuity. Within the new demands for technological progress through scientific knowledge, many regarded water as one of the main features of nature subject to human intervention.

Toward the end of the eighteenth century, architects and engineers proved forceful advocates for the development of infrastructure, especially those trained in elite institutions such as the at the École des Ponts et Chaussées. The control of water was key to the physiocrats' new emphasis on expanding agriculture; they developed new techniques for canalizing rivers in order to harness natural resources and provide new transportation options, improving the exchange of goods and population movement. They experimented with new materials and technologies for lifting, strengthening, and extending bridge spans. They even proposed the construction of a sewerage system for Paris, although this would not be concluded until the time of Haussmann. The new developments would not only prevent natural catastrophes, they argued, but would also showcase the nation's dedication to science and reason. In any case, as architect and scholar Juan Calatrava maintains, water was the catalyst for a range of developments: supply, circulation, urban hygiene, the embellishment of cities, the organization of territories, and creation of wealth through agriculture and manufacture.[8]

Water and Salt in Ledoux's Route

The expansion of water infrastructure proved a catalyst in the regional development of the Franche-Comté. The availability of wood and coal for fuel, while abundant, was not enough; reliable sources of water for production and transportation were needed.

Ledoux, assuming that the road network and the canals planned in the Franche-Comté, Charolais, Nivernáis and Berry provinces—joining the Loire, the Rhone, and the Saônes rivers—situated the site of the salt mines, at the center of European markets. Rural and regional projects gave Ledoux the opportunity to unite themes such as forest reform and its management, which, along with his interest in modernizing agriculture and promoting rural industry, became a central theme in his theoretical ideas and in his creative practice.

Ledoux's design for the *saline* was an attempt to break with the archaic methods used in other French *salines* by creating conditions for large-scale production, where water and its potential for fostering regional development occupied a fundamental role.

In the introduction to his treatise "Architecture Considered in Relation to Art, Morals, and Legislation," Ledoux did not withhold his criticism of the existing *salines*:

> Those lavish buildings erected on a whim, some already destroyed, and others about to be, those worthless and hideous materials, those ruinous maintenance costs, those versatile combinations that last less than a lease contract; the sumptuousness of the saline of Dieuze, the preserved undergrounds of Salins, the city built by the abundant of its resources, here, indeed, are the reasons for the decision taken.[9]

Traditional *salines* consisted of underground wells, the porter's accommodation, an evaporation building or stove room, a storage place where the salt was stored and conditioned. Annexed to the director's house there was a storehouse.

The *saline* at Arc-et-Senans answered the increasing demand for this most useful of commodities. The existing facilities at Salins-les-Bains precluded simple extension because of its location in the valley and its natural limits. Unlike older *salines* such as the Salines de Salins, also located in the Franche-Comté, officials located the Arc-et-Senans *saline* near its fuel source (the Chaux forest), as Ledoux

Figure 2.1 Salins-les-Bains, brine conduction, 2015.

Source: Photograph by Carmelina Martinez.

mentions in his treatise: "It was easier to bring the water in, than to carry a chopped forest."[10] Of course, to do this required major overhauls to the terrain. From the Salins-les-Bains salt mine (Figure 2.1), the water flowed through a 21 km wooden duct to the Arc-et-Senans Royal salt mine, where an aqueduct made of wood and a double pipeline were added to the *saline* itself. Ledoux introduced a new technique in the form of a large "graduation" building, in which the water underwent partial evaporation. In this project, water was visibly tamed and geometrically ordered in the different deposits to be industrially treated to extract its wealth.

The Saline Royal d'Arc-et-Senans: Materialized Urban Project

Exploring Ledoux's urban vision in his projects for the *saline* at Arc-et-Senans, it is important to distinguish between those aspects constructed and those planned and published but never materialized.[11] Ledoux conceived three projects, an initial project, the second, realized one, and another project included for the City of Chaux, all of them published in his treatise "Architecture Considered in Relation to Art, Morals, and Legislation." In his treatise, Ledoux brought together several of the designs made for different types of buildings from the 1770s to the 1780s. He presented an ellipse formed by two semicircles joined at their limit by straight lines, as the genesis of the City of Chaux: an unbuilt project.

According to Ledoux himself, his initial design for the *saline royal* was unsatisfactory, as it "had been conceived before knowing the lay of the land." He blamed "junior agents who made decisions in the shadows."[12]

As he learned more about the site, he realized that his initial plans were inadequate, and that he needed to reflect more on issues of site, safety, and hygiene in order to develop an optimal solution. Early designs had included an enfolding square of galleries grouping the different activities under several buildings interconnected by oblique corridors, which resembled the ancient Greek *Stoas*. These corridors were flanked by 144 columns. The building was symmetrical, the geometric distribution of the spaces gave the chapel and the oven the same importance, located on both sides of the main access. The building intended for the desiccation of the salt followed the installation patterns shown in the plates of the *Encyclopedia*. This approach had been inspired by the conventional designs of similar constructions of the era. On the façade and section, he used the sloping roof in the traditional way, as indicated in the Encyclopedia of Mineralogy. Other representations of that time, such as that of Jean Baptiste Lallemand (1716–1803), of the boiler's interior of the *saline* at Lons-le-Saunier in the Franche-Comté, seemed rustic when compared to the interiors of Ledoux's project.

However, in his realized project (Figure 2.2), Ledoux opted for a different design approach, incorporating gardens in a semicircle to improve social wellbeing, and separated the pavilions according to their functions. Ledoux found greater virtue in the curve line as he mentioned in his treatise: "Its shape, very similar to that of the celestial vault, is pure and pleasant to the eye. I agree, it lacks the drawback of the obtuse angles that compartmentalize extension, and the acerbic shapes that damage

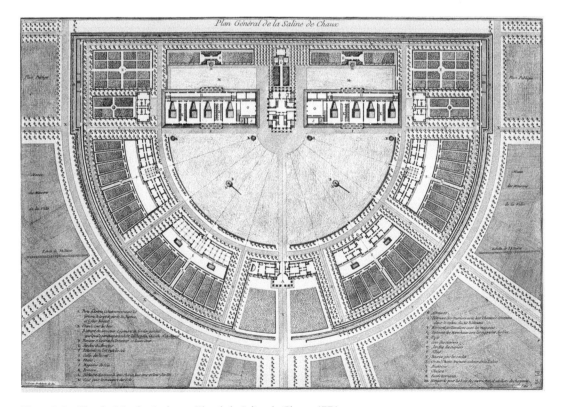

Figure 2.2 Claude-Nicolas Ledoux, *Plan de la Saline de Chaux*, 1774.

Source: Illustration courtesy of Wikimedia Commons.

Figure 2.3 Portico access, Arc-et-Senans *saline*, 2015.

Source: Photograph by Carmelina Martinez.

aesthetic."[13] The industrial facilities built at Arc-et-Senans *saline* consisted of 11 buildings projected from a 370-meter diameter semicircle, with radial lines that defined the location of the different edifices and gardens. A portico with a cave like archway (Figure 2.3), guides the visitor into a courtyard with a semicircular array of buildings. The central edifice includes the director's house and the chapel (Figure 2.4), as envisioned in the published plan. On both sides of the director's house, Ledoux located the salt evaporation buildings, followed by the edifices of the commissioners along the transverse axis. Additional structures include workers' housing, the cooper's accommodations (including the warehouses), and the marshal's quarters, with the storerooms and warehouses for the iron needed for the fabrication of the barrels being used for salt storage.

Two Readings of the Saline at Arc-et-Senans: Wellbeing and Control

In his treatise, Ledoux insisted on the character of utilitarian buildings. When speaking of the buildings destined for the desiccation of salt, he commented:

> The multiplicity of needs that must be taken into consideration, the lines prolonged by the necessity for successive workshops, seem to exclude those folds dictated by theory to oppose the masses against each other. I do not believe that this theory allows these tormented planes at all, nor that pompous ostentation of the servile or scholastic procedure that governs most conceptions.[11]

Between Technology and Architecture

Figure 2.4 Claude-Nicolas Ledoux, *Vue perspective de la Ville de Chaux*, 1804.

Source: Claude-Nicolas Ledoux, *Architecture Considered in Relation to Art, Morals, and Legislation* (1804).

In fact, Ledoux's architectural and urban program brought together diverse social groups and hierarchies into the same spatial envelope. His realized proposal, as well as the ideal one, provided a shared space for all of them, using architectural symbolism during a time of transformation. The director, for instance, was not only a symbol of power, but also the emblem of the highest morality: the father, the priest, the teacher. Symbolism was used to uplift elevate values related to cultural, moral, spiritual, and social life. It was not merely a theatrical representation, nor a formalism.

The gardens were also symbolic and not just an utilitarian element. They provide space for recreation and for the sustenance of inhabitants by serving as an allotment for vegetable cultivation. At Chaux, Ledoux proposed and improved society that could live and work, either within the *saline* itself or in the surroundings. Sustainable, by having orchards to harvest, economically sound by locating it near its fuel source. In this approach, the infrastructure conceived under Ledoux's particular physiocratic vision offered solutions that allowed improvements to social conditions and addressed the challenges of industrial production and the rupture between industry and agriculture.

In the context of the consolidation of the monarchical state of Louis XV, a revising of the royal *saline* at Arc-et-Senans highlights the use of architecture as a representation of power. According to Michel Foucault, at the end of the eighteenth century, architecture began to be linked to considerations of population control, hygiene, and public health. Designed spaces were not neutral backdrops for human activity; rather, architects, engineers, builders, and officials deployed spatial organization in buildings to extend power through capillary forms.[15] In this way, design added new layers of control to common types of buildings such as prisons, schools, asylums, and factories.[16] This is evident in the plan of the *saline* at the City of Chaux (Figure 2.4), where Ledoux placed the buildings in a symbolic interrelation: the director's house at its center (Figure 2.5), connected along a longitudinal central axis to the church and courthouse, with everything on the premises supervised under an optics of surveillance and control.

Figure 2.5 The director's house and the chapel, Arc-et-Senans *saline*, 2015.

Source: Photograph by Carmelina Martinez.

Final Considerations

The *saline* at Arc-et-Senans was not an unfinished work or the "embryo" of a utopian project: it was a concrete, realized idea.[17] Ledoux proposed, in this his most important project, that infrastructure and architecture intertwined in a virtuous circle. Through this project he tried to solve the practical needs of a factory while bearing in mind the wellbeing of those who would work there. Ledoux managed to solve "the physical accommodation for workers in the social structure of production and architectural expression, capable of providing the industry with a language that would reinforce both surveillance and common life."[18] His project, and much of the work of French architects and engineers in the eighteenth century, reflect the growing tension between the bourgeois dedication to reason and the presumptive power of the sovereign and the state, a tension that would eventually erupt in violent revolution.

Notes

1 Cf. Jacques Delille (1782), *Les jardins, ou l árt d'embellir les paysages* (Paris: Chaspal, Libraire-Éditeur, 1844); Louis-Sébastien Mercier (1770), *El año 2440. Un sueño como no ha habido otro*, trans. Ramón Cotarelo (Madrid: Akal, 2016); Jean-Jacques Rousseau (1761), *Julia, o la nueva Eloísa*, trans. Pilar Ruiz Ortega (Madrid: Akal, 2007).
2 *Encyclopédie, ou dictionnaire raisonné des sciences, des arts et des métiers, etc.*, eds Denis Diderot and Jean le Rond d'Alembert, Vol. 10: 58. The University of Chicago: ARTFL Encyclopédie Project (Autumn 2017 Edition), Robert Morrissey and Glenn Roe (eds), http://encyclopedie.uchicago.edu/.

3 Norbert Elias, *El proceso de la civilización*, 3rd edn (Mexico: Fondo de Cultura Económica, 2012), 119.
4 Ibid. 119.
5 Jean-Paul Desprat, *Mirabeau: L'excès et le retrait* (Paris: Perrin, 2008), 44.
6 Elias, *El proceso*, 121.
7 *Encyclopédie*, Vol. 6: 538; The University of Chicago: ARTFL Encyclopédie Project (Autumn 2017 Edition), Robert Morrissey and Glenn Roe (eds), http://encyclopedie.uchicago.edu/.
8 Juan Calatrava, *Arquitectura y Cultura en el siglo de las Luces* (Granada: Universidad de Granada, 1999), 57.
9 Claude-Nicolas Ledoux, *La Arquitectura considerada en relación con el arte, las costumbres y la legislación* (Madrid: Akal, 1994), 38.
10 Ibid. 39.
11 Cf. Herrmann, "The problem of chronology in C.-N. Ledoux engraved works," *Art Bulletin*, Vol. XLII, Sept. 1960; Daniel Rabreau, *Claude-Nicolas Ledoux (1736–1806)* (Paris: William Blake & Co., Art & Arts, 2000); Emmeline Scachetti, "La Saline d'Arc-et-Senans de Ledoux: du texte à la réalité," in *Autour de Ledoux: architecture, ville et utopie*, eds Gérard Chouquer and Jean-Claude Daumas (Besançon: Presses Universitaires de Franche-Comté, 2008), 39–56.
12 Ledoux, *La Arquitectura*, 156.
13 Ibid. 66.
14 Ibid. 118.
15 Michel Foucault, "El ojo del poder," in *El Panóptico*, ed. Jeremías Bentham, trans., Julia Varela and Fernando Álvarez-Uría (Barcelona: La Piqueta, 1980), 4.
16 Michel Foucault, *Vigilar y castigar* (Mexico: Siglo XXI, 2009), 252.
17 Daniel Rabreau, *Claude-Nicolas Ledoux (1736–1806)* (Paris: William Blake & Co., Art & Arts, 2000), 103.
18 Ángeles Layuno Rosas, "Las primeras 'Ciudades de la industria'. Trazados urbanos, efectos territoriales y dimensión patrimonial. La experiencia de Nuevo Baztán (Madrid)," *Revista electrónica de geografía y ciencias sociales* 17: 451, www.ub.edu/geocrit/sn/sn-451.htm.

3
CEMENT AS WEAPON
Meta-Infrastructure in the "World's Last Cement Frontier"

Robby Fivez and Monika Motylińska

With cement being one of the major materials for infrastructural development, cement plants constitute a form of meta-infrastructure. As the infrastructure for infrastructure itself, cement plants preceded almost every large-scale road, dam, port, and military project in the twentieth century. Since stories of 'successful' infrastructure projects are often part of the ammunition for colonial apologetics or neo-colonial thinking, debunking this myth of undivided success is important: without an anchoring in material conditions, infrastructure is all too often recruited into success stories of 'progress' and global modernity.' This is particularly the case in the context of (post-)colonial sub-Saharan Africa, where these meta-infrastructures form a powerful weapon to fight the ideas of colonial success that persist in the (few) concrete infrastructural projects of bygone colonial eras that are still operational. In our chapter, we argue for an approach to the study of infrastructure that is grounded in the materiality of production, attentive to unexpected actors, alert to complex power relations, and encompassing both stories of failure and success.

In the June 1954 issue of the *Colonial Building Notes*, a monthly bulletin intended for the Public Works Departments of British colonies, the colonial liaison officer, George Atkinson, stressed that "few commodities of mineral origin are more important to the development and progress of the less advanced areas of the world than is cement." In particular, "for the construction of hydro-electric and other dams, bridges, harbors, factories and so forth," cement was considered to be indispensable.[1] This colonial delirium over cement and its concrete infrastructures clearly echoes into the present. Today, national governments, multilateral agencies, economists, construction companies, engineers, and architects continue to see cement as "the primary input for the development of basic infrastructure from roads, rails and ports to hospitals, schools, shops and housing […] an integral part of economic growth and development."[2] Because of this sustained belief in cement as the material condition for 'development'—and in Africa as the continent that needs to be 'developed'—Africa is widely considered to be the world's 'last cement frontier.'

In this chapter, we challenge this developmentalist logic by re-writing the genealogy of cement in Africa.[3] Adding historical depth to the ubiquitous building material, we counter the idea that cement is a material of Western 'modernity.' By relocating cement's history to Africa, it becomes clear how Africa is anything but the last cement frontier.

Although relocating cement's history, it is not our intention to 'provincialize Europe' in its development. We surely acknowledge that cement was to a large extent invented in the West. After all, in the nineteenth century the likes of Saint Léger, Vicat, or Aspdin still quarreled over 'their' invention, and none of these debates were situated out of Western Europe. However, if we want to write a history of cement, we should not confine ourselves to this particular period or geography. Although some historians have shown how a focus on cement production already complicates the narrative (e.g., early expansion of the cement industries in the U.S.A.), most cement histories only focus on a series of technical developments starting in Europe in the early nineteenth century.[4] Taking cues from Cyrille Simonnet's suggestion that "the history of constructing in cement, in concrete, does not only concern the laboratory of the engineer," we argue that the most crucial antidote to this European centrality in the development of cement is to look beyond these moments and places of 'invention' to the actual places of production.[5]

The title of this chapter pays homage to Sérgio Ferro's groundbreaking essay *Concrete as Weapon*. Ferro's work is highly relevant for a critical engagement with the concept of infrastructure.[6] In his Marxist approach to architectural history and theory, he calls for a renewed interest for the material in architecture. Far ahead of Adrian Forty, he understood that it is through the material that architectural history and theory can become socially relevant again. By ignoring how construction processes functioned as tools for the "subordination of labor at the building site," Ferro contends that architectural histories and theories that do not account for the material processes of building are "complicit in rendering these questions invisible and apparently irrelevant for the field." While this turn toward construction is highly relevant for every architectural object, it is particularly valuable in the investigation of infrastructure. After all, viewing infrastructure as an object detached from the material processes that produced it obscures many of its messiest aspects, such as the state expropriation of land, the varied labor conditions, the massive extraction of resources, and the devastating environmental impact. In our chapter, we argue for an approach to the study of infrastructure that is grounded in the materiality of production, attentive to unexpected actors, alert to complex power relations, and encompassing both stories of failure and success.

Cement formed the material basis of hundreds of massive infrastructure projects in sub-Saharan Africa from the colonial period through independence to the present. Therefore, rather than focus on a single infrastructural project, this chapter examines multiple ways in which the insatiable need for cement has turned cement plants into *meta-infrastructure*—that is, infrastructure *underlying* infrastructure. In particular in the context of Africa, where in colonial times 'traditional' materials were discarded as being unhygienic or '*non-durable*,' concrete and cement are often considered to be one of the most direct 'legacies' of Western involvement.

Our analysis of the African cement industry that follows is structured in three main time periods: pre-colonial, colonial, and post-independence until nowadays. In tracing these lineaments, we zoom in on particular moments in time and representative case studies following a reverse chronology. The inverted chronology provides us with an opportunity to challenge the progressive narrative of infrastructure so common to the logic of development. Since we are not after a success-driven narrative, we trace our story backward to show how development schemes arose, analyzing the complex histories of cement production, the failures, and eventually even the continuity between precolonial hydraulic binding agents and the cement industry on the continent.

Expanding Infrastructure of Post-Independence (after 1957)

Although there are numerous contemporary articles (both scholarly and popular) that point out the feverish investments of Chinese, African, and European cement companies on the African market, this does not necessarily mean a sudden spike in cement producing plants. Often, these 'new' investments are grafted onto existing infrastructures of cement production (Figure 3.1).

Rather than a cement wasteland, a map of Africa's cement production plants in 1970 shows how in the 1960s Africa saw the largest increase in cement production of any world region. For instance, in the course of only three years, between 1966 and 1968, cement plants or mills in Ukpilla/Okpella and Calabar, Nigeria, Monrovia, Liberia, Loútété, Republic of the Congo, and Dar es Salaam, Tanzania, among others, started production, all of them directly related to infrastructural projects of the post-independence period.

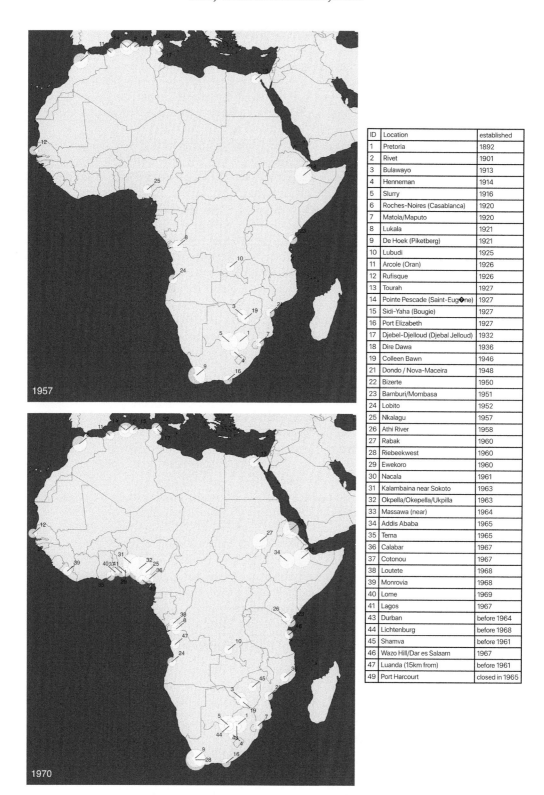

Figure 3.1 Cement production in sub-Saharan Africa (based on a literature survey conducted by the authors).
Source: © Robby Fivez, Monika Motylinska.

In Nigeria, the Okpella plant and its extensions are situated at a strategically important node, close to the A2 highway connecting the northern and central part of the country with the Edo and Delta states.[7] Nowadays, the plant is run by the largest African cement producer, Dangote Cement Plc, through its subsidiary Okpella Cement. For the extension in 2016, a deal was struck with Sinoma International (a subsidiary of China National Material Group), one of the largest Chinese enterprises providing cement equipment and engineering on the global market for the erection of the clinker line. The machinery itself has been supplied by a variety of specialized internationally active companies such as the Gebr. Pfeiffer from Germany, which delivered the mills. The satellite footage demonstrates the heavy impact of limestone extraction and cement production on the local landscape and long-lasting spatial and environmental consequences of the decision-making processes dating back to the 1960s.

The ties to German actors can be also traced back to the 1960s, when the project of the Okpella cement plant was developed and executed by a syndicate of German enterprises, in which Friedrich Krupp Rheinhausen provided the mechanical equipment, whereas Philipp Holzmann AG and Continho Caro & Co. were structural engineering contractors (Figure 3.2). This complicated cluster of transnational actors is not a recent phenomenon. However, it is rather emblematic for production of cement across the twentieth century. This varied set of profit-driven actors, easily transgressing state boundaries, already shows the limited nature of the success stories of (neo-)colonial infrastructure, usually portrayed as a one-on-one relation between colonizer and colonized.

The initial plant in Okpella had a daily capacity of 500 tonnes of ordinary Portland cement and operated on the dry process (which is considered to be more efficient but also to have a more harmful effect on laborers and the environment due to dust sedation). It was located in the proximity of a limestone quarry and removed from the town. The actual production site consisted of an ensemble of silos and other storage facilities, as well as smaller edifices such as barracks. The most prominent feature, the rotary kiln, was surmounted by a longitudinal shed, the preheater, which was supported by a vertical structure.

Such efforts to boost local production of construction materials were typical for the early post-colonial period. For instance, in Congo/Brazzaville the cement plant was constructed in order to reduce the dependency on cement imports and boost infrastructural investments, even if its capacity remained limited. The plant in Dar es Salaam was directly linked to the expansion of the economic capital with its transport infrastructure (including, inter alia, a harbor and a new airport). Moreover, the fact that both in Nigeria and Congo/Brazzaville cement plants were constructed by German companies suggests that the recently independent African nations sought to overcome the monopoly of companies

Figure 3.2 Okpella/Ukpilla cement plant, after 1966.

Source: © Berlin-Brandenburgisches Wirtschaftsarchiv e.V. (*BBWA*), 1500/13 (Altsignatur), 41527 (Vorlagen-Nummer).

from the former metropoles.[8] However, as we will show, the simple connection between the colony and the metropole was never the case—neither in sub-Saharan Africa nor elsewhere.[9]

Although this wave of investments in the 1960s indicates a partial rupture between the colonial era and post-independence eras, there were also striking consistencies in infrastructure development and, hence, cement plant investments. For example, the Inga dam scheme—a highly visible nation-building project of the Mobutu regime—had already been partially elaborated in the 1950s under Belgian occupation. After calculating the enormous amounts of concrete needed for its construction, the engineers quickly realized that the whole project would only be economically viable if the cement could be locally produced in the colony. Besides, the general need for a new cement plant in the Bas-Congo had been clear to the administrators much earlier, independently from this particular investment. Faced with numerous obstacles, the colonial regime never launched the project. However, in 1970 the Democratic Republic of Congo government built the Cimenterie Nationale in Kimpese, precisely to revive the Inga dam, to this date a recurrent infrastructural dream.

Whether rooted in colonial thinking or not, these varied cases demonstrate the correlation between erection of cement plants and infrastructure, underscoring centrality of cement as meta-infrastructure.

Cementing the Colonial Project (1920s)

The first major wave of investment in the African cement industry occurred shortly after World War I. During this period, colonial officials envisioned and built numerous transport and industrial projects across colonial Africa, including harbors, dams, and railway lines. These projects served to buttress the extractive economy and to deepen (oftentimes very frail and superficial) control over territory. To provide material for the construction of infrastructure, colonial officials sited cement plants across sub-Saharan Africa, for instance in Rufisque near Dakar in the French colony of Senegal (first plans dating back to 1928) and in Matola, close to the capital of the Portuguese colony of Mozambique, Lourenço Marques (first planned in 1920). European engineers emphasized the importance of boosting the capacity of local cement production in order to reduce the costs of transportation. For them, local production of construction materials was the necessary prerequisite of strengthening, in other words, cementing, colonial power,[10] which, as we posit, follows the logic of meta-infrastructure.

A focus on the Belgian Congo provides a case in point, as it was exceptionally early in producing cement on the African continent. As long ago as 1932, a French cement producer observed with some jealousy that due to the installment of two cement plants in the early 1920s: "In these privileged regions [i.e. Belgian Congo], the [infrastructural] works in concrete and reinforced concrete can be executed with a minimum of uncertainty or disappointment, and with a minimal cost."[11] Despite this appraisal, the troubled history of the first cement plant in Congo—installed for the reconversion and electrification works of the railway between Matadi and Kinshasa—shows how the European *cement men* struggled to cope with local realities. Although the Lukala plant was supposedly operational from 1921, the Société des Ciments du Congo (CICO) faced mounting difficulties throughout the decade. Instead of choosing state-of-the-art technology, the company decided to invest in second-hand machinery from Germany. Although the manager was aware that "in a European industry, this machinery would have been replaced ages ago,"[12] due to its cost-efficiency a vertical cement kiln was considered ideal for the Belgian Congo (Figure 3.3). Such kilns had already been closed down in Europe and the U.S.A. because of their dangerous operating conditions—yet the company saw their African laborers as cheap, easily available, and replaceable through the state recruitment system if they would dare to speak up against the dangerous working conditions. A general strike only months after the installment of the kiln, instigated by Senegalese and Togolese immigrant laborers, not only proved the company wrong, but it also brought it to the brink of bankruptcy.

However, it would be an oversimplification to assume that state-of-the-art technology was absent from the Belgian Congo during the 1920s. At the cement plant in Lubudi—which was of strategic importance for the whole mining industry in the province of Katanga—engineers installed a newly

Figure 3.3 Vertical kiln of Lukala.

Source: © Belgian State Archives (BSA), Fonds Finoutremer, no 1052.

patented model of a rotary kiln designed by G. Polysius, a German firm specializing in the design and construction of cement plants. As described in the advertisement brochure, this technology proved to be safe and efficient, so that "from start, the plant is working without any trouble and to full satisfaction of the committers [sic] though it is operated by natives under the supervision of a European staff reduced to the minimum admissible." In addition to such rhetoric of progress, the brochure provides rather rare depictions of factory employees. Strikingly, the visual propaganda of the German company also included a local 'staffage' of sorts, as the external view of the cement plant was embellished with drawings of straw huts supposedly built in the direct proximity of the plant, even if this would have

Figure 3.4 Cement plant in Lubudi depicted in a brochure by G. Polysius, after 1926.
Source: © Landesarchiv Sachsen-Anhalt, Dessau (LASA), I 414, Nr. 435/3.

been hazardous due to the circulation of fine particulates from the production process (Figure 3.4). However, from the point of view of the company in question, such 'exoticization' was deemed necessary in order to embed the project in the local landscape—even if it was an imagined one.

Alternative Genealogies (pre-1920s)

If we move further back in reconstructing cement genealogies of sub-Saharan Africa, we will encounter other, earlier examples of cement plants that were perceived by colonial powers as a necessary meta-infrastructure of large colonial investments, especially in the domain of transport infrastructure. From 1909 to 1913, the German firm G. Polysius drew up plans for a cement production site at Pongwe in German East Africa (nowadays Tanzania). The plans include a limestone quarry, the cement factory with surrounding housing facilities for the European personnel, and two railway stations. In preparation, the firm's engineers thoroughly mapped the topography of the terrain, as well as the lime and clay deposits meticulously. Had it been erected, the Pongwe facility would have been among the first cement plants in sub-Saharan Africa, apart from three plants in Southern Africa, namely Pretoria Portland Cement Company, established in 1892, and Premier Portland Cement Company of Bulawayo, and Blue Circle Cement Ltd. Company established in South Rhodesia in 1913 and 1914, respectively.

German colonial officials deemed the location of the Pongwe to be crucial both for the construction of the railway and the extension of the nearby harbor in Tanga. By 1891, the stations "Steinbruch" (stone quarry) and "Pongwe" had already been constructed along the line, and were among the first to be established. Meanwhile, the firm of G. Polysius had already established itself as a specialized global player prior to World War I. However, in Pongwe it faced competition from Vogtländische Plantagengesellschaft, an export agriculture operation aiming to expand its operations through production of construction materials. Both companies aimed to acquire plots between the Steinbruch and Pongwe stations, where a disused limestone quarry already existed. After a flurry of correspondence between G. Polysius headquarters in Dessau and the colonial government, the company managed to secure a concession in 1910. Under the terms of this "public-private-partnership," the colonial government and the company constructing the railway, Koloniale Eisenbahn-Bau-und Betriebsgesellschaft, were allowed to acquire limestone and other mineral products of the quarry. The pleas of the second firm were purposely ignored by the colonial bureaucracy.

However, correspondence between the owner of the enterprise from Dessau, Otto Polysius and his notary in Dar es Salaam, reveals that rapid construction had never been the company's intention. On the contrary, the aim was to postpone the investment for as long as possible in order to gather sufficient capital and stocks. The only reason for hasty bidding was to outplay the competitor, Vogtländische Plantagengesellschaft. But now faced with an unfeasible schedule, the contract was still unfulfilled in 1913, and the German cement plant in East Africa never came into being. While a cement plant would eventually be erected in the same location, this case clearly demonstrates how the territories of colonial expansionist planning were simultaneously sites of speculation for capitalist firms, whose ambitions surpassed national boundaries and constraints, extending into colonial territories.[13]

With the meta-infrastructure of cement still underdeveloped in German East Africa in the early twentieth century, colonial officials turned to burnt lime as a substitute and thus were dependent on local expertise. Traces of this dependency can even be found in official sources such as the contract between German colonial government and the construction company Philipp Holzmann for erection of one of the major railway lines (from Dar es Salaam to Kigoma in German East Africa), which directly stated that: "The use of lime or trass as a partial or total substitute for cement is only permitted with the explicit approval of the Railway Commissioner," thus giving us an important clue that this was a common solution to shortages in cement supply in colonial infrastructural projects. Lime, of course, had been used for centuries along the Swahili coast as a bonding agent for mortar and render.

A similar example can be found in the Congo Free State. For the construction of the quay wall in the harbor of Dolo—the first harbor of Kinshasa—officials conducted an investigation in 1899 into local limestones. Numerous lime samples were tested and, after burning, some showed significant promise for use in construction, with hydraulic and strength properties close to the cements imported from Europe. After this success, a prototype lime kiln was developed and built in Dolo. The secretary of interior affairs of the Congo Free State, who saw the economic importance of producing such a cement-like material in the colony, even envisioned building lime kilns all over the Congo if the experiment in Dolo proved successful:

> it will be important to construct as many lime kilns as needed [for the equipment of the colony], and to write a report as detailed as possible, giving us all the information about the production of burnt lime in Africa.

Apparently, the lieutenant who was responsible for the execution of the works was "not the '*right man the rigth place*' [sic]" as the francophone official commented, resulting in a stillborn project.[14]

Despite the difficulties faced when installing these colonial cement plants and lime kilns, so far this cement history still largely confirms rather than questions the European centrality in the production of cement in Africa. However, in this early period, questions arise on the role of local expertise in what can be considered a lime burning industry, as already observed based on indirect clues from the railway contract. For instance, when in 1911 the vice governor of Katanga wanted to find a substitute

Figure 3.5 Termite hill lime kiln. In the foreground three figures (probably an African woman and two colonial officials wearing pith helmets) can be discerned, giving an idea of the enormous scale of the kiln.

Source: © Africa Archives, Belgian Ministry of Foreign Affairs *(BMFA)*, 3DG(1822)8.

for expensive South-African cement, he investigated the possibility of replacing cement with locally produced lime. The state inspector commissioned to find a solution reported back about a giant lime kiln in Mikola, close to Elisabethville (present day Lubumbashi). Although the lime kiln was exploited by two Italians, his report stated explicitly that it already existed "when they took over production."[15] The fact that the kiln was installed inside a huge termite hill strongly suggests an African agency in the production of burnt lime that was never acknowledged in official colonial discourses (Figure 3.5). Numerous other snippets in colonial archives and colonial literature suggest that such African lime burning industries existed long before the arrival of European colonizers in Africa. In a map made by the French botanist Michel Adanson, for instance, as early as 1754 lime kilns were mentioned along the coast of Senegal.[16] Also in Ghana, Togo, Sudan, and Mali, early European travelers mentioned the practice of lime burning in the eighteenth century. On the other coast, several German, French, and British sources mention a local lime burning industry in Tanzania, Madagascar, and Zanzibar.

Conclusion: Materializing Infrastructure

It is only recently—following the material turn in social sciences—that Ferro's Marxist approach to the production processes of architecture has gained momentum. His attention to material production has found its way into architectural history and theory through several sources, including: urban and construction historians interested in social aspects of the construction site; anthropologists and sociologists investigating the processes of building; and insights from science and technology studies applied to built environments.[17] Throughout our chapter, we have aimed to show how this material approach is even more important when studying infrastructure. Without an anchoring in material conditions, infrastructure is all too often recruited into success stories of 'progress' and 'global modernity.' This is particularly the case in the context of sub-Saharan Africa. Since stories of 'successful' infrastructural projects are often part of the ammunition for colonial apologetics or neo-colonial thinking, debunking this myth of undivided success is even more important here than elsewhere.

In this chapter, we have challenged the success stories of cement production in sub-Saharan Africa, through inverting their chronology and investigating a wide variety of sources. Taking the materialities of infrastructure into account, a nuanced picture emerges, encompassing different sets of actors such as laborers, indigenous craft practitioners, on-the-ground engineers, and construction managers, all engaged in ambiguous interdependencies with and independence from (post-)colonial powers. While the former Belgian and German colonies are only two of numerous possible sites for investigation, what has become clear is that histories of infrastructure grounded in overdetermined and unilinear narratives of progress must give way to a range of other stories—to local alternatives, indigenous knowledges, false starts, and dashed dreams.

What also becomes visible in our examination of cement as meta-infrastructure are different geographies and scales, revealing how intertwined production and commodity chains functioned throughout the twentieth century, establishing transnational connectivity much earlier than the 1970s "shock of the global" period.

Finally, this approach enables us to observe different temporalities, defined not only by ruptures but also by important continuities. These vectors of obdurance and change not only arise out of supposed path dependencies but are simultaneously rooted in the local landscape. As cement production is dependent on the (local) supply of raw materials such as lime (a rare mineral in many parts of sub-Saharan Africa) and clay, it is no surprise that we are dealing with a spatially fixed industry, with all the vagaries that come with real sites and places. If a location for a cement plant was chosen at the beginning of the twentieth century, it is not only very probable that the plant still exists there nowadays, but it is even very likely that these locations echo the locations of pre-colonial lime burning sites. Thus, in so many ways the history of cement as a material opens up a view of infrastructure not only as a finished object or network, but also as an assemblage of inputs unevenly distributed, episodically planned, haphazardly extracted, and politically embedded, all with varying degrees of failure and success.

Notes

1. Colonial Geological Surveys Mineral Resources Division, "Cement in the Colonial Territories: A Review," *Colonial Geology and Mineral Resources* 3, no. 3 (1953). Reprinted in *Colonial Building Notes*, no. 22 (1953): 6–9.
2. Lyal White, "The Case of Cement," in *Africans Investing in Africa*, ed. Terence McNamee, Mark Pearson, and Wiebe Boer (New York/Hampshire: Palgrave Macmillan, 2015), 124.
3. This research was conducted in several archival collections in Europe and Africa: the Belgian State Archives (BSA); the Belgian Ministry of Foreign Affairs (BMFA); the Archives Nationale du Congo (ArNaCo); the Economic Archive at the Institute for Urban History, Frankfurt am Main (IfS); the State Archive of Saxony-Anhalt in Dessau (LASA); Berlin-Brandenburgisches Wirtschaftsarchiv (BBWA).
4. Salvatore Aprea, "German Concrete: The Science of Cement from Trass to Portland 1819-1877," in *Treatise on Concrete*, ed. Roberto Gargiani (Lausanne: EPFL Press, 2016). For the US context, cf. Amy E. Slaton, *Reinforced Concrete and the Modernization of American Building, 1900–1930* (Baltimore/London: The Johns Hopkins University Press, 2001).
5. Cyrille Simonnet, *Le Béton. Histoire d'un Matériau* (Marseille: Parenthèses, 2005), 28.
6. Sérgio Ferro, "Le Béton comme Arme," in *dessin/chantier*, trans. Cyrille Simonnet (Collection École d'architecture de Grenoble, Paris: Éditions de la Villette, 2005).
7. 1966, BBWA, 42471.
8. Ibid. 39626.
9. U.S. Department of Commerce, "Translations on Sub-Saharan Africa," no. 686 (February 1968).
10. Karl Krüger, *Tropentechnik: Kolonialtechnik im Querschnitt* (Kolonial- und Tropentechnik 1, Berlin: Elsner, 1939).
11. "Les Super-Ciments Et Leur Adaptabilité D'emploi Aux Bétons Exécutés En Pays Chauds," *Le Ciment*, no. 9 (1932).
12. 1927, BSA, Fonds Finoutremer, 1820.
13. Cf. Marc Linder, *Projecting Capitalism: A History of the Internationalization of the Construction Industry*, Contributions in Economics and Economic History (Westport, Conn.: Greenwood Press, 1994), 158.
14. 1899, BMFA, RF(1713)22a.

15 1911, BMFA, 3DG(1822)8.
16 Michel Adanson, "Carte particulière des environs de l'Isle du Sénégal," (1754), Bibliothèque nationale de France, département Cartes et plans, File n° GE C-21960.
17 For scholarship and understanding of the social and cultural importance of the construction site, in an anglophone and francophone context, respectively, see Christine Wall, *An Architecture of Parts. Architects, Building Workers and Industrialisation in Britain* (Abingdon: Routledge, 2013); Jacob Paskins, *Paris under Construction* (Abingdon/New York: Routledge, 2016). For an anthropological analysis of construction see Tim Ingold, *Making: Anthropology, Archaeology, Art and Architecture*, 1st edn (Abingdon/New York: Routledge, 2013). For an STS approach to built environments, see Albena Yaneva and Bruno Latour, "Give Me a Gun and I Will Make All Buildings Move: An Ant's View of Architecture," in *Explorations in Architecture: Teaching, Design, Research*, ed. Reto Geiser (Basel: Birkhäuser, 2008).

4
NOTES FROM THE UNDERWORLD
Excavation as Architectural Counter-History
Stefano Corbo

The deepest existing mines are at least four times deeper than the height of the tallest skyscraper—the Kingdom Tower in Jeddah (1008m). Both structures (mines and skyscrapers) require the same technological apparatuses: elevators, complex ventilation systems, telephones, electricity. But the connection between skyscrapers and underground spaces is not merely symbolic or illustrative. The construction of a super-tall tower requires tons of steel, concrete, glass, and aluminum. This implies the mining and exploitation of iron, limestone, bauxite, coal, and many other minerals. As a symmetrical counterpart of the vast vertical expansion that characterizes the global cities' skyline, subterranean spaces are a repository: an inventory of architectural forms and strategic intentions. Such spaces are not discrete and bounded, but rather are profoundly entangled with the world above. At the same time, underground structures only represent a limited portion of a wider and more articulated terrene: the Underworld. The Underworld can be read as an interpretative category that includes all those secret and hidden episodes——urban infrastructures, habitable environments, military and religious structures, architectural ruins, left-over spaces—that, despite their apparent marginality or their current state of conservation, have a relevant impact on our cities: because their role has been historically specular to the one played by the visible vertical architectures. In other words, the Underworld is not a state of exception; rather, it constitutes a complementary aspect of the capitalist and late-capitalist condition.

Beginning in the second half of the nineteenth century, a series of radical transformations swept across the major European cities. Georges-Eugène Haussmann famously carried out a comprehensive operation of urban renewal, demolishing part of the historic Medieval fabric and inserting commodious new thoroughfares bracketed by carefully controlled and modulated building forms. In Barcelona, Catalan urban planner Ildefons Cerdà envisioned an expansion of the historic city through a homogeneous grid composed of a single octagonal block typology repeated over and over again. In Stockholm, a great ornate iron tower gathered together 5,000 connecting wires strung through the air for the newly consolidated telephone company. Parallel to these vaunted episodes of urban reorganization are less well-known yet equally relevant projects to reconfigure the city below ground, changing the way people live, move, and communicate. Indeed, by 1913, Stockholm's telephone company had buried all of its telephone wires underground, consigning the great tower to obsolescence and effectively rendering communication infrastructure invisible.

Throughout the nineteenth century, architects, engineers, and planners looked to the space below to extend the working systems of the city. One such underground reconfiguration was the Thames Embankment project, launched in 1862 (see Figure 4.1). The Embankment was a subterranean structure which incorporated a sewage system and an underground railway to relieve traffic congestion. The desire for a modern network of sewers was not new; it had been proposed in 1666 after the Great Fire. In the nineteenth century, however, chronic cholera outbreaks in 1832, 1849, and 1854

Figure 4.1 Cross section of the Victoria Embankment, London. From *The Illustrated London News*, 1867.
Source: Illustration courtesy of Wikimedia Commons.

galvanized municipal officials and urban reformers around the construction of an extensive sewer system. As described by Lynda Nead in *Victorian Babylon*, the sewers were not the only public infrastructure to be built in London at the time.[1] On the contrary, sewers, along with gasworks, artificial lightning, and gardens shaped a new geography of spaces that radically transformed the city. When the Embankment work commenced, it involved narrowing the River Thames and creating three different sub-districts: the Victoria, Chelsea, and Albert Embankments. The quantities of materials employed give us some idea about the scale of these works: 650,000 cubic feet of granite, 80,000 cubic yards of brickwork, 140,000 cubic yards of concrete, and 500,000 cubic feet of timber.[2] While the aboveground surface was enriched with statues and monuments, some of London's frenetic circulation began to move underground. For the first time, the subterranean world emerged as a complementary part of city life.

Such a radical transformation was not simply a matter of removing muddy pockets from the city center. Just as in Paris, where the supposedly hygienic urgency to demolish the overcrowded areas of the city served as pretext to put into place a spatial regime of surveillance and repression, the remaking of the Thames Embankment served specific ideological interests. Through technological innovation, moral hygienism, and social control, the Embankment project represented the continuation belowground of a manifest strategy: to transform London into a global capital—the epicenter of an empire characterized by colonial practices and maritime hegemony. Thus, in nineteenth-century London the subterranean gains extraordinary relevance: it permits the modernization of the city, celebrates its status and determines its functioning.

London's Embankment is just one of many examples of the specular relationship emerging in the nineteenth and twentieth centuries between the visible and the invisible, the above and below the ground. In his book *Vertical*, Stephen Graham points to the entangled connection between skyscrapers and mines, referring to an intriguing diagram presented by OMA/AMO at the 2014 Venice Architecture Biennale. The diagram compared the rising heights of skyscrapers over the last 150 years with their topological negative—the excavations downwards in mines. It revealed a surprising finding: the deepest existing mines (4 km deep) are at least four times the linear measurement of the current highest skyscraper—the Kingdom Tower in Jeddah (1008 m).[3] At the same time, both mines and skyscrapers derive their functioning from the same technological equipment: elevators, complex ventilation systems, telephones, electricity. And the construction of a tower requires tons of steel, concrete, glass, and aluminum, which implies the mining and exploitation of limestone, bauxite, iron, coal, and other minerals. In other words, skyscrapers and mines represent a continuous and extended domain, subject to the same means of production and to the same macro-economic dynamics.

The Underworld

If we shift our focus from skyscrapers and mines to the whole set of artifacts that characterize the human-built world, we need to start looking at architecture's history not only for its visible manifestations above ground, but also for its hidden subterranean spaces. As an analogue counterpart to the vast vertical expansion that characterizes the global cities' skyline, in fact, subterranean spaces are a repository: an inventory of architectural forms, material extractions, bizarre experiments, and ambiguous episodes.

Mines, dwellings, vernacular architectures: in delineating a taxonomy of old and recent episodes, more urgent issues arise. These subterranean spatial products are not simply scattered or isolated cases. In their diversity, they constitute a whole, a well-defined territory. The name we will give to this composite field is Underworld.

The following pages aim to demonstrate two different hypotheses. The first hypothesis is that the study of the Underworld allows to outline a comprehensive history of the built environment and of its transformations, which takes into account space beyond formal or aesthetic qualities, and investigates architecture's role in the so-called Anthropocene. Although humans, since early ages, have tended to colonize any possible corner of the earth for different purposes, it is only after the Industrial Revolution that the degree of ambition and awareness with which natural resources have been exploited has gradually shaped an invisible domain, parallel and complementary to our visible built environment. The Underworld includes, but is not limited to, subterranean examples. It reaches beyond its most literal interpretation to incorporate all those secret and hidden elements whose spatial articulation is not completely revealed, or whose internal logic derives from above-the-ground inputs. Underground spaces belong to the Underworld, but the Underworld is not always belowground: it can be inaccessible or far from the public gaze, yet located in urban centers. Bunkers, catacombs, aqueducts, and, more recently, data centers, and seed banks: all of these examples belong to the Underworld. The Underworld manifests itself not as a specific physical location or collection of objects, but a set of socio-technical and spatial relations that shape our cities.

The second hypothesis informing the structure of the paper is that the Underworld's character—its conception, its materialization, its functioning—is essentially infrastructural. The Underworld exists to guarantee efficiency and to complement some of the services provided above ground; but it also exists to deploy a range of activities that otherwise would be prohibited or difficult to be performed elsewhere—with this respect, the Underworld often coincides with the most sinister manifestations of late capitalism, representing its black hole but also the deep reason of its prolongation and hegemony. In other words, one may say that the Underworld does not constitute a state of exception: its *raison d'être* derives from the same forces triggering the above-the-ground realm: settlement, trade, migration, warfare, epidemics. As François Fourquet argues, the city can be read as an ensemble of collective apparatuses distributed through space both horizontally and vertically. It collects, registers, catalyzes, and stores visible (objects) and invisible (information) flows.[4] In this sense, the study of the Underworld becomes all the more relevant, as it shapes socio-technical relations, distributes resources and mobilities (unevenly), and expands forms of surveillance and social control.

In addition, the Underworld is a field for the operation of biopower, a spatial realm governed by what Michel Foucault called the *dispotif*. When outlining his concept of dispositive—that heterogeneous ensemble of discourses, institutions, laws, administrative statements, scientific enunciations, philosophic and moral propositions—the French philosopher also mentioned the role played by architecture and described how, especially in the eighteenth and nineteenth centuries, political intentions manifested mainly through infrastructures, dwellings, and public spaces.[5] In looking at the Underworld as a composite constellation of all apparatuses that fuel biopolitics, we can detect the instrumental character of any design process: whether they served to protect entire countries from enemies, or to store sensitive data, underworld spaces are the ideal terrain to investigate the relationship between power, surveillance, and individuality.

Command and Control

Foucault's notion of *dispotif* is particularly useful in accounting for the long history of the design and production of infrastructures of control. His own account begins famously with the Panopticon. A social experiment ideated by philosopher Jeremy Bentham in 1791, the Panopticon represents the metaphor of how any institution—cultural, social, political—can establish forms of vigilance and punishment over its citizens. Its circular architecture is characterized by a series of rings: each ring accommodates several individual cells. In the middle, a single, all-seeing Eye—a tower representing the invasive presence of Power, which sees everything without ever being seen. And yet, while the Panopticon introduced the notion of constant observation and absolute isolation, it is largely an aboveground enterprise.

By contrast, the so-called Old Newgate prison in East Granby, Connecticut suggests a variant lineage of control, one involving the Underworld as a governing spatial logic. At the beginning of the eighteenth century, copper was discovered in the region and a system of tunnels was dug for its extraction. Ore from the mine was shipped to Boston and then to England to be refined. In 1773, the Connecticut General Assembly transformed the tunnels into a prison and employed its inmates as miners. Additional underground rooms were excavated, and the prisoners were forced to live and work below the ground. At Newgate, and thousands of other prison-mines around the world, panopticism is not a design requirement for control; it is enough to govern and secure the points of access, trapping prisoners in a world below ground.

The Underworld is also commonly produced and deployed for the exercise of state power and military control. In times of war, the Underworld expands rapidly through engineering works such as bunkers, tunnels, and shelters. Trench warfare during World War I found millions of soldiers living and dying in the sinuous networks carved out of farms and forests along the front lines. From 1940 to 1944, the London Underground itself served as an extensive air raid shelter for huddling and terrified civilians. During the Cold War, the fear of nuclear attacks led to the construction of a massive underground defense system, from missile silos and command bunkers to millions of designated fallout shelters in the basements of apartment buildings, hospitals, courthouses, and city halls. Today, especially in Western countries, most of these spaces have been simply abandoned or reconverted into public venues, such as museums and art galleries.

However, the expansion of the Underworld in times of war is not simply a defensive preoccupation. Often, the Underworld has been conceived as a weapon, a prolongation below the ground of warfare by other means. To some extent, warfare can only be fully understood in its three-dimensional character, as aerial views and maps offer a very partial picture. During the Cold War, for example, the U.S. Strategic Air Command built over one thousand intercontinental ballistic missile (ICBM) silos across the country (see Figure 4.2). Although well hidden from American citizens, the Soviet Union maintained detailed knowledge of the sites through satellite imaging and espionage reports. Moreover, while typically secreted away in remote deserts or plans, most of the missiles targeted high profile population centers,

Figure 4.2 Titan II ICBM at the Titan Missile Museum in Arizona, 2012.

Source: Photograph courtesy of Steve Jurvetson, Wikimedia Commons.

specifically the cities of Soviet republics and China. Successive generations of silo technology required different construction and maintenance specifications, but nearly all silo complexes include two or three missile tubes, a power station, and an underground command center. The largest warhead ever carried by an ICBM belonged to the Titan I, for which 52 silo complexes had been built across the Western deserts between 1963 and 1981. Titan II missiles were designed to be launched in less than a minute. However, in 1981 improvements to the Atlas missile program rendered the Titan II ICBMs obsolete, and they were destroyed, along with all but one of their silo complexes. The remaining Air Force Facility Missile Site 8, seen in Figure 4.2, was turned into the Titan Missile Museum, a sort of Cold War *memento mori*.

If the Soviet Union was a constant yet silent enemy, the United States conducted a more traditional war campaign in Vietnam. Here the Viet Cong ideated and deployed highly tactical guerrilla warfare by reusing and expanding a capillary network of tunnels devised to obscure their movements and to throw the Americans off guard (see Figure 4.3). The tunnels beneath the Cu Chi district in Saigon were actually dug in the 1940s first during the war against Japanese invaders, and then against the French colonial army. But when the United States increased its presence in Vietnam in the mid-1960s, the tunnels were reactivated and for long time were used to resist the American offensive. Their entrances camouflaged and booby-trapped, they served as hiding places during combat and as transport for weapons, food, and messengers. The tunnels even housed hospitals and other structures for soldiers, such as theaters and music halls. For much of the war, the U.S. military had great difficulty detecting and destroying these structures. In 1967, when American soldiers raided the Viet Cong headquarters of Cu Chi, they found documents containing Viet Cong strategy and maps of U.S. bases.

Figure 4.3 Cu-chi Tunnels, Vietnam: camouflage and the art of war.

Source: Photograph courtesy of Thomas Schoch, Wikimedia Commons.

Vietnamese authorities estimate that 45,000 men and women lost their lives defending the Cu Chi tunnels, which have been preserved as public memorial parks.[6]

Similar dynamics unfold today in the Gaza Strip, where, over the last twenty years, the Arab–Israeli conflict has moved partially underground. As documented by Eyal Weizman in his *Hollow Land*, while construction of tunnels already started in the 1970s, it is only after the second Intifada (2000) that the use of tunnels accelerated, when Israel sealed off the Gaza Strip from the outside world.[7] Throughout the years, the Israeli army has adopted a systematic body of invasive actions aimed to take possession of the airspace, water aquifers, and the underground of the area, although Palestinians are supposed to control a portion of territory on the basis of the Oslo Accords (1993). To avoid being spotted, the tunnel entrances and exits are generally located inside buildings. Most tunnels have several access points and routes, starting in homes or rural structures, joining together into a main route, and then branching off again into several separate passages leading to buildings on the other side. In this way, if one entrance is shut down, others can still be used.[8] For a depressed economy such as Gaza's, the construction of tunnels has become a profitable operation, and a relevant source of income. Typically, tunnels are built by private contractors who employ local diggers and engineers. The construction quality is slightly better than Vietnam's tunnels, since they are made of concrete and wired for electricity. In surveilling the area by drones and other devices, the Israel Defensive Forces (IDF) can detect the presence of tunnels when excess landfill or sand is identified. Sensors and transmitters have also been deployed to discover these invisible structures and, since 2014, thirty-two tunnels have been destroyed with explosives, according to Israeli numbers.

Storage and Retrieval

Another widespread use of the underground is for the sequestering of valuable commodities, including money, computer data, and servers. Bank vaults have long been located underground in order to reduce the risk of breach. The Torrione of Niccolò V, a tower and underground vault built by Bernardo Rossellino between 1451 and 1455 in Vatican City, provides a case in point. Originally a prison inside the Leonine Walls, today this structure is the headquarters of a controversial bank: the Istituto per le

Opere di Religione (IOR). While it was founded as a local bank for Vatican citizens, the IOR later became an offshore entity, and over the years rumors have proliferated about the bank's activities of money laundering, occult funding, and obscure geopolitical affairs. Their opaque presence is also emphasized by the image of the Torrione: a sort of bunker, whose 30-foot-thick walls protect its secrets from any process of transparency that similar banks are subject to around the world. For many years, mystery has haunted the IOR's activities; it was rumored to have 130 employees and about 44,000 saving accounts. Customers were identified through a code number only, and operations were not traceable. Its business was known only to the pope and a few other Vatican authorities. In 2012, for the first time in its history, the IOR opened its doors to journalists. In 2013, the bank published its financial holdings. Such underground vaults often carry a double significance; they project an air of security and impenetrability, while simultaneously occluding their operations in a shroud of mystery.

While tens of thousands of underground bank vaults continue to serve their intended purpose, today our most valuable commodity is information, stored in the form of data and located materially on computer servers. The need to store and retrieve computer data has constituted one of the most generative technological and infrastructural challenges of the last seventy-five years. In the 1950s and 1960s, universities, governments, and corporations built massive warehouses dedicated to housing punch cards and magnetic tape. In the 1970s and 1980s, many tech writers imagined that the microprocessor revolution would obviate the need for massive physical storage facilities. However, with the proliferation of the internet in the 1990s, the need for information storage grew exponentially. In some cases, conventional buildings, originally designed for other purposes, were converted to accommodate cables, computers and servers. In Downtown Los Angeles, for example, is a 39-story tower—a construction with a regular façade and with no peculiar formal qualities. Designed by SOM in their San Francisco branch, the building was supposed to house offices—window areas were in fact maximized to provide light and views for the occupants.[9] In 1992, the tower—One Wilshire—became a carrier hotel, and on the fourth floor a large meet-me-room (MMR) was installed—a space where different telecommunication companies could physically connect one to another and exchange data. In contradicting the modernist principle which inspired its construction—form follows function—One Wilshire solidifies a double contradiction: outside is a conventional tower, reflecting Fordist models of labor organization. Inside is an interconnected world of cables, data, and information—one of the crucial hubs for Western U.S., where most of the traffic from the U.S. to Asia passes through the building.[10] In addition, One Wilshire proves how virtual space needs physical space. Or, virtual space needs infrastructures.

Over the past twenty years, architects and engineers have developed a new building typology colloquially known as the "server farm." These facilities are essentially highly advanced technological warehouses designed to ensure fast connectivity, security, and nonstop operation. Data centers are similar to industrial complexes and demand a huge amount of electricity to function. Their presence is normally isolated from city centers and protected from interference. Since the internet is frequently a target of espionage or cyberwar—an extension of the Cold War in the twenty-first century—the design of data centers has military and political implications. However, the information we have about these structures is mainly limited to centers run by internet service providers, whose main goal is to store their own servers and not to necessarily safeguard sensitive data.

Meanwhile, the common thread between the military world and data protection is evident at Pionen White Mountain, a former nuclear bunker in Stockholm, located 100 feet below Vita Berg Park. Originally built in 1943 to protect government activities from enemy attacks, the bunker was transformed in 2008 into a data center designed by architect Albert France-Lanord. Light, plants, water, and technology are imported from the surface in order to transform an inanimate rock interior into a living organism occupied by humans and other living beings. Home to the WikiLeaks servers, among others, Pionen White Mountain is still a bunker—an impassable fortress that serves as ironic contrast to the transparency and free access implicit in information technology. Although White Mountain is one of the first attempts to rethink the image of data centers and to move away from the utilitarian

Figure 4.4 Svalbard Global Seed Vault, Norway: the only visible part of the structure.

Source: Photograph courtesy of Miksu, Wikimedia Commons.

aspects of its spaces, its inaccessibility exemplifies the contradictions and ambiguities that come with new building typologies.

Another form of data archive can be found on the island of Spitsbergen in Norway, 800 miles from the North Pole: the Svalbard Global Seed Vault, the biggest repository of agricultural biodiversity in the world (see Figure 4.4). A hybrid structure—part seed bank, part bunker, part data center—it was funded by the Norwegian government and opened its doors in 2008. The government owns the building but not its content, which is why different countries, from the United States to North Korea, agreed to deposit copies of their plant seeds in Svalbard. Its purpose is twofold: to preserve genetic diversity and protect seeds from natural disasters or other accidents. Designed by Peter W. Søderman MNAL of Barlindhaug Consult, the building is accessed by a cement monolith partially wedged into the ice and rock. Inside, a 390-foot-long tunnel runs straight through the permafrost, where three underground rooms store the seeds at a temperature of −0.4°F, which will significantly delay aging.

By 2017, the vault was storing more than 930,000 seeds, but it has the capacity to store up to 4.5 million crop varieties—each variety containing an average of 500 seeds. Compared to the other 1,700 seed banks around the world, the Norwegian government intended the Svalbard Global Seed Vault to provide optimal conditions and tight security. Scientists consider the location ideal because Spitsbergen is roughly 430 feet above sea level—high enough to protect the vault from rising waters when the ice melts. Yet, despite such precautions, the facility flooded in 2017 due to ice and permafrost melt from unusually high temperatures. Intended to function for long periods without human intervention, the vault is now under twenty-four-hour watch, with emergency waterproofing being added.[11]

At the End of the Journey

Fredric Jameson identified in the Bonaventure Hotel the crystallization of postmodernism, or the cultural logic of late capitalism, because of its reflective surfaces, and its position in relation to the surrounding urban context of a sprawling, centerless Los Angeles.[12] However, it might be just as reasonable to see data centers, seed banks, and carrier hotels as harbingers of late-capitalist spatial production. Indeed, few projects underscore the relationship between the Underworld and late capitalism more than the development of the dark fiber connection between the Chicago Mercantile Exchange and the Nasdaq data hub in Carteret, New Jersey. Constructed by Spread Networks (now owned by Zayo Group Holdings, Inc.), the project consists of a large bundle of optical cables laid in a 1,331 kilometer trench and tunnel between the two points. While fiber optic lines generally follow existing underground sewer and utility ducts as well as railroad corridors, the Spread Network trench plies the straightest line possible, even boring through mountains and crossing farm fields to do so. At an initial cost of $US300 million, the cable provides "dark fibre" (lines that lay dormant until called upon) for stockbrokers and other clients to reduce latency by shaving three milliseconds off trading time—a crucial advantage in the high-speed, algorithm-driven world of arbitrage.[13]

Over the last century, then, a constellation of new landforms and building typologies has emerged in relation to changing socio-technical conditions. In this sense, a journey through the Underworld helps draw some conclusions about its physical and symbolic role. First, the Underworld constitutes an inverted infrastructural terrain—the mirrored continuation of spatial politics. Issues of territorial control, defense, labor, land exploitation, privatization of public spaces, all continue downwards in the remote and dark areas of our cities. Second, the Underworld reveals a spatial paradox: the more immaterial and intangible our everyday communicative world becomes—from cloud storage to big data—the more obscure, segregated, and inaccessible are the infrastructure forms that support it. Hidden behind Victorian houses, or buried 100 feet below the ground, the physical presence of the Underworld is inversely proportioned to the contents it stores. This apparent contradiction does not weaken late capitalism's image; on the contrary, it enhances it. And third, while its surfaces are often hidden, abandoned, neglected, or denied, the Underworld nevertheless presents a field of possibilities. Rather than imagining it only as a negative and threatening realm, we can study its intertwined articulations and the relationships these produce between humans and objects, bodies and spaces, data and images. By doing so, we will better understand spatial and ideological conditions behind architecture, and, ultimately, we can develop a more comprehensive understanding of the relation of infrastructure to power.

Notes

1 Lynda Nead, *Victorian Babylon: People, Streets, and Images in Nineteenth-Century London* (New Haven: Yale University Press, 2000).
2 Frederik Gosman, *Seven Days in London: A Practical Descriptive Guide* (London: C. Smith & Son, 1884), 68.
3 Stephen Graham, *Vertical* (Brooklyn: Verso, 2016), 202.
4 François Fourquet and Lion Murard, *Les équipments du pouvoir* (Paris: Union Générale d'Éditions, 1976).
5 Michel Foucault, "Space, Knowledge, and Power," interview with Paul Rabinow, in *Architecture Theory since 1968*, ed. Michael Hays (Cambridge: MIT Press, 2000).
6 Gordon Rottman, *Viet Cong and NVA Tunnels and Fortifications of the Vietnam War* (New York: Osprey Publishing, 2006), 51, 56–57.
7 Eyal Weizman, *Hollow Land. Israel's Architecture of Occupation* (London: Verso, 2007), 255.
8 Ibid. 254.
9 Robert Summel and Kazys Varnelis, *Blue Monday. Stories of Absurd Realities and Natural Philosophies* (Barcelona: Actar, 2007), 63.
10 Dave Bullock, "A Lesson in Internet Anatomy: The World's Densest Meet-Me Room," *Wired*, March 3, 2008.
11 James Bridle, *New Dark Age. Technology and the End of the Future* (London: Verso, 2018), 52.
12 Fredric Jameson, *Postmodernism, or, The Cultural Logic of Late Capitalism* (Durham: Duke University Press, 1991).
13 Donald MacKenzie, "Capital's Geodesic: Chicago, New Jersey, and the Material Sociology of Speed," in *The Sociology of Speed: Digital, Organizational, and Social Temporalities*, eds J. Wajcman and N. Dodd (New York: Oxford University Press), 56–62.

PART II
Embodiments

5
VIRTUAL GARDENS
Gendered Space in the History of Afghanistan's Telecommunications

Hannah Ahlblad

This chapter explores the twentieth century evolution of telecommunications infrastructure through political and cultural shifts in Afghanistan as it relates to historic concepts of a woman's "place" in Afghan society, particularly in Pashtun society. Afghanistan's relative delay in nationalized infrastructure and control enabled women to perform in virtual media spaces without established constraints. Until the Soviet occupation in 1978, multiple foreign powers had constructed telegraph lines and radio towers as a means of monitoring one another's operations in Iran and the Indian subcontinent, with minimal involvement in Afghan society. The Taliban rejected adoption of the internet and limited women's physical mobility and visibility. After the launch of 2G phones with internet access, women quickly gravitated to social media as a public space in response to physical limitations. While other Islamic republics built their own internet services and architecture, Afghanistan was inundated with a range of international internet and mobile data service providers and built a decentralized digital infrastructure. The development of wireless and satellite providers made it difficult for any one political body to control and censor the country's internet content. Today, reinforced by an active diaspora of Afghan women, mobility, power, and independence depend more on access to the internet, radio, and messaging than to the urban streets. The physical construction of modern communication systems in Afghanistan have become an evolving virtual forum for women in an otherwise constrained physical environment.

Afghanistan's geographic proximity to Iran, Pakistan, China, and the former Soviet Union has resulted in a highly uneven and episodic history of infrastructure development, as foreign powers with military or ideological agendas continually enter and depart. The country's telecommunications history in particular has played a profound role in shaping society over time, most dramatically women's roles and identities. Despite European, Soviet, and American investments in communications infrastructure over the past century, Afghanistan's geopolitical maneuvers continually deterred any lasting monopoly of their communications infrastructure and its content. In this way, the country has developed a poorly connected basic infrastructure, layered over by the more recent expansion of globally connected cyberspace. The disjuncture between these systems has provided an opening for women in Afghanistan and across the diaspora to reclaim their role as storytellers and artists within a digitally inflected Afghan identity.

As women take increasingly to the digital realm, Islamic scholars continue to debate women's roles within the Pashtun code of conduct, the *Pakhtunwali*, centering primarily on physical relationships with men and bodily presence in the public sphere. For decades, male politicians in Afghanistan have sought legitimization through the strategic veiling and unveiling of women. At the same time, Western scholarship and media frequently read women's mobility and freedom outside the home within a narrowly compassed framework. Western feminist scholars in particular have drawn problematic conclusions about female empowerment in terms of the *chadaari*, or covering, as opposed

DOI: 10.4324/9781003093756-8

to women's actual practices and presence in space. In this chapter, however, I will show that the physical "veil" does not automatically determine a woman's political and intellectual influence and presence. In fact, the ability to connect to cities and countries from behind a screen, not a veil, is the most significant expression of freedom—the right to participate, enabled through the expanding digital infrastructure.

For centuries, societal rules controlled women's physical location and literal visibility, but not their ideological visibility. In 1881, the first known lithograph of Afghan poetry was published in Kabul. The choice of the publishing house was *Diwan-e Ayesha*, a posthumous collection of poems by Ayesha Durrani, the wife of Timur Shah Durrani, the second ruler of the Durrani Empire.[1] Oral Pashtun poetry by the wives and relatives of warriors valued the power of a woman's fierce loyalty and empowering voice. Among the Afghan Hazara and Tajik communities, and in pre-Islamic Zoroastrian dynasties, women have been political advisors. And the interpretation of Islamic codes of conduct has varied considerably, not only between the multiple groups that comprise Afghanistan, but also in the varieties of Islam that have moved in and out of currency over time.

While previous Afghan governments have alternately banned and encouraged women to be in school, the workplace, and public spaces, women have had a growing presence and under-recognized power in the realm of communications. First as authors of ancient Persian and Pashto poetry, and later in the avid production of Afghanistan radio, television, and telephone networks, women have been at the forefront of the country's evolving telecommunications infrastructure. Indeed, the arrival of telephone boards and radios brought women into the modern workforce in the early 1940s long before the Soviet and United States' political involvement. But the tumultuous history of Afghanistan in the twentieth century frequently disrupted the production of hardscape infrastructure, leaving substantial gaps that would eventually be filled by digital technologies. Over the past two decades, satellite and cellular networks have expanded, and the lack of organization of Afghanistan's telecommunications has worked to women's advantage, offering an alternative space to the binary debates around *purdah*. Decentralized telecommunications infrastructure engenders women's relative freedom of speech on mass media platforms compared to the more physical restriction of their spatial territories. As such, the internet, and specifically the social media networks that connect women across South Asia and to diasporic communities, plays a crucial role in the narrative and cultural formation of present-day Afghanistan.

Strategic Connection: 1912–1940

The disparate and fiercely defended tribal territories from the Hindu Kush to the arid deserts of the Helmand long formed a geographic block against a uniform infrastructure system. By 1872, telegraph lines connected East Bengal to Great Britain, but wrapped outside the edge of Afghanistan's southern border. The investment and establishment of telegraph and telephone infrastructure in Persia and India was a strategic intelligence tool for the British Empire. A 1912 War Office map of infrastructure shows a deliberate circumambulation of Afghanistan by British telegraph lines and alternately Russian and British railroad systems with different gauges (Figure 5.1). Through the vast open space labeled "Afghanistan," a network of dirt roads and rivers cross through villages. Telegraph lines creep up to the edges of Afghan territory but remain outside of it.[2] During the three Anglo–Afghan wars, Britain monitored arms smuggling by strategically placed telegraph and later telephone lines along major roads at the Iran–Afghan border.[3] After a 1919 stalemate, the British Protectorate left Emir Amanullah Khan with national jurisdiction over a large mosaic of ethnic groups, religions, and cultures. However, British officials continued to assert their interests in the country, often sparring with Germany for influence.

In the 1920s, a campaign by the British Foreign Office convinced the Emir to route Afghan international post mail circuitously through Bombay.[4] Ten years later, the British convinced a new monarch, Muhammad Nadir Shah, to route telegraphs with western destinations, eastward through British

Virtual Gardens

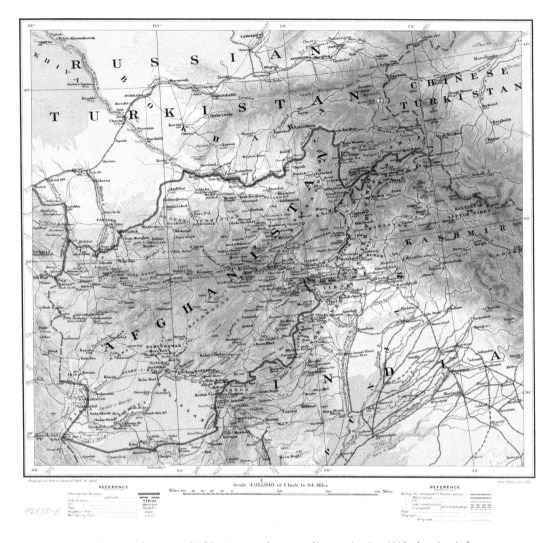

Figure 5.1 British War Office map of Afghanistan and surrounding territories, 1912, showing infrastructure as a strategic element.

Source: Courtesy of the Library of Congress.

India.[5] Britain gained more control of Afghanistan's communications without physically re-colonizing Afghanistan. Germany countered British control of the postal service with moves to electrify Kabul and Kandahar, and to connect Afghanistan's provinces to power and communications networks. The presence of multiple foreign investors grew with the 1921 Afghan–Soviet Treaty, and the 1923 German Afghan Trade Commission, diminishing concentrated power over the new state's infrastructure. Between 1923 and 1928, the Soviets established a telegraph office in Kabul, a civil air link between Tashkent and Kabul, and initiated the North–South Salang Pass highway.[6] In 1925, the German Siemens Corporation lay cables, paved roads, bridges, and telegraph lines.[7] Emir Amanullah Khan purchased two German V-41 broadcasting transmitters from the Telefunken company for Kabul and Kandahar.[8] A German-built recording studio opened outside Kabul.[9]

Despite these expansions in the 1920s, the majority of Afghanistan remained rural and disconnected from global markets. Women's protected physical status remained confined to local sites of domesticity or agriculture. Gender separation responded to the majority's Islamic values and to even older nomadic tribal customs. More than religious, protecting a woman's *namus*, her virtue and honor, had a long history among the nomadic Pashtuns who protected and avenged anyone who threatened lineage, property, or loved ones.[10] Archaeologist and ethnologist, Louis Dupree, writes that some of the desire to control women's appearance and presence defends against a Pashtun aggression called "woman-stealing." Because they were most frequently in charge of domestic life while men were out, women carried their family's household wealth and thereby their honor, enrobed in velvet gowns embroidered with gold and bedecked in coins.[11] In 1928, Emir Amanullah presided over a *Loya Jirga*, the traditional assembly of Tribal Elders. His wife, Queen Soraya, and over 100 other women attended, unveiled. To amend the outrage that followed, Amanullah issued a reversal of mandatory girls education, ordered the closure of women's hair salons, and re-established the *purdah*.[12] Women were of course absent from building or operating telecommunications networks.

After the Afghan Civil War of 1928–1929 damaged radio infrastructure, Mohammad Zahir Shah consolidated power in 1933, and purchased a new set of radio transmitters from Germany.[13] By the end of the 1930s, 70% of new technological infrastructure in Afghanistan was German.[14] During the Third Reich, previously private German infrastructure work fell under the purview of Organisation Todt.[15] Earlier broadcasting systems and radio telegraphy in Afghanistan had been begun by Siemens Technologies, Maschinenbau, and Telefunken. During World War II (WWII), these projects were completed by the Nazis, and used as part of Germany's South Asian warfare operations.

Accelerated Connection: 1939–1978

Telecommunications infrastructure was used internally by the government to improve Afghan economic systems across disparate regions, and externally, to serve foreign investors' geopolitical aims. Although Mohammad Zahir Shah repeatedly reinforced Afghanistan's neutrality during WWII, he favored German telecommunication systems. In 1939, transmission technology and workers arrived from Germany to launch the first broadcast on August 23, 1940 that could reach all over Afghanistan. The Third Reich used their communications infrastructure in Afghanistan to establish an *Anwehr* outpost where military intelligence officers under the guise of "scientists" for the Organisation Todt conducted sabotage against telecommunications infrastructure along the border with British India with support from the Faqir Ipi's Pashtun guerrilla movement.[16] By 1942, the CIA had detected German intelligence surreptitiously routing radio traffic between Berlin and Kabul, pretending to communicate with a Kabul Skoda Works factory.[17] The vast majority of Afghanistan lacked basic literacy through most of the twentieth century, and though nefariously built, these radio systems would later become the nation's first means of mass communication. After the Nazi surrender in 1945, Afghanistan was silently divided between Soviet and American technicians in the northern and southern provinces, respectively.

Prime Minister Sardar Muhammad Daoud Khan outlined goals for the economic development of Afghanistan in 1954 as part of the first of several Five-Year Plans. In 1960, the nation's largest city, Kabul, had a literacy rate of 5.9%, the highest of anywhere in the country.[18] Afghanistan's population relied on the telephone wire and radio signals that traversed the country and by 1968 made up 59% of budgetary spending.[19] During the 1960s, the Afghan Ministry of Planning issued annual reports in English describing telecommunications infrastructure and construction spending with the tabulated number of Soviets or alternately Americans leading each project. Given widespread illiteracy, these English-language reports seem intended for the USSR, U.S., and other foreign governments to keep tabs or compete for influence through infrastructure investment. Booklets from the Afghanistan's Government Publishing House claim a national ownership of telecommunications infrastructure, although the telephone system in Kabul was

Virtual Gardens

Figure 5.2 Telephone wire at a cotton processing plant in Kunduz, northern Afghanistan, 1961.

Source: Ministry of Planning of the Royal Government of Afghanistan.

directly funded by the Soviets. In 1961, the Ministry of Planning reported a tenfold growth telephone line connections from 2,500 in 1955 to 25,000 in 1960. The report notes international call connections between Kabul and New York, London, Paris, Bombay, Tehran, Tashkent, and Moscow, and the anticipation of upcoming work that would connect Kabul to Tokyo, Rome, Munich, and Calcutta.[20]

A 1960 bilingual Dari–English publication from the Ministry of Planning advertises telephone towers and operator switchboards in rural areas. Turrets of telephone wire skim past a gleaming white modernist factory in the northern city of Kunduz (Figure 5.2). In another photo, women sit at the switchboard, with their hair coiffed in trendy European styles, "connecting calls between Kandahar and Kabul" (Figure 5.3).[21] Since switchboard operators and radio broadcasters were physically invisible, whether or not women employees covered their hair is only relevant to the reader of the Ministry of Planning's publications, not to the women's work. It suggests that the image of unveiled women was more global marketing than overwhelming reality.

Historian Nancy Dupree observed a distinction between women in urban and rural communities in reaction to new infrastructure. Urban women left *purdah*, or seclusion, and removed their chador in cities. Meanwhile, in agricultural communities that had grown wealthier from better transportation and communication, nomadic women settled down and remained in *purdah* because the ornamental,

Figure 5.3 Construction of telephone lines between Kabul and Kandahar, and switchboard operators, 1961.
Source: Ministry of Planning of the Royal Government of Afghanistan.

luxurious veils indicated their family's upward mobility and ability to pay servants to do tasks that were otherwise not accommodated by more conservative covering.[22] As of 1964, a woman's "dignity, compulsory education, and freedom to work" was guaranteed by the nation's secular constitution.[23] Muhammad Daoud Khan's economic ambition and autocratic rule opened higher education and vocational training to women. Radio and telephone allowed women to be heard more than seen. The emergence of widespread telecommunications effectively created a new spatial territory in Afghanistan that had not yet been evaluated in terms of gendered space by religious scholars or long-term cultural establishments.

Women on daytime radio in Afghanistan fulfilled the culture of women in a sphere separate from men. In 1976, radio secretary and singer, Farida Mahwash received the honor of *Ustadh*, master musician, from the government.[24] That same year, management professor Francine Gordon compared American and Afghan women working in communications. Careers in telephone and radio operation were well suited to women because of the hours, the comfortable distance between men and women, and the "depersonalization" of the work environment.[25] Since the cultural tradition obligated a separation of genders based on occupations, telecommunications offered an acceptable space in which women could work behind the screen of an operations board or sound engineering set. Prime Minister Daoud Khan usurped power in a 1973, abolished the monarchy, and announced his presidency on Radio Afghanistan.[26] But Daoud Khan's 1977 constitution did not satisfy an increasingly divided public opinion on gender issues. The country's delicate balance of old and new, Afghan, American, and Soviet power was finally thrown off in 1978 with the assassination of President Muhammad Daoud Khan and the Soviet-backed Saur Revolution.

Socialist Connection: 1978–1987

A few months earlier, the Japanese International Cooperation Agency (JICA) had completed a two-year project to construct and set-up a television studio in Kabul. The television studio, which remained in operation through 1996, included five studio cameras and editing tools, along with an outdoor broadcasting van with three camcorders, and ten Electronic News-Gathering units (ENGs).[27] Japan hoped that its media infrastructure contract with Kabul would bring Afghanistan closer into a pan-Asian alliance against growing Soviet power. However, it was too late. When Afghanistan's socialist leader, Nur Muhammad Taraki, rose to power in 1978, Radio Television Afghanistan began to broadcast two hours of daily programming on the country's only television channel.[28]

Soviet and American infrastructure projects gradually turned more antagonistic. A 1965 memorandum between the Turkmen Communist Party and the Soviet Union requested a far-reaching 150kW radio transmitter to broadcast communist propaganda into Afghanistan—to counter the Voice of America's anti-Soviet broadcasting in Iran near Afghanistan's northwest border.[29] While the United States created targeted news broadcasting and propaganda through the 1960s in neighboring countries, Voice of America only began to broadcast radio into Afghanistan through third-party countries after 1978.[30] Radio Kabul's programming shifted from the popular and folk music and news in Dari and Pashto to re-broadcasted propaganda, directly from the USSR. Afghanistan's Revolutionary Council increased the presence of women in political media outlets. Dr. Anahita Ratebzad was named Minister of Social Affairs, and reached tens of thousands on a radio broadcast speech that promoted women's role in the country's socialist movement:

> [The] Duties of women and mothers, who shape the future of the country [are] to bring up sons and daughters who are sincere and patriotic […] and take steps to consolidate your revolutionary regime as bravely as the heroic and brave men of this country.[31]

During the 1980s, female Russian intellectuals came to Afghanistan to instruct co-educational computing classes at the Polytechnic University in Kabul. Aggressive anti-religious policies and media control set the Pashtun and Islamic beliefs at odds with Soviet infrastructure advancement. The Soviet invasion of Afghanistan was the first time a foreign government had both implemented communications infrastructure and steered its application by the internal population. These years engendered a subsequent reversal and physical destruction of Afghanistan's infrastructure and new opportunities for political participation.

Strategic *Dis*connection: 1989–2001

In 1989, the Soviet Union retreated from Afghanistan. During the Soviet occupation of Afghanistan, the computer engineering programs at the U.S.-backed Kabul University had been eliminated, with technical engineering courses heavily developed at the Soviet-sponsored Kabul Polytechnic University. Along with the exit of Soviet professors, scientists, and an Afghan intellectual exodus, went the knowledge base to coordinate and cultivate a foundation of Afghan-led computing infrastructure. The Taliban's radicalized religious students and mujahideen opposed the corruptive potential of widespread mass communications systems. By the time the Taliban emerged as the dominant force in Kabul in 1996, broadcasting infrastructure was destroyed. In addition to the mandate of the *burqa* across cities, televisions and printed images of women were banned. Radio Kabul was renamed *Voice of Sharia*, and it was the only permitted radio station.

During the 1980s and 1990s, Taliban men had encouraged religious women to be vocal activists against secular communist rule. By 1996, the Taliban had shifted their attitude completely. Women were no longer allowed in politics, media or education. Nonetheless, women protested in public against Taliban policies. One Taliban official in the Attorney General's office explained the *burqa* in 1997: "The face of a woman is a source of corruption for men who are not related to them."[32] The Taliban was aware that Afghan women heavily influence public opinion. Violence against dissidents, particularly women, revealed the Taliban's ideological vulnerability and tenuous grip on power.

Anytime a woman left home, she was to be accompanied by a male escort, fully concealed and silent. No auditory presence; neither speaking nor laughing was permitted. Part of the Taliban's 1996 adjustments included suspending women from their jobs, many of whom were the sole providers for their families.[33] The Taliban's conceived cocktail of Wahhabi and Pashtunwali beliefs restricted the mobility of women more than any other period of modern history. The country's estimated 15,000 to 20,000 telephones were concentrated in securitized public bazaars, outside a woman's reach.[34] Many telephone poles and connections had been knocked down through the war's explosive violence, and served the Taliban's paranoid policy to limit the communications infrastructure. International calls were mostly made by crossing the border into Pakistan, where there was broader access to telephones.

The neighboring Pakistani government oversaw an expansion of its internet services and access to internet cafes and personal computers during the late 1990s. So did the Kingdom of Saudi Arabia, which adopted a public internet connection in 1998 routed through King Fahd City for Technology and Science. With the distribution of internet access and routers to their citizens, Saudi Arabia also constructed firewalls and systematic censorship of internet content as early as 1998.[35] In contrast, the Taliban did not find any reason to expend on infrastructure only to block access. However, like the rest of the world during the dot-com boom, the Taliban leadership was curious to peek into the new internet. Their solution: a single computer in Afghanistan was allowed internet access, routed through a Pakistani internet service provider, and managed and "monitored" by a "reliable person."[36] On August 25, 2001, Mullah Muhamad Omar Mujahid issued a *fatwa* that banned the internet from being established in the Islamic Emirate of Afghanistan. After 9/11 and the U.S. invasion of Afghanistan, the internet arrived under the U.S.-backed government of President Hamid Karzai in 2002.

Today: How Do You Veil the Net?

The Afghan–American-owned, Afghan Wireless Communications Company (AWCC) began to install cell-phone towers in 2002. Previously, AWCC had signed a contract with the Taliban in 1998 for wireless GSM infrastructure, giving 20% company ownership to the government, and ingratiating themselves with both Taliban and U.S. factions.[37] In the first decade of the 2000s, American finances dominated telecommunications and specifically internet infrastructure projects in Afghanistan through the DoD and USAID. NATO expanded its Virtual Silk Road Highway to Kabul University in 2004, as part of a program to connect the former Soviet republics of the Caucasus and Central Asian Republics internet by satellite service to the Deutsches Elektronen–Synchrotron (DES) in Hamburg.[38] AfghanSAT1 was later manufactured by European Aeronautic Defence and Space Company (EADS), sold by the French company EutelSAT funded by NATO, and launched from French Guiana, a safe distance from Taliban counterinsurgency.[39]

An influx of internet and mobile service providers in Afghanistan parallels that of the early twentieth century. President Ashraf Ghani's diversification of telecommunication investors parallels Amanullah

Virtual Gardens

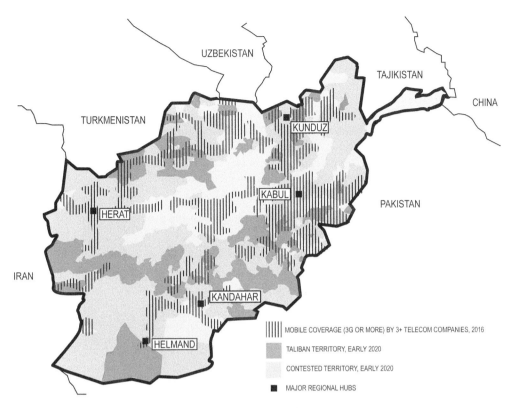

Figure 5.4 Cellular data coverage and Taliban-held territory, Afghanistan.

Source: Map drawn by Hannah Ahlblad, using aggregated public open-source data from The Islamic Republic of Afghanistan, Ministry of Communications; Foundation for Defense of Democracies; The Islamic Republic of Afghanistan, Telecom Regulatory Authority.

Khan's strategic balance of foreign investment in roads, postal mail, and telegraph lines in the 1920s. The Afghan Ministry of Telecommunications and internet Technology now lists several authorized mobile networks managed by firms in the United Arab Emirates, Monaco, South Africa, China, Switzerland, and the United States, each with different vested political interests. Among all the countries involved, the Taliban views local Afghan telecom providers with the highest level of suspicion.

Unable to ban VPNs, and create firewalls, the Taliban react with physical violence, a mostly futile campaign to ravage physical telecommunications towers and wires. A map of Taliban-controlled territories corresponds to the urban areas shown with the greatest number of GSM providers, which indicate the ongoing success of mobile phone penetration (Figure 5.4). In September 2019, Taliban fighters in the Northwestern provinces of Afghanistan destroyed fifteen major national wireless network towers as a protest against democratic elections[40]. Before the support of internet satellites, Afghanistan's estimated internet penetration in 2009 was 3.5%.[41] Today's divisions endanger Afghanistan's development and stability, but also enforce the power of social media. Information campaigns are in the hands of many people instead of any one regime. Since 2014, the Taliban has tried to ban smartphones across controlled-provinces;[42] They thereby reduce their own access to messaging. Today's sophisticated plethora of ways to navigate past firewalls, conceal small phone hardware, mask IP addresses, and escape censorship on the world wide web means that Afghanistan's internet freedom will likely persist. The Diaspora of refugees and emigrants also preserve the legacy of Afghanistan beyond the narrow historical scope of the Taliban.

An internet-savvy generation of women influencers counter Taliban narratives. The told history and present political role of women sit on phones inside and outside the physical borders of Afghanistan.

Social media provides an opportunity for Afghan women in their native country and abroad to connect across the world. Afghan students at Kabul University and in California responded to the Black Lives Matter protests of summer 2020 as an occasion to speak out against the abuse of migrant Afghan workers in Iran, and the violence against the Shi'ite Hazara community by the Taliban.[43] Every day, young women in Kabul "like" and comment on photos of their online friends in Stockholm, New Delhi, Dubai, Tehran, and Los Angeles. In the post-Bin Laden world, Instagram and TikTok provide young women with a platform to create their own vibrant narrative of Afghan identity.

Today no country need provide Afghanistan with a recording studio. With phones, women can geotag themselves across Afghanistan's beautiful valleys, deserts, and mountains or post from the seemingly infinite confines of their own homes. In one selfie at a textile bazaar, a mirror reflects an Afghan–Swedish travel blogger, Sana, the iPhone concealing her face from onlookers (Figure 5.5). Unlike their

Figure 5.5 Instagram selfie taken by @Sanaaqt's at a bazaar in Kabul, November 2019.

Source: Used here with permission

grandmothers, whose select careers and voices in public affairs on national radio in the 1960s and 1970s exposed them to the critique of rural conservatives, today's transnational Afghan influencers express that sharing curated content online adds nominally to the everyday risks of life in a war-torn country. For many women, the gain—connection, knowledge, and influence is worth that risk.

Nearly ten years ago, Dinah Zeiger suggested that online outlets were "merely a world stage that reinforces a stereotypical Western understanding of the 'Orient' as passively locked within ancient custom and religious law."[44] Today's Afghan millennials are not preoccupied by an appeal to Western audiences. They post stories of a pan-Asian history with photos, poetry, and music collaged from Bollywood, Iran, China, and Japan. In 2020, during a Q&A session on her Instagram story, a broadcaster for Radio Television Afghanistan attributed her success to a bachelor's degree in Malaysia, and an MBA from China. While American and British presence is associated with invasions and wartime, China does not carry a negative or overwhelming cultural influence on young Afghans.

Chinese education and technology in Afghanistan parallels the rise of German dominance in the 1930s, but now targets Afghan women. Mobile smartphones from ZTE and telecom providers like Huawei provide Afghanistan with relative freedom of speech. Driven by financial domination, China supports both ends of the political spectrum: aiding the Taliban in building telephone infrastructure and supposed surveillance systems in 2001, and more recently, funding women in study-abroad programs in business and technology.[45] Today, China is the largest investor in Afghanistan, as part of the massive expenditures of the Digital Silk Road initiative begun as a component of the Belt and Road Initiative in 2015. One day, China's Digital Silk Road may face-off against the rising threat of the Islamic State's completely different brand of authoritarianism.

Conclusion

Christine Noelle-Karimi describes the debate over women's place in society as one that was based on external visibility: "Marking the boundary between the inner (female) and outer (male) worlds, veiling served as an emotionally laden symbol for all parties involved."[46] In addition to the domestic sphere, the inner world also refers to the mind, and a psychology and philosophy of self. While men are more visually present on city streets, rural dust roads, and across leading political and commercial institutions, the visual presence of women in Afghanistan has reflected a cultural, political, and psychological concept of place. Due to the past century's focus on physical gender barriers, telecommunications infrastructure and an open internet accessed from a phone offers a chance for women to expose the inner world and beauty of Afghanistan to the entire world.

In today's fight for attention online, the words of the Taliban are one in a million. Their approach to technology remains a physical one because the reality of a virtual world is, as the rest of the world has discovered, borderless. Meanwhile, the voices of Afghan women increase tenfold. Conflicts of the region during the twentieth century produced a Diaspora population estimated at over three million. Online "branding" images, reactions, musings, and political opinions of thousands of women in the country and in the Diaspora echo across borders. In contemporary Muslim discourse, there is also now a question of what women's mobility implies. Mobility is no longer just about physical presence, but the presence of ideas. Those who seek to contain it cannot, and furthermore, these words and commentaries on our world today reflect a modern rebirth of the origin heroine-poetess.

Notes

1 Ayesha Afghan Durrani, *Diwan-e Ayesha*, Bā bayārī-i Maṭbaʿ-i Sarkārī-i shahr-i Kābul-i gulgul bishkuft, Kabul: 1881–1882.
2 Michael Mann, "The Deep Digital Divide: The Telephone in British India 1883-1933," *Historical Social Research/Historische Sozialforschung* 35, no. 1 (131) (2010): 188–208, 198.

3 Robert M. Burrell, "Arms and Afghans in Makrān: An Episode in Anglo-Persian Relations 1905-1912," *Bulletin of the School of Oriental and African Studies* 49, no. 1 (1986): 8–24.
4 Coll. 35/10 "Afghanistan: Entry into International Postal and Telegraph Unions; Reorganization of Posts and Telegraphs Services (1923-1938)," *British Library: India Office Records and Private Papers*, IOR/L/PS/12/4112, in Qatar Digital Library.
5 Ibid.
6 J. Bruce Amstutz, *The First Five Years of Soviet Occupation* (Washington, D.C.: National Defense University Press, 1986), 12.
7 Conrad J. Schetter, *Kleine Geschichte Afghanistans* (Munich: Verlag CH Beck, 2010), 14.
8 Shahjahan Sayed, "Radio Afghanistan: Historische Entwicklung und Aufgabe," *Communications* 18, no. 1 (1993): 89–102, 89–90.
9 Schetter 15.
10 Palwasha Kakar, "Tribal Law of Pashtunwali and Women's Legislative Authority'" (Unpublished legal paper, Harvard University Library, 2004).
11 Louis Dupree, *The Role of Folklore in Modern Afghanistan* (Washington, D.C.: American Universities Field Staff, 1978). Accessed July 1, 2020 via 1989 photocopy scanned on *Afghan Digital Libraries*: 242.
12 Haleh Afshar, "Women, Wars, Citizenship, Migration, and Identity: Some Illustrations from the Middle East," *The Journal of Development Studies* 43, no. 2 (2007): 237–244.
13 Adrian Peterson, "Kabul Radio Memories," *Radio Heritage Foundation*. Broadcast September 2001. Available online through radioheritage.net.
14 Ibid.
15 Milan Hauner, "The Significance of Afghanistan: Lessons from the Past," *The Round Table* 70, no. 279 (1980): 240–244.
16 Milan Hauner, "Afghanistan between the Great Powers, 1938-1945," *International Journal of Middle East Studies* 14, no. 4 (1982): 481–499.
17 Memoranda for the Chief, Situation and Planning Branch, United States Central Intelligence Agency, "Information from Radio Sources other than the Federal Communications Commission," June 26, 1942. Available at CIA online archives.
18 *Population and Agricultural Survey of 500 Villages*, Research and Statistics, Ministry of Planning, Kabul, 1963. University of Nebraska-Omaha Center for Afghan Studies.
19 Ibid.
20 *Afghanistan: Ancient Land with Modern Ways*, Ministry of Planning of the Royal Government of Afghanistan, 1961: 109.
21 Ibid. 110.
22 Nancy Hatch Dupree, "Behind the Veil in Afghanistan," *Asia* Jul/Aug 1978: 10–15. Accessed via *Afghan Digital Libraries*: 12.
23 Nancy Hatch Dupree, "Revolutionary Rhetoric and Afghan Women," New York City: *Afghanistan Council*, Asia Society, Jan. 1981: 2. Accessed via *Afghan Digital Libraries*.
24 John Baily, *War, Exile and the Music of Afghanistan: The Ethnographer's Tale* (Abingdon: Routledge, 2016), 81.
25 Francine E. Gordon, "Telecommunications: Implications for Women," *Telecommunications Policy* 1, no. 1 (1976): 68–74.
26 Todd Anthony Rosa, *The Last Battle of the Cold War Begins: The Superpowers and Afghanistan, 1945–1980* (Washington D.C., The George Washington University Press, 2006) 53.
27 Abdul Rahman Panjshiri, "The Current State and Challenges of Broadcasting Stations in Afghanistan," *The 24th JAMCO Online International Symposium 2016*, Japan Media Communication Center.
28 "What's on! Today's Television," *Kabul New Times*, January 1, 1983.
29 "Memorandum to CC CPSU from Turkmen CC on Extending Turkmen Foreign Broadcasting," April 29, 1965. Archives of the Central Committee of the Communist Party of the Soviet Union.
30 Rosa 56.
31 Dupree (1981), 4.
32 M.J. Gohari, *The Taliban: Ascent to Power* (Oxford: Oxford University Press, 1999), 108.
33 Barnett R. Rubin, "Women and Pipelines: Afghanistan's Proxy Wars," *International Affairs* 73, no. 2 (1997): 283–296, 287.
34 Siri Birgitte Uldal and Muhammad Aimal Marjan, "Computing in Post-War Afghanistan." *Communications of the ACM* 49, no. 2 (2006): 19–24, 20.
35 H.A. Al-Shahrani, "A Brief History of the Internet in Saudi Arabia," *TechTrends* 60 (2016): 19–20.
36 "Taliban Decree of 25 Aug 2001." Published in English on the *Internet Assigned Number Authority*, January 13, 2003. Accessed on May 27, 2020 via www.iana.org/reports/2002/af-redelegation/taliban-decree-25aug01.html.

37 Bruce Girard, Jo van der Spek, and Radio Reed Flute, "The Potential for Community Radio in Afghanistan," *Comunica* (August 8, 2002): 8.
38 "Afghanistan links to the Virtual Silk Highway," *NATO Newsroom*, October 10, 2004.
39 John F. Sopko, "Afghanistan's Information and Communications Technology Sector: US Agencies Obligated Over $2.6 Billion to the Sector, but the Full Scope of US Efforts is Unknown," *SIGAR 16-46 Audit Report* 2016. Accessed via: The Defense Technical Information Center Online.
40 "Takhrib-e poonzdah anten mobeel toosat Taliban wa qetaa ertebat dar walayat shomali Afghanistan," October 1, 2019. *BBC Persia*. Accessed on May 20, 2020 via www.bbc.com/persian/afghanistan-49876440.
41 World Bank Data, International Telecommunication Union (ITU) World Telecommunication/ICT Indicators Database.
42 "Da'esh estefadeh az telefon ha-ye hamrah houshmand ra mamnou-aa kard," January 12, 2015, *Shafaqna Shia News Association*.
43 Stefanie Glinski, "Afghan Car Blaze Deaths Prompt Fury Over Mistreatment of Refugees in Iran," *The Guardian*, June 8, 2020.
44 Dinah Zeiger, "Afghanistan Blues: Seeing Beyond the Burqa on Youtube," in *Land of the Unconquerable: The Lives of Contemporary Afghan Women*, ed. Jennifer Heath and Ashraf Zahedi (Palo Alto: University of California Press, 2011), 103.
45 Barbara Keleman, "China & the Taliban: Pragmatic Relationship," *CEIAS Insights*. June 26, 2019. https://ceias.eu/china-the-taliban-pragmatic-relationship/
46 Christine Noelle-Karimi, "History Lessons: In Afghanistan's Decades of Confrontation with Modernity, Women Have Always Been the Focus of Conflict," *The Women's Review of Books* 19, no. 7 (2002): 1–4, 3.

6
MOBILIZING LABOR FOR INFRASTRUCTURE IN NORTHEAST BRAZIL, 1915–1932

Laura Belik

This chapter analyzes Brazil's large infrastructural projects built in the early twentieth century by focusing on the process of recruitment of workers, and particularly the role of concentration camps in the northeast region throughout these operations. Built between 1915 and 1932, these contested spaces officially served both to host and quarantine refugees from the droughts in Ceará State, and to secure cheap labor for projects across the country. Northeast Brazil faced severe drought periods between 1887 and 1932. The inland populations, which were the most affected, started abandoning their lives to look for help elsewhere. Refugees from the droughts directed to the camps were often allocated by the government in what was called the "drought industry," taking advantage of their unstable situation. The concentration camps, built mainly in the outskirts of Fortaleza, were an idea pushed by influential colonial elites who dreaded the masses reaching their city. The camps were presented as a form of aid, but they were truly aimed at isolation, as well as recruitment centers. Forced and induced migrations were part of a nationalistic discourse in a recently independent country that was trying to secure its status and identity throughout its territory, attaining its borders, and "modernizing" and exploring its resources. National infrastructure, thus, is as much a social as a physical construction.

From the late 1870s until the early 1930s, Northeast Brazil witnessed some of the most severe drought periods ever registered, popularly known as the Terrible Years (1877/1915/1932). Groups of migrant families from the inlands, the *sertanejos*, who worked as stock growers and farmers were forced to relocate into the coastal and capital cities of the region. Residents in these cities referred to these drought refugees as *flagelados* (people who were regularly whipped or beaten), a demeaning term used strategically to reinforce their position as poor and landless people. As a response to this state of emergency, officials tried to establish strategies for dealing with refugee populations in need, while also seeking to invest in larger ideals of modernization, progress, and development.[1] The consequences of climate vulnerability, the nation's recent abolishment of slave labor (1888), and the drive for rapid construction of new infrastructure led to the "drought industry," in which the state used the poor and landless as a cheap labor force for public works (see Figure 6.1).[2]

Focusing on the State of Ceará, this chapter draws attention to the history of the drought refugees (*flagelados*) and the ways in which local and national governments have dealt with the migrant crisis, culminating in the construction of concentration camps first in 1915, and again in 1932.[3] I argue that the camps played an important role in the building of Brazilian infrastructure, and should be considered crucial sites in Brazil's history and modernization. This chapter introduces the social and historical context of the creation of the camps and tracks how these spaces operated and became institutionalized as sites for the organization and control of labor power. The goal is to emphasize the history of these camps particularly through the spaces they create, their multiple scales and

Mobilizing Labor in Northeast Brazil

Figure 6.1 Refugee migrants working on Ceará's rail system connecting Fortaleza to former Ramal de Itapipoca (today's Ramal João Felipe) at kilometer 57 in Umari, Ceará, February 1920.

Source: Acervo da Fundação Biblioteca Nacional, Brazil.

perspectives, and their relationship to what it meant to build infrastructure in Brazil in the first half of the twentieth century.

Migration and Political Order

Throughout the years, several attempts had been made by local and national governments to deal with the droughts in *Nordeste* (Northeast Brazil Region) and its impact on resident families. Often, *sertanejos* (rural, back country people) survived by migrating to other states. However, in Ceará State the majority of the population of *flagelados* during the 1877 drought moved toward the coast and capital cities by foot or by train. The drought of 1877 marked an important moment in Ceará's history. This was the first time masses of migrants were being directed toward the cities instead of other rural inland areas. "Migration by 1877 was not anymore about the movement between dry lands and humid areas, but between the countryside and the cities."[4] And while the "drought" was certainly an environmental issue, its impact and effects had profound social and political implications. Governmental authorities had few tools at their disposal to overcome the dry period, and instead turned their attention to controlling the circulation of refugees, particularly in Fortaleza, Ceará's capital.

By the turn of the twentieth century, this massive migratory wave had increased Fortaleza's population from 25,000 to 114,000 people.[5] The sudden growth coincided with a period of renovations in the capital city, influenced by the European *Belle Epoque*, when salons, clubs, and cafés were becoming increasingly popular amongst the intellectuals and elites.[6] Fortaleza's bourgeoisie played

Figure 6.2 Lodging for a drought refugee family working for Ceará's rail company, Umari, CE, February 1920.
Source: Acervo da Fundação Biblioteca Nacional, Brazil.

an important and influential role within the local government, persuading decisions related to how the city was being built and administered.[7] While the local bourgeoisie was never a fully coherent or unified group, they converged around a view of the *flagelados* as a mass of people disposed toward crime, violence, and radicalization—a significant threat to the established order.[8] They were particularly fearful of uncontrolled settlement as migrants set up makeshift homes wherever they could find available space (Figure 6.2). In response, local authorities designated specific areas of the city to gather, isolate, control, and assist this body of people: the *abarracamentos* (shack concentrations), and later the concentration camps.

Modernizing Fortaleza

The proposal for the *abarracamentos* (shack concentrations) in 1878, and for the concentration camps, in 1915, started as an urban strategy for modernizing the capital city of Fortaleza. Cloaked in the noble mantle of an "aid" policy, the concentration of migrants in specific locations unfolded primarily as a zoning method to control settlement, sanitation, and disease. Planners and government officials selected locations strategically to isolate this group of newcomers from contact with the city center.

In 1863, Architect Adolfo Herbster was hired to design and implement a master plan (*Plano de Expansão*/Expansion and Growth Plan) of Fortaleza, focusing particularly on hygienics, moral order, and infrastructural improvements, inspired by Baron Haussmann's 1853 plan for Paris. Fortaleza was growing because of enslaved labor cotton exporting businesses led by local colonial merchants and international companies. Even as the capital gained commercial attention, the 1877 drought brought the arrival of the first waves of large numbers of migrants in Fortaleza, rapidly changing the city's dynamic.⁹ Following similar principles of spatial organization from Herbster's plan, the local government responded to the crisis by isolating the *flagelados*, creating a series of thirteen "*abarracamentos*" within the city's boundaries. These spaces sheltered incoming migrants, and served as a recruiting ground for cheap labor in new public works such as dams, civic buildings, and sanitation projects.[10] Local authorities justified the low wages by noting the help that they had already given to the refugees.[11]

Historian Frederico de Castro Neves highlights how the establishment of these public works in the capital city and its surroundings served two purposes: first, it provided much-needed employment to migrants, however low the wages; and second, it justified directing public money toward aid distribution that would not just look charitable, but that contributed to local ameliorations and modernization in the bargain.[12] Another important characteristic of the *abarracamentos* had to do with controlling a newly proletarianized population. By keeping a close eye on migrants, authorities would prevent revolts and rebellions and curtail crime and "immoral" activities.[13] Historian Kênia de Sousa Rios argues that control of the *flagelados* and the development of the city were deeply entangled processes; urban renewal projects produced public benefits while providing an opportunity to submit drought refugees to a regime of labor discipline.[14]

The Shift to Migrant Camps in 1915

In the early 1900s a series of technological developments transformed life Fortaleza, including sewage and sanitation (1908), automobiles (1909), electric trams (1913), and electric lighting in public and private spaces (1913).[15] The next major drought period in 1915 and the arrival of a new wave of migrants to a newly modernized Fortaleza led the government to rethink the *abarracamentos* arrangements. The new order was to promote the concentration of refugees within a single and isolated location in the outskirts of the capital: the *Alagadiço Concentration* Camp. According to Governor Colonel Benjamin Barroso (1914–1916), these measures would facilitate distribution of aid and allow better, more humane treatment for the refugees through the allocation of food, shelter, and public services. Nevertheless, the influx of migrants proved higher than expected, and the *Alagadiço Camp*, designed to host around 3,000 people, eventually registered more than 8,000 refugees sharing a single delimited space.[16] Both the *Abarracamentos* and the 1915 concentration camps in Fortaleza lacked the most basic hygienic conditions, clustering large groups of people in fragile, ephemeral constructions made of sticks and straws or under the shade of cashew and mango trees.[17] Despite the presence of some medical aid, the lack of sanitation, insufficient food rations, and proliferation of diseases resulted in precarious conditions and increased deaths.[18]

The shift between using multiple *abarracamentos* into sheltering refugees on the concentration camp was a way to further limiting access of the *flagelados* within the city's premises. The *abarracamentos*, while isolated, where less restrictive, and where still located within the urbanized areas of Fortaleza. The Alagadiço camp was placed in the outskirts of the city by the Alagadiço train station, where the so called "invaders" would have little to no contact with the rest of the population. Governor Colonel Benjamin Barroso's goal by building the camp was to avoid scenes of begging, crime, and prostitution in the city center that were recurring during earlier drought crises. Due to lack of documentation, it is hard to estimate the size and other physical characteristics of the Alagadiço camp. Unlike the experiences of concentration camps built in 1932, the focus of the 1915 camp was to isolate and monitor newcomers, being their placement in work fronts an important but secondary endeavor.[19] By the end of the drought, the Alagadiço camp was dismantled, people were dispersed, and no traces of this camp's facilities can be found today.

The Consolidation of Camps during the 1932 Drought

Despite experience of the 1915 camps, as the next big drought period arrived in 1932, government officials promptly redeployed this strategy. Idelfonso Albano, Mayor of Fortaleza between 1912 and 1914 and 1921 and 1923, and Governor of Ceará State between 1923 and 1924, passionately defended the concentration camp policy, proposing not only its continuation, but to add facility units throughout the state in order to avoid the periodical "invasion" of migrants into the capital city.[20] Ceará State already had a strategy of controlling the movement of migrants during less intense drought periods, either by assigning them to inland public works (roads, dams, railroads) or offering tickets for families to move to the North or South regions of the country. With the advent of the great drought of 1932, however, Albano's defense won the day, and state officials implemented five concentration camps in locations around the Ceará region (in addition to the two camps within the capital's borders). These new enclosures would now directly implement "regular work and rigorous routine."[21] Kênia Sousa Rios shows that while mobilizing the *flagelados*' labor for infrastructure started in 1877, these practices gained traction over the next half-century, finally to be consolidated as state and local policy during the drought of 1932.[22]

This consolidation came under the auspices of a new political regime. The Brazilian Revolution of 1930, also known as the *1930s Coup d'état*, ended the period called "Old Republic" (1989–1930), and made Getúlio Vargas the new president of an authoritarian and centralized regime that lasted until 1945. Vargas' administration would heavily invest in Brazil's image of "modernization," an effort to shift the nation from an agrarian onto an industrial footing. This perspective on labor and production incentivized the use of concentration camps as sites of production and not just aid. Lúcia Arrais Morales distinguished the 1932 camps from earlier efforts, arguing that under Vargas they became part of a nation-building endeavor. While the main goal of the Fortaleza concentration camp in 1915 had been to isolate and control migrants, in 1932 camps became a central feature in the mobilization and control of a labor force for public works in the North and Northeastern regions of the country.[23]

To this end, Vargas relied on his Minister of Road and Public Works, José Américo de Almeida. José Américo was originally from Paraíba, another Northeast State highly affected by the drought periods, and he recognized that beyond isolating the *flagellados*, authorities could mobilize their labor power while absorbing them into a nation-building discourse, "disciplining their minds and bodies," as Américo would put it.[24] The s*ertanejos flagelados* brought with them their mixed ancestry, descended from Portuguese colonists, escaped black slaves and native indigenous people. As such, they were seen as the quintessential Brazilians, and perfectly situated as subjects for Vargas' cultural and economic modernization efforts. At the same time, the *sertanejos* faced high levels of racial and class prejudice, perceived by urbanites as culturally backward, condemned to a primitive state because of their heritage and long adaptation to a harsh climate.[25] Therefore, Vargas and his ministers convinced themselves that initiatives such as the work fronts and the concentration camps in *Nordeste* were helping *sertanejos*' drought migrants, saving these people by disciplining them.

In order to centralize all services related to *flagelados*' assistance, Minister Américo directed the support received by the National Government in 1932 to IFOCS (Federal Superintendence of Drought Works).[26] This agency was responsible for: (1) building new public and private dams; (2) building new roads; and (3) controlling the circulation of drought migrants.[27] Investments in the Northeast region during the 1932 drought corresponded to about 10% of the national budget that year—in comparison to 1% in previous years.[28] Considering this as a crisis period, once the drought was over, expenditure ceased as well. Nevertheless, by the mid-1930s the significant improvements in access and infrastructure in Ceará were all attributable to the state-mobilized labor of the *flagelados*.

Camp Planning and Development

The Ministry of Road and Public Works established two main criteria for the installation of the 1932 camps. First, the ministry ordered that they should be spread around the state's territory in order to reduce access to the capital city of Fortaleza and other heavily populated cities, guaranteeing an even territorial occupation. Second, they needed to be connected to a source of public works, especially large infrastructure-building projects (Figure 6.3).[29]

Mobilizing Labor in Northeast Brazil

Figure 6.3 Pirambu Concentration Camp in Fortaleza, CE, 1932.

Source: Relatório da Comissão Médica de Assistência e Profilaxia aos Flagelados do Nordeste, National Department of Public Health, August 30, 1933. Rio de Janeiro: Heitor Ribeiro & Cia. 1936/Acervo DNOCS.

The "migration geography" of drought refugees largely followed the railways, as trains facilitated migrants' journeys.[30] Even with the suspension of the distribution of tickets, refugees continued to arrive in Fortaleza during 1932, traveling from far-distant regions.[31] Therefore, it was precisely by the "*pontos de trem*" (train stops) that the government chose to install the concentration camps in an effort to control the flow of refugees more rigorously. Once established in these locations, the camps received large numbers of migrants. Official documents from medical expeditions in 1932 and 1933 report that 70,000 men, women, and children sought refuge or assistance at camps that year, although it is likely that twice that number passed through during the 1932 drought.[32] Because federal assistance was conditional on proof of labor recruitment, camp administrators focused on enrollment, often overlooking the quality of their services or the wellbeing of the people they were sheltering.[33]

The design and administration of the camps reveal the state's concern for the moral and physical discipline of *sertanejos* as part of the larger nation-building project. The facilities and infrastructure of the 1932 camps were not very different from earlier iterations. Camps' spaces consisted of large fenced or walled areas. Usually planned to host between 2,000 and 5,000 people, sometimes these facilities ended up receiving more than 50,000 *flagelados*.[34] Besides sharing similar principals of use and spatial organization, each camp in 1932 had different sizes, characteristics, and rules. Most of the camps consisted of large temporary sheds made out of sticks, where families would take refuge from the sun and heat. Access to drinkable water was also a determining factor for the government to choose the location of the camps. This water would be coming either from the local dam where refugees would be working, a local pond, or being pumped or collected with a draw-well from the underground (see Figure 6.3). Camps would also have designated spaces for (insufficient) hospital care, a chapel, and a kitchen for distributing food. Buriti Camp, located near Juazeiro do Norte (a pilgrimage site) and on the border between three different states, housed about 70,000 people. There were three doctors and four guards hired to assist these refugees, and one rudimentary hospital

Figure 6.4 Former Train station at Campo do Patu, in Senador Pompeu CE. This is the only camp with physical remnants, and it is currently being considered for Ceará State landmarking process.

Source: Photograph by Laura Belik, 2018.

facility with approximately 100 beds available. Obituary books from Buriti Camp registered more than 500 deaths every month.

All camps and their activities officially ended before mid-1933, when the first rains of the season enacted the end of the drought. Newspapers defended ideas such as distribution of tickets for refugees to go back to their homes in the inlands, or move elsewhere to other states if they were not already allocated to any public work construction project. At the same time, they would also insist that the people who were currently working in urban improvements in Fortaleza should stay in order to provide a ready pool of cheap labor. Nevertheless, this systemic desire of control from the elites on the migratory movements of the *flagelados* was not put into practice. Some migrants did go back to the inlands, but others stayed in the capital without following any pre-determined governmental rules."[35] Once these spaces were no longer in use, camps were left to decay. Today, out of the seven concentration camps built in 1932, only Campo do Patú, in Senador Pompeu, has physical traces remaining (see Figure 6.4).[36]

Conclusion

Despite being an important part of Ceará's history, configuring urban and social dynamics and establishing early relations of power and exclusion in Fortaleza, the existence of the camps is very little known even by local populations. Assistance for drought refugees and mass migrations are topics broadly understood and present in people's lives, but a closer look at the government's aid and infrastructural strategies—and their biased goals—are mostly erased or untold. While projects and policies such as the concentration camps were no longer put into practice after the events of 1932, we can recognize later governmental programs that followed similar logistics in Ceará. One example is the case of the *Pousos* recruitment centers, built in the early 1940s to house volunteers sent to the Amazon region to work as latex farmers producing rubber for the Allies during World War II.[37] We can also recognize the effects of the camps' policy in Fortaleza's landscape today, where the area formerly used by more than 6,000 refugees at Campo do Urubú in 1932 comprises the largest slum community in the city, with over 115,000 residents.[38] But the most important legacy of the camps is less direct, based not on physical remnants of the camps themselves, but on the roads, dams, and other infrastructure projects built by the hard labor of the migrants concentrated in temporary locations. They tell us a story of how building infrastructure in Northeast Brazil is (and continues to be) as much a social as a physical construction, as much a project of nation-building as an effort to discipline and control a rural proletariat on the move. While neglected, the camps are a crucial part of Brazil's history, and their consequences still reverberate today.

Notes

1 José de Américo de Almeida, *O Ciclo Revolucionário do Ministério da Viação* (Rio de Janeiro: Imprensa Nacional, 1934), 161.
2 This term was coined by Brazilian journalist Antônio Callado (*Correio da Manhã*, 1958).
3 By the late 1930s, local newspapers would try using other ways to name these spaces, as the term "concentration camp" started gaining a very specific connotation with the rise of the Nazi Party and European extermination camps.
4 Frederico de Castro Neves, *A Multidão e a História: Saques e outras ações de massa no Ceará* (Rio de Janeiro: Relume Dumar; Fortaleza: Secretaria de Cultura e Desporto, 2000), 50.
5 Ibid. 48.
6 Raimundo Girão, *Geografia Estética de Fortaleza* (Fortaleza: Editora UFC Casa de José Alencar/ Programa Editorial, 1997 [1979]), 181.
7 Fortaleza's bourgeoisie was mainly formed by former colonial elites, land owners raising cattle and/or growing cotton, and merchants involved with international trade.
8 Rios identified two main diverging groups amongst the elites: the commercial bourgeoisie, and the conservative Catholic bourgeoisie. See Kenia Sousa Rios, *Isolamento e Poder: Fortaleza e os campos de concentração na Seca de 1932* (Fortaleza: Imprensa Universitária da Universidade Federal do Ceará /UFC, 2014), 34.
9 Margarida Julia Farias de Salles Andrade, *Fortaleza em Perspectiva Histórica: Poder Público e Iniciativa Privada na Apropriação e Produção Material da Cidade 1810–1933* (São Paulo: Universidade de São Paulo, 2012), 131.
10 Many of the newcomers were sent to *abarracamentos*, but the precise number is unknown. See Neves, *A Multidão e a História*, 48.
11 Andrade, *Fortaleza em Perspectiva Histórica*, 132.
12 Neves, *A Multidão e a História*, 52.
13 Dalila Arruda Azevedo, "'Curral dos Flagelados': disciplinamento e isolamento no campo de concentraçãp na obra 'O Quinze', de Raquel de Queiroz," i *Encontro de Pesquisa e Pós-Graduação em Humanidades* 2 (2011): 11.
14 Rios, *Isolamento e Poder*, 46.
15 Andrade, *Fortaleza em Perspectiva Histórica*, 167.
16 Frederico de Castro Neves, "Curral dos Bárbaros: Os Campos de Concentração no Ceará (1915-1932)," *Revista Brasileira de Historia* 15, no. 29 (1995): 96.
17 We can find brief descriptions of these big open and crowded spaces in Neves, *A Multidão e a História*, 48; Rachel de Queiroz, *O Quinze* (São Paulo: Siciliano, 1993 [1930]), 87; and Yzy Maria Rabelo Câmara and Rabelo Câmara Yls "Campos de Concentração no Ceará: Uma realidade retratada por Rachel de Queiroz em O Quinze (1930)," *Revista Entrelaces* 5, no. 6 (2015): 178.
18 Neves describes medical aid facilities within the camps' premises in Neves, *A Multidão e a História*, 55; Neves, *Curral dos Bárbaros*, 97.
19 Lúcia Arraes Morales, *Vai e Vem, Vira e Volta: As rotas dos soldados da borracha* (São Paulo: Annablume/Fortaleza: Secult, 2002), 142.
20 Ildefonso Albano, *O secular problema da seca* (Rio de Janeiro: Imprensa Oficial, 1918).
21 Neves, *Curral dos Bárbaros*, 105.
22 Rios, *Isolamento e Poder*, 48.

23 Morales, *Vai e Vem, Vira e Volta*, 139.
24 Neves, *Curral dos Bárbaros*, 107.
25 Eve E. Buckley, *Technocrats and the Politics of Drought and Development in the Twentieth-Century Brazil* (Chapel Hill: The University of North Carolina Press, 2017), 12.
26 IFOCS (*Inspetoria Federal de Obras Contra as Secas*/Federal Superintendence of Drought Works) is known today as DNOCS (*Departamento Nacional de Obras Contra as Secas*/National Department of Drought Works).
27 Bárbara Bezerra Siqueira Silva, *O poder político de José Américo de Almeida: a construção do americismo (1928-1935)* (Unpublished dissertation, Universidade Federal da Paraíba, João Pessoa, 2015), 85.
28 "*Departamento Nacional de Obras Contra as Secas (DNOCS),*" FGV CPDOC. www.fgv.br/cpdoc/acervo/dicionarios/verbete-tematico/departamento-nacional-de-obras-contra-as-secas-dnocs. Last Accessed June 20, 2020.
29 Neves, *Curral dos Bárbaros*, 108.
30 Rios, *Isolamento e Poder*, 20.
31 Ibid.
32 This information can be found at *Relatório da Comissão Médica de Assistência e Profilaxia aos Flagelados do Nordeste* (Report from the Medical Assistance and Prophylaxis Commission for Northeastern Flagellated Population) presented to Mr. Director General of the National Department of Public Health on August 30, 1933, written by Dr. J. Bonifacio P. da Costa, Commission Chief, Rio de Janeiro: Heitor Ribeiro & Cia. 1936/ Acervo DNOCS.
33 Neves, *Curral dos Bárbaros*, 113.
34 Rios, *Isolamento e Poder*, 93.
35 Ibid. 78.
36 Neves, *Curral dos Bárbaros*, 110. Campo do Patú became a municipal landmark in 2019, and is in the process of recognition as a state heritage site.
37 Part of the Washington Agreements (1942) between President Vargas and U.S. President Theodore Roosevelt.
38 Sandra Paula Evaristo Monteiro, *Projeto Vila do Mar no Grande Pirambu: Avanços e Retrocessos* (Fortaleza: Universidade Federal do Ceará/Faculdade de Geografia, 2018), 35.

7
EVERYDAY LIVING IN CAIRO'S CITY OF THE DEAD

Reem Saad Sardina, Sherif Elfiki, and Ahmed El Antably

Because of severe housing shortages in Cairo, several historic cemeteries have become home to a unique form of urban life forged by squatters. The City of the Dead (Qarāfah) comprises three of these historic cemeteries, where inhabitants either live in mausoleums or in self-built constructions around the tombs. Sometimes they are stigmatized for living among the dead. At other times, they are looked upon with an eye of sympathy for not fully fitting within the normalized dwelling traditions. Regardless, many families have been living there for three or four generations, establishing a range of spatial accommodations for dwelling in a necropolis. Through a variety of bodily and architectural practices, they have been able to rewrite, redefine, and appropriate their spaces. This chapter explores the many ways that the living inhabitants negotiate the spaces of the dead in the conduct of their everyday routines. We argue that these negotiations are temporally dynamic, and that the physical spaces of the City of the Dead are crucial catalysts in shaping the everyday experience of the living inhabitants. This in turn blurs the distinction between life and death and between what is an acceptable and unacceptable way of dwelling in the world. We also argue that the inhabitants' practices challenge taken-for-granted spatial dichotomies such as indoor/outdoor and public/private.

The City of the Dead (Qarāfah) is a name given collectively to three historic necropolises in Cairo, Egypt: the Eastern Cemetery, the Southern Cemetery, and Bāb al-Nasr. With their walls, tombs, streets, and pathways, they comprise a substantial part of Cairo's necropolitan infrastructure. Simultaneously, with the shortage of housing in the city, they have become home to a unique kind of squatter settlement.

The unconventional combination of death and life in the City of the Dead places its inhabitants in an ambivalent position relative to their fellow Cairenes. Sometimes they are stigmatized for dwelling in the necropolises. At other times, they are regarded with a sympathetic eye for not fully fitting within Cairo's dwelling traditions. For their part, the inhabitants appropriate the tombs in ways that produce hybrid spaces accommodating funeral and non-funeral activities. Today, many families consider the tombs as their home, with some having lived there for up to four generations. Through various bodily and architectural practices, they have been able to redefine and appropriate their everyday spaces.

This chapter explores the negotiations between the necropolitan infrastructure—that is, the spaces, routes, networks, and flows of death—and the everyday bodily practices of its living inhabitants. The argument put forward here is that the inhabitants' continuous appropriation of the tombs blurs the distinction between acceptable and unacceptable habitat, indoor and outdoor environments, and public and private spaces. This work relies on the findings of fieldwork conducted in the Eastern Cemetery in 2017.

The Historic Necropolises of Cairo

The City of the Dead, along with other significant historic districts and monuments, is a part of Historic Cairo, which is a UNESCO World Heritage Site. It contains many impressive Islamic mosques and mausoleums, mostly dating back to the Mamlūk period, 1250–1570 CE. According to Galila El Kadi, the necropolis is as old as Cairo itself. Early tombs had little to do with the living. However, the Fatimid and Ayyubid periods started a building boom in the necropolis that reached its peak later in the Mamlūk period. Places for religious ceremonies, prayer, and learning started to attract Sufis. The Mamlūks did build mausoleums and complexes that included schools and khanqāhs out of the belief that these would extend their good deeds after their death. They also donated food during religious festivals to the urban poor, students, and residents of the khanqāhs. Housing estates began appearing around the schools until 1459 CE, when authorities banned permanent residence in the necropolis due to the plague.[1] The ban continued through Muhammad Ali's reign, whose government tried to restrict the necropolis to only burials and death-related religious activities. Meanwhile, the tombs were built to provide residence to caretakers, the City of the Dead's first inhabitants.[2]

From the end of the nineteenth century onwards, the Cairene population increased dramatically, creating a severe housing shortage, which consecutive governments failed to address. People started to consider cemeteries as a permanent housing alternative. Some moved to live inside the mausoleums or in constructions they built in the vicinity of the tombs. Rents for the tombs, at the time, were reasonable. Those who could not afford them could still live there in exchange for becoming tomb caretakers tasked with funerary-related jobs. It is challenging to estimate the population of the City of the Dead today. The difficulty lies in the extremely porous edges between the spaces of the living and those of the dead. However, Max Rodenbeck claims that, in the 1990s, it accommodated over two million people.[3]

Other than low rents, inhabitants favored the City of the Dead over other Cairene squatter settlements due to the fact that the geographic location of the three cemeteries allows for easy access to daily commutes in Cairo. For example, the Eastern Necropolis, which is a strip of land about 600 meters wide and 3.5 km long, is bordered from the west by Fatimid Cairo and Salāh Sālim Road (an arterial road), from the east by al-Nasr Street (a ring road) and Manshīyat Nāssir (an informal settlement), and from the south by Salāh al-Dīn Citadel. The adjacent major roads have another effect on the cemetery: they stunt its horizontal growth, pushing residential buildings to eat into the funerary infrastructure.

The Infrastructure of the Dead (the Eastern Cemetery)

Looking from above at the Eastern Cemetery from Salāh Sālim Road, the calmness of death prevails. The cemetery contains many architectural masterpieces in its domes, minarets, and tomb walls. Even though wide avenues separate the buildings along with dusty paths, there is very little traffic. Compared with other Cairene informal settlements, there is a low density of housing and a relatively high concentration of greenery. In some instances, the urban fabric looks haphazard, and in others it looks like it has been formally planned. However, the view from Salāh Sālim Road shows minimal traces of life. The walls, angles, and other elements of the cemetery hide traces of living inhabitants and their diverse daily spatial practices (Figure 7.1).

There is more than one type of Muslim tomb in Egypt. The type used in the City of the Dead typically has an underground burial room for males and another for females. Several stone slabs cover the opening of the tomb. Removing the stones reveals the stairs leading down to the two burial chambers. The covered opening is usually in an open courtyard. However, in some examples, it is located inside a shelter. Both locations are identifiable by the gravestone and yet not easily noticeable for outsiders. The stone slabs are lifted only for burial events and are replaced immediately afterwards.

Everyday Living in Cairo's City of the Dead

Figure 7.1 The view of the cemeteries from above, showing its quietness and minimal traces of living.

Source: Photograph by Reem Saad Sardina.

The cemetery's built fabric can be categorized into three spatial registers, namely funeral, non-funeral, and hybrid. The funeral spaces are open yards with multiple tombstones that do not provide a place for shelter. The non-funeral spaces are the residential constructions that were built in between and around the tombs. They are conventional squatter homes, which are sometimes used for commercial activities. Also, official governmental schools, small coffee houses, and a police station are present. The hybrid spaces are those that accommodate both funeral and non-funeral activities. They are walled graveyards containing a courtyard used both for burial and shelter (Figure 7.2). The shelter typically consists of a room or two, initially designed for extended family visits or caretakers' accommodation.

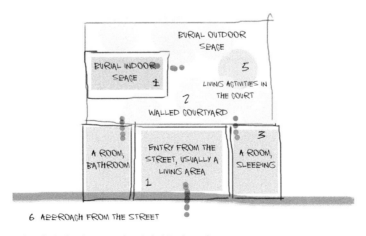

Figure 7.2 An example of a hybrid space of an inhabited tomb.

Source: Drawing by Reem Saad Sardina.

87

Those shelters are a part of the graveyard and each is owned by the family of the deceased, who authorizes the caretaker to inhabit them.

As for the street network, the cemetery is bordered by main thoroughfares with heavy traffic. Inside the cemetery, there are two types of streets. First, there are the relatively wide vehicular roads that are found around mosques, schools, or conventional residential areas. In between these main roads are the avenues surrounding the graveyard constructions. Some of them can accommodate vehicles during funeral events. Others are pedestrian-only pathways or alleys, which are calm and provide access to more than one tomb. Many of the inhabitants' daily activities are conducted in those alleys.

Everyday Practices

The tomb dwelling boundary generally starts from its street approach and largely depends on the tomb's width. If the approach is a narrow alley that is not frequented by cars, the alley becomes an extension of the domestic activities happening inside the tomb, like cooking or sleeping on hot days. If it is a broader street, it may be used as a socializing space for men or a small convenience store that sells simple everyday goods (e.g. cigarettes, snack food, confectionery, and soft drinks) to cemetery residents and funerary visitors. The "store" is sometimes a 1.5 × 1.5 m wooden kiosk or simply a woman selling goods from her dwelling window (Figures 7.3 and 7.4).

The tomb dwelling's entrance usually leads directly to the main indoor living area, connecting to the courtyard and the other rooms. The courtyards will often have some combination of a television, seating area, sink, and stove. There is no space for a purpose-built kitchen, so residents will perform food preparation and cooking tasks either in the burial courtyard or in the outdoor extension in front of the tomb. In rare instances, cooking takes place inside the tomb using the gravestones as a working surface. Many inhabitants have creatively adapted the wood coffins into ironing boards, tables, and benches.

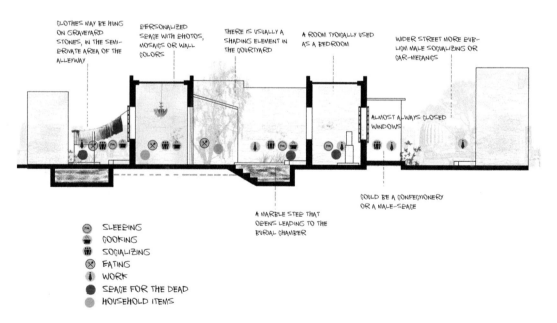

Figure 7.3 An illustrative section, showing an example of different street approaches. A wider street usually does not accommodate daily activities, while a narrow private alleyway does.

Source: Drawing by Reem Saad Sardina.

Everyday Living in Cairo's City of the Dead

Figure 7.4 Example of the confectionery.

Source: Photograph by Reem Saad Sardina.

Figure 7.5 A shared sleeping space. On the left is the gravestone of the deceased and on the right is the bed of the living inhabitant.

Source: Photograph by Reem Saad Sardina.

Residents often allocate spaces for activities according to the weather. If the weather is nice, they will place a movable table in the alleyway in front of the tomb for dining. When it is hot, they dispense with the table and eat on the floor inside the tomb, protected from the direct sunlight and heat. A similar practice is observed for sleeping. In summer, residents stay awake until late at night, then sleep in the courtyard. When napping or resting, they learn to follow the shadow of the trees to protect themselves from the sun. In inclement weather, the living inhabitants may join the dead inside the built rooms of the tomb (Figure 7.5).

The social status of the dead extends to the living people too, as residents often relate themselves to their deceased neighbors. According to one resident, the dead are much quieter and cause him no problems, unlike his living neighbors. When asked, many of the participants claimed they prefer living in the cemeteries for they are quiet and everyone is "minding his own business." Not only do they accept their dead neighbors, but they take pride in them. For example, an interviewee boasted that his dead neighbors are princes and pashas. However, this is only reflected in the material quality of the tomb, which is more spacious and better ornamented; but, being present in the tomb of a notable person, according to him, improves his social status among other inhabitants.

Contrary to most residents of Cairo, the presence of death does not disturb the inhabitants of the cemetery. Death has become a normal part of their everyday landscape and routine to such an extent that it may go unnoticed. The infrastructure created for the repose and conveyance of the dead into an afterlife has been appropriated by the living as functional, commodious, and felicitous habitat.

Death as an Agent in Everyday Living

Cairo's City of the Dead reveals the mutually constitutive relationship between social and spatial production.[4] As they cohabitate, the living and the dead negotiate mutually advantageous social relations, where the dead contribute to the lives of the residents and vice versa. The dead provide a quiet place to live, and the living protect the dead by maintaining infrastructure and guarding against thieves.

At the same time, tomb dwellers are often at odds over spatial uses and social meaning with those who own the tombs.[5] The owners and the inhabitants exist in a symbiotic relationship that they both disparage. Similar to the practice of house sitting in the West, the owners allow the inhabitants to occupy the tombs in exchange for "tomb sitting" and cleaning. While the inhabitants pay little or no rent, they live in the tombs under sufferance, with no leases or legal protections. As such, they are vulnerable to eviction if the owners are displeased with their efforts. They struggle to meet the owners' expectations, even in the tiniest details of their home living. Meanwhile, the inhabitants want to establish a sense of place, a home. They tend to adorn the tombs—their homes—with whatever they see reflecting their identity, like hanging wall pictures, changing paint colors, or adding mosaic tiles (Figure 7.6). One of the inhabitants relates that, while she pays no rent, living in a tomb nevertheless incurs costs. She claims that it is expensive to make the tomb suitable for living, like painting or tiling it. In doing so, she provides free maintenance for the tombs on behalf of the owners, which they do not seem to appreciate.

During their visits to their deceased family members, the owners expect to see the tomb in a pristine condition. The inhabitants should stay entirely out of sight, along with any traces of their everyday practices. They are expected to be invisible. It deprives them of their right to manifest themselves in space or practice the simple everyday activities that leave traces in the space which they see as defying the norms of living.

In a few cases, the inhabitants and the owners agreed that the latter must notify them before their visit, during which the residents must clear the tombs from any living traces and leave.

The inhabited tomb, in that case, is suffused with a multiplicity of meanings that shift with the change of the social setting, as exemplified by the forced disappearance of inhabitants at the times of tomb visits. In this sense, the meaning of home changes for those who live there. This tension between owners and inhabitants, in Jill Stoner's terms, is a tension between turning the "smooth" spaces into strictly "striated" ones.[6] Smooth spaces of the inhabited tombs here are not in themselves liberatory, but they inhabit a struggle, face challenges, and invent small new spaces where the inhabitants live fluidly in opposition to the same space perceived as a strictly functional striated one.

According to Michel de Certeau, space planners are "seeing the whole from a solar eye, looking down like a god." They conceive the space to be only a burial place neglecting that it is lived in ways that they may not understand. "It's hard to be down when you are up."[7] The tomb owners perceive it as a place of memory, devotion, and reverence, where they have the right to come at any time and visit

Figure 7.6 An interior of a tomb, personalized by its living inhabitants.

Source: Photograph by Reem Saad Sardina.

their deceased. The tomb custodians appropriate the tomb owners' perceived space tactically to fulfill their everyday needs or modify it according to their preferences. The tombs inhabitants, in this case, are in a continuous flux between their two spatial productions: the tomb and the home.

Blurred Boundaries

Courtyards are a common feature in traditional Cairene Islamic architecture. They are present in public and residential buildings alike. They provide an introverted spatial configuration well adapted to the cultural demands for privacy and intimate social life. They also offer an environmental solution to the Cairene hot and arid climate. Graveyards in the City of the Dead follow the same pattern. They are built around a courtyard. Figure 7.2 is an example of an inhabited tomb with an approach from a relatively wide thoroughfare. One enters from the cemetery street through a door and then there are two steps down into an inner lobby. The lobby leads to a courtyard and additional rooms. According to Jeffrey Nedoroscik, the number of rooms expresses the wealth, power, and social status of the owning family. Some tombs contain plantations in the courtyards, beautifully crafted cenotaphs, and entry gates.

In the City of the Dead, the streets and alleys function simultaneously as public thoroughfares and as extensions of the private domain of homes. The boundary of a private home in the Eastern Cemetery is determined, to some extent, by car access. For example, tombs surrounded by main streets accessed by cars have less privacy than ones surrounded by narrower pathways. Women may perform some daily household activities outdoors in these extended spaces. Boundaries further delineated women's dress code.[8] Inside the realm of what women consider the privacy of their home, they will freely wear their informal clothes. If they cross that perceived boundary, they have to change into formal dress and put on their veils. When women cook in alleyways, their hair is uncovered, and their outfit is informal and comfortable. Following old Egyptian customs still in use in many parts of the country, when a stranger passes by, particularly a man, he must declare his presence by making a sound—a courtesy cough—to alert women of the household of his presence so that they wear their veils.

Because their private interior courtyards are often cramped and confined, women typically set up clotheslines in the semi-public alleyways. The location of the clotheslines allows the inhabitants to monitor them from within the household. Although an alleyway is considered elsewhere as a semi-public space where male socializing activities can take place, in the City of the Dead, residents consider these to be extensions of the private home, which precludes many public functions, but which provide women more space for tasks and socializing with one another. As such, smoking shisha (water pipe)—a male socializing activity—always takes place in coffee houses located in the broader streets and never in alleyways.

The hierarchy of privacy in the City of the Dead does not only apply to domestic spaces but also to streets. According to an interviewee, some streets are considered primarily private and others primarily public. That distinction is made according to the movement of vehicles in the City of the Dead. Any street easily accessible by a car is considered public, and therefore not convenient for tomb living. Other streets, where cars do not pass by frequently, are regarded as private streets that can afford families living there. The street approach is usually an extension of the home activities. In the case of a wide street, it is used as a male gathering/seating area. In other incidents, it is used as a confectionery outlet with the selling happening from the inside.

Work and home are intertwined in the City of the Dead—not in a sense that inhabitants work from their home, but that home is their work. Families (mainly women) deploy their labor in keeping their homes, and by extension the tombs, clean and well-maintained. They understand that this practice is what secures their free stay. They are responsible for taking care of the plants, scrubbing walls and surfaces, and keeping their homes tidy and ready for the family of the dead to visit any time. Another opportunity for women is operating a small confectionery shop. This is usually a window overlooking the street, which operates according to the housewife's available time. She stores the goods in her home and operates her business from the inside too.

A range of everyday activities continually blurs the distinction between indoor and spaces in the Eastern Cemetery. Windows open to the outside of a home are rare. The sense of openness, most of the time, comes from the connection between the indoor spaces of the home with the well-planted courtyard. Inhabitants welcome guests to the courtyard, the most pleasant area of their "home." They say "come here, come inside" in a way that reflects how they perceive the courtyard, open to the elements, as the main interior space of their dwelling.

The presence of a funerary element changes the social setting of the space. For example, the presence of a gravestone changes a space from a private to a semi-private one. An inhabited tomb is always shifting between the three facets of "perceived," "conceived," and "lived" space in Lefebvre's terms. For example, the tomb owners always aspire to keep it clean and ready for a visit. They perceive it as their own for hosting their dead family members. Meanwhile, the tomb inhabitants perceive it as their home and their source of living. They subvert the wills of the owners by appropriating the graveyards. Moreover, they deal with death as if it is just a routine part of everyday life; they clean tombs and see death-related spatial manifestations yet they pursue their daily practices unfettered by their presence.

Living with the Dead

The City of the Dead is a place of negotiation between the sacred and the secular, the living and the dead. Janet Abu Lughod referred to the strange paradox that the City of the Dead hosts more living people than the living city of Fūstāt.[9] In the City of the Dead, the relationship between the living and the dead is intertwined. The City of the Dead affords the sanctity of death and the profanity of life simultaneously.

Besides being perceived as social misfits, many strict Muslims consider living with the dead as ḥarām (forbidden by Allāh) and often condemn the entire community for this activity.[10] This perspective has resulted in the continuous stigmatization of the inhabitants living there as profane. Such ideas have negatively influenced the inhabitants' perception of themselves and their dwellings. They imagine that living with the dead is a punishment for the weight of their sins. They perform socially perceived irreverent acts of everyday life, like marital sex, over the tombs' burial place. (In a society that is considered conservative, non-marital sex is a sin and a taboo that is socially and religiously unacceptable. However, even marital sex is regarded as a sinful act if it is performed in a graveyard.)

Tomb dwellers do not necessarily display different characteristics from the majority of Cairo's urban poor. However, the rest of the city's residents condescend to tomb dwellers. This, according to El Kadi, and in keeping with governmental neglect of the area, has contributed to the marginalization of the tomb dwellers. The Egyptian film "Innī Lā Akdheb wa lakinnī atajammal" ("I am not lying, I am prettifying"), based on a novel by Ihsan Abdel Quddous, famously depicted this phenomenon in 1981. The protagonist struggled to hide that he was residing in the City of the Dead. When his secret was revealed, his colleagues and his lover rejected him for not fitting in with their perception of proper dwelling.

Even the cemetery's epithet "City of the Dead" neglects the fact that other people reside in it. This results in a state of ambiguity and ambivalence in official channels. On the one hand, the government failed to provide appropriate housing alternatives and publicly demanded the residents' eviction. On the other hand, it provides them with electricity, schools, a police station, paved roads, and other public infrastructure. Meanwhile, the inhabitants are fully aware of the negligence and inability of the state institutions to fulfill their needs in the future. That is why they accept minimal provisions in exchange for cheap housing in geographic proximity to most city services.

The tomb dwellers were able to stake small claims in the great city's interstitial spaces and build homes there. However, now, even those small spaces are at risk of disappearing. As this chapter is being written, bulldozers are moving in to demolish some tombs or walls separating tombs from the main street, as they are getting in the way of constructing a flyover. A massive bulk of concrete will cut through the cemetery to transport speeding cars to the speculative new cities of the desert. The government mandates the Housing Ministry and the Governorship of Cairo to make substitute arrangements for any residences, commercial outlets, or graveyards that block its path. The flyover will be named Al-Ferdaws, which ironically translates to "paradise." The government asserts that this is for the public good and that monuments will not be affected. Underneath the broken stone and bricks are the traces of both the dead and the living. Some families had to go through the agony of moving the skeletal remains of their dead to places which were spared demolition. The unlucky ones had to transport their remains to different cemeteries.

The necropolitan infrastructure of Cairo raises some concerns. The cemeteries contain numerous monuments beautifully attesting to the history of Cairo. Nevertheless, the authorities continue to neglect them and have taken no steps toward their preservation as heritage. They have no plans for their development as areas of unique qualities hosting both living and dead inhabitants. The authorities favor demolition of the cemeteries for the sake of enhancing the living city's infrastructure over the wellbeing of its inhabitants. The living inhabitants of the City of the Dead are not only invisible in the eyes of the tomb owners, but also in the eyes of the authorities.

Notes

1. G. El Kadi And A. Bonnamy, *Architecture for the Dead: Cairo's Medieval Necropolis* (Cairo, New York: The American University in Cairo Press, 2007).
2. Jeffrey A. Nedoroscik, *The City of the Dead: A History of Cairo's Cemetery Communities* (Westport, Conn: Bergin & Garvey, 1997).
3. Max Rodenbeck, *Cairo: The City Victorious* (New York: Vintage, 1998).
4. Henri Lefebvre, *The Production of Space*, trans. Donald Nicholson-Smith (Malden, Mass., Oxford: Blackwell, 2009).
5. Reem Saad Sardina, "Space and Everyday Life in Cairo's City of the Dead" (Unpublished Masters Thesis, Cairo, Egypt: Arab Academy for Science, Technology, and Maritime Transport, 2019).
6. Jill Stoner, *Toward a Minor Architecture* (Cambridge, Mass: MIT Press, 2012).
7. Michel de Certeau, *The Practice of Everyday Life* (Berkeley, Calif.: University of California Press, 2008).
8. Mohamed Gamal Abdelmonem, "The Practice of Home in Old Cairo: Towards Socio-Spatial Models of Sustainable Living," *Traditional Dwellings and Settlements Review* 23, no. 2 (2012): 35–50.
9. Janet L. Abu-Lughod, *Cairo: 1001 Years of the City Victorious* (New York: Princeton University Press, 2005).
10. Hassan Ansah, *Life, Death, and Community in Cairo's City of the Dead* (New York: iUniverse, 2010).

PART III

Natures

8
DAMS, LAKES, AND WATER SPORTS
Building a Hybrid Landscape in Belgium's Eau d'Heure Valley, 1933–1987

Marie Pirard

The construction of a dam and artificial lake in Belgium's Eau d'Heure valley radically transformed the landscape into a hybrid site of production and consumption. This chapter traces the micro-history of the site in order to understand how such a hybrid assemblage between a productive and recreational landscape was built over the long term. It starts with 1930s modernists' theoretical experiments that served as a background for the postwar hydraulic project. It describes the 1950s to 1970s multi-scale political controversies that surrounded the dam. And finally, it ends with the dam site implementation and development between 1971 and 1987. The case study thus addresses both the history of public infrastructure building and that of the rise of a leisure culture from the 1930s to the 1980s. Two a priori antagonistic visions toward the territory and its natural resources are at stake. On the one hand, outdoor leisure practices such as boating and sailing depend upon the attributes of an environment considered as healthy and conducive to recreation. On the other hand, the dam materializes a national-scale productive effort to manage the country's freshwater stocks and flows. Situated at the intersection between these two visions, the case study explores their interactions over time. It reveals an emerging narrative surrounding the Belgian landscape that collapsed its material and cultural dimensions into an account of human welfare. And it provides the opportunity to study, from a long-term perspective, the architectural and urban design culture that flourished around the project, and to question how the design professions both shaped and reacted to the hybrid and artificial character of the site.

The story begins at the end: a postcard, probably from the 1980s, showing two adults and a child, presumably a nuclear family, sailing on a blue lake under a blue sky (Figure 8.1). Their almost naked bodies are as orange as the hull of their catamaran, matching the colors of the sails. In the background lies the crest of a hydraulic dam, overlooked by two rough concrete towers, connected by a steel bridge, and accompanied by a neoclassical colonnade. The framing of the picture focuses on the coordinated action of the sailors and the massive concrete infrastructure that overlooks the site's geography. The tanned, athletic sailors are captured in action, immersed in the operation of the boat. No natural topography is visible. Only the inconspicuous presence of a strip of vegetation reminds us that something exists behind the dam.

Obviously, the anonymous photographer wanted to bring two worlds together: water sports and hydraulic dams. In doing so, he or she tells us something about the aesthetic and cultural codes that framed the infrastructural project of the dam, located upstream of the Eau d'Heure river, 30 km south of the industrial city of Charleroi, in Belgium. This chapter aims at dissecting such an implicit testimony. What is the story of this hybrid assemblage? Why does it seem so appealing to put the two worlds together? What does it tell about the interaction between the material and cultural backbone of the Belgian welfare state? These questions will be addressed in two parts: first a 1930s modernist background, which allows us to study an antecedent to the postwar project and helps us to situate the Eau d'Heure valley in the Belgian

Figure 8.1 Sailing on the Plate-Taille Lake.
Source: Private collection © photo-studio d, Ans.

landscape; then the hydraulic dams project itself, starting with the 1950s national infrastructure modernization plans and the controversies they initiated; and finally, crossing the stages of the site development between 1971 and 1987.

Modernism and Regional Space

In 1933, the Belgian committee prepared its contribution for the fourth CIAM conference (*Congrès internationaux d'architecture moderne*) under the topic of the Functional City. Clear instructions were given—fixed graphic codes and scale—to display and compare 33 cities analyzed by different national groups.[1] But the Belgian committee decided to break partially out of the framework, as Raphaël Verwilghen explains in his preparatory notes: "Belgium is the densest country in the world. It tends to become a single large urban agglomeration (conurbation). Therefore, it is more interesting to study the process of the formation of urban groupings in Belgium, than to study a few large cities in isolation."[2] They thus decided to present the analysis of such a conurbation stretching from Antwerp (seaport and commercial metropolis), over Brussels (geographical, political, administrative, and economic center), to Charleroi (industrial basin). This conurbation is, as they pointed out, supported by a single hydraulic communication axis, the ABC (Antwerp–Brussels–Charleroi) canal (Figure 8.2). Their approach was representative of two recurring themes within the Belgian modernist movement: the idea that urbanization goes beyond the scale of the city and must be organized at a regional scale (or even a national scale in the case of a small country); and the model of an urban corridor that follows the infrastructures framework.[3]

Figure 8.2 An urban corridor (the ABC modernist conurbation), two recreational patches (Upper Belgium and the coastline), and the postwar management of freshwater (the Deltaplan and the Eau d'Heure dams).

Source: Drawing by Marie Pirard.

As a corollary, the model of an urban corridor crisscrossing the territory created its negative: a pattern of residual patches that remain at a distance from the infrastructure network. The coastline to the North and, on a larger scale, the Upper Belgium to the South of the Sambre-Meuse industrial valleys, constituted quiet zones, away from the main axes. Hence, when modernist architects and planners became interested in these territories, they described them as natural and rural reserves with recreational value for the rest of the country.[4] In a study for the magazine *Bruxelles*, Victor Bourgeois—then Belgian CIAM committee chairman—clearly illustrated the split: he drew the capital city and its green suburbs as the center of the country, surrounded by two remote satellites, the coastline and Upper Belgium, labeled as vacation areas.[5]

Once the views are assembled, a two-sided project for Belgium emerges: a productive landscape supported by the infrastructural network completed, in its voids, by an idealized rural and recreational landscape. The model was, of course, a cultural construction, which would, if implemented, tend to create an artificial boundary in a regional space far more interconnected than the modernist narrative suggests. In practice, it remained a largely speculative endeavor. In the 1930s, when the drawings were produced, the political majority was not conducive to urban planning while the process of industrialization was already well underway.[6] As Victor Bourgeois argued in his report of the fourth CIAM meeting, the country, despite its small size, was then one of the most industrialized in the world.[7] There was no blank page available for the modernist architects and urbanists to plan from scratch, but instead a rapid ongoing development. Nevertheless, this imaginary portrait of Belgium proved important as a background influence on the postwar developments examined below.

Establishing the Eau d'Heure Valley as Pivotal Site

After the fourth CIAM meeting, Victor Bourgeois carried on the urban analyses originated from the ABC case study. From 1935 to 1946, he produced multiple drawings related to his native city, Charleroi, the third pole of the conurbation. One of them, the axonometric view of a speculative plan, is of particular interest as it introduces the Eau d'Heure valley location (Figure 8.3).[8] Rather than zooming in to the urban center, Bourgeois' drawing focuses attention onto the broader surroundings. A landscaped forest occupies the foreground of the image, while the industrial city, represented in dark, inhabited by slag heaps and chimneys, is relegated to the background. To the existing wooded areas, crossed by several small streams, he added white lines—representing pedestrian and cycle paths—and placed three recreational sites: a sports stadium, an open-air theater, and a swimming lake.

Figure 8.3 A speculative plan for Charleroi, 1935–1946.

Source: © CIVA, Brussels, Fonds Bourgeois.

This is where the Eau d'heure river comes into play as the swimming lake was planned to be built on its course, although closer to the city center than the postwar dam. One could consider this as a simple coincidence. More than fifty years separates the two projects which, beyond their position in the hydrographic network, have little in common. Yet, I argue that Victor Bourgeois' speculative plan still participated in raising opportunities regarding the valley that would later mark the development of the postwar project. Once placed in the modernist territorial narrative, the Eau d'Heure valley appears as a pivotal site: at the crossroads of the ABC urban corridor and the recreational territory of Upper Belgium. By choosing it to host his swimming lake, the architect put a finger on the hybrid potential of the valley and subsequently questioned the transition between industrial and recreational spheres of influences.

In the 1930s context of the first paid vacations, Victor Bourgeois was an advisor for the Ministry of Public Health, for which he conducted feasibility studies for the development of leisure and vacation sites. Within this institution, it soon became clear that Belgium was lacking bathing opportunities. The feasibility studies attested to this, as they mainly dealt with industrial sites—former quarries and man-made reservoirs—to be reinvested and transformed into swimming facilities. In the speculative plan for Charleroi, Victor Bourgeois reinterpreted his previous research by integrating a swimming lake but also an open-air theater and a stadium, all three voluntarily artificially dug in the ground.[9] In *Charleroi, terre d'urbanisme*—the 1946 book in which the speculative plan was finally published – the architect described his fascination for earthworks and excavators that could quickly transform landscapes. He saw them as the means to build a new monumentality, able to represent collective action by hosting new leisure practices.[10] The codes of the industrial and extractivist society were thus intentionally borrowed but distorted, reclaimed outside the sphere of economic production. Contrary to what the modernist territorial division suggests, the architect's attitude toward the recreational landscape was not contemplative or protectionist at all, but fully interventionist. He even spoke of an *architecture de terre* (architecture of earth) that does not simply occupy the forest but intends to remodel it. Thus, according to Victor Bourgeois, the *Eau d'Heure* valley is a pivotal site and, therefore, it can be worked as a porous border, a place of ambivalent contamination and cultural experimentation rather than as a clear dividing line.

Victor Bourgeois' plan never materialized. The momentum of public interest in recreation during the 1930s was slowed by World War II. Although Bourgeois' projects were held up as examples by the administration under the German occupation, little was built during the war.[11] Some of his prewar projects were demolished under the bombardments, while a large part of the Belgian modernist avant-garde was discredited in the eyes of the resistance by its tolerance toward the German administration.[12] When the dams were put on the table once again during the *Trente Glorieuses*, the social and architectural context had changed dramatically, and their implementation required many more actors at the table.

From Postwar Reconstruction to the *Trente Glorieuses*

After the war, the first steps of Belgian reconstruction were mainly carried out on an emergency basis. Few long-term investments were undertaken before 1955 and the launching of the "Program Acts" by Omer Vanaudenhove, Minister of Public Works. The modernization plan was divided into three parts: the Road Fund, the ten-year Port of Antwerp extension plan, and the Canal Act. Once again, at a governmental scale, the infrastructure network provided the catalyst and pivot point for territorial development.[13] More specifically, two out of the three plans were hydraulic infrastructures, linked to the availability of a raw material—the national freshwater stock—whose role in the story must now be more broadly introduced, before returning to the particular case of the Eau d'Heure valley.

Everything started with the project to extend the port of Antwerp toward the Rhine estuary. The 1955 Program Acts guided the extension of the port to reach a future canal that would link it to the Meuse–Rhine delta, thereby creating a new strategic maritime connection.[14] But the canal would be partly situated on the Dutch side of the border and, moreover, its connection to the sea would risk introducing salt water into the freshwater lakes that the Netherlands was building via the Deltaplan (flood barriers between the North Sea and the lakes of Zeeland).[15] To resolve this conflict, a bilateral agreement was negotiated. It led to the 1963 Scheldt–Rhine Treaty, stipulating that, in compensation for building the canal, Belgium would guarantee a constant water flow into the delta from the mouth of the Meuse, a river that crosses southern Belgium before reaching the Netherlands. The challenge was not to increase available quantities of water but to eliminate seasonal variation, in order to maintain a constant lightly polluted flow all year long. From that demand emerged the idea of building dams. They were to be built in Upper Belgium, in rural tributary valleys of the Meuse and Sambre rivers, in order to control the flow from upstream, and ensure the supply of the strategic estuary.

The treaty was therefore the founding act of the dams, far from the de-commodified character of Victor Bourgeois' speculative plan. It constituted a "missing link" between the Program Acts and the dams, based on a compensation mechanism, a compromise between two countries in full economic boom, which shared the same predatory vision toward their territories and resources. Hence, it has been deemed as one of the first milestones in the European integration project. At the same time, it created additional tensions between the two regions of the country—Wallonia in the south, Flanders in the north—since the freshwater reserves of the Sambre-Meuse basins, in the south, would be harnessed to allow the extension of the port of Antwerp, in the north. Walloon industrialists were worried that the Sambre-Meuse valley would lose its industrial vocation to became "an aqueduct carrying drinking water to the Netherlands."[16] These dissents probably participated in feeding the progressive regionalist polarization of the country, later leading to its federalization.

Although they may not have been aware of it, the people depicted in the postcard enjoyed their outing against the backdrop of large-scale territorial and political plans, in which water emerged as an object of technological control, power struggles, and political bargaining. This situation connected these Belgian holiday-makers to a broader recreational landscape or "waterscape" shared with their Dutch neighbors, who, on the far end of the network, were also sailing on the newly created artificial lakes of the Deltaplan (Figure 8.2).[17]

It took another six years between the signing of the treaty and the establishment of clear political guidelines for its implementation. A royal commission studied the issue between 1966 and 1969, and prescribed raising the existing dam of *La Gileppe*, as well as building three new series of dams in southwestern Belgium. In the meantime, the issue had been broadened and rebranded as "*Le problème de l'eau.*" According to the commission, the need for centralized management of freshwater flows would not only address the 1963 treaty but also serve wider purposes, like meeting the increasing domestic demand for drinking water and supporting regional industrial activity. Constant river flow would dilute pollution generated by the heavy industries along the Sambre-Meuse rivers and supply the canals that had been enlarged through the provisions of the Canal Act.[18] It would feed the cooling system of the Tihange power plant, as well as several new water inlets for domestic use. The report of the commission thus depicted the dams as necessary for the economic interests of the Sambre-Meuse industrial basin as well as for the port of Antwerp. It presented them first and foremost as an industrial proposition, but also as a necessary component of electricity, water, and goods provision, grounded in the expanding consumer culture of the *Trente Glorieuses*.[19]

Shaping the Postwar Leisure Landscape

Dam projects faced mounting opposition in the decades following World War II. From 1965 to 1978, each public announcement of a dam project in the Semois, Lesse, and Eau noire valleys met with opposition by citizen groups. They relayed scientific doubts concerning the efficiency of the dams and pointed out small-scale alternatives.[20] They criticized the state's governance model, arguing that their own interests had not been integrated in the decision-making. Finally, they expressed a strong desire to protect the traditional rural lifestyle closely associated with their valleys, embodied by practices such as hunting, fishing, poaching, and the resistance actions of the *maquisards* during the war.[21] These local movements, combined with regional tensions, made the construction of the dams highly controversial. As a result, only the Eau d'Heure valley dam series made it to the construction phase.

Unlike the other proposals, the Eau d'Heure valley site raised comparatively little opposition. Because the area was sparsely populated, few expropriations were needed, and the amount of land required was further reduced by the subdivision of the water reserve into two sites: a lower lake on the *Eau d'Heure* and an upper lake that worked as a pumped storage unit in the adjacent Plate-Taille valley. This division reduced the span of the site in the main valley, and, subsequently, prevented the village of Cerfontaine from flooding. Moreover, the Ministry of Public Works sought acceptance among local residents by tying the project expressly to leisure and recreation. Drawing on the territorial narrative established through Victor Bourgeois' feasibility studies, ministry planners argued that Belgium lacks bathing opportunities, and that the construction of the dams would enhance the Upper Belgium region as a vacation area. Thus, an official discourse emerged that framed the dams as a win–win proposal: on the one hand, to support the management of the national hydraulic network, and on the other to provide bathing opportunities and reinforce the attractiveness of Upper Belgium for tourists.[22]

This notion of binding the Eau d'heure dams with leisure took shape in the Ministry of Public Works in the early 1970s through interdepartmental meetings. Discussions with experts of the Department of Sports and Tourism or with the *Plan Vert* (green plan) were recorded in meeting minutes and explanatory brochures. From these varied conversations, two key ideas emerged. First, the Plate-Taille lake would be enlarged, in order to host a water sports center. Second, three smaller dams would be built upstream of the Eau d'Heure lake, equipped with forebays to regulate the flow of water. Their purpose was to reduce tidal variation by controlling the supply to the downstream network during the summer. These infrastructure elements would thus minimize the build-up of unpleasant muddy areas that appear on the lakeshores, especially during the peak of summer tourism.[23] As a result of such a federal commitment, embodied by these two decisions, the local authorities were convinced that the infrastructure could help drive the regional economy. The Ministry of Public Works charged them with developing lakeshore tourism and recreational facilities. In the mid-1970s, two intermunicipal structures, Intersud and BEPN, became part of the overall project and would slowly—and not without criticism—plan the touristic exploitation of the site.[24]

The process of shaping the site for leisure was thus arguably used as a political instrument, developed in response to the dam controversies in order to build a consensus with local authorities and citizens. But this commitment to a regional leisure landscape was present from the first blueprint, and was thus by no means a subsidiary aspect of the project.

The Decorated Dam: Absorbing the Artificiality of the Site

While the planning and construction of the Eau d'Heure dams proceeded rather smoothly, the project was by no means an ideologically neutral technical exercise. Once accepted and underway, it generated great enthusiasm among authorities. The large-scale presence of the dams and lake in the landscape evoked the power of the postwar infrastructure-driven Welfare State, made concrete and dynamic by delivering leisure opportunities such as sailing and swimming to a broad population. But, in terms of image, the project, divided in two dams, three pre-dams, and as many lakes, was not so easy to grasp. The dam on the Eau d'Heure main valley is made of rockfill—a construction method that blends it in the landscape—while the forebays or pre-dams are mainly underwater. Not surprisingly, when it came to create a site marker, attention turned to the Plate-Taille secondary dam, which consists of a concrete retaining wall directly linked to the biggest lake of the site (Figure 8.4).

The Ministry of Public Works commissioned an engineer–architect, Jean Barthelemy to transform the dam into a recognizable monument. His intervention was published in the Belgian architectural magazine *A+* in 1983, two years after the lakes formed.[25] He designed the pumping-storage unit as well as two concrete towers, a steel bridge, a colonnade, curved lampposts, and railings superimposed on the retaining wall of the dam (Figure 8.1). At first glance, the *A+* article which promotes structural design,

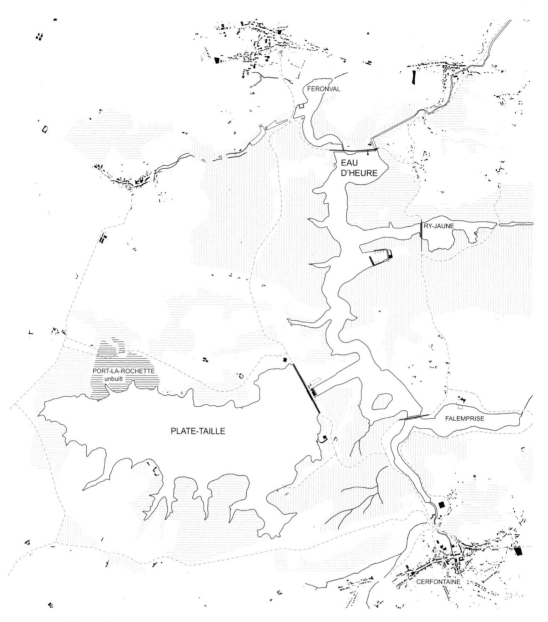

Figure 8.4 The Eau d'Heure dams.
Source: Drawing by Marie Pirard.

leads to believe that Jean Barthelemy falls into line with the modernist legacy: looking for structural truth and eager at exploring the particular monumentality of an industrial infrastructure. But, unlike Victor Bourgeois' *architecture de terre*, he only paid attention to the retaining wall of the dam, without any concern toward the general site shaping and its earthworks. Moreover, he did not interfere with the design of the concrete wall itself, but rather decorated it through adding external references such as the neoclassical language of the colonnade and the organic metaphor that underlies the observation tower spiral plan and the curved railings. His intervention focuses on association and symbolism, both concepts that were put on the agenda by the post-modernist discourses.[26] And indeed, the intervention proved to have lasting iconic value: the Plate-Taille tower, colonnade, and dam were captured extensively in postcards and even postage stamps, influencing the long-term image of the site in the collective imagination.

Barthelemy's design had an unexpected collateral effect. Making the Plate-Taille retaining wall the focus of the site detached it from the whole *organic machine* that had encompassed it.[27] Thanks to his intervention, it was possible to visit the dam, climb the observatory tower, and explore its pumping-storage unit. The Plate-Taille dam became the officially presentable part of the infrastructure. It captured the hybrid and artificial charge of the infrastructure, indirectly purging the rest of the site of its plural connotations and allowing it to function as "simply natural" in contrast with the artifice of the concrete wall. A few years later, in 1987, the urban planner Raymond Lemaire published an unbuilt project for a new resort town, Port-la-Rochette, on the shore of the Plate-Taille lake (Figure 8.4). The location was chosen for its sunny aspect but also to escape the view of the dam. The town, then, would unfold without any reference to the infrastructural status of the lake. For Lemaire, hiding the view of the retaining wall from the town was sufficient to deny the artificiality of the site, which he deemed incompatible with a resort. This proves the effectiveness of Jean Barthelemy's intervention, making the decorated dam the only holder of the hybrid status that it absorbed and fixed. This diversionary tactic "freed" the site of its artificial character and paved the way for the generic waterside real estate development launched in the 2000s.

Conclusion

In order to trace the micro-history of the Eau d'Heure valley, we had to foil Jean Barthelemy's ruse: starting from the postcard but broadening the site analysis to explore its multiple agencies. For that purpose, it was necessary to decentralize the gaze from the Plate-Taille retaining wall; to study the reshaping of the whole site's landscape by the Ministry of Public Works; to zoom out until reaching the macro-economic and political issues that marked its development; and to go back in time in order to ground its cultural framework in the 1930s modernist vision of territorial planning and de-commodified leisure.

Such a movement has revealed the hybridity of the site. The dams have proven to be simultaneously part of the material and cultural backbone of the Belgian welfare state by answering to a double ambition: both productive—to manage the national freshwater resources—and recreational—for tourists to bathe in the reservoirs thus created. Within the productive facet, no clear dividing line was found between technological and political issues: managing freshwater was simultaneously a technical challenge—calculating water flows, designing infrastructures—and a political stake—source of controversies at the European, regional, and local levels. Likewise, no clear-cut existed between the intellectual construction of the modernist "idea of nature"—idealized as bodily or spiritually regenerative—and its material counterpart—the radical artificialization of a landscape to tie it to leisure.

Throughout the story, each architectural or landscape intervention appears on its own as a minor or incomplete piece of Belgian architectural history. The modernist territorial narrative, as well as Victor Bourgeois' speculative plan for Charleroi, were never explicitly taken seriously by the political spheres. The state's postwar development ambition associated with the building of dams has never been fully realized, as only one new dam site was constructed. After the *Trente Glorieuses*, Belgians shifted their vacation preferences to sunnier destinations, putting Upper Belgium at risk as a tourist attraction. Jean Barthelemy's designs for the dam were important for the project's signification, but by no means remarkable on their own. And the construction of facilities on the Eau d'Heure lakeshores by intermunicipal agencies stalled for many years before being activated by public–private partnerships.

What can we learn from this puzzle, then, where each piece reflects missteps, shortcomings, even failures? I argue that something relevant emerges from the case study not by taking its stages into account independently, nor by contrasting them with each other, but rather by exploring them in their ensemble results. Over several decades, the many approaches and attitudes of those who participated shaped the Eau d'Heure landscape, constructing a powerful regional imaginary—the one conveyed by the postcard—through impressionistic touches, composing a heterogeneous cultural form just as hybrid as the Eau d'heure valley itself.

From the "manifesto of hybridity" constituted by Victor Bourgeois' concept of *architecture de terre*, through the interdepartmental approach that took place in the Ministry of Public Works to tie the site to leisure, to the "capture chamber" created by Jean Barthelemy's monument, there was no continuity of purpose nor shared discursive field to govern the project from start to finish. But neither were the interventions independent of each other. The modernist territorial narrative gave rise to the idea of developing tourism in Upper Belgium by building dams, although these dams created a landscape that contradicts the modernist vision of urban corridors clearly delineated from recreational patches. The call for a leisure-oriented monumentality, which was embodied in the obviously artificial *architecture de terre* by Victor Bourgeois, was, to a certain extent, implemented discreetly by the Ministry of Public Works. And, concurrently, it was overused by Jean Barthelemy, whose monumental design scheme both captured and watered down the artificial nature of the site. In the postwar context, the prewar modernists' concepts were reclaimed and hybridized with new political, economic, and cultural developments. Reciprocally, the postwar implementations delineate, *a posteriori*, the scope of the prewar experimentations. From such implicit long-term relationships, an heterogenous architectural culture emerges, making the Eau d'heure infrastructure project concurrently rich, ambivalent, unclassifiable, and opaque.

Notes

1 Eric Mumford, *The CIAM Discourse on Urbanism, 1928–1960* (Cambridge: MIT Press, 2000), 59–65.
2 Geoffrey Grulois, "Le Grand Bruxelles: Généalogie d'une figure métropolitaine dans la Belgique de l'entre-deux-guerres," Inventer le Grand Paris. 1919-1944: Actes du colloque des 4 et 5 décembre 2014.
3 Pieter Uyttenhove, *Stadland Belgie, Hoofdstukken Uit De Geschiedenis Van De Stedenbouw* (Ghent: A&S Books, 2011); Michael Ryckewaert, *Building the Economic Backbone of the Belgian Welfare state, Infrastructure, Planning and Architecture 1945–1973* (Rotterdam: 010 Publishers, 2011).
4 Marie Pirard, "Regards 1848-1977," in *Guide Architecture Moderne Et Contemporaine 1893-2020, Namur Et Luxembourg*, eds Jean-Paul Verleyen and Cécile Vandernoot (Cellule Architecture de la Fédération Wallonie-Bruxelles, 2020).
5 Iwan Strauven, "Victor Bourgeois 1897–1962: Radicaliteit En Pragmatisme, Moderniteit En Traditie" (PhD thesis, Universiteit Gent, Université Libre de Bruxelles, 2015).
6 Guy Vanthemsche, "De Mislukking Van Een Vernieuwde Economische Politiek in Belgïe Vóór De Tweede Wereldoorlog: De Orec (Office De Redressement Economique)," *Revue belge d'Histoire contemporaine* 2, no. 3 (1982): 339–389.
7 Victor Bourgeois, "4me Congrès International D'architecture Moderne, Extrait Du Rapport Sur L'urbanisme En Belgique," *L'émulation, architecture et urbanisme* (1933), 46.
8 Strauven, "Victor Bourgeois 1897–1962; Fonds Bourgeois, P-1932-04, CIVA, Brussels.
9 Marie Pirard, "Constructed Landscapes for Collective Recreation: Victor Bourgeois's Open-Air Projects in Belgium," in *Architecture and Collective Life*, eds Penny Lewis and others (Abingdon: Routledge, 2021).
10 Victor Bourgeois and René de Cooman, *Charleroi, Terre D'urbanisme* (Brussels: Art et Technique, 1946).
11 Pierre Gilles, "L'urbanisme Sauveur, L'assainissement Et L'aménagement D'Antoing," *Reconstruction* 11 (1941): 20–25.
12 Uyttenhove, *Stadland Belgie*, 178–218.
13 Michael Ryckewaert, *Building the Economic Backbone of the Belgian Welfare State, Infrastructure, Planning and Architecture 1945–1973* (Rotterdam: 010 Publishers, 2011), 18–79.
14 Ibid. 81–96.
15 Charles Christians, "Le Problème de l'eau et la Liaison Escaut-Rhin," *Hommes et Terres du Nord* 2, no. 1 (1965): 96–97.
16 Ibid.
17 Filippo Menga, and Erik Swyngedouw (eds), *Water, Technology and the Nation-State* (New York: Routledge, 2018), 3.

18 Eugène Valcke and Georges Boby, *Le problème de l'eau en Belgique* (Ministère des travaux publics, Voies hydrauliques, 1964).
19 Archives Régionales du Ministère des Travaux Publics, February 1969, OIP/CESRW/200509/4/06 Rapport final du Commissariat Royal au Problème de l'Eau, Namur.
20 Archives Régionales du Ministère des Travaux Publics, November 1966, OIP/CESRW/200509/4/03 Etude réalisée par le bureau d'études Eau et Relief pour l'asbl Défense de la Semois, Namur.
21 Benjamin Hennot, *La bataille de l'Eau Noire* (Belgique: Ere doc, 2015); Omer Marchal, *Lesse, le village qui ne voulait pas mourir* (Brussels: Pierre de Meyere, 1967).
22 L'Equerre, *Programme de Développement et d'Aménagement du Sud-Est: Atlas et Projet* (Brussels: Bureau d'architecture et d'urbanisme l'Equerre, 1963).
23 Archives Régionales du Ministère des Travaux Publics, Août 1971, OIP/CESRW/200509/2/3 Le complexe des barrages de l'Eau d'Heure, Namur.
24 Freddy Joris, "La Station Touristique De L'eau D'heure," *Les Cahiers de l'Urbanisme* 47 (2003): 32–40.
25 Jean-Marie Huberty, "Les barrages, de la digue du castor au mur de 200 m (Barrage de la Plate-Taille)," *A+* 85 (1983): 25–27.
26 Robert Venturi, Steven Izenour, and Denise Scott Brown, *Learning from Las Vegas: The Forgotten Symbolism of Architectural Form* (Chicago: MIT Press, 1977).
27 Christine Macy and Sarah Bonnemaison, *Architecture and Nature, Creating the American Landscape* (London, New York: Routledge, 2003).

9
PEDAGOGIC LANDSCAPES
Recreation, Play, and Danish Infrastructure Design
Margaret Birney Vickery

In Denmark, there has long been an emphasis on outdoor learning as a means of developing an individual's creativity, and respect for the natural world, which would subsequently encourage a cultural identity. N.F.S. Grundtvig's ideas for folk schools in the early nineteenth century and C.T. Sørensen's designs for junk playgrounds in the 1930s, together with early green infrastructure and a human-centered scale for Denmark's capital city, Copenhagen, provided experiential learning experiences. Recreation in the outdoors introduced construction techniques, hydrology, and natural systems to the public, while forging human connections. What is sometimes called soft infrastructure—the preservation and development of green spaces within an urban fabric — has been an integral part of the development of Copenhagen since the early twentieth century. This chapter examines how such outdoor opportunities are featured on several new "hard" infrastructure projects completed in the last several years such as the Sølrogård Wastewater treatment plant, the Køge Water filtration park, and Copenhill, a new waste to energy plant designed by Bjarke Ingels' firm BIG. It examines Danish attitudes toward education, recreation, and play, in order to contextualize these new hybrid infrastructures, which produce clean water, heat, and electricity, while offering experiential learning and accidental encounters with the natural world.

Throughout the twentieth century, large scale infrastructures such as power plants and wastewater treatment facilities have generally been isolated and out of sight except in the underserved areas where they are most often found. Ignored and forgotten, it is easy to take for granted clean water from our taps or the sources producing electricity for our homes. As Mitchell Schwarzer notes: "It is the invisibility of the systems that sustain our splendid artificial environments that leads to the neglect of ambient nature, urbanity, and infrastructure itself."[1] This neglect and ignorance about the production of these vital systems can be understood as part of much larger issues such as environmental protection and climate change. Recent Danish infrastructure, however, reveals a proclivity for transparency, connection, and openness toward the public. From electric compressor stations to power plants and wastewater treatment systems, Danish design reflects what Leo Marx calls a "complex pastoralism" which unites utility with landscape and promotes human connection to the natural world through built forms.[2] This chapter examines the history, meaning, and design signatures of this infrastructural openness. I argue that these projects are part of a broader Danish tradition of popular education where recreation, outdoor activity, and play lead to deeper connections with nature. Within this framework, Danish designers have come to regard infrastructure as performing functional as well as pedagogical roles, arguing that both are necessary in the provision of public goods and the building of a healthy society.

Danish Infrastructure and Popular Education

Denmark is a small country of about five million people. It is frequently lauded for its well-educated citizenry, high living standards, happiness quota, and advances in green energy production. Scholars have looked at the Danish model of government and public participation to understand how and why the Danes have been so successful at promoting green infrastructure and power while other countries have struggled to implement their climate goals as determined at venues such as the Global UNFCCC and the resulting Paris Agreement of 2015. Julie L. MacArthur's research has delved into how public participation, government policy, and industry have worked together in Denmark to make the country a leader in "participatory renewable design."[3] The key to success, according to MacArthur, is a focus on public inclusion, from the planning process on through to community ownership. She argues that the strong public stake in large-scale projects is crucial for fostering citizen knowledge about the complexities of energy production, creating a shared financial stake in renewable energy projects, and moving toward more reflexive design and implementation.[4] And the "Danish Energy Model," a government tract issued by the Danish Energy Agency, cites the critical role the public plays in helping Denmark reach its goal of being fossil free by 2050. Summarizing its aims and achievements, the agency concludes that "Energy policy is well rooted in the everyday lives of Danish citizens, with significant public engagement in all aspects of the low-carbon transition."[5]

Denmark has a long tradition of egalitarian educational and community engagement. The strong social cohesion may be due to a particular nationalism that developed in the nineteenth century, in the aftermath of Denmark's defeat in the Second Schleswig War. In the search for a national identity many Danes turned to the ideas of N.F.S. Grundtvig, the priest, poet, and nationalist who lived and wrote during the mid-nineteenth century. Grundtvig rejected the education of the elite in the universities, with its emphasis on classical subjects and Latin, and argued instead for a form of education for the people that celebrated the Danish language, and Danish history, and tradition. These ideas coalesced in the development of folk high schools which proliferated in the last quarter of the nineteenth century. Intended for students 18 years or older, the folk schools offered courses in agriculture, music, and physical fitness. While supported by the government they often began as local efforts. According to Lars Bo Kaspersen, "These bottom-up initiatives provided a strong educational foundation for the population and contributed to a rising self-consciousness and self-confidence."[6] The American folklorist Olive Dame Campbell documented the Danish folk schools in 1928, commenting that: "The folk school is firmly attached to the soil. It seeks to relate the culture of books and art to the culture of the soil."[7] In addition to an effort to bolster national pride, the folk schools offered "outdoor education, for and through one's own nature."[8] Today, these ideas are manifested in the *udeskole* (outdoor classroom), and the nation's educational objectives include regular connections with nature.[9]

This approach to education is exemplified by the Danish adventure playground movement. In the early 1940s, the highly regarded modernist landscape architect, C.T. Sørensen designed the Emdrup junk playground. This was an idea he had floated since 1931 in his book, *Parkpolitik I Sogn og Købstad (Park Policy in Parish and Market Town)* in which he stated that "children's playgrounds are the city's most important form of public plantation."[10] In 1943 the architect Dan Fink invited Sørensen to be part of the design team working on a new housing estate in the town of Emdrup, in Jutland. This was an opportunity for him to realize his ideas. The housing units surrounded a central courtyard that was enclosed within a tall berm, thus shielding views of the inner space from the houses. Instead of a set of permanent playground structures, children were given old cars, remnants of construction equipment, packing crates, and branches to play with. The result for the children was a freedom to explore the capabilities of materials, to discover, without much risk, how a structure stands and why it falls, where puddles form and why they drain, and how to make and care for spaces (Figure 9.1). Sørensen's invention, while not popular with parents whose children returned home dirty from their construction projects, developed into what is still lauded today as the adventure playground. Certainly, Sørensen had no regrets. In 1951,

Figure 9.1 C.T. Sørensen/Det Kongelige Akademi, junk playground, Emdrup, Denmark, 1940–1941.

Source: Royal Danish Academy of Fine Arts.

he wrote: "of all the things I have helped to realize, the junk playground is the ugliest; yet for me it is the best and most beautiful of my works."[11]

In the same article Sørensen reflected on the children's activities at Emdrup. These included dismantling an old car and re-using the parts to create an energy producing windmill, as well as any number of shelters and gardens constructed with twigs and branches. Once the "twigs and branches have served their time as building material for wigwams, kraals and Stone Age houses they are chopped up in bundles for firewood for bakers' ovens: waste paper is collected and exhibitions are held."[12] Such sites stimulated children's ingenuity and creativity, fostered their self-confidence and understanding of how machines and materials functioned, and instructed them about energy production and waste management.

These adventure playgrounds continued to develop in Denmark throughout the twentieth century. By 1980, authors Edna Michelle and Robert T. Anderson published their findings of Danish play spaces. They wrote: "The adventure playground encourages children to build houses from scrap lumber, to have experiences with natural materials such as dirt, water, growing of plants and animals, and to organize themselves in play."[13] Sørenson's concept led to a design approach to play wherein children can freely explore their natural world and their own environment. The importance of such exploration should not be underestimated. Studies abound about the importance of connecting children with nature. In their article about this connection, Jamie Huff Sisson and Martha Lash draw on Richard Louv's notion of "nature-deficit disorder." They agree with Louv that traditional education policies fall short by rendering environmental education a merely passive activity. Like Louv, they argue that "hands-on learning is needed for children to build a relationship with nature that will lead to caring for the environment in the future."[14] Long before sustainability became a policy goal, Sørensen understood that a sustainable society depends on the commitment of successive generations, which, in turn, requires a broad-based, engrained understanding of the relationship between the built and the unbuilt environment. He recognized that the activity with abundant power to teach children about the world around them and to care for it is play.

Concurrent with Sørensen's modernist landscape designs and his junk playground, Peter Bredsdorff and Sten Eiler Rassmussen (both prominent Danish architects), developed plans for Copenhagen's Finger Plan published in 1947. This built on the earlier 1936 Green Network Plan that had laid out extensive park and greenways systems primarily to the northwest of the city. The Finger Plan, named for its hand-like shape, included "fingers" of green spreading west and south of the city. "The plan highlighted the importance of reserving a regional coherent network of green space areas to provide easy close-by access to recreational experiences for the urban population."[15] While not a politically powerful tool in the two decades following, it did help to guide the city's development through the 1950s and 60s and it has been strengthened since the 1970s.[16] These green fingers stretching out from the palm-like center of the city of Copenhagen, included walking trails, bike paths, and even beaches for the public to the south of the city. Ensuring recreational spaces within an urban context provides what Beery et al call "incidental" experiences in nature consisting of unplanned and surprise encounters with flora and fauna. The authors contrast these spontaneous experiences with "intentional" events such as planned hikes, bike rides, or outings to the beach. All these encounters, whether they arise through deliberation and forethought or simple serendipity, offer contacts with nature that improve mental and physical health.[17]

The Danish architect Jan Gehl expanded on these ideas in his urban plans. Active since the 1960s, Gehl has been lauded as a prescient planner who advocated for bike lanes, sidewalks, and human scaled cities during the auto-centric 1960s. He has been credited with Copenhagen's transformation from a city of cars to one of bicycles and public transportation. In an interview from 2013, Gehl argued, "The best thing you can do in city planning is to invite people to perform some natural activities every day; that's much better than a million fitness centers."[18] Moving people through cities and towns on foot or by bicycle offers both the health benefits to which Gehl refers, and opportunities for both accidental and intentional connections with the natural world as advocated by Beery and his colleagues.

This brief survey of the work of key figures in Danish educational philosophy and design from the nineteenth through the twentieth century illuminates a common belief in the importance of time spent in nature for the health and well-being of Danish citizens. While I do not posit a direct causal link between Grundtvig's folk schools or Sørensen's junk playground, I do argue that the hard infrastructure projects discussed in the following pages can be better understood within this wider cultural context and intellectual tradition. Experiential learning in the outdoors, an urban fabric that affords easy access to nature, and a human-scaled built environment have long underpinned the traditional planning of green or "soft" infrastructures. The architects and landscape architects discussed below have adapted these principles into their designs for large, hard infrastructure projects that produce clean water, heat, and electricity.

Danish Infrastructure: Transparency, Recreation, and Productive Systems

The pages that follow examine three key infrastructure sites recently opened in Denmark. Though there are other examples to be found, these projects unite productive infrastructural systems with recreational landscapes that encourage play and exploration. In a very real sense, they illustrate Sørensen's commitment to learning through play by connecting the public to their sources of clean water and energy through recreation in the landscape.

In an article for *Places* in 1989, Anne Whiston Spirn noted that:

> Like a primordial magnet, water pulls at a primitive and deeply rooted part of human nature. Water is a source of life, power, comfort, fear, delight; it is a symbol of purification, of both dissolution of life and its renewal.[19]

However, as many scholars have noted, the technologies developed over the nineteenth and twentieth centuries for the capture and conveyance of water in cities have attenuated our connection to it, obscuring the natural hydrological cycles. "As rain falls to the ground," Spirn continues, "it is quickly directed to drains and carried off; after we use water, it is flushed away into underground pipes and transported to sewage treatment plant[s], which like garbage dumps, are touched into forgotten corners of the city."[20]

A desire to re-establish basic human connection with water informed the development of the recently opened Køge Waterworks outside Copenhagen (Figure 9.2). Designed by Gottlieb Paludan Architects, and opened in 2018, it is situated near three schools in a modest-sized town just southwest of the capital. The large water filtration building comprises a glass curtain wall supported

Figure 9.2 Gottlieb Paludan Architects, Køge Waterworks, Køge, Denmark, 2019.

Source: Gottlieb Paludan Architects.

by a steel frame resting on stone walls. The glazed transparency is a deliberate means of illustrating the varied processes involved with water treatment and testing that happen within. In addition to containing the water tanks and filtering equipment, the structure houses administrative offices for the client, the utility company Klar Forsyning, and labs that are open to universities and commercial ventures researching new methods of water treatment and testing.

A sloped roof directs rainwater off the building like a water curtain where it is then funneled into corten steel runnels. Staggered in height, these long rectangular channels, angled across the landscape, carry the rainwater to a small lake. The lake is designed to absorb rainwater from the plant and to manage major weather events such as torrential cloudbursts. The lake water is then pumped into the processing plant and treated for public consumption. Part of the brief for the architects and engineers was to tell the story of water and to illustrate for visitors both natural and human-made filtering systems.[21] The zig-zagged arrangement of the channels and their placement low to the ground invite children from the neighboring schools to come and play with the water, splashing, damming, and experimenting with its flow. In a society with the cultural legacy of Grundtvig and Sørensen, such play is understood as a means of connection to and education about our interactions with this most vital resource. The overt connections between the water cycle and nature as expressed in the landscape of the Køge waterworks, together with the transparent inner workings of the plant are designed to educate the local population, from schoolchildren to professional academics about their water supply and the larger water cycle. Because of the cultural tradition, play and recreation are essential methods of learning about those relationships.

Such goals also inform the recently opened, Sølrogård Climate and Energy Park in Hillerød Denmark (2019). A collaboration between the local water and waste treatment company, Hillerød Forsyning, local government, and architects from Gottlieb Paludan, Henning Larsen, and C.F. Møller, the park includes a new wastewater treatment plant, a large recycling center, and a visitors' center for administration and education. Significantly, it also includes a bat hotel, a bird tower, numerous water retention ponds, paths, and boardwalks for walking and biking, as well as the archeological remains of an old mill dating from 1572. Visitors to the park can learn about the history of water and wind power in Denmark as the archeological work there continues. Future plans include the construction of solar arrays and a geothermal heating plant. When the company was tasked with building a new wastewater treatment plant and a more efficient recycling center, local politicians required that the development of a new site include both recreational and educational facilities.[22]

Overall, the landscape plan has echoes of classic English landscape design with meandering paths and carefully constructed views across water features. It brings to mind the works of Capability Brown. Silhouetted against the sky are no faux temples, rotundas, or follies of a lordly estate, but rather the new recycling facility, and the Climate and Environment Center. This was designed by Gottlieb Paludan Architects. Three rectangular volumes unite around a glassed-in central gap, the "transparent heart of the complex."[23] The building houses administrative offices for staff, workshop spaces, and parking within a crisp, corten steel façade. It is powered by solar panels, insulated with a green roof, and it stretches out across a landscape of grassy meadows and wetlands. An efficiently organized recycling center with sorting stations arranged in a trapezoidal plan abuts the eastern edge of the park. Cars and heavy trucks are kept separate from each other so the act of dropping off recycling is distinct from its removal off-site. The heart of the center is an open area with a trussed roof of white pyramidal forms that provide protection from the elements and define areas for disposal of hazardous waste. A green space with a small pond, replenished by rainwater, serves as a gathering space for visitors, staff, and schoolchildren who come regularly to the park to learn about the facility. Director Støvring announced that local children will visit the park at least five times a year for formal instruction about waste, recycling, and water treatment.[24]

In 2019, the Sølrogård Wastewater Treatment plant opened in the park (Figure 9.3). Traditionally in the US and Europe, smelly and unattractive facilities that treat our most basic waste are kept out of sight (and mind). But here in Hillerød, the plant nestles beneath a low rise in the park. Paths

Figure 9.3 Henning Larsen Architects, Sølrogård Wastewater Treatment, Hillerød, Denmark, 2019.

Source: Henning Larsen Architects. Photograph by Jacob Due, used with permission.

traverse the building's low roof, which is planted with colorful sedums, while angular skylights allow views inside. Special filters trap the odors. As people bike and walk through the park, a diversion to the roof of the plant affords views across the landscape and down into the workings of the site. The structure itself is bifurcated by a central path with a small temporal creek running through it, which offers visitors an understanding of how nature processes water. Large windows line the facades of the central alley to provide further views inside. Like the junk playground, casual recreation engenders learning, in this case exposing the visitor to the processes involved in wastewater treatment, while providing opportunities for exercise and accidental encounters with the natural world. This plant builds upon the central tenet of the Climate and Energy Park, that nature, habitat, and humans need to co-exist.

In the March 3, 2020 edition of the Danish architecture magazine, *Arkitekten*, Brigitte Kleis reviewed the newly opened Amager Bakke Waste-to-Energy plant in Copenhagen. She introduced the article by effusing that: "Copenhagen has been given a new attraction, which—like a Kinder Egg—is truly three things at ones: combustion plant, architectural fixing point, and a playground for all of us."[25] This new power plant represents what its designer, Bjarke Ingels' firm calls "hedonistic sustainability."[26] Designed by BIG and SLA landscape architects, the plant includes a ski slope and hiking trails on the twisting green roof, and a climbing wall up the north facing façade (Figure 9.4). It is sited on a modest industrial peninsula surrounded by water, sports facilities, and a marina, with new apartments framing views of the plant and restaurants and music venues nearby. In addition to year-long skiing on the specially designed rooftop ski-slope, SLA landscape architects designed the green roof with a pastoral assortment of trees, grasses, and wildflowers whose seeds will spread across the landscape after blooming. While the Copenhageners' waste is burned for electricity within, residents are offered views of the inner workings of the plant after their hike to the top or their ski to the bottom.

Danish Infrastructure Design

Figure 9.4 SLA Landscape Architects, Copenhill, Copenhagen, Denmark, 2021.
Source: © SLA.

While some have hailed Amager Bakke as an engineering triumph and recreational marvel, others have critiqued Bjarke Ingels for his hedonistic approach to sustainability and argue that the "playful" features trivialize the emissions of the plant.[27] There is certainly a good deal of hype over this project, and it is as yet unclear whether it will live up to its touted promise. Yet, Ingels' goal of connecting the public to its source of energy via play echoes C.T. Sørensen's junk playground at Emdrup. Both understand recreation and play as a means of connection to larger systems, be they natural or infrastructural.

The infrastructure projects discussed above intentionally combine fun with their function. They share with the efforts of Grundtvig, Sørensen, and Gehl a pedagogical approach to outdoor recreation. Through various methods of exposure, the architects and landscape architects responsible for these projects connect the visitor with the plants' functions and offer opportunities for both fortuitous and deliberate interactions with nature. They embody the principles advocated by Anne Whitson Spirn, who has argued for a new aesthetic for landscape architecture, one that "engages all the senses, not just sight, but sound, smell, touch and taste as well. This aesthetic includes both the making of things and places and the sensing, using and contemplation of them."[28] For Spirn and the scholar Elizabeth Meyers, contact with sustainable environments

> can result in the appreciation of new forms of beauty that are discovered ... because they reveal previously unrealized relationships between human and nonhuman life processes ... [and] through the experience of different types of beauty we come to notice, to care, and to deliberate about our place in the world.[29]

The Danish infrastructure projects at Køge, Hillerød, and Copenhill manifest a re-focusing on infrastructural production, and create new connections between that production and the public. Such connections encourage individuals to think about (and care for) both infrastructure *and* the natural world.

The aesthetics of recent Danish infrastructure design encourages users to "notice, to care" about the sources of power and water upon which Danish society depends, as do we all in the twenty-first century.[30] The recreational opportunities they provide are not superficial additions to the plants. Rather the design elements are dictated by and integral to the functioning of the plant itself. The bucolic rises and wetlands at Sølrogård have aesthetic allure, but play a crucial role in filtering rainwater. And the playful water channels at Køge feed the rainwater from the roof to the lake. The aesthetic design of such infrastructure highlights the processes while engaging the public and fostering a concern with and connection to these productive sites. This is part of a culturally embedded goal of promoting an informed, educated citizenry.

While architects and landscape architects around the globe are frequently asked to include visitors' centers and accommodations for school field trips in their designs for infrastructure, the Danish examples build play and recreation into the structures themselves as pedagogical tools. In the tradition of C.T. Sørensen and his junk playground, recreation is understood as a vital means of teaching visitors the environmental principles surrounding the production of energy and clean water. Immersed in experiential learning in the water channels at Køge or peering in at the sorting and combustion of waste through the climbing wall at Amager Bakke, children and adults connect with and participate in generative systems while enjoying aesthetically designed, inviting environments. In these examples play does not trivialize the water cycle or the waste stream. Rather it integrates these vital systems into the public consciousness and makes them part of the realm of everyday. Through the beauty of nature, and the joy of play and exercise, such projects are designed to help us to "notice, to care, and to deliberate about our place in the world."[31] With the growing threats of climate change and habitat loss, an informed and well-educated public is vital to understanding and addressing the issues we face. Rather than passive learning through lectures and signage, these projects inform the Danish public through experience, fostering connections to nature even in urban environments, and a deep understanding of how we interact with and experience both nature and infrastructure.

Notes

1 Mitchell Schwarzer, "The Conceptual Roots of Infrastructure" *Intelligent Infrastructure: Zip Cars, Invisible Networks, and Urban Transformation*, ed. T.F. Tierney (Charlottesville and London: University of Virginia Press, 2016), 57.
2 Leo Marx, "Does Pastoralism Have a Future?" *Studies in the History of Art* 36, Symposium Papers XX: The Pastoral Landscape (1992): 218.
3 Julie L. MacArthur, "Challenging Public Engagement: Participation, Deliberation and Power in Renewable Energy Policy," *Journal of Environmental Studies and Sciences* 6 (2016): 635.
4 Ibid. 637.
5 "The Danish Energy Model," accessed June 1, 2020, https://ens.dk/sites/ens.dk/files/contents/material/file/the_danish_energy_model.pdf.
6 Lars Bo Kaspersen, "The Creation of Modern Denmark: A Figurational Analysis," *Historical Social Research* 45, no. 1 (2020): 182–206, 200.
7 Olive Dame Campbell, *The Danish Folk School: Its Influence in the Life of Denmark and the North* (New York: Macmillan Co., 1928), 184.
8 Carmen Rotaru, "The Triad: Grundtvig, Haret, Gusti: Outdoor Education in the History of the International Pedagogy," *Procedia: Social and Behavioral Sciences* 142 (2014): 532.
9 Rotaru, "The Triad," 533.
10 Sven-Ingvar Andersson og Steen Høyer, *C.T. Sorensen: Landscape Modernist* (Copenhagen: The Danish Architectural Press, 2001), 18.
11 C. Theodor Sørensen, "Junk Playgrounds," *Danish Outlook* 1, no. 4 (1951): 314.
12 Ibid.
13 Edna Michelle and Robert T. Anderson, "Play Spaces in Denmark," *Young Children* 35, no. 2 (January 1980): 4.
14 Jamie Huff Sisson and Martha Lash, "Outdoor Learning Experiences Connecting Children to Nature: Perspectives from Australia and the United States," *Young Children* 72, no. 4 (September 2017): 10.

15 Beery and others "Fostering Incidental Experiences of Nature," 723.
16 Ibid.
17 Ibid. 718.
18 Violet Law, "Jan Gehl," *Progressive* (December 2012/January 2013): 37.
19 Anne Whiston Spirn, "The Poetics of City and Nature: Toward a New Aesthetic for Urban Design," *Places* 6, no. 1 (1989): 91.
20 Spirn, "The Poetics of City and Nature," 91.
21 "Køge Waterworks," accessed May 15, 2020, www.gottliebpaludan.com/en/project/k-ge-waterworks.
22 Søren Støvring, Administrative Director, Hillerød Forsyning, "Background Facts on Solrødgård," statement in support of the Danish Landscape Award (2019), www.gottliebpaludan.com/en/project/k-ge-waterworks. Given to author by Sten Sødring, Jan. 1, 2020.
23 "Solrødgård Climate and Environmental Center," accessed May 20, 2020, www.gottliebpaludan.com/en/project/solr-dg-rd-climate-and-environmental-centre.
24 Støvring, "Background Facts on Solrødgård."
25 Brigitte Kleis, "Amager Tray: The Kinder Egg" (March 10, 2020), https://arkitektforeningen.dk/arkitekten/amager-bakke-kinderaegget/.
26 Hattie Hartman, "Eco-Humanism is the Future," *Architects' Journal* 237, no. 8 (February 2013): 24.
27 Alex Ramiller and Patrick Schmidt, "Making Radical Change Real: Danish Sustainability, Adaptability, and the Reimagination of Architectural Utopias," *Utopian Studies* 30, no. 2 (2019): 288.
28 Spirn, "The Poetics of City and Nature," 108.
29 Elizabeth Meyers, "Sustaining Beauty: The Performance of Appearance: Can Landscape Architects Insert Aesthetics into Our Discussions of Sustainability?" *Landscape Architecture* 98, no. 10 (October 2008): 120.
30 Ibid.
31 Ibid.

10
A VAST DEMOGRAPHIC VOID
Infrastructure, Ecology, and the Amazon
Catherine Seavitt Nordenson

The Brazilian state has consistently identified the territory of the Amazon basin as an expansive hinterland to be mapped, defended, and exploited for resources through the implementation of regional infrastructure. Riverine systems, telegraph lines, and highways were deployed to support economic development. During the colonial period, the Brazilian naturalist Alexandre Rodrigues Ferreira mapped the fluvial routes of the Amazon River and its tributaries from 1783 to 1792. After the declaration of the First Brazilian Republic in 1889, the connection of the hinterland to coastal population centers became an urgent nationalist concern for protecting sovereign borders. In 1906, the Comissão Rondon was initiated by the Ministry of War with the Ministry of Agriculture, Industry, and Commerce. Led by Cândido Rondon, the objective of the nine-year project was the implementation of a telegraph line and a series of stations between the cities of Cuiabá in the state of Mato Grosso and Porto Velho in the state of Amazonas, thereby connecting the farthest reaches of the hinterland to the coast. During the developmentalist military dictatorship that began in 1966, the newly defined "Amazônia Legal" was considered an unfortunate "grande vazio demográfico." In 1967, President Humberto Castelo Branco launched Operation Amazon, an effort to penetrate the forest with the Trans-Amazonian Highway. His successor, President Emílio Médici, initiated the National Integration Program in 1970, a plan to implement social and economic infrastructures in the Amazon region through the development of agricultural and grazing plantation projects. International corporations were encouraged to participate in this nationalist project. A significant shift in this developmentalist trajectory was marked by the testimony of noted landscape architect Roberto Burle Marx to the Federal Senate in 1976. Citing the rapacious deforestation practices of Volkswagen do Brasil at its experimental cattle ranch in the Amazon, a new nationalist movement in support of environmental protection was launched.

"Owning" the Amazon has always been bound up in questions of sovereignty. And sovereignty has long been framed by authoritative claims of territorial possession. An extensive history of settler colonialism defines Brazilian attitudes toward the landscape of the Amazon basin, long considered *um vazio demográfico*—a demographic void, a great emptiness to be filled, or at least threaded with a connective infrastructural web at a massive scale. Deployed over centuries, this pervasive infrastructure of possession is an extractive imperial, colonial, and nation-building project, one that sought to connect the coastal centers of government and trade with the vast expanse and immense resource wealth of the Amazon basin. But the colonial reading of demographic emptiness is at odds with the rich, biodiverse ecology of multiple actors within the rainforest's tropical biome—including its indigenous peoples—that in fact comprise the region. Indeed, the complex interactions between the Amazon's soils, waters, flora, fauna, and people produce an entangled ecology that presents significant resistance to these infrastructural lines.

The Portuguese in the Amazon

During the colonial period in Brazil, Portuguese-backed explorers known as *bandeirantes* slashed and burned their way through the immense hinterlands of Brazil in an attempt to establish and defend territorial borders for the Portuguese crown. They copied the practice of *coivara*—the burning of forested lands to clear territory for settlement and agriculture—from indigenous peoples, though these nomadic groups generally managed much smaller parcels of land and migrated often, allowing the forest to regenerate. The *bandeirantes* sought to exploit and mine the land for profit; yet one Brazilian-born explorer, Alexandre Rodrigues Ferreira (1756–1815), took a more "naturalist" approach to his expedition through Amazon territory. Ferreira's botanical interests in Brazil's Amazon region were a contemporaneous foray into the tropical botanical supply chain developing along the equatorial belt of the Portuguese colonies, including India, the West Indies, and East Africa.

Born in the captaincy of Bahia in the Portuguese Viceroyalty of Brazil, Ferreira studied natural history at the University of Coimbra in Portugal. He was sponsored by Queen Maria I of Portugal to explore and map the little-known captaincies in the Amazon basin—Grão-Para, Rio Negro, Mato Grosso, and Cuiabá—to gain an understanding of the economic possibilities of these often disputed territories. Traveling along the fluvial routes of the Amazon River and its tributaries from 1783 through 1792, Ferreira and his team drew maps and collected samples of flora, fauna, and minerals, as well as tools and objects made by the indigenous peoples he encountered. He also wrote philosophical and political commentaries about his observations, included in his report to the crown, *Diário da Viagem Filosófica* (*Diary of a Philosophical Voyage*). Predating Alexander von Humboldt's travels through the Spanish-owned territories of the Amazon and equinoctial regions of South America from 1799 to 1804, Ferreira's account provided a first-hand report of a region rich in flora and fauna, as well as numerous illustrations and ethnological reflections on its indigenous peoples—the territory was certainly not empty. Ferreira's diary and collections, deposited at the Royal Museum of Ajuda and the Royal Museum of Natural History in Lisbon, would not be studied or published until almost 100 years later.[1]

The Amazon territory's floral wealth was not rigorously collected, documented, and classified until the beginning of the nineteenth century, when Dom João VI, succeeding his mother Maria I in 1816 and reigning over the Portuguese kingdom from his throne in Rio de Janeiro, opened Brazil to European scientific expeditions. He welcomed the Austrian Scientific Mission to Brazil in 1817, led by botanist Carl Friedrich Phillip von Martius (1794–1868) and zoologist Johann Baptist von Spix (1781–1826). They began a three-year scientific expedition from Rio de Janeiro in 1817, traveling first overland northward through the eastern inland provinces and then westward along the Amazon River to Tabatinga, and finally returning to Europe in 1820. Brazil's tropical flora and fauna was collected, classified, and remitted to Europe. *Flora Brasiliensis*, initiated in 1840 by Martius but only completed postmortem in 1902 by his colleagues, was the expedition's monumental publication, documenting over 8,000 species of native flora with thousands of lithographic prints.[2] The work included over fifty plates illustrating typical landscapes throughout the country, as well as Martius's map that classified the country into five floristic or phytogeographic regions. Each of the five domains was named after a Greek nymph; the Amazon basin was designated by Martius as the Naiades region, after the nymphs of freshwater rivers and lakes.

The Amazon and Nation-Building

After Dom João VI's son Pedro I claimed independence from Portugal in 1822, declaring himself Emperor of Brazil, agents of the newly established state continued to think of the Amazon as an expansive territory to be mapped, but also defended from other national interests and economically exploited for its valuable resources—particularly rubber and hardwoods. Yet the indigenous populations were significantly ignored in this territorial claim—an irritant to be swept aside in the pursuit of sovereignty, resources, and profit. Upon the overthrow of the emperor Pedro II and the declaration of the First Brazilian Republic in 1889, strengthening the connection of Brazil's so-called empty hinterlands to its burgeoning coastal cities became an urgent nationalist preoccupation, given the concern to protect the Republic's sovereign borders. The westernmost extents of the Amazon at the borders of Bolivia, Peru, and Brazil were particularly contested, due to the valuable rubber trade booming in the Amazon basin at the end of the nineteenth of the century. The highest quality rubber latex was extracted from the wild rubber trees known as seringueira (*Hevea brasiliensis*) dispersed throughout the western territory of Acre.

In 1905, after Brazil had acquired part of Acre from Bolivia, a joint Peruvian-Brazilian expedition was launched, with the intention of peacefully determining the border between the two nations. Euclides da Cunha (1866–1909), the Brazilian author, sociologist, and engineer, embedded himself with the joint expedition. Da Cunha was preparing his second book about the Amazon, tentatively entitled *Lost Paradise*. Due to his untimely death in 1909, this book would never be completed, but a series of seven essays were published posthumously, also in 1909, with the title *À margem da história* (*The Amazon: Land without History*). Da Cunha's descriptive passages of the Amazon region remain powerful today: he wrote of the land as ephemeral, undermined and disappearing as sediment through the riverine networks of the Amazon basin. "Country without land, land without country…Such is the river, then, and such its history: tumultuous, disorganized, incomplete."[3] Yet da Cunha's perspective as author was focused primarily on Brazil's nationalist project of territorial expansion and control. Unlike Ferreira or Martius, he does not describe the diverse flora or fauna, and makes almost no mention of indigenous peoples—and when he does, it is with dismissive disgust. Da Cunha does, however, describe the peak of the rubber boom and its impact on the contract laborers, known as *freguês*, who tapped the wild rubber trees for latex. He sympathized with these men and called for reform; specifically, a labor law ennobling human efforts that would link humans and the land. And in a prescient suggestion for infrastructure in support of both expansion and the labor of extraction, da Cunha's last essay, "Transacreana," includes his proposal to build a railway across the state of Acre. Though the railway was never built, the idea prefigured the BR-364, a diagonal interstate highway project initiated in the 1960s, connecting the southeastern state of São Paulo to the northwestern state of Acre.

In 1907, an exploratory Brazilian government venture, the Comissão de Linhas Telegráficas Estratégicas de Mato Grosso ao Amazonas (CLTEMTA: Commission for a Strategic Telegraph Line from Mato Grosso to Amazonas) was initiated by the Ministry of War in partnership with the newly established Ministry of Agriculture, Industry, and Commerce. Led by Lieutenant Cândido Mariano da Silva Rondon (1865–1958) of the Corps of Military Engineers, the objective was to establish a telegraph line and a series of telegraph stations between the Amazon cities of Cuiabá in the state of Mato Grosso and Porto Velho in the state of Amazonas (Figure 10.1). This nine-year project, extending from 1907 to 1916, became known as the Comissão Rondon.

While the telegraph provided a means of communication between the farthest reaches of the hinterland and the coast, the ambition of the commission was much more than simply laying a cable through the dense forest. It was also a scientific expedition, this time conducted by Brazilians for the purposes of understanding the westernmost reaches of the Amazon basin.[4] The botanist Frederico Carlos Hoehne (1882–1959) of the Museu Nacional joined the Comissão Rondon from 1908 through 1909, identifying and collecting fifty-eight new plant species. Areas of the basin that might be suitable for colonization, agriculture, and grazing were mapped. As part of his team's scientific activity, Rondon collected rich visual documentation, particularly on the indigenous peoples of Mato Grosso, through the commission's innovative Cinematography and Photography Section, led by Thomaz Reis. Lieutenant Rondon himself was half-indigenous, from his mother's side, and in 1910 he would become the first director of Brazil's Serviço de Proteção ao Índio (Indian Protection Service, now Fundação Nacional do Índio/FUNAI). The spirit of scientific inquiry evident in the Comissão Rondon reflected

A Vast Demographic Void

Figure 10.1 Comissão Rondon, construction of the telegraph line at the Rio Jamarí, Amazonas (now Rondônia), ca. 1911.

Source: Photo by Joaquim de Moura Quineau/Acervo do Museu do Índio/Fundação Nacional do Índio, Brazil.

the growing influence of positivism throughout Brazil's elite military academies during the First Brazilian Republic.[5] Positivist ideas supporting progress and development through a rational methodology appealed to the new republic's desire for economic independence and modernization through infrastructure.

Dictatorship and Infrastructure

By the time the First Republic was overthrown with the Revolution of 1930, establishing Getúlio Vargas (1882–1954) as president, Rondon's completed telegraph line was a key infrastructural thread stitched through the Amazon basin. However, riverine transportation along the Amazon River and its tributaries remained the main conduit of access, communication, settlement, and economic development. Domestic resource extraction focused on just two forest products: wild rubber from the

Hevea brasiliensis tree and the wild Brazil nut (also called the Pará nut) from the *Bertholletia excelsa* tree. The prices of both fluctuated significantly on commodity markets, subject to boom and bust cycles.

With the establishment of Vargas's Estado Novo political dictatorship in 1937, the infrastructural links to the Amazon were expanded dramatically. Vargas' *Marcha para o Oeste* (March to the West) initiative, launched in 1938, encouraged agricultural colonization of Brazil's sparsely settled inland territories by subsidizing the migration of poor and working class citizens to the Amazon region.[6] With the promise of a "new life in the Amazon," their migration would not only relieve population pressures in the eastern cities, but would also populate the "void" with citizens loyal to the Brazilian state (Figure 10.2).

Meanwhile, American business interests had already taken hold. The American industrialist Henry Ford (1863–1947) established a rubber-tree plantation at the company town of Fordlândia in the eastern Amazon state of Pará in the 1920s and 1930s, seeking to harvest natural rubber latex for the Ford Motor Company—but the initiative was abandoned by 1934.[7] In 1942, in the context of World War II, Vargas agreed to supply the Allies with wild rubber latex to support wartime mobilization. American finances were directed toward the relocation of thousands of Brazilian migrant workers

Figure 10.2 Jean Pierre Chabloz, *Vida Nova na Amazônia*, Estado Novo recruitment propaganda produced for SEMTA (Special Service for the Mobilization of Workers for the Amazon), 1943.

Source: Jean Pierre Chabloz Collection/Art Museum of the Federal University of Ceará, Brazil.

for the labor-intensive task of tapping naturally occurring rubber trees in the western Amazon state of Acre. But as the synthetic rubber industry developed in the United States in the 1940s, American investment in the Amazon basin would shift rapidly toward hardwood and mineral exploitation, particularly iron ore, manganese, and bauxite. The deforestation and heavy extraction required by both practices required highway infrastructure.

Vargas was deposed as president in 1945 by another military coup, but he would be elected once again in 1954 and his influence would remain throughout Brazil's Fourth Republic, which extended from 1946 until the imposition of the military dictatorship in1964. A new Constitution was drafted in 1946; in addition to reestablishing the separation of powers and basic individual rights, the document asserted the important role of the state in the development of the nation's economy. The 1946 Constitution directed three percent of all federal revenue toward increasing the "economic worth" of the Amazon region.[8] In 1953, the Superintendência do Plano de Valorizaçao Econômica da Amazônia (SPVEA) was established to administer these constitutionally mandated funds, coordinating regional development programs. This would establish both the infrastructural and ideological foundations for subsequent state projects implemented by the military dictatorship in the late 1960s.

During the military dictatorship in Brazil, which began with yet another coup (and the collusion of the United States government) in 1964 and continued for 21 fraught years, the "empty" Amazon again loomed large. In 1966, President Humberto de Alencar Castelo Branco (1897–1967), the first president of the dictatorship, launched *Operação Amazônia* (Operation Amazon), an effort to strengthen the regional economy of the Amazon basin as well as support the migration of landless peasants from Brazil's arid northeast to the Amazon basin. The operation included the establishment of financial and tax incentives to attract private investors.[9] Emphasizing the commonly held perception of the Amazon as a demographic void, Castelo Branco's policy slogan, *Integrar para não Entregar* (Integrate or Surrender) exhorted a clearly nationalist position toward the territory—the Amazon region must be "integrated" socially, culturally, and economically through development, or Brazil would risk abdicating its territory to other nations. As in previous decades, the Brazilian state viewed colonization and occupation of the Amazon region through farming and ranching in newly cleared areas as a necessary step toward securing national borders and alleviating poverty.

General Artur da Costa e Silva (1899–1969) succeeded Castelo Branco's presidency in late 1967, followed shortly afterward by General Emílio Garrastazu Médici (1905–1985) in 1969. Both men significantly hardened the regime, imposing censorship, dissolving Congress, suspending habeas corpus, and sponsoring significant human rights abuses, including torture. Yet at the same time, the regime's new developmentalist policies led to massive economic growth, the so-called *milagre econômico brasileiro*—the Brazilian Miracle. Médici elaborated the ongoing colonization program in the northeast and Amazon regions by initiating the Programa de Integração Nacional (National Integration Program) and launching the Rodovia Transamazônica (Trans-Amazonian Highway) BR-230 east-west highway project in 1970, with significant international funding from the World Bank and the Inter-American Development Bank.[10] The development mission of the military regime shifted significantly to embrace international interests and funding sources for accessing and occupying the Amazon; this direction would continue with Médici's successor, General Ernesto Geisel (1907–1996), who served as president from 1974 through 1979.

As the regime sought to penetrate the interior of the forest with road infrastructure, it incentivized deforestation by both state-owned and international corporations in order to support the development of new agricultural and grazing projects (Figure 10.3). The Rodovia Transamazônica was seen as a pathway to the inexpensive land of the Amazon region through the establishment of physical infrastructure, not unlike Rondon's telegraph line fifty years earlier. Internationally supported farming and ranching initiatives were viewed as extensions of the regime's ongoing interest in resource extraction and economic development.

The military regime's embrace of international interests was exemplified by its support of the Jari Florestal e Agropecuária project, located on the Jari River in the eastern Amazon state of Amapá.

Figure 10.3 Automobiles traversing wooden plank bridges during the construction of the BR-230 Rodovia Transamazônica in Manaus, Amazonas, 1984.

Source: Folhapress, São Paulo, Brazil.

The Jari project included a massive paper-pulp tree plantation of the non-native species *Gmelina arborea* (gamelina or gamhar, native to India) and *Pinus caribaea* (Caribbean pine), and an enormous floating cellulose pulp mill and production factory constructed in Japan and shipped to Brazil. The project was masterminded in 1967 by the American entrepreneur and billionaire Daniel K. Ludwig (1897–1992), a shipping magnate, and continued through 1981.[11] Like the Fordlândia project, this tree plantation initiative would also fail, in part due to the misunderstanding of the nutrient-poor soils of Amazonia—the region's soils lacked phosphates, a condition to which native plant species were well adapted, but that doomed agricultural projects based on large-scale clearance and plantation-scaled cultivation. As with other similar projects, the ongoing incremental social and environmental impacts of the Jari project would prove disastrous.

Burle Marx and the Rise of Environmentalism

Looking back at this long timeline of infrastructural tendrils and resource extractions within the Amazon basin—and the resultant environmental damage—one wonders who grasps the higher moral ground in the questions of Amazon integrity and sovereignty? Enter a radical environmental advocate of the twentieth century: Roberto Burle Marx (1909–1994), the modernist Brazilian landscape architect and activist. His history was not uncompromised—for seven years, Burle Marx served as an appointed member of the military regime's Conselho Federal de Cultura, the Federal Cultural Council, advising the government on cultural matters during an era of censorship and human rights abuses. Yet he was boldly critical of many of its developmentalist policies, particularly those impacting the environment. Several of Burle Marx's eighteen position pieces presented to the council and cultural minister during his tenure from 1967 through 1974 address the destruction of stands of the threatened native tree species *Araucaria angustifolia*, the Paraná pine or araucária, in the southern states of Paraná, Santa Catarina, and Rio Grande do Sul. Through these deliberately environmentalist speeches, Burle Marx positioned nature, conservation, and ecology as inseparable from the national and cultural expression of a rapidly modernizing Brazil.

In 1969, Burle Marx addressed the deforestation of the northern states of the Amazon basin for agricultural and grazing purposes in a speech entitled "Forest Politics and the Destruction of Forests." Here, he recounted the Amazon research executed by the forester Dr. Dammis Heinsdijk and others, who argued against the rapid and selective lumbering exploitation and extraction of native tree species, including *Swietenia macrophylla* (mahogany or mongo) and *Cordia goeldiana* (freijó) hardwoods as well as *Cedrela spp.* (cedar or cedro) softwoods.[12] In 1976, two years after stepping down from the council, Burle Marx returned to the Brazilian Senate to present a landmark deposition that advocated for the environmental protection of the Amazon region. He argued against the regime's policies of agricultural colonization and economic exploitation. He sought to recast the vast forest as site of national ecological and cultural heritage, meriting protection and preservation by the state. His speech attacked the regime's ongoing support of international corporations profiting from the Amazon. He reframed the forest through a nationalist lens, as an environmental resource and point of pride for Brazilian citizens. He specifically addressed an inherent problem within Brazil's Forestry Code: the stipulation that a property owner could legally deforest 50 percent of the native trees on a site—often cleared with fire—and replant it with non-native species for a harvesting profit.[13] This, he argued, was not reforestation, but an irreversible act of environmental destruction.

In the same Senate deposition, Burle Marx described a contemporary version of *coivara*, the slash-and-burn clearing of the forest by fire. He cited evidence of "the largest fire in the history of the planet, detected by satellites," an enormous forest fire over thousands of acres of land intentionally set by the multinational corporation Volkswagen do Brasil to clear trees from its experimental cattle ranch, the Fazenda Cristalino, in the southeastern corner of the Amazonian state of Pará.[14] Initiated by the São Paulo-based German car manufacturer Volkswagen do Brasil in 1973, with profitable economic incentives provided by the Brazilian military regime, the Fazenda Cristalino was a 140,000 hectare (540 square mile) territory along the Rio Cristalino, a tributary of the Rio Araguaia at the eastern state line of southern Pará. In 1975, Volkswagen do Brasil initiated a massive clearing fire, as part of a plan to transform 70,000 hectares (270 square miles) of the territory's native forest into cattle pasture—at half of its total area, this was the maximum that could be legally deforested per the Forestry Code. The size of the fire, seen in imagery captured by the United States NASA space station Skylab, was significantly exaggerated in the international press, and Burle Marx too exaggerated its scale—intentionally or not—in his Federal Senate deposition, describing the fire as destroying a forest "the size of Lebanon."[15]

Wolfgang Sauer (1930–2013), the German chief executive of Volkswagen do Brasil, was upset by the bad publicity. But Burle Marx refused to back down when asked, via a letter from Volkswagen's public relations group on July 8, 1976, to rescind his exaggerated comments to the Senate. Rather, he wrote a scathing response—and indeed, an articulate argument in defense of nature, and the Amazon—in a personal letter addressed to Sauer on November 4, 1976, stating that:

> I will never make such a denial … I don't believe in selective, trained fires. In addition to "weeds," it is likely that the fire also burned "noisy" macaws, "filthy" armadillos, "vicious" jaguars, "venomous" snakes, certainly large trees and perhaps even some "treacherous" Indian. Do you know that the "shrubs and other types of forest" that you mentioned were objects of admiration and fascination for such illustrious Germans as Martius and Humboldt, who traveled to the Amazon in the nineteenth century—and by 1810, Martius, outraged, denounced the massacre of such precious flora. You have to understand that it is my obligation to oppose everything that I consider an ecological crime … the sacrifice of nature is irreversible."[16]

By characterizing Volkswagen do Brasil's Fazenda Cristalino fire as an ecological crime, Burle Marx poignantly shifted the opinion of Brazilian citizens—and their legislators—toward a recognition that the Amazon represented something much more valuable than an undeveloped territory with potential economic profit. An ethical and nationalist sentiment was invoked: the Brazilian forest should not be sacrificed to exploitative international interests. Its so-called demographic emptiness, the *vazio demográfico*, was not empty at all—its biodiversity was measureless, yet vulnerable. In many ways, its infrastructure was complete: its interconnected ecological network was as vast as the very scale of the basin.

By 1986, the experimental Fazenda Cristalino cattle ranch would be undone by both labor abuses and environmental failures. However, it was not until 1989 that the main recommendation of Burle Marx's Senate deposition would be actualized, with control of the Amazon region released from the Ministry of Agriculture's profit-driven legislative grasp and transferred to Brazil's federal environmental agency, SEMA. The biologist Paulo Nogueira Neto (1922–2019) formed SEMA, or the Secretaria Especial do Meio Ambiente (Special Secretary for the Environment) in 1973. The environmentalist view supported by Burle Marx and others suggested that the Amazon should be understood and protected as an environmental asset—indeed, the lungs of the planet—rather than as an underdeveloped territory to be brought to heel with massive infrastructure projects that would expand agriculture, farming, ranching, and mining initiatives for international profit.

Conclusion

Today, scientists note that the Amazon rainforest fixes huge amounts of the planet's carbon dioxide emissions, serving as a massive carbon sink. In turn, it produces twenty percent of the world's oxygen. The biodiversity of the Amazon's tropical and subtropical broadleaf forests is extraordinary, providing habitat for over 40,000 plant species, 2.5 million insect species, 2,200 fish species, and 400 mammal species.[17] Yet the settler-colonialist view of the Amazon as a great void to be occupied—and an untapped source of wealth—created the path dependence of infrastructural development as necessary to support agriculture, mining, and timber extraction. This perspective of the forest as tabula rasa has been difficult to countermand, despite appeals for environmental protection by Roberto Burle Marx and others. Deforestation rates in Brazil have been trending upward since 2012, rapidly escalating during Jair Bolsonaro's presidential term that began in January 2019. The Bolsonaro administration has refused to enforce environmental protections, and has actively encouraged the rapacious clearing and burning of the forest, returning to an earlier conception of the Amazon basin as a source of wealth and profit for both the state and private investors.

The dire impact of these forest politics are clear: as early as July 2018, ten prescient Brazilian scientists concluded that "the abandonment of deforestation control policies and the political support for predatory agricultural practices" would make it impossible for Brazil to reduce its carbon dioxide emissions in accordance with the 2016 Paris Agreement of the United Nations Framework Convention on Climate Change. Wholesale clearance for farming and livestock has destroyed habitat and put the entire Amazon ecosystem at risk (Figure 10.4).[18] In the dry months of 2019 and 2020, forest fires increased significantly, and the crisis around the COVID-19 coronavirus pandemic has not only disproportionately impacted the indigenous peoples of the Amazon basin, but has served as a distraction for even more clearing fires to occur without oversight.

Given our understanding of the global scale of the climate emergency, we possess a broader understanding of the relationships of the equator and the poles, of the emission (or sequestration) of carbon, and of the influence of the atmosphere on the oceans. Though we must think differently of sovereignty and borders, infrastructure and networks, with new post-territorial concepts of biomes and watersheds, of atmospheres and oceans, we must not risk falling into a settler colonialist variant of environmentalism that views the Amazon as yet another resource for all. It has never been a *vazio demográfico*, despite that construction by the Brazilian state. Rather, it is an ancestral homeland to indigenous

A Vast Demographic Void

Figure 10.4 Cattle grazing on a tract of cleared Amazon forest, near Novo Progresso in the state of Pará, 2014.

Source: Photograph by Lalo de Almeida/*The New York Times*/Redux.

occupants who have lived there for tens of thousands of years. Indeed, as Burle Marx would assert half a century ago, "the sacrifice of nature is irreversible." Yet a multisovereign policy of protection and management of the Amazon rainforest that acknowledges and respects the presence of indigenous peoples while holistically addressing our global environmental condition is a necessary way forward.

Notes

1 "Diary of a Philosophical Voyage" (*Diário da Viagem Filosófica*) was published in the *Revista do Instituto Histórico e Geográfico Brasileiro* in 1887.
2 Carl Friedrich Philipp von Martius and August Wilhelm Eichler, *Flora brasiliensis: Enumeratio plantarum in Brasilia* (Munich and Leipzig: R. Oldenbourg, 1840–1906). Martius's works also include *Nova genera et species plantarum brasiliensium* (1823–1832) and *Historia naturalis palmarum* (1823–1850).
3 Euclides da Cunha, *The Amazon: Land Without History*, trans. Ronald Sousa (New York: Oxford University Press, 2006), 11.
4 According to anthropologist Edgar Roquette-Pinto (1884–1954), who joined the Comissão Rondon in 1912, "the construction of the telegraph line was the pretext. The activity of scientific exploration was everything." See his field diary, *Rondônia: Anthropologia—Ethnographia*, Archivos do Museu Nacional do Rio de Janeiro, Vol. 20 (Rio de Janeiro: Imprensa Nacional, 1917).
5 Dominichi Miranda de Sá, "Inventário da natureza do Brasil: As atividades científicas da Comissão Rondon," *História, Ciências, Saúde-Manguinhos* 15, no. 3 (July–September 2008): 779–810.
6 Cassiano Ricardo, *Marcha para Oeste: a influência da bandeira na formação social e política do Brasil* (Rio de Janeiro: José Olympio, 1940).
7 For an excellent analysis, see Greg Grandin, *Fordlândia: The Rise and Fall of Henry Ford's Forgotten Jungle City* (New York: Metropolitan Books, 2009).
8 *Constitution of the United States of Brazil, 1946*, Title Nine, General Provisions, Article 199: "In the execution of the plan to increase the economic worth of the Amazon Valley, the Union shall invest, during at least

twenty consecutive years, an amount not less than three per cent of its tax revenue." English translation by the American Brazilian Association, New York, 1946.
9 SUDAM, *Investimentos privilegiados na Amazônia* (Belém: SUDAM, 1966), 226. See also SUDAM, *Operação Amazônia: Discursos* (Belém: SUDAM, 1968). The territory of Amazônia Legal (the administrative unit defined in 1966 as the Brazilian states of Acre, Amapá, Amazonas, Pará, Rondônia, Roraima, Tocantins, part of Mato Grosso, and most of Maranhão) today comprises 59% of the area of Brazil, but holds less than 12% of the nation's population.
10 Decreto-Lei No. 1.106, signed into law on June 16, 1970 by President Médici, established the *Programa de Integração Nacional* and launched the construction of the Trans-Amazonian Highway. See www.planalto.gov.br/ccivil_03/decreto-lei/1965-1988/Del1106.htm, accessed July 1, 2020.
11 Loren McIntyre, "Jari: A Billion Dollar Gamble," *National Geographic* 157, no. 5 (May 1980): 686–711.
12 Roberto Burle Marx, "Politica florestal e destruição das florests" (Forest Politics and the Destruction of Forests) *Cultura: Conselho Federal de Cultura* (Ministério da Educação e Cultura) 3, no. 21 (March 1969): 34–41.
13 The Código Florestal Brasileiro (Brazilian Forestry Code) was instituted by Decreto No. 23.793 on January 23, 1934, during the Vargas administration; it was revoked and replaced by Lei No. 4.771 on September 15, 1965, under the military dictatorship's President Castelo Branco. For the full text of the 1965 Forestry Code referenced by Burle Marx, see www2.camara.leg.br/legin/fed/lei/1960-1969/lei-4771-15-setembro-1965-369026-publicacaooriginal-1-pl.html, accessed July 1, 2020. The most recent update to the Código Florestal, Lei No. 12.651, was signed into law on May 25, 2012, by President Dilma Rousseff (b. 1947).
14 Roberto Burle Marx, "Depoimento no Senado Federal," June 1976, reprinted in *Arte e Paisagem: Conferências Escolhidas*, ed. José Tabacow (São Paulo: Nobel, 1987), 71. Translation from the Portuguese by the author.
15 For an excellent history of the Fazenda Cristalino, see Antoine Acker, *Volkswagen in the Amazon: The Tragedy of Global Development in Modern Brazil* (Cambridge and New York: Cambridge University Press, 2017).
16 Roberto Burle Marx, "Conviver com a natureza," in *Burle Marx: Homenagem à Natureza*, eds Paulo e Lucia Victoria Peltier de Queiroz and Leonardo Boff (Petrópolis: Editora Vozes Ltda., 1979), 93–94. Translation from the Portuguese by the author.
17 Juan de Onís, *The Green Cathedral: Sustainable Development of Amazônia* (Oxford: Oxford University Press, 1992), 34. See also the World Wildlife Fund, www.worldwildlife.org/ecoregions/nt0168, accessed July 1, 2020.
18 Pedro R.R. Rochedo and others, "The Threat of Political Bargaining to Climate Mitigation in Brazil," *Nature Climate Change* 8 (July 2018): 695–698, https://doi.org/10.1038/s41558-018-0213-y, accessed July 1, 2020.

PART IV

Flows

# 11

VISUALIZING THE VALENS AQUEDUCT IN EARLY MODERN ISTANBUL

Fatma Sarıkaya Işık and Pelin Yoncacı Arslan

The fourth-century Valens Aqueduct has sustained its continuous operation of supplying water to Istanbul, to the Byzantine and Ottoman capital city. The intra-mural water bridge is a monumental link between the Third and the Fourth hills occupied by the two most prestigious Ottoman complexes, and for centuries, it prevailed as the main water distribution point to the higher grounds of the city. Thus, the Aqueduct of Valens figured prominently in the early-modern depictions of the city. Artists illustrated the water structure in city maps, bird's eye views, miniatures, portolan atlases, and panoramic depictions starting from the fifteenth century. Indeed, representations of Istanbul's topographical and symbolic transformations never failed to include the aqueduct as a prominent feature of the urban landscape. As early as the fifteenth century, the Byzantine monument was embedded in the Ottoman historical topography and the collective memory of Constantinople/Istanbul. To analyze the ways in which this water infrastructure was represented in the following three centuries, this paper presents a selection of city depictions that reveal the aqueduct's turbulent status and changing reception in Early Modern Istanbul. The investigation uncovers alterations in the reception, which translated it from a water-conveyer into a resilient monument in the Ottoman capital.

In A.D. 356, the orator Libanius of Antioch extolled his native city's superiority by praising its water abundance.[1] The flourishing springs accompanied by fountains and aqueducts were among the most admired features of a city he described as the "capital of the Nymphs." He then disparaged the empires newly designated capital, Constantinople, for its crucial defect in the matter of water. Despite its strategic location over the Bosporus and the well-protected natural harbors, the "New Rome," unlike "old" Rome, had long been compelled to transport water into the densely populated city center.[2] Without abundant supply, the expanding capital extended infrastructure across the Thracian Peninsula in order to reach remote water sources. Thus, it is no surprise that the completion of the 971 meters-long aqueduct made the emperor Valens the true founder of Constantinople. During Valens' decennial ceremony in 373, Senator Themistius praised the emperor, saying that he had "turned the beloved from an inanimate to an animate state" as he "breathed life into this beautiful and desirable body," and that "the city is truly a city and no longer a mere sketch."[3]

As one of the essential components of the new capital's *opera publica*, the Thracian Water Network was first initiated by Constantius II as a long-distance supply line reaching from the Istranca Mountains and finalized by building a monumental aqueduct between the Third and Fourth hills inside the city walls. Named after Valens, this fourth-century aqueduct is one of the rare surviving Late Antique monuments in Istanbul today (Figure 11.1). The long bridge is partially double-arched and reaches 28–29 meters at its maximum height.[4] For many centuries, it prevailed as the main water distribution point of the *intra muros*.[5] Following its waterline entering the city from the north of the Gate

DOI: 10.4324/9781003093756-16

Figure 11.1 A contemporary view of the Valens Aqueduct over Atatürk Boulevard, Istanbul.

Source: Photograph courtesy of Joseph Heathcott.

of Charisius (*Edirnekapı*), the monumental aqueduct was positioned in near-parallel to the northern arm of the Mese, the main east–west thoroughfare of the city.[6] It bridged the imperial complexes, the Forum of Theodosius and the Church of the Holy Apostles. Distributing water to the city's higher grounds at an elevation of about 56–57 meters above sea level, the aqueduct supplied any structure over the 35m contour level, including the reservoirs of the Mokios, Aetius and Aspar, Constantianae, Anastasianae, and Carosianae Baths, the Nymphaeum Maximum near Theodosius' Forum, the Binbirdirek covered cistern and the cistern of the Forty Martyrs situated on the Mese.[7] Sources indicate considerable expenses for the structure's restoration and maintenance operations throughout the Byzantine rule.[8]

After the Ottoman conquest, as part of Mehmet II's substantial re-glorification process, engineers enhanced the former urban water distribution layout and restored many Byzantine structures, including the Valens Aqueduct and the Thracian Water Network.[9] Consequently, due to the abundant water provision options, the immediate environs of the aqueduct emerged as a prominent position in the city, accumulating new imperial monuments as a result. Mehmed II constructed the First Ottoman Palace (1458) on the eastern end of the aqueduct, close to the former Forum of Theodosius. The vast market area built up around the Palace transformed this region into a crowded residential and commercial zone. On the western end of the water structure, the sultan placed the first Friday mosque of the capital, the Fatih Mosque Complex, on the Holy Apostles' former site. Additional water supply lines were constructed as well, namely the Halkalı Channels, feeding the Imperial Palace of Topkapı at the eastern tip of the peninsula, ensuring a broad intra-mural water distribution network connected to the system of Valens Aqueduct.[10] Reaching from the north-west of the city's Land Walls at an altitude of 55–65 meters, these lines were recognized as the higher channels of the city, distributed through the Valens Aqueduct.

Reflecting the monument's crucial bridging role within the water supply systems, as well as its strategic position between the two most prestigious Ottoman complexes, the Aqueduct of Valens figured prominently in the early-modern depictions of the city. Artists illustrated the water structure in city maps, bird's-eye views, miniatures, portolan atlases, and panoramic depictions starting from the fifteenth century. Indeed, representations of the topographical and symbolic transformations of Istanbul never failed to include the aqueduct as a prominent feature of the urban landscape. As early as the fifteenth century, then, the Byzantine monument was embedded in the Ottoman historical topography and the collective memory of Constantinople/Istanbul. However, what is less often recognized is the ways in which this water infrastructure was represented in the following three centuries. In order to trace subsequent representations of the Valens Aqueduct, we will examine a selection of images that reveal this artifact's turbulent status and changing reception in Early Modern Istanbul. The investigation uncovers alterations in the aqueduct's reception, which translated it from a water-conveyer into a resilient monument in the Ottoman capital.

Beyond the Functional Operations

Among many bird's-eye views from Christoforo Buondelmonti's *Liber Insularum Archipelagi*, the late fifteenth century Düsseldorf manuscript has been identified as remarkably different due to its inclusion of details that could have only been derived from first-hand experience following the Ottoman conquest (Figure 11.2).[11] As Ian R. Manners has argued, the drawing was the first to speak to the conquest and the subsequent urban transformation while still demonstrating Buondelmonti's typical cityscape: buildings with domes and visually imposing columnar monuments scattered around the partially double-walled city.[12] The Düsseldorf view is one of the earliest to celebrate the cultural hybridity of Ottoman Istanbul, affirming the city's changeable, rather than eternal, status.[13]

What is remarkable for our purposes is that this version was the first map depicting the Aqueduct of Valens as a significant feature of the urban landscape. In the image, the water bridge conspicuously occupies the central focal point and connects the Fatih Mosque and the Old Palace to the Hippodrome and the Topkapı Palace. The structure is depicted in oblique perspective and detailed with a water channel over its bold arches, alluding to the city's restored Byzantine waterways. Of course, the map does not offer a "real" fifteenth-century urban picture, yet the incorporation of the aqueduct demonstrates the significant presence and materiality of the bridge, and would have required the first-hand experience to draw.[14] Its continuous rhythmic columnar facade forms the backdrop for the label "Constantinopolis." Here, at a very central point of the illustration, the artist assigned more than a functional role to a water bridge: it symbolizes Mehmed II's renovated cityscape both in terms of its monumentality as well as its role in supplying water for the sultan's two principal architectural structures: his mosque complex and the Topkapı Palace. As such, contemporaries would have recognized this large-scale infrastructural project as a symbol of the "new" capital's glory.

The aqueduct visually connects the Ottoman Sultanate to a long history of imperial glory by placing his own commissioned works into dialogue with the city's colossal Byzantine monuments like the Column of Justinian. A mid-fifteenth century traveler to the city effused over the great size of the Valens Aqueduct:

> … There is also a bridge there, one of the wonders of the world; her breadth puts the rapporteur in such a position to describe her, that he comes to the point of being pulled. At last pictures are so much so that they cannot be described.[15]

The Aqueduct of Valens was definitely one of the most "visible" monuments of Early Modern Istanbul, and its inclusion in the Düsseldorf version contributed to the establishment of a multifaceted imperial identity for the young Ottoman state.[16] Buondelmonti's representation reserved a permanent seat for the aqueduct in the subsequent images of the capital.

Figure 11.2 Map of Constantinople by Cristoforo Buondelmonti, Düsseldorf copy, ink drawing, ca. 1481.

Source: By permission of the University and State Library Düsseldorf. University and State Library Düsseldorf, Ms G 13, fol.54r., urn:nbn:de:hbz:061:1-36224

Embedded in the Ottoman Cityscape

During the Early Modern period, the empire developed several cartographic traditions, including diverse samples of the private, scientific, religious, and artistic forms of mapmaking and the state-sponsored illustrations for military, administrative and architectural use.[17] Among these, the *şehnames* constitute one essential and common Ottoman cartography genre. Developed under the sultans' patronage, the *şehnames* comprised illustrated royal histories of the empire's cultural, political, and military achievements, often with the capital's urban landscape as background.[18] Several examples of this cartographic genre include depictions of the Valens Aqueduct.

The first of these, the miniature map of Matrakçı Nasuh from the manuscript *Mecmu-i Menazil*, also known as *Beyan-ı Menazil-i Sefer-i Irakeyn-ı Sultan Süleyman*, displays a representative collection of monuments of sixteenth-century Istanbul (Figure 11.3). At that time, Süleyman I's assertion as true heir of the Byzantine legacy underlined the condition of a universal state unified under one single rule.[19] Reflecting this policy, numerous old religious buildings were converted and adapted to new usages; yet the Byzantine architectural traces were still perceptible within the cityscape, even after sixty years of Ottoman rule.[20] In the manuscript, Matrakçı placed the map in a double-page composition, where the walled peninsula stood on the right half and the districts of Üsküdar, Galata, and Eyüp on the left. Two axes provide a visual anchor: the north–south axis connects Galata Tower to the Old Palace, and the east–west axis connects the Hagia Sophia Mosque to the Fatih Mosque.[21] The Valens Aqueduct, a single-story, eight-arched bridge with a reduced span, is not depicted on one of these emphasized pictorial axes, yet lies very close to the latter, to the left of its actual position

Figure 11.3 Map of Constantinople in *Beyan-ı menazil-i sefer-i Irakayn-ı Sultan Süleyman*, ca. 1537.

Source: By permission of the Istanbul University Library, TY05964/8b-9a.

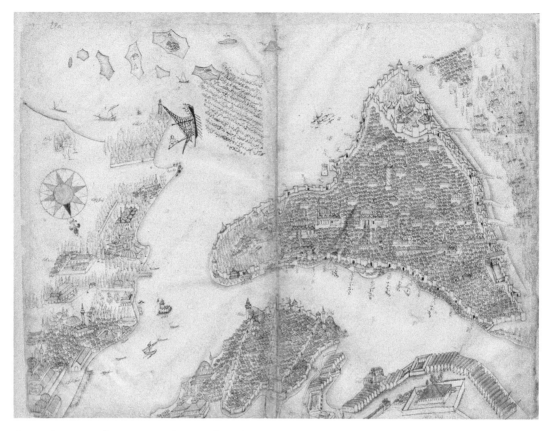

Figure 11.4 Map of Constantinople in *Kitab-ı Bahriye*, ca. 1629.

Source: © STAATSBIBLIOTHEK ZU BERLIN: Preussischer Kulturbesitz, Orientabteilung, Diez A fol. 57. By permission of the Staatsbibliothek zu Berlin-Preussischer Kulturbesitz, Orientabteilung.

between the Fatih Mosque and the Old Palace. Visible from elevation, the water structure creates an illusion of a colonnaded street mirroring the imperial thoroughfare, the "Divanyolu," extending between the *Edirnekapı* and the northern section of the Byzantine *Mese*. Despite this topographical inaccuracy, the bright blue color placed under each archway evokes flowing water as a tactile reference to the *raison d'être* of the structure.

In the seventeenth century, however, Ottoman portolan charts record a more expansive topographical illustration of the capital. The Berlin-57 version of Piri Reis' *Kitab-ı Bahriye*, for example, presents a broader Istanbul with Galata and Üsküdar districts and the Princes' Islands in a bird's-eye view from a northern point (Figure 11.4). Within the peninsula's triangular borders, the residential texture covers the entire urban landscape interwoven with the palaces, Byzantine colossal columns, and the frequent mosques with domes and minarets. Next to the Fatih Mosque, one sees the Valens Aqueduct labeled as *Eski Kemerler* (Old Arches) depicted in elevation view against the oblique view of the composition. The view displays a strong sense of place when locating the water bridge accurately in front of the Şehzade Mosque. Most notably, the topographical condition bridged by the aqueduct, namely the level difference between the ends, is clearly depicted by the flat upper line and the gradual decrease in the arches' heights underneath—showing the inclination of the terrain.

Our final maps are the Ottoman water supply maps documented by a central group of royal architects in the form of long rolls. These drawings recorded the water structures including the aqueducts, sewers, water domes, and distribution pools. Specifically, they provide elaborate visuals displaying the

Visualizing the Valens Aqueduct

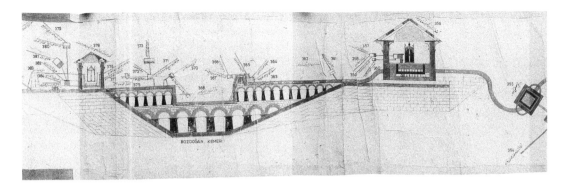

Figure 11.5 Süleymaniye Water Supply Map, second half of the eighteenth century.
Source: By permission of the Turkish and Islamic Arts Museum, Istanbul, H. 3337.

intra-mural flow of various water networks and the structures they feed. Multiple architectural and topographical details regarding the Valens' water bridge and the urban layout are visible in Köprülü (1672) and Beylik (1748) and Süleymaniye (the second half of the eighteenth century) Water Distribution Maps.[22] Among these, the Köprülü Map renders the city in profile view along with monuments drawn from elevations.[23] The two sides of the waterline are viewed from opposite directions. In the line of the monuments, the aqueduct is represented as two fragments of a stylized bridge with a collapsed section in between. This part depicts the eastern upper section destroyed after the earthquake of 1509 and restored by Bayezid II immediately.[24] It is labeled as "big arch at *At Pazarı*." The Beylik Water Distribution Map, however, illustrates a more realistic picture by showing the two-story arched structure sitting on the topography with one end collapsed.[25] The damaged end and the water channels passing at the top of the structure represents the monument "as it is" in the eighteenth century. Similar to the Köprülü Folio, its label refers to the place and reads "the big arch at *At Pazarı*."

Different from the Köprülü and Beylik folios, the Süleymaniye Water Supply Map provides a technical drawing of the aqueduct (Figure 11.5).[26] It represents the water structures supplying the Süleymaniye Mosque Complex, with detailed depictions and labeling of the pools, water towers, dams, cisterns, and other elements. The map includes in-situ specifications marking the points of distribution, the destroyed section, and the water tower. The aqueduct's outline is shown as a double-line drawing in blue (representing the water flow) and arches are seen in elevation with a single-line cross-hatched grid showing the construction pattern. The lower arches form large squares composed of massive stone blocks, while the upper arches are small, with small stones and brickwork, all reflecting accurately the physical condition of the standing Aqueduct.

The examples discussed above reveal that the intra-mural water infrastructure was already among the Ottoman capital's innumerable wonders in the sixteenth century. The depictions did not necessarily situate the aqueduct as one of the city's icons, yet suggest that it was hardly possible to miss such a large-scale urban artifact so close to the Fatih Mosque. In *Beyan-ı Menazil*, a work filled with many symbolic interpretations, the first image one encounters is Istanbul's miniature map.[27] Among many other politically and religiously significant buildings, the otherwise utilitarian Valens Aqueduct stands in monumental form. The book was commissioned as part of Süleyman I's preparations for the military campaign to control Mesopotamia, and it illustrated in miniature the one hundred and thirty cities, towns, and places where the sultan visited during his marches with the Ottoman army. Therefore it reflects an extended concern of the Ottoman Empire's power and legitimization for military expansion.[28] In this context, without a doubt, the Valens Aqueduct strongly manifested and further strengthened the Byzantine water infrastructure's role in the symbolical portrayal of the capital.

The *Kitab-Bahriye*, on the other hand, provides a more convenient setting for the water bridge to emerge as an undisputed urban landmark. In the view, the standardized residential features in the background accentuate the palaces, the aqueduct, and the other Byzantine structures along with the monumental mosques that dominated the city from the sixteenth century onwards. The Byzantine structure is underlined as a comparable urban node within this Islamicized topography. As the *Kitab-ı Bahriye* manuscripts covers the entire Mediterranean region, the image of the imperial capital within the book further manifests "the Ottoman self-representation within the global view of Mediterranean."[29] In this context, the Byzantine water bridge was included in a wider picture denoting the symbolic affirmation of the Ottomans in the region.

Perhaps most importantly, the water distribution maps illustrate the water infrastructure in detail from the natural source to the city's heart, bringing the entire cycle of water into the representation of the Ottoman imperial landscape. The drawings depicts the water network extending from the hinterlands and connecting to the urban core defined by the Land Walls, thus recorded the Ottoman rule over the natural sources. both These folios render multiple elevations of the aqueduct along with the continuous flow of supply lines in both technical and representational terms. By doing this, the views did not implement a complete city layout, yet still documented the significant landmarks and critical water structures. In these depictions, the most notable and recognizable element of infrastructure is the Aqueduct of Valens, which emerges as the leading water actor sustaining urban life within the capital.

The Lasting Edifice in the Ever-Changing Skyline

None of the attempts for visualizing the Ottoman capital had achieved the level of accuracy as Melchior Lorichs' panoramic description.[30] His long-profile view of Istanbul (1559), as Nigel Westbrook demonstrates, presents an empirical observation supported by perspectival geometry and allegorical pulse.[31] From sheets, VII to IX, the artist situates "the center of the city" that was bordered with the Column of Constantine and the Mosque of Beyazıt. At the intersection of sheets XI and XII, Valens' water bridge gently ascends through the sky over other structures. It is rendered with substantial precision since the illustrator most probably relied on the information recorded from several observation points in Pera.[32]

Lorichs' viewpoint is not an exception. From the sixteenth to the nineteenth century, European artists created textual and pictorial renderings scanning the northern ridges of the city horizontally.[33] This was after the reformulation of the northern cityscape by the chief architect Sinan's massive mosque complexes built atop the vacant hills—the most symbolic of all being the Süleymaniye Mosque.[34] The urban development built on the northern terraces that rose from the Haliç Sea Walls, and the commercial and residential districts along the waterside created an alternative representational front for the city. This crucial shift in the viewing standpoint gave the Byzantine aqueduct, one more time, a leading role as it figured prominently in the monumental panoramas of the city.

In Lorich's panorama and many others, the Ottoman urban landscape has been conceptualized as a collage of old and new buildings. The peninsula is detached and underlined by the body of water, with the low-rise sea walls, city gates, and continuous rows of harbor facilities on the waterfront. The colossal mosque complexes with multiple domes and vertical minarets dominate the horizon. These impressive complexes create visual gravity that simultaneously highlights the natural topography in a rather indirect manner. Finally, the minarets and columnar monuments as vertical posts appear as the punctuating finishes of the city views. In these depictions, the Valens Aqueduct presents prominent horizontal accent stretching between the hills just below the level of the mosque complexes. Its strong relationship with the topography establishes the "imageability" of the water bridge, which further promotes the skyline's significance.[35] As such, the topography is augmented through the water bridge, and the bridge has been recognized with the urban landscape. Furthermore, the linear body of the infrastructure determines the upper "edge" of the capital, thus anchoring the aqueduct to the panorama's spatial configuration. This association established the aqueduct as vital in every subsequent panoramic view. The city's celebrated and embellished northern heights became inseparable from the monumental water infrastructure. The nineteenth-century traveler Thomas Allom further affirmed this condition by pairing the aqueduct with the monumental Süleymaniye while reporting from Pera: "… the aqueduct of Valens stretching from hill to hill, and seen in almost every direction … In the perspective is, the city of Constantinople, displaying its most conspicuous objects—the Mosque of Solimanie, and the Aqueduct of Valens."[36]

The Life-Giving River

The Valens Aqueduct sustained its critical role in Constantinopolitan life throughout the centuries. Successive emperors and sultans expended immense sums on its maintenance and security. The urban representations discussed here reveal the varied approaches to visualizing the city as a topographical entity and the aqueduct as an embedded structure within. Putting aside the pictorial distinctions, they constitute episodic portraits representing changing views of the aqueduct's status in the urban landscape. The rhythmic repetition of its arches proved a powerful visual register of rulers' efforts to solve the most fundamental problem of the *payitaht* (the Ottoman capital); the insufficient supply of fresh water. Thus, the frequent displays of the water bridge in the Ottoman imperial landscape imagery have been visually linked to the broader representation of aspired, attained, and flowed water to the *intra-muros*. Thus, beyond its utilitarian function, the aqueduct has achieved the status of a monument, a process underscored and amplified through the numerous depictions of the bridge in city portraits—in Buondelmonti's drawing, for example, it literally connects the old Byzantine city to the new Ottoman capital. Moreover, the diverse panoramic views produced for travellers recognized the aqueduct as a palpable marker on the skyline. As such, the water structure eventually accumulated most of the attributions of a landmark: function, conspicuous design, symbolic meaning, and historical prominence.[37]

Several literary accounts from Byzantine and Ottoman periods have cast the city's transported water within allegory, often referring to it as a human-made river. From the fourth-century Constantinople, the archbishop Gregory of Nazianzus described the Thracian Water Network as a "subterranean and aerial river," thus, recognized the extensive water line as a stream.[38] As we read from Themistius in the beginning, the Thracian Network had a primary significance in "animating" the city where it had not been capable of making a "revelry" before the water flowed through the aerial river of Valens. It was the aqueduct's water that brought pleasure and joy to numerous *nymphaeums*. In Ottoman Turkish, the aqueduct is called *kemer-i* (arches) *âb-ı revan* (stream).[39] Ottomans sources reported the freshness and liveliness of the capital when sufficient water circulated through the fountains, pools, baths, and ablution wells of the city.[40] As the sixteenth-century poet Eyyübi writes, such plentitude "brought all friends to new lives," which is "like the water of life."[41] Moreover, Ottomans bolstered the water narratives by relating them with the watery genesis of the world and the heavenly springs, as seen in the Quranic verse "… we made from water every living thing."[42] During one of the Ottoman renovations, a couplet was etched on the forty-fifth pier that reads: "Şad-ab kılıp alemi izzile Sultan Mustafa, Bala-yı tak-ı ser—bülend maü'l-hayata navedan,"/"the Sultan Mustafa has supplied the world with the honorable water and made the long bridge a lofty vessel for the water of life."[43] The Byzantine aqueduct was indeed praised for its central place among the city's monuments. Its lengthy body was the great artery of the city, a river bringing Istanbul "*âb-ı hayat*"—the water of life.

Notes

1 Libanius, *Or.* 11.270.
2 *Codex Justinianus*, 11.42.7. For a comprehensive survey regarding the water supply system, see James Crow, Jonathan Bardill, and Richard Bayliss, *The Water Supply of Byzantine Constantinople* (London: Society for the Promotion of Roman Studies, 2008).

3 Themistius, *Oratio*, 11.151a-2b and 11.151c–152b; cf. 150a–d.
4 Crow, Bardill and Bayliss, *The Water Supply*, 118. Also see Paul Magdalino, "Aristocratic Oikoi in the Tenth and Eleventh Regions of Constantinople," in *Byzantine Constantinople: Monuments, Topography and Everyday Life*, ed. Nevra Necipoğlu (Leiden: Brill, 2001), 68.
5 Paolo Bono, James Crow, and Richard Bayliss, "The Water Supply of Constantinople: Archaeology and Hydrogeology of an Early Medieval City," *Environmental Geology* 40 (October, 2001): 1325. Also see Jer. *Chron.* s.a. 373; Them. *Or.* 11.150d–152b, 13.168a–c; 14.183c; Greg. Naz. *Or.* 33.6; Soc. 4.8.7; *Parastaseis syntomoi chronikai* 74; Cedrenus, *History*, 543, 544; Theoph. a.m. 5860; Zon. 13.16.33–35.
6 Malalas, 18.17; Chron. Pasch, 618–619; Cedrenus, *History*, 1.685.
7 Crow, Bardill, and Bayliss, *The Water Supply*, maps 13, 14, 15.
8 Paul Magdalino, "Medieval Constantinople," in *Studies on the History and Topography of Byzantine Constantinople*, ed. P. Magdalino (Aldershot: Variorum, 2007), 19; Mango, *Le développement urbain de Constantinople (IV–VII siècle)* (Paris, 1985; 2nd edn. Paris: Diffusion de Boccard, 1990), 20, 41, 60.
9 Mertol Tulum, *Tursun Bey: Tarih-I Ebü'l-Feth* (İstanbul: İstanbul Fetih Cemiyeti, 1977), 67, 68–70.
10 Kazım Çeçen, *İstanbul'un Osmanlı Dönemi Su Yolları* (İstanbul: İSKİ, 1999), 142–143. For the map, see Çeçen, *Halkalı Suları* (İstanbul: İstanbul Büyükşehir belediyesi, 1991), 37–39, maps 1 and 2. For their connection to the Topkapı Palace, see Gülru Necipoğlu, "Virtual Archaeology in Light of a New Document on the Topkapı Palace's Waterworks and Earliest Buildings, circa 1509," *Muqarnas* 30 (2013).
11 Ian Manners, "Constructing the Image of a City: The Representation of Constantinople in Cristoforo Buondelmonti's Liber Insularum Archipelagi," *Annals of the Association of American Geographers* 87, no. 1 (1997): esp. 87–94.
12 Ibid. Also see Çiğdem Kafescioğlu, *Constantinopolis/Istanbul: Cultural Encounter, Imperial Vision, and the Construction of the Ottoman Capital* (University Park: Penn State University Press, 2009), 143–144.
13 On the revitalization of the multicultural and multinational Ottoman capital, see Giovan Maria Angiolello, *Viaggio di Negroponte*, ed. Cristina Bazzolo (Vicenza: Neri Pozza, 1982), 24, 37; Gülru Necipoğlu, "From Byzantine Constantinople to Ottoman Konstantiniyye: Creation of a Cosmopolitan Capital and Visual Culture Under Sultan Mehmed II," in *From Byzantion to Istanbul: 8000 Years of a Capital* (İstanbul: Sakıp Sabancı Museum, 2010), 262–277.
14 Manners, "Constructing the Image of a City," 75.
15 Franz Taeschner, "Der Bericht des arabischen Geographen Ibn al-Wardi liber Konstantinopel," in *Beitrage zur historischen Geographie- Kulturgeographie- Ethnographie und Kartographie- vornehmlich des Orients*, ed. H. Mzik (Leipzig: F. Deuticke, 1929), 84–91.
16 Necipoğlu, "From Byzantine Constantinople," 266.
17 For a detailed corpus on Ottoman cartography, see Ahmet T. Karamustafa, "Introduction to Ottoman Cartography" and "Military, Administrative, and Scholarly Maps and Plans," in *The History of Cartography: Cartography in the Traditional Islamic and South Asian Societies*, Vol. 2, eds J.B. Harley and David Woodward (Chicago: The University of Chicago Press, 1992), 3–11 and 209–227.
18 J.M. Rogers, "Itineraries and Town Views," in *The History of Cartography: Cartography in the Traditional Islamic and South Asian Societies*, Vol. 2, eds J.B. Harley and David Woodward (Chicago: The University of Chicago Press, 1992), 228–236.
19 İffet Orbay, "Istanbul Viewed: The Representation of the City in Ottoman Maps of the Sixteenth and Seventeenth Centuries" (Ph.D. diss., MIT, 2001), 49.
20 Walter B. Denny, "A Sixteenth-Century Architectural Plan of Istanbul," *Ars Orientalis* 8 (1970): 49–63.
21 Ibid. 58.
22 The Köprülü Water Supply Map is in Süleymaniye Library of Islamic Manuscripts, H. 197. For the image, see Bilge Ar, "Osmanlı Dönemi Su Yolları Haritalarında Roma ve Bizans Yapıları," *Sanat Tarihi Defterleri* 13–14 (2010): 15–54. The Beylik Water Supply Map has two copies, one in Fatih Millet Library no. 930; and the other is in Topkapı Palace Museum Archive E. 12481.
23 For detailed examination, see Çeçen, *Halkalı Suları*. Also see Ar, "Osmanlı Dönemi Su Yolları," 17–20.
24 Necipoğlu, "Virtual Archaeology," 315 and 320.
25 Ibid. Also see Çeçen, *İstanbul'un Osmanlı Dönemi Su Yolları*; Necipoğlu, "Virtual Archaeology," 315.
26 For detailed examination, see Çeçen, *İstanbul'un Osmanlı Dönemi Su Yolları*, esp. 157; Crow and others, *The Water Supply*, 87.
27 For detailed examination of the map, see Orbay, "Istanbul Viewed," 29–68; Hüseyin G., Yurdaydın, *Beyan-I Menazil-I Sefer-I Irakeyn-I Sultan Süleyman Han* (Ankara: Türk Tarih Kurumu Basımevi, 1976).
28 Orbay, "Istanbul Viewed," 32–33.
29 Ibid. 292.
30 Melchior Lorichs' panoramic depiction is in the University of Leiden, the Netherlands. For the image, see Nigel Westbrook, Kenneth Rainsbury Dark, and Rene van Meeuwen, "Constructing Melchior Lorichs' Panorama of Constantinople," *Journal of the Society of Architectural Historians* 69, no. 1 (2010): 62–87.

31 Westbrook and others, "Melchior Lorichs' Panorama," 68.
32 Karl Wulzinger, "Melchior Lorichs Ansicht von Konstantinopel als topographische Quelle," in *Festschrift Georg Jacob*, ed. Theodor Menzel (Leipzig: Harrassowitz, 1932), 355–368.
33 Some of the well-known early-modern profile views and the panoramas of the city are the anonymous panorama in the Vienna Bibliothek (1570), the conspicuous panoramas by Cornelis de Bruyn (1698) and Cornelius Loos (1710), the panoramic view of Philipp Ferdinand von Gudenus from 1740 and a pair of rare panoramic views in the Istanbul Pera Museum (eighteenth century).
34 For the ideological and symbolical aspects of the Süleymaniye Mosque Complex, see Gülru Necipoğlu, "The Süleymaniye Complex in Istanbul: An Interpretation," in *Muqarnas III: An Annual on Islamic Art and Architecture*, ed. Oleg Grabar (Leiden: E.J. Brill, 1985), 92–117.
35 For the term "imageability," see Christian Norberg-Schulz, *Genius Loci: Towards a Phenomenology of Architecture* (New York: Rizzoli, 1980), 20.
36 Thomas Allom, *Constantinople and the Scenery of the Seven Churches of Asia Minor*, Vol. 1, ed. R. Walsh (London: Fischer & Son,1839), 14–15, 23–25.
37 John Bougher Rowland, *Features Shown on Topographic Maps* (Washington, D.C.: Geological Survey Circular, 1955), 8.
38 Gregory of Nazianzus, *Or.* 33.6.
39 For the use of *kemer-i âb-ı revan* in Ottoman literary accounts, see Eyyübi, *Menakıb-ı Sultan Süleyman: Risale-I Padişahname*, ed. Mehmet Akkuş (Ankara: Kültür Bakanlığı Yayınları, 1991), 162 and 166; Gelibolulu Mustafa Ali, *Künhü'l Ahbar*, 65. Also see the dictionary Şemseddin Sami, *Kamus-ı Türki*, ed. P. Yavuzarslan (Ankara: Türk Dil Kurumu Yayınları, 2015), 21.
40 See, Eyyübi, *Menakıb*, 156–265.
41 "Zemin içre akuben geldi çün ab/Hayat-ı ab buldı cümle ahbab/Akar her çeşmenün ab-ı hayatı/Niçe çeşme suları ab-ı hayvan." See Eyyübi, *Menakıb*, 247. For the cosmological mentions of water, see 247–250.
42 Ibid. The Quranic verse is repeated at 255–257. Also see *The Quran*, trans. A.Y. Ali, 21.30.
43 Semavi Eyice, "Bozdoğan Kemeri," in *İslam Ansiklopedisi* 3 (İstanbul: Türkiye Diyanet Vakfı, 1988), 320.

12
THE AIRPORT TERMINAL
Circulation and Soft Power
Menno Hubregtse

This chapter examines how airport infrastructure in general, and the passenger terminal specifically, operate not merely as functional nodes in a system of transportation, but also as a form of soft power to project and reinforce national status. Beginning with early airfields, I consider how architects have adjusted this built form in response to functional and technical requirements such as innovations in aircraft design, threats to security, and ground transportation networks. I also illustrate how architects incorporate spectacular elements to create globally recognizable terminal buildings and how they design the interior in order to encourage passenger spending. After a brief overview of airport development and the types of land tracts they are built upon, I discuss the varied challenges that architects face in designing air terminals. Like many contemporary elements of the built landscape, these transportation systems evoke an aesthetic of smooth circulation that often obscures a range of uneven processes of development and mobility. I then look at the ways that air terminal circulation has changed to amplify consumption around the 'captive audience' of the air traveler. Finally, because airports are imbricated so thoroughly with a country's image, I examine why some protest movements choose to interrupt the airport's flows as a means to demonstrate against the state.

A vast infrastructure system underpins the world's commercial air travel network. Material entities such as runways, control towers, terminals, and aircraft serve to transport passengers between destinations, and telecommunication technologies such as computer networks, databases, and radar systems process and order the flows of passengers and their luggage. At the same time, the terminal serves as the key pivot between air and ground infrastructure, and as such constitutes a site for the accumulation of meanings associated with mobility in a rapidly globalizing age. This chapter examines how airport infrastructure in general, and the terminal specifically, operate not merely as functional nodes in a system of transportation, but also as a form of soft power to project and reinforce national status. As an architectural typology, the terminal emerged unevenly over time through trial and error around a range of design considerations. These include elements such as cost, engineering, security, access, flow, and logistics, all geared for optimal performance. Meanwhile, as the terminal converged around a standard suite of architectural features, a countervailing trend arose whereby national and local governments deploy spectacular design signatures to differentiate their airports within a globally competitive travel market.

After a brief overview of airport development and the types of land tracts they are built upon, I discuss the varied challenges that architects face in designing air terminals. Like many contemporary elements of the built landscape, these transportation systems evoke an aesthetic of smooth circulation that often obscures a range of uneven processes of development and mobility. I then look at the ways that air terminal circulation has changed to amplify consumption around the 'captive audience' of the air traveler. Finally, because airports are imbricated so thoroughly with a country's image, I examine why some protest movements choose to interrupt the airport's flows as a means to demonstrate against the state.

Placing the Airport: Finding Flat Land for the Runways

The main requirement for an airport is a vast, flat area of land for its runways, which need to be oriented in relation to the prevailing winds.[1] In addition, the site should be close to an urban center and accessible via ground transportation networks. Some of today's busiest airports began as small airfields built before World War II.[2] For instance, Mexico City's Benito Juarez International Airport began its life in 1910 as a dusty airfield owned by the Braniff family on the Plain of Balbuena. The Dutch military developed Amsterdam's Schiphol as an aerodrome in 1916, and it gradually transformed into a civilian airport after World War I ended. Over the past century, it has been expanded and renovated several times in order to serve an ever-increasing number of air travelers. Madrid-Barajas and Frankfurt Airport were airfields without paved runways when they began their commercial operations in 1933 and 1936. Both sites now encompass wide areas that contain several runways, taxiways, hangars, and terminal buildings.

In some cities, additional airports are built in different locations to meet this growing demand for aviation. When Charles de Gaulle opened in Paris in 1974, for example, it was expected to handle the surge of mass air travel that came with the introduction of wide-body jet aircraft such as the Boeing 747 in the early 1970s. The existing Paris airports, Le Bourget and Orly, had been operating since 1919 and 1932, respectively. Le Bourget stopped serving commercial air travel a few years after Charles de Gaulle opened. Orly, however, is still a central hub for domestic and international flights. Today, at least 28 cities around the world have more than three airports in their metropolitan areas. London and New York have six each, Los Angeles and Seattle five, and many cities have four airports from Melbourne to Moscow, and from Tokyo to Stockholm. The number of airports does not correlate with city size, but instead reflect major nodes of national and international travel.

One of the largest airports built in recent years is Istanbul Airport. It opened in October 2018 and replaced Atatürk Airport, which had reached its capacity, as the country's major international passenger hub.[3] All commercial passenger flights ceased to land and depart at Atatürk Airport in April 2019, and airlines had to transport their equipment to the new site, which is located 32 kilometers to the north. Istanbul Airport is designed to process 90 million passengers per year, and it will be expanded to handle 200 million passengers per year. It is expected to be a central hub that connects Europe, Asia, and Africa, and it will compete with Dubai's airport, which is one of the world's busiest in terms of international passenger traffic.

Charles de Gaulle and Istanbul Airport were built on existing plots of land adjacent to the city. In some cases, new airports need to be built on reclaimed land within a water body. Osaka's Kansai International, which opened in 1994, is the first large-scale airport to be built on a manufactured island. Planners chose to build the complex within Osaka Bay since the flat plots of land in this mountainous region were already developed. It was designed to absorb seismic movement and has sustained little damage from earthquakes, although the island has been sinking faster than anticipated, which has increased the airport's maintenance costs.[4] Like Kansai International, Hong Kong International is situated on an island in the seawater next to the city. When this mega-complex opened in 1998, it replaced the city's existing airport, Kai Tak, which was located closer to the city's center in Kowloon. The new airport is built upon two islands, Chek Lap Kok and Lam Chau, which were levelled down to make way for the runways, terminal, and ground transportation network. Seoul's Incheon International is built upon a manufactured landmass between Yongyu Island and Yeongjong Island in the Yellow Sea. When the airport opened in 2001, it overtook Seoul's Gimpo International as South Korea's primary airport. Gimpo International, however, remains in operation; it serves flights to regional destinations.

While plots of reclaimed land are costly to build, planners are able to optimize the airport's layout since they do not need to adjust the design to pre-existing structures. At Kansai International, Hong Kong International, and Incheon International, planners designed the ground transportation network in conjunction with the air terminal. In each of these cases, the rail station is situated at the center of the terminal's landside. This is indeed helpful for circulation since passengers do not need to walk a long distance between the station and the terminal. Thus, while passengers might perceive such connections as a matter of effortless convenience, these intermodal nodes and paths are part of a highly engineered landscape designed not only for frictionless mobility, but also for urban and national prestige.

The Air Terminal

The terminal building has seen many adaptations over the past century, and architects have looked to other structures such as railway stations, which also regulate passenger flows. Early airfields often used hangars as terminals. By the late 1920s, airports such as Schiphol and London's Croydon had constructed more permanent buildings. Many were expanded in subsequent years and offered amenities such as restaurants and rooftop viewing terraces. During the 1950s and 1960s, architects such as Eero Saarinen created open-spaced buildings that evoked the spirit of flight. Security concerns arising in the 1970s, however, dampened these daring designs, and architects built terminals with interiors partitioned by many corridors. This tendency waned in the 1990s, after Foster + Partners and JSK Architekten introduced large concourses with high ceilings and glass walls (Figure 12.1).

Figure 12.1 JSK Architekten, Terminal 2, Frankfurt Airport, Germany, 1994.

Source: Photograph by Menno Hubregtse.

These buildings offer passengers impressive views within this vast space as well as vistas outwards onto the surrounding apron. The departures and arrivals areas are usually situated on separate levels; the former is generally above the latter. Terminals with this configuration have upper and lower roadways that align with these levels. Many contemporary terminals, such as Hong Kong's Terminal 1, Madrid-Barajas's Terminal 4, and Seoul Incheon's Terminal 2, incorporate a series of bridges in the interior that lead from the upper roadway to the departure area's check-in counters. These elevated walkways allow for an expansive view of the building's height and breadth. These views provide legibility by allowing passengers and visitors to see the interior layout as they enter the building, while also offering a spectacular visual-aesthetic effect.

While the terminal's elevation is a significant part of its design and the most visible aspect for visitors, architects generally concentrate on the structure's footprint before attending to other details. They examine the runways' layout as well as the projected volume of traffic, and then they calculate how the terminal can efficiently process incoming and outgoing flights. Moreover, the runways determine which direction the terminal should face and how many piers should extend out from the main structure. Terminals designed for new airports often have a symmetrical footprint. For instance, Hong Kong's Terminal 1, Incheon's Terminal 1, and Bangkok's Suvarnabhumi have an axis of symmetry that runs from the building's landside to its airside; when passengers enter the building at its midpoint from the access road, they are aligned with this center line—their view to the right mirrors their view to the left. At Hong Kong's Terminal 1, Foster + Partners designed the ceiling's vaults and skylights such that they run parallel to this axis; they are visible on the departures level, and they draw the passenger's eye in the direction they need to go in order to access pre-boarding security and gates. The girders and skylights at Incheon's Terminal 1 also suggest this directional flow; however, they radiate outwards in conjunction with the crescent-shaped building's footprint.[5] Fentress Architects designed the exterior wall facing the landside access road with a concave shape. The airside's exterior wall has a convex shape, and it has a number of air bridges that link with the aircraft. There are also two piers with additional gates that spread outwards into the apron.

These terminals built for new airports contrast with the types of terminals that serve airports with longer histories. Schiphol's current terminal, which has been expanded numerous times since it first opened in 1967, has a complex asymmetrical footprint.[6] Marius Duintjer designed the original terminal structure, while Benthem Crouwel Architects designed most of the additions. This includes Terminal-West, which opened in 1993 as a second building conjoined with the original terminal. The firm also designed Schiphol Plaza, the airport's new entrance and railway station that opened in 1995, as well as a number of additional piers. Like Schiphol, Frankfurt's agglomeration of terminal buildings and piers has an asymmetrical footprint. Frankfurt's Terminal 1, which opened in 1972, has been expanded numerous times to account for increased passenger traffic and changes in aeronautic technologies. When Frankfurt's Terminal 2 opened in 1994, it was the first terminal in the world designed to accommodate the Airbus A380.[7] The airport's planners and the terminal's designers, JSK Architekten, knew that Airbus was developing the A380, and planned ahead to accommodate the massive craft, which held its first test flight in 2005 and entered service two years later. Terminal 2 was built to the east of Terminal 1, and they are joined together via a corridor on the airside. On the landside, passengers and visitors can transfer between Terminals 1 and 2 via a rail shuttle built in 1994. The Pier A-Plus, completed in 2012, is the most substantial addition to the building. Gerkan, Marg and Partners designed the 800-meter-long extension not only to provide extra space, but also to increase the number of gates at Frankfurt Airport that can service the Airbus A380.[8]

Charles de Gaulle also presents a collection of terminals built over time, though they are spread further apart. Terminal 1, which opened in 1974, is a circular concrete structure that resembles a fortress.[9] Paul Andreu's unusual Brutalist terminal design consists of a multi-level concrete structure with three floors of automobile parking above the arrivals and departures levels. Passengers transit between these levels via escalators that crisscross through the building's circular courtyard (Figure 12.2). The gates are located in seven separate satellite buildings, which are accessed via underground passageways.

Figure 12.2 Paul Andreu, Terminal 1, Paris Charles de Gaulle Airport, France, 1974.

Source: Photography by Menno Hubregtse.

Terminal 2, which began operating in 1981, is located approximately two kilometers southeast. Andreu partitioned the terminal into two curved halls straddling an access road. Each terminal presents a concave façade to the road, composed of repeated modules topped by a roofline that evokes an airplane wing in section. His designs for Halls 2C and 2D use a similar layout. Andreu took a different approach to Halls 2E and 2F, however. Completed in 2003 and 1998, respectively, these terminals' landside areas are dimly lit, an unusual feature in an era of increasingly transparent exterior façades. Their airside interiors, by contrast, are brightly illuminated by abundant skylights, with Hall 2E presenting a curvaceous tubular ceiling, while passengers in 2F pass below a pitched, hangar-shaped roof structure. Passengers can walk between Terminal 2's separate halls via passageways. Terminal 3, which services low-cost airlines, is situated approximately one kilometer north of Terminal 2, and presents a far more utilitarian design. Like Frankfurt Airport, an automated train allows passengers to travel between these three terminals.

Charles de Gaulle is not an anomaly in its jumbled accumulation of forms and styles. For example, London Heathrow consists of five terminals situated in three separate areas, and Madrid-Barajas's Terminal 4 is located three kilometers away from the airport's Terminals 1, 2, and 3. John F. Kennedy airport has had ten terminals in its 73-year history, but through a near-continuous process of demolitions, consolidations, and new construction, the airport now has six terminals of varied size and style.

Architects began to create naturally lit and open-spaced terminals after Foster + Partners introduced a new type of design for London's Stansted Airport, which opened in 1991.[10] The firm placed the baggage handling systems in the basement and created an expansive interior that contrasted with earlier and contemporaneous air terminals, which generally had narrow corridors and low ceilings. Frankfurt's Terminal 2, which was completed in 1994, is also more characteristic of current terminal design (Figure 12.1). Its departures area is situated in a concourse with a 30-meter-high ceiling illuminated by skylights. Airport authorities welcomed these new types of bright open spaces, and they expected that these less claustrophobic interiors would improve the passenger's experience. These high-ceilinged concourses also allow for unobstructed sightlines in the interior, which are integral to passenger wayfinding.[11] For instance, a view of the aircraft on the apron indicates where the gates are located. A clear view of the ceiling and the building's exterior walls also helps passengers orient themselves in the space.

Shopping

Contemporary high-ceilinged concourses are indeed easier to navigate, and they require fewer signs and maps for wayfinding. This lends to a less busy visual environment, where passengers are perhaps less concerned with navigating the interior. However, some open-spaced terminals, such as London Stansted, are filled with shops and restaurants which obscure one's view of the concourse.

Retail and restaurant sales are a central concern for airport authorities since they rely on these profits, as well as landing fees and parking revenues, to pay for the airport's operating costs, renovation projects, and expansions. In short, the airport's principle users—air passengers and meeters and greeters—help fund this infrastructure via their expenditures on food, travel accessories, gifts, and souvenirs. The majority of the airport's stores and restaurants are typically situated in the terminal's post-security airside and only serve air travelers. Yet, some airports, such as Schiphol, Hong Kong International, and Kuala Lumpur International, have shopping malls located on the landside and are intended to attract non-travelers from the surrounding region.

A number of airports force travelers to pass through shopping spaces—but these are usually situated after the check-in point. In the previous decade, planners at airports such as London Gatwick, London Stansted, and Charles de Gaulle have installed walkthrough duty-free stores.[12] Passengers encounter these retail spaces immediately after they exit the pre-boarding screening area. They have no choice but to walk into these shops, and they must follow a route lined with watches, sunglasses, liquor, and perfume. In some cases, these pathways include a number of curves in order to increase the passenger's exposure to retail goods. While only some air terminals incorporate walkthrough duty-free stores, all airports have a variety of shops in the post-security airside. These typically include well-known multinational brands like Victoria's Secret. Airports that largely serve international passengers also feature luxury brands such as Burberry, Gucci, and Chanel. These exclusive shops suggest that the airport's region is a place of affluence and a significant center for global commerce. In some cases, an upscale shop will have its own distinctive storefront design. For instance, the Louis Vuitton store at Singapore Changi's Terminal 3, which opened in 2017, has a spectacular six-meter-tall high-resolution LED display that surrounds its entrance.

Access Roads and Rail Lines

A central concern for architects is whether the terminal offers a smooth interchange with ground transportation networks. A design which offers an efficient link between the roadways, parking, and rail access undoubtedly bolsters the nation's reputation among those visiting the airport. Gyo Obata tried to minimize the distance between the parking and the gate in his design for the four new terminals that opened at Dallas/Fort Worth in 1974 (Figure 12.3).[13] These buildings have an identical semi-circular

Figure 12.3 Aerial view of terminal buildings and highway through the airport at Dallas/Fort Worth International Airport during construction, ca. 1973.

Source: Courtesy, *Fort Worth Star-Telegram Collection*, Special Collections, The University of Texas at Arlington Libraries.

footprint. Each terminal encloses its own parking area within its inner curve, which faces an expressway. Obata chose this configuration since the terminal's outer curved wall would allow more planes to access the terminal. While this design simplifies the access between the parking space and the gate, it vastly increases the distance that passengers need to travel when transferring between terminals. Obata, however, incorporated an innovative automated people mover that would whisk people from building to building. Obata envisioned a number of other identical terminals to be built beside the four original buildings, which are on both sides of the expressway. The airport opened a fifth terminal in 2005, and it is planning to build a sixth terminal.

Charles de Gaulle's Terminal 2, as described above, has a similar configuration of curved halls facing a roadway. Andreu's design, however, did not include a people mover to facilitate travel between the terminal's halls. But, passengers and visitors have been able to access the terminal via rail since it began operating in 1981. The airport's first railway station, which opened in 1976, serves the city's and its suburb's RER network. This concrete building is situated near Terminal 3 and Roissypole, an area containing airport hotels and offices. In 1994, the Société nationale des chemins de fer français (SNCF) opened a second station at Charles de Gaulle Terminal 2 that could accommodate its high-speed TGV trains. This station, which Andreu designed in collaboration with

Jean-Marie Duthilleul, not only facilitates rapid connections to locations across France but also introduces travelers to a significant French innovation in rail technology. In 2007, the airport opened the CDGVAL, an automated rail shuttle which travels between the two rail stations, Terminal 1, and two parking lots. Prior to its completion, passengers relied on buses to transfer between these stations, terminals, and car parks.

At Hong Kong International, Foster + Partners fully integrated a rail station into the new terminal's design. When the airport opened in 1998, the city's Mass Transit Railway (MTR) began operating a 35-kilometer airport express line that connected the terminal with three new rail stations in Tsing Yi, Kowloon, and central Hong Kong. The latter two stations extend the airport into the city since they have counters where passengers can check their luggage. While this express line encourages people to travel to the terminal via mass transit, passengers and visitors can also drive to Hong Kong International via a six-lane toll road built specifically for the airport.

At Incheon International, Terry Farrell & Partners' Ground Transportation Centre has a markedly different design than Fentress Architects' Terminal 1 (Figure 12.4). The station evokes a futuristic aesthetic due to its complex curves and its airfoil, which is situated above the building's oculus and resembles a spacecraft. The Ground Transportation Centre is a node for buses, taxis, and a rail line to Seoul, which is located 45 kilometers east of the airport. When the building opened in 2001, critics lambasted the lack of rail service, noting that the entry tolls and expensive bus fares were unreasonable expenditures for the airport's low-wage workers.[14] In 2007, a train line to Gimpo International Airport came into service, and the line was extended to Seoul Station in 2010 so that passengers no longer needed to transfer to a separate subway line to access the city.

Figure 12.4 Terry Farrell & Partners, Ground Transportation Centre, Incheon International Airport, South Korea, 2001.

Source: Photograph by Menno Hubregtse.

While Incheon International initially lagged behind other Asian hubs in terms of rail access, it became a center for new rail technologies when South Korea's government decided to build a maglev test track at the airport in 2007. The line, which uses magnets to levitate the train above the rail, stretches for 6.1 kilometers and includes six stations on the island the airport is situated upon. The train, which can travel at speeds up to 110 km/hr, departs from the Ground Transportation Centre and stops at the airport's long term parking and adjacent areas with hotels and businesses. It opened to the public in 2016, and passengers can travel for free. A brochure available via the airport's website states that this project will "lead the world with domestic technology."[15] Indeed, the maglev line is intended to bolster South Korea's status as a technologically advanced country, and it showcases innovations developed by national firms such as Hyundai Rotem.

The most remarkable maglev line that services an airport is at Shanghai Pudong International. The 30-kilometer line, which began commercial operations in 2004, connects the air terminal with Longyang Road Station. There are no stops along the way, and the train reaches speeds up to 431 km/hr. At Longyang Road Station, passengers can transfer to three of the city's metro lines. This significant high-speed transit line, however, is a German innovation. Siemens and ThyssenKrupp led the project's development, and German Chancellor Gerhard Schröder traveled to Shanghai for the maglev's inaugural trip in December 2002.[16] That being said, most passengers likely do not know who designed the project, and the maglev suggests that China is standing at the forefront of transportation infrastructure design.

Airports on the World's Stage: Spectacles, Protests, and Politics

As major ports of call, airports often undergo significant renovation in preparation for large-scale global events. National and local governments view this infrastructure as a way to garner attention while in the global spotlight, so investment is meant to bolster the host country's reputation. When Beijing Capital International Airport completed its new Terminal 3 prior to the 2008 Summer Olympic Games, it was the world's largest air terminal. Three weeks before the 2018 Winter Olympic Games in PyeongChang, Incheon International opened its new Terminal 2—the airport's most substantial expansion since it began operating in 2001. In some cases, new rail links to the airport are built to serve the influx of visitors attending these events. Vancouver's transportation authority opened the rapid transit Canada Line, which connects the airport with the city's downtown core, in advance of the 2010 Winter Olympic Games. The Delhi Metro Rail Corporation expected to open its new Airport Express line in time for the city's hosting of the 2010 Commonwealth Games. Unfortunately, its construction was delayed, and it did not begin carrying passengers until February the following year.

While New Delhi missed the opportunity to showcase its new rail line in time for a global event, protests forced Shanghai's municipal government to suspend its plans for a 37-kilometer extension of the airport's maglev line to the city's Expo 2010 site and its second airport, Hongqiao International. In 2007 and 2008, many of the city's residents rallied against the extension because of evictions and concerns regarding safety, noise pollution, and magnetic radiation.[17] The protesters had even written to German Chancellor Angela Merkel to intervene, since Siemens and ThyssenKrupp were expected to work on the maglev line's expansion.

In the United States, demonstrators occupied a number of airports throughout the country in January 2017 to protest against President Donald Trump's executive order that targeted Muslims traveling from Libya, Sudan, Somalia, Syria, Yemen, Iraq, and Iran.[18] The order, which Trump signed one week after his inauguration, forced the nation's border agents to detain arriving passengers, some of whom were ailing and elderly. In New York, thousands of activists assembled at John F. Kennedy's Terminal 4, which handles many of the airport's international flights and where a number of Muslim travelers were apprehended and questioned. Scenes of the protests were broadcast around the world. Trump, however, did not acquiesce to their demands, and he continued to enact similar travel restrictions throughout his presidency.

More recently, pro-democracy activists in Hong Kong have occupied the city's airport and blocked its ground transportation links to convey their political message to an international audience. In August 2019, demonstrators occupied Terminal 1's publicly accessible areas and forced a number of flight cancellations. They were protesting against a proposed bill that would permit Hong Kong's government to extradite its residents to mainland China. Media organizations across the world distributed photos and videos of the concourse's large open space filled with a throng of activists, and this imagery illustrated that a vast number of Hong Kong's residents were opposed to the bill. In response to this protest, police tightened their security measures at Hong Kong International. Nonetheless, activists captured the world's attention once again on September 1, 2019, when they blocked the airport's access road and express line. Three days later, Hong Kong's China-backed government succumbed to the protesters' demands and withdrew the bill.

Conclusion

During the last century, airports have gradually grown from small airfields to large sprawling complexes with many buildings and runways. Planners have continually refined the airport's layout in response to increased passenger traffic, new aviation technologies, security concerns, and innovations in mass transit systems. In addition, architects have adjusted the terminal's design such that it includes plenty of space for shops and restaurants, as airport authorities rely on passenger spending to pay for their operations. At the world's busiest airports, architects are often tasked with creating a soaring terminal building that is meant to impress the nation's citizens as well as visitors. While high-ceilinged concourses and glitzy storefront designs might bedazzle the airport's visitors, an easy-to-navigate interior space certainly appeals to passengers who need to rush to their gate. Local and national government bodies recognize the value of a spectacular and efficient airport design, and they often commission improvements to this infrastructure prior to a major global event that will bring a surge of visitors to the city, where the terminal will be their first experience of the destination.

Throughout its history, the terminal has drawn media attention. The early airport's rooftop terrace allowed visitors to view the latest aircraft designs. During the nascent jet age, people would visit the terminal to catch a glimpse of celebrities passing through the airport. This, however, waned with the rise of mass air travel and an increase in airplane hijackings during the early 1970s. Indeed, the terminal is now a highly surveilled space. Yet, demonstrators in recent years have transformed this controlled zone into a place of protest. Their interruption of the airport's operations certainly captures the world's attention, but it also undermines the nation's wish to have the airport appear as a smooth functioning transit hub for the world's aviation industry.

Notes

1 Brian Edwards, *The Modern Airport Terminal: New Approaches to Airport Architecture*, 2nd edn (New York: Spon Press, 2005); Robert Horonjeff and others, *Planning and Design of Airports*, 5th edn (New York: McGraw-Hill, 2010).
2 Marc Dierikx and Bram Bouwens, *Building Castles of the Air: Schiphol Amsterdam and the Development of Airport Infrastructure in Europe, 1916–1996* (The Hague: Sdu Publishers, 1997); Hugh Pearman, *Airports: A Century of Architecture* (New York: Harry N. Abrams, 2004); Alastair Gordon, *Naked Airport: A Cultural History of the World's Most Revolutionary Structure* (Chicago: The University of Chicago Press, 2008).
3 Gerhard Hegmann, "Istanbul Sets New Standards," *Die Welt (English)*, April 8, 2019, Nexis Uni.
4 Anne Graham, *Managing Airports: An International Perspective*, 5th edn (London: Routledge, 2018).
5 Donald Albrecht, ed., *Now Boarding: Fentress Airports + The Architecture of Flight* (London: Scala Publishers, 2012).
6 Koos Bosma, ed., *Megastructure Schiphol: Design in Spectacular Simplicity* (Rotterdam: NAI Publishers, 2013).

7 "Frankfurt Airport Celebrates 25th Anniversary of Terminal 2," *ENP Newswire*, October 25, 2019, Nexis Uni; "Dr. Wilhelm Bender: 'Frankfurt Airport is on the Path to Becoming a Leading A380 Hub'," *PR Newswire Europe*, April 28, 2005, Nexis Uni.
8 "Frankfurt Airport Opens Pier A-Plus as Scheduled," *News Aktuell*, October 2, 2012, Nexis Uni.
9 Philip Jodidio and Paul Andreu, *Paul Andreu, Architect* (Basel: Birkhäuser, 2004).
10 Kenneth Powell, *Stansted: Norman Foster and the Architecture of Flight* (London: Fourth Estate, 1992).
11 Menno Hubregtse, *Wayfinding, Consumption, and Air Terminal Design* (London: Routledge, 2020); Menno Hubregtse, "Passenger Movement and Air Terminal Design: Artworks, Wayfinding, Commerce, and Kinaesthesia," *Interiors: Design/Architecture/Culture* 7, nos 2–3 (2016): 155–179. https://doi.org/10.1080/20419112.2016.1215678.
12 Ibid.
13 Gordon, 243–244.
14 "Airport Opening," *The Korea Herald*, March 20, 2001, Nexis Uni.
15 "Incheon Airport Maglev Line," Incheon Airport, accessed June 20, 2020, www.airport.kr/ap_file/ko/file/maglevLine_brochure_en.pdf.
16 "Zhu Promises Second Maglev Line after Shanghai Trip," *Deutsche Presse-Agentur*, December 31, 2002, Nexis Uni.
17 "Shanghai Residents Protest Transrapid Extension," *Spiegel Online*, March 13, 2007, Nexis Uni.
18 Andy Newman, "Highlights: Reaction to Trump's Travel Ban," *The New York Times*, January 29, 2017, Nexis Uni.

13
THE POROUS INFRASTRUCTURES OF SOMALI MALLS IN CAPE TOWN

Huda Tayob

This chapter takes as its subject a series of contingent mixed-use urban markets that have been established in Cape Town, South Africa, by migrants, refugees, and asylum seekers from various parts of the African continent. Known colloquially as 'Somali malls,' these markets typically occupy once-vacant or underused office blocks, filling them with multiple small shops, services, and residences. Read through the lens of infrastructure, these spaces of flows tie Somali diasporic communities into transnational networks of sociality and exchange. Through novel forms of organization, procurement, display, and hospitality, proprietors optimize the spaces internally within buildings while at the same time constructing networks that exceed the building envelope, creating a flexible, multiscalar set of practices. Women comprise the large majority of traders in the Somali malls, carving out spaces not only for merchandising and earning a living, but also for the construction of migrant sociality in a new and unfamiliar world. This research approach is grounded in broader anthropological approaches and architectural fieldwork methods. The resultant multiscalar reading of informal migrant markets, not usually found in spatial archives, questions dominant readings of infrastructures in post-colonial contexts.

Since the mid-1990s in greater Cape Town, a series of contingent mixed-use urban markets has been established by migrants, refugees, and asylum seekers from various parts of the African continent. Among these are a spatial typology widely known as Somali malls, named for their main proprietors, Somali refugees. In the peripheral northern Cape Town suburb of Bellville, these multi-story office conversions host various functions including residential accommodation, shops, and various services that primarily cater to east African new entrants. Over the past three decades, they have emerged as key spaces of infrastructure and flows in the exchange of goods among migrant communities, and a feature of Cape Town's urban landscape.

This chapter reads into the fine grain of the Somali mall in order to draw out broader urban and architectural entanglements across scales.[1] Rather than approach the markets as fixed objects in space and time, I examine them as unstable sites that both expand within and contract beyond their physical bounds. As E. Summerson Carr and Michael Lempert assert, scale is not given, but is made in the world.[2] In this sense, even as the scalar exertions of commerce map onto particular geolocations, they simultaneously fold into and exceed their bounded framing, suggesting a porosity across space and time. Working through the implications of these sites across borders is central to recognizing them as historically constituted, to follow Edward Said.[3] Reading these Somali malls across scales can reveal how migrant social and spatial practices escape neatly drawn boundaries. It is this porous, fungible nature of the markets in greater Cape Town that have made them a central feature of migrant life in post-apartheid South Africa.

In his discussion of the poetics and politics of infrastructures, Brian Larkin asserts that infrastructures are "unruly," in that they cannot be understood as objects alone. He argues that, "what distinguishes

DOI: 10.4324/9781003093756-18

infrastructures from technologies is that they are objects that create the grounds on which other objects operate, and when they do so they operate as systems."[4] Following Larkin, I read the Somali Malls as infrastructural, in that they provide a nodal point for amplifying and enabling the flow of goods, services, and people. Furthermore, these Somali malls are not unique to Cape Town, but are also found in Nairobi, Dubai, and Minneapolis.[5] They should therefore be read within a wider system of similar spaces.

In the following sections I take a close look at the 'Somali mall' at three scalar registers: the urban neighborhood, the building, and the individual shop. I show that the porosity and flexibility of these registers reveal how migrant communities have constructed spaces of flows. By examining the Somali mall and its environs across varied scales and borders, the importance of these spaces as part of the commercial infrastructure for everyday migrant life stands out in sharp relief.

Bellville

Bellville is an area approximately twenty-five kilometers north of the city center, and currently within the metropolitan boundaries of the City of Cape Town. From the 1950s, newspaper articles describe the area as the urban cultural heartland of 'white' Afrikaans speakers in the region, an Afrikaner CBD in contrast to the city of Cape Town.[6] On September 7, 1979 the area of Bellville was granted city status, and by the 1980s newspapers suggested that "it was in Bellville [...] that the Afrikaner has found his feet and become a co-builder of South Africa's future."[7] Following the end of apartheid, and the formation of the Cape Town Metropolitan Municipality in 2000, Bellville lost its city status, and became an area within the wider Cape Town region. This period coincided with 'white' flight from the area to nearby gated communities. Black South African residents as well as African migrants from Somalia, Ethiopia, and The Congo quickly moved into the area, drawn by good transport links, high levels of formal infrastructure, and inexpensive rentals.[8] The decline in investment and change from city status to suburb was instrumental in Bellville becoming a pan-African space, facilitating and enabling both mobility and a form of settlement for non-citizens.

The most significant changes occurred in the former central business district (CBD), between the Bellville train station and Voortrekker Road, a key urban artery. Shifting radically from a 'white' heartland under apartheid to a largely 'Black' space in recent years, it challenges the still dominant view of Cape Town as an unchanging 'white' apartheid city.[9] However, the changes in Bellville were not only demographic, but also spatial, as migrant groups forged new patterns of inhabitation and transformed buildings and landscapes to suit their needs. It is in this context that the Somali mall emerged as a new node in the commercial and social infrastructure of Bellville (Figure 13.1).

The term "Somali mall" refers to multi-story markets in Bellville which have dominant Somali or east African populations; in 2015 there were approximately fourteen in the former CBD area. These mixed-use markets have been created from old multi-story office blocks or large individual commercial spaces. It is unclear where the term itself comes from, yet it is widely used in the area to refer to these mixed-use spaces. While primarily given over to commercial enterprises, they also house numerous social and religious services, including churches, mosques, nursery schools, community organizations, English language schools, travel and transportation agencies, money exchanges, restaurants, coffee shops and residential accommodation. The pattern and proliferation of these markets has coincided with the changing refugee policies and border permeability. As such, Somali malls are perhaps better understood as arcades, where the "passage is a city, a world in miniature."[10] In Bellville, it is rumored that within these few city blocks, the Somali population alone swells to 7,000 on a Sunday, as refugees gather. The increasing visibility of the malls, and their infrastructural role in the lives of migrants, points to their significance in post-apartheid urban space in spatial, economic, and cultural terms.

Figure 13.1 Advertisement for a Somali mall in Bellville, Cape Town, 2014.

Source: Photograph by Huda Tayob.

Nevertheless, not everyone in Cape Town looks upon the malls and their environs favorably. Newspapers describe the area as a site of "urban decay," and as "crime-ridden and rundown."[11] Articles emphasize the "dirt and waste" that accumulate in the busy streets and alleys, and lament that migrants are "invading" and "taking over," turning the area into a "slum."[12] It is only when xenophobic attacks occurred in surrounding areas that there was minimal recognition of Bellville as a "safe haven" for migrants.[13] Many refer to the area derisively as "little Somalia" or "little Mogadishu," a foreign space.[14] The negative perception of the area is racially charged through its association with 'Black' African character.

The dystopic view is shared by the City of Cape Town, which established the Voortrekker Road City Improvement District (VRCID) as a vehicle to "turn the area around."[15] Between 2012 and 2014, the VRCID identified 15 "problem buildings" where they hoped to evict current tenants. In November 2013, for example, officials evicted residents from the Anabora Shopping Centre, which had housed shops, a school, several restaurants, and residences. According to the VRCID manager, the mall was a space of irregular, informal and unacceptable occupation.[16] He did not recognize that for many refugees and asylum seekers, these malls provide access to space in a property market that is otherwise inaccessible and unwelcoming to non-citizens.[17]

Despite having experienced significant disinvestment after 'white' flight, Bellville maintains a high level of formal and physical infrastructure, with running water, electricity, phone lines, and good

Figure 13.2 Som Shopping Centre, Cape Town, 2014.

Source: Photograph by Huda Tayob.

connection to existing road and rail networks. The improvisatory nature of the Somali malls and the ad hoc additions and sub-divisions builds on these existing infrastructure affordances to establish new spaces of flows suitable to the incoming populations (Figure 13.2). In buildings that were previously solely commercial, the Somali malls offer instead a porous range of private, public, and familial spaces. While AbdouMaliq Simone's work emphasizes these immaterial connections between bodies, this chapter suggests that these networks extend into the manipulation of the architectonic fabric itself, and are hosted in distinct material and spatial sites.[18] As Benjamin and Lacis said of Naples, "building and action interpenetrate in the courtyards, arcades, and stairways."[19] While such occupation is contingent, and at times precarious, the inhabitants of Bellville have nevertheless invested substantial material and cultural capital into the activations of these spaces for everyday social and commercial life.

Som City

Som City was one of the first Somali malls established in Bellville (Figure 13.3). From the outside, the building has the appearance of a neat, if slightly worn, office block. A small sign with the Somali flag displays the mall's name. Below the sign, double glass doors open onto a small foyer with peeling, faded, yellow walls. Straight ahead is a defunct lift, and to the right, the main staircase for the building. In the foyer are small advertisements for "Jubba Internet Café" and "Som City." The first flight of stairs leads to a small landing with various notices displayed. To the left of the landing is "Mubarak Restaurant" which serves East African dishes, along with snacks, tea, and coffee. To the right of the landing is a corridor that runs the length of the building with small shops on either side; these shops are between one and six square meters and most are run by women. They sell food items, women's clothing, and miscellaneous household goods, piled high on shelves, hung on the walls and in front of windows; I was told

Figure 13.3 Som City, Cape Town, 2014.

Source: Photograph by Huda Tayob.

that it is the best place to buy clothing for festive occasions. There is also a laundry, phone service, and internet café on this floor. The floors above house one of several lodges in Bellville, which are living quarters consisting of small, shared sleeping spaces.

Until 2004, the Som City building was a regular office block. Ahmed, the current manager, described travelling over land to South Africa, fleeing violence in Mogadishu.[20] When he first arrived in Cape Town in 2000, he worked as a street trader in various parts of the city, saving where possible. When 20 Kruskal Avenue became available for rent, Ahmed and two friends saw the opportunity to turn it into a Somali mall. The Oriental Plaza, the first Somali mall across the street, was a prosperous precedent, along with the Somali malls Ahmed had seen in Eastleigh, Nairobi, on his way to South Africa. In Eastleigh, Ahmed had personal experience of the potential of Somali Malls to provide affordable residential accommodation and services for new entrants and itinerant traders. When they gained occupation of 20 Kruskal Avenue, they subdivided spaces to create small affordable trading spaces on the lower two floors, and a residential lodge above. Ahmed lived in the lodge himself for the first two years that Som City was open.

The naming of this Somali Mall "Som City" underscores Ahmed's canny spatial conceptualization of the interior as an arcade—and alternative world brought into Bellville. Beyond Benjamin's reading of the arcade as a city, this is an arcade that calls itself a city, named after a country. "Mubarak Restaurant," Moqdishu Trading, and Jubba internet café, among others, tell their own spatial stories of arcades elsewhere, and of the porous relationships between Somali malls in Cape Town and those in Nairobi, Minneapolis and Dubai. Therefore, while Som City and various other pan-African markets in the area are linked to existing social and physical networks within the city of Cape Town, they extend beyond their particular material and spatial envelopes. In both conceptualization and operation, they exceed the bounded framing of the nation state, and instead rely on personal negotiations and kinship networks that link into transnational networks, movements, and practices. The multi-scalar nature of these spaces as highly localized and intimately connected elsewhere becomes particularly evident when looking at the scale of individual shops and the goods within them.

Moqdishu Trading

Moqdishu Trading is a single store within Som City, which is run by Sara, a female trader. Within the arcade-like space, this is one of the many similar shops that is characterized by the dense accumulation of goods (Figure 13.4). Most of the stores sell similar "Somali goods" which include items such as Banadir One Coffee, spices for Somali tea, masallahs (straw mats), perfumes, attar (natural oil

Figure 13.4 Interior of a shop in Som City, Cape Town, 2014.

Source: Photograph by Huda Tayob.

perfumes), hair oils, henna, abayas, sandals, hijab, clothes for weddings, imported cosmetics, flax seed oil, sesame oil and spaghetti. Most also stock Anchor Milk powder, Hilwa chicken stock, and Foster Clark's juice mixes. These goods are often sold alongside toothpastes, shampoos, and bags of rice. As Caroline Skinner has noted, informal trade is a key occupation for new entrants to South Africa as their irregular status means few are able to access the formal job market.[21]

Sara's shop is one of many in a country where the majority of informal trade is undertaken by women.[22] These shops are further gendered in that they host domestic practices which include caring for families, overseeing after-school homework by their children, organizing meals, and extending hospitality to family and friends. The parceling of spaces into smaller increments, from Bellville to Som City to an individual shop accords with a gendered gradation in scale from the urban to the domestic. Yet, the goods themselves reveal the imbrication of these arcades with spaces and people located elsewhere, and at a transnational scale.[23]

My first introduction to Som City was with Fatima, a trader who runs a shop next door to Som City. She took me on a tour of the Somali malls in the area. This introduction to the Somali malls coincided with an introduction to several of her friends and family members, many of whom had their own small shops, and all of whom offered us a place to sit and a cup of tea. Our visits extended beyond an introduction, to a discussion of daily life in Bellville, conversations about schools, and updates on the latest marriages, births and deaths, or violence in surrounding areas of Cape Town. Always included was the latest news on new arrivals in the city along with recent departures. As a result of both the goods sold and the uses of space, these small shops are key social spaces for Somali women in Cape Town.

Long operating hours means that the women who run these stores spend most of their day in Bellville and in their shops, from around nine in the morning to nine at night. The day is punctuated with visits from family and friends who stop to eat lunch together, or drink tea throughout the day. All of the small shops have extra chairs, and visits can last from ten minutes to several hours. Within the shops, women arrange elaborate and dense displays to show case their wares and to create a sense of familiarity for a very particular clientele—Somali people who have been forcibly displaced and are attempting to reconstruct a sense of home. The provision of a product such as "Banadir One Coffee" involves more than just the buying and consumption of the coffee; it also sparks conversations and story-telling in a familiar language, and imbibing a familiar taste from home.

As an assemblage of materials and practices, the shop is the end point of an extended infrastructural system—a space optimized around the flow of goods from varied locations beyond the city, into the confines of a mercantile operation, and finally into the homes of Somali migrants. According to Som City manager Ahmed, a great many of the goods sold in the shops are sourced out of Dubai, procured in several ways. First, a group of women might send a list of goods they wanted, either by fax or email, to a relative in Dubai. She would buy the things, and ship them as personal packages on payment. This was easy to do, yet depended on a well-known and trustworthy intermediary. Ahmed noted, "If you ask any Somalian if they got relatives in Dubai, they will tell you yes, they have relatives there. Some of them stay there, they have businesses, they have property there."[24] Indeed, Dubai since the 1980s, prior to the outbreak of civil war 1991.[25] In this way, family networks are crucial to the operation of many small shops in Somali malls.

A second, more cost-effective procurement method is for women to travel to Dubai in order to purchase goods directly. For example, Sara travels to Dubai around three times per year. She takes a commercial flight, stays with relatives, shops for the goods there, and depending on the quantity either brings the goods in her luggage, sends them back to South Africa by air cargo, or in a shipping container. She also sources goods from Kenya and Saudi Arabia.[26] In other cases, a group of women will pool their money to send one of them to Dubai to collect the goods for everyone. This is usually cheaper than the first option, as the buyer could shop around for the best prices. However, this method depends on one of the women having the "right papers." Most Somali refugees in Cape Town do not have a passport, and therefore could not leave the country through official means.[27]

A third procurement method involves one woman with a passport acting as a cross-border trader. Fatima confirmed that this was how most goods were sourced in Bellville. She added that due to the small scale of her shop, it was this third way that she preferred, as it did not involve putting up large sums of money in advance, or securing necessary travel documents.[28] Like most Somali migrant traders, she sources most of her goods from Dubai or directly from family in Kenya, and none from within the South African borders. Narrowing down the scale of focus from the building to the shop to the particular items reveals the porosity inherent in the spatial organization of these commercial flows. However, while the parceling of space into small individual shops suggests a reduction in scale, the sourcing of goods talks to trans-national relationships.

However they procure their wares, the networks themselves often remain opaque to outsiders.[29] As Carla Freeman notes, the engagements of women traders across borders belie the "slippery equation between local and woman/gender that has effectively eclipsed the latter from the macromodels of globalization."[30] Moreover, standard architectural narratives that focus only on buildings obscure the critical role that female migrants play in using architectural space to facilitate the transnational flows of goods and to build felicitous communities in exile. Therefore, while the signage and names suggested a spatial history fixed in particular spaces in Somalia and Mogadishu, these networks pointed to a more fluid, opaque, and unstable set of connections with architecture and urban space.

Porous Infrastructures

Ahmed's understanding of Som City as connected to sites in Nairobi and Minneapolis mirrored Sara and Fatima's experience of sourcing and procuring goods for their stores from wider networks of similar markets and associated cross-border traders. The logistical configurations for trade, sourcing, procuring, and facilitating the movement of goods at a transnational scale points to the infrastructural nature of these Somali malls. The research explicitly locates the Somali malls in Cape Town as part of a wider infrastructural network beyond South Africa. They have a history that is linked to formal infrastructures, refugee policies, colonial planning, and state dispossession, and they are tied into the ongoing racialization of migration. The opaque nature of these infrastructures is however highlighted by their invisibility to the city and state. Despite the centrality of Somali malls to migrant groups, they are under constant threat of evictions from the city and public–private partnerships under the guise of regeneration and city-improvement guidelines. This has the dual impact of both adding to the unstable precarity of these sites and adding a layer of opacity to the services and resources the Somali malls provide. These sites therefore operate at the unstable locus of precarity and possibility.

In this chapter, recognizing both the physical and intangible networks of support and cross-border trade as infrastructure enables a view of the centrality of these spaces to migrant groups' livelihoods, and simultaneously points to their longer history as architectures tied into global informal trade. Adopting a critical infrastructural lens opens a wider and more systemic view of the spatiality that operates across scales and across national borders. In contrast to the emphasis often placed on the improvisatory nature of infrastructures for informal trade in the global south, a multi-scalar view of Somali malls points to the very real existence of physical built forms, and to the concrete spatial and material affordances of what often gets glossed over as ad hoc or improvisatory. While such spaces are often contingent and precarious, inhabitants nevertheless invest labor, capital, and cultural meaning in them to serve the diasporic community. I build on AbdouMaliq Simone's concept of *people as infrastructure*, yet suggest that in addition to thinking through the immaterial networks of improvisation which Simone emphasizes, these Somali malls reveal spatial and material negotiations ramified through built form. Rather than focusing on the absence of infrastructures, we see dislocated people assembling new spatial nodes as a way of overcoming formal exclusion.

None of this is to suggest that globalization is a smooth even field of unlimited, unregulated flows. Instead, the precarity of these Somali malls as infrastructures points to the deep inequalities in global trade, while simultaneously drawing out how marginalized groups negotiate these networks.[31] The transnational interdependency of Somali malls reveals the concerted effort among diasporic communities to establish alternatives to exclusionary circuits of capital. Reading these spaces as porous infrastructure allows us to hold their multiple scales and associated places together at the same time, across vast geographies. By reconfiguring the architectural space of the common office block, Somali migrants create new nodes in the transnational circulation of people, goods, and cultural forms and meanings.

Notes

1. This chapter is reworked from a previously published article: Huda Tayob, "Architecture-by-Migrants: The Porous Infrastructures of Bellville," *Anthropology Southern Africa* 42, no. 1 (2019): 46–58.
2. E. Summerson Carr and Michael Lempert, *Scale: Discourse and Dimensions of Social Life* (Oakland: University of California Press, 2016), 2.
3. Edward Said, "Representing the Colonized: Anthropology's Interlocutors," *Critical Inquiry* 15 (1989): 205.
4. Brian Larkin, "The Politics and Poetics of Infrastructure," *Annual Review of Anthropology* 42 (2013): 329.
5. Mulki Al-Sharmani, "Contemporary Migration and Transnational Families: The Case of Somali Diaspora(s)," paper delivered at a conference on *Migration and Refugee Movements in the Middle East and North Africa*, The American University in Cairo, Egypt, October 23–25, 2007; Kenneth Omeje and John Mwangi, "Business Travails in the Diaspora: The Challenges and Resilience of Somali Refugee Business Community in Nairobi," *Journal of Third World Studies*, 31 (2014).
6. Reg Weiss, "Great Plans Mature at Bellville," *Cape Argus*, October 31, 1957.
7. Staff Reporter 1982.
8. Interview with John, August 25, 2014; Interview with Patel, August 25, 2014.
9. Edgar Pieterse, "Post-apartheid Geographies in South Africa: Why Are Urban Divides so Persistent?" *Proceedings of the Conference Interdisciplinary Debates on Development and Cultures*, University of Leuven, 2009.
10. Walter Benjamin, *The Arcades Project: Walter Benjamin* (Cambridge MA: Harvard University Press, 1999), 3.
11. Bronwynne Jooste, "Lifeline for Cape Town's Suburbs of Decay, *Cape Argus* (2012).
12. Clayton Barnes, "Bellville CBD and Surrounds: 'I Don't Go into the CBD: It's Filthy'," *Cape Argus* (12 November 2010): 4; Clayton Barnes, "Spare Us the Hype, Just Deliver a Cleaned-up CBD, Bellville Voters Tell Candidates," *Cape Argus* (18 April 2011): 4; Zara Nicholson, "Loud Calls to Prayer Raise Ire of Residents," *Cape Times* (11 April 2011): 8.
13. Zara Nicholson, "Somalis find a safe haven in Bellville," *Cape Times* (11 May 2012): 8.
14. Gabriel Tati, "The Immigration Issues in the Post-Apartheid South Africa: Discourses, Policies and Social Repercussions," *Space Population Societies* 3 (2008); Interview with Patel, August 25, 2014; Interview with James, January 6, 2015.
15. Staff Reporter, "Cape Town Plans to Turn Around Voortrekker Road," *Cape Argus* (August 1, 2012); City of Cape Town, "Urban Regeneration Programme Stabilises Areas, Improves Lives," City of Cape Town, November 22, 2013.
16. Interview with Willem, November 19, 2014.
17. Iyonawan Masade, "Where Is Home? Transnational Migration and Identity Amongst Nigerians in Cape Town," in *Imagining the City*, eds Sean Field, Renate Meyer, and Felicity Swanson (Cape Town: HSRC Press, 2007).
18. AbdouMaliq Simone, "People as Infrastructure," *Public Culture* 16, no. 3 (2004): 407–429.
19. Walter Benjamin and Asja Lacis, "Naples [1924]," in *Reflections: Essays, Aphorisms, Autobiographical Writings* (New York: Schocken Books, 1986).
20. Interview, with Ahmed, February 6, 2015.
21. Caroline Skinner, "Street Trade in Africa: Review," *School of Development Studies*, Working Paper 51 (2008).
22. Debbie Budlender, *Street Traders and Their Organisations in South Africa* (Geneva: International Labour Organization, 2003); Skinner.
23. Arjun Appadurai, *The Social Life of Things: Commodities in Cultural Perspective* (Cambridge, UK: Cambridge University Press, 1986).
24. Interview with Ahmed, February 6, 2015.

25 Peter D. Little, *Somalia: Economy Without State* (Bloomington: Indiana University Press, 2003), 147; Omeje and Mwangi.
26 Interview with Sara, February 7, 2015.
27 Interview with Fatima, September 1, 2014; Interview with Ahmed, February 6, 2015.
28 Interview with Fatima, September 1, 2014.
29 Simone, "People as Infrastructure."
30 Carla Freeman, "Is Local: Global as Feminine: Masculine? Rethinking the Gender of Globalization," *Signs* 26, no. 4 (2001): 1007–1037.
31 Francis B. Nyamnjoh, "Globalisation, Boundaries and Livelihoods: Perspectives on Africa," *Identity Culture and Politics* 5, nos 1–2 (2004): 44.

PART V

City Making

14
BRIDGING THE BOSPORUS
Mobility, Geopolitics, and Urban Imaginary in Istanbul, 1933–1973

Sibel Bozdoğan

The completion of the first suspension bridge across the Bosporus Straits in Istanbul in 1973 marked the culmination of a century-old dream to connect Europe and Asia. From its emergence as a daring but unrealistic idea during the late Ottoman Empire, to the first unrealized proposal in the 1930s and its gaining traction after 1950 following Turkey's economic liberalization and international realignment in the Cold War, the story of the Bridge compellingly illustrates how geopolitical ambitions, competing national agendas and trans-national flows of technical expertise intersected in the making of an iconic structure that transformed the city's urban morphology and metropolitan imagination in unprecedented ways. The chapter traces this earlier story of the Bosporus Bridge using primary sources and some untapped archival material. The overall argument is that engineering works like the Bosporus Bridge are more than technical and aesthetic objects: they embody myriad political, symbolic, historical and cultural meanings. Far from being smooth processes, their conception, design, construction, and reception involve contentious processes and unintended consequences—in this case, the phenomenal expansion of Istanbul towards its hinterland, as well as the unleashing of a ubiquitous instrument of modern Turkish politics: namely, the linkage of infrastructure with populist propaganda.

The Bosporus is the 31 km-long, winding and narrow strait (700 meters wide at its narrowest point) separating Europe and Asia and connecting the Black Sea with the Sea of Marmara and the Mediterranean—a route along which commercial ships and colossal oil tankers travel every day. From the earliest, quasi-mythical crossing of King Darius' Persian armies in the fifth century BC over a "floating bridge" of ships joined together, to the fifteenth-century crossing of the young Ottoman Sultan Mehmed II on his way to conquer Constantinople, it has assumed enormous historical, cultural, and symbolic significance as a kind of civilizational East–West boundary.[1] But it would not be until the late twentieth century that a span linked the two shores of the strait with a massive suspension bridge. Today, heavy traffic crosses over the Bosporus on three great bridges, the northernmost of which carries the Trans European Motorway, while huge oil tankers wind through it carrying Caspian oil to the Mediterranean and beyond. The density of this traffic daily reaffirms Istanbul's unique urban identity as a city sitting on cross roads. It is a "hinge-city" as urban theorist Richard Sennett has called it: "… a city, just like Venice, which is the European prototype of this particular urban form, built on trade with distant places and the impermanence in time of foreigners inhabiting a cosmopolitan space."[2]

When it did finally open to great fanfare in October 1973, the first suspension bridge across the Bosporus marked the culmination of a century-old dream to connect Europe and Asia (Figure 14.1). This chapter looks at how geopolitical ambitions, specific national agendas of successive governments and trans-national flows of technical expertise intersected over many decades in the making of an iconic

Figure 14.1 First Bosporus Bridge (Atatürk Bridge), Istanbul, by the engineering firm of Freeman, Fox & Partners; completed in 1973.

Source: Photograph by Uğurhan Betin.

structure that would eventually transform the urban morphology and metropolitan imagination of a unique world city in unprecedented ways. The primary argument of the chapter is that engineering works like roads, tunnels, and bridges are not just technical/utilitarian solutions to problems of urban mobility and transportation, but also symbolic objects charged with political meanings that shift over time. Their design, construction, and public reception involve multiple actors, contentious processes, unrealized intentions, and unintended consequences.

Historical Precedents

In his famous *Voyage d'Orient* of 1911, Le Corbusier took notice of this geographical peculiarity of Istanbul—a city bisected by waterways with three landmasses facing each other across bodies of water: the historic peninsula in the south and Galata-Pera to its north, separated by the estuary Golden Horn on the European side of the Bosporus and Üsküdar, the third urban hub of the historic city, farther away on the Asian side. While the steep topography of the city allowed unique views and vistas across these waterways and bridges existed across the Golden Horn since mid-nineteenth century, one could cross the Bosporus straits only by small boats or passenger ferries that served this cosmopolitan city of over one million people at the turn of the twentieth century. Further north, Bosporus shores remained a distant suburban landscape of sparsely settled small villages.

The desire to span this unique body of water stretches back into the nineteenth century, not merely as a technical dream, but as a political project to expand imperial influence and control. Several unrealized Bosporus bridge proposals testify to the intersection of European strategic interests with Ottoman ambitions for the technological modernization of the Empire, also underscoring the late

Empire's economic dependency on European powers under the façade of its political sovereignty. A drawing of one such example, a "proposed bridge across the Bosporus" by Carl Von Ruppert was displayed in the 1867 Paris Exhibition.[3] The sturdy iron structure of this cantilever bridge with double parabolic girders not only presents a stark visual contrast with the picturesque Bosporus landscape but also exemplifies what the engineering community saw as the primary technical problem at the time, namely "how to make suspension bridges rigid enough to carry a railway train" as the journal *The Engineer* put it in 1884.[4]

The primary actors who initiated such projects were Constantinople's foreign-owned tram and railroad companies and their French, British and other European stakeholders who saw lucrative profits in the idea and lobbied their respective governments, citing the great commercial, military and geopolitical benefits of a Bosporus crossing. In 1900, for example, Istanbul's Bosporus Railroad Company commissioned the rather fantastic Hamidiye Bridge, an Orientalist bridge design that supported its suspension structure by masonry pylons topped with neo-Memluk towers replicating Cairene precedents. That the Hamidiye Bridge proposal was conceived as part of the Baghdad railroad project—an Ottoman concession to Germany after the historical alliance between Kaiser Wilhelm II and Sultan Abdulhamid II, testifies to the imperial geopolitics of the time.

As the Germans were coveting the Middle East, the British were also entertaining their own imperial dreams of bridging the Bosporus, not just as a connection between the two shores of the straits, but as a railway passage to India that would also fortify the strategic military significance of the straits against Russian expansion. An 1893 article in *The Engineer* observed:

> Turkey's geographical position is an enviable one, but like many other good positions it is surrounded with responsibilities. Her situation as the guardian and owner of the Bosporus is a crucial one. The custodian of the Bosporus ought to be strong; fit for fulfilling *the duties of sentinel* which the situation naturally requires of her.[5]

This overtly geopolitical role assigned to the Ottoman Empire at the end of the nineteenth century is remarkably similar to the one that would admit Turkey into NATO in 1952 and accelerate the process that would eventually give Istanbul its bridge as I discuss later.

Such projects remained fantasies however, through the tumultuous historical events of World War I, the collapse of the Ottoman Empire, and the proclamation of the Turkish Republic in 1923, the year when the national capital was moved to Ankara resulting in Istanbul's loss of its formal imperial glory. Throughout the 1920s, Istanbul was a shadow of its former self, having lost nearly half of its turn-of-the-century population to wars, population exchanges, and the departure of Europeans, Levantens, and non-Muslims, who had constituted the most economically dynamic groups of the late Empire. Yet, in a paradoxical relationship to this shrinkage of population, Istanbul also experienced an expansion of its urban footprint towards the north of the city and along the long stretches of its coastline. This was largely the result of middle and upper classes moving out of the historic city to the newly developing and more modern residential neighborhoods in the north, and to the new villas and summer residences that began dotting the shores of the Bosporus and the Marmara. It was becoming increasingly evident that the dreamed of Bosporus bridge needed to be part of a more comprehensive transportation planning.

An Ill-Fated Interwar Project

One German émigré, the prominent Weimar veteran architect/planner Martin Wagner who came to Turkey in 1936 and became a consultant to Istanbul municipality, was the first to systematically observe the problem of access and mobility as the central issue to be tackled. Based on detailed analyses of demographics and existing modes of urban transport, he emphasized the urgent need to connect the separate pieces of the dispersed city and facilitate access to the center.[6] This recommendation would become the primary mandate for Henri Prost, the French urban planner who prepared Istanbul's first Master Plan approved in 1939. It was a regulatory plan to introduce zoning and an efficient road network. Although it fell short of proposing a Bosporus bridge, Prost's report suggests that there were ongoing discussions to pursue the idea. He argued that if a bridge were to be built in the near future, the best location would be the narrow crossing between Rumeli Hisarı and Anadolu Hisarı[7]—a location far north of the bridge's actual location (but one that would eventually be the site of the second bridge in 1988).

It should be noted that these deliberations took place in a dramatically altered historical context. It was no longer the imperial geopolitics of pre-World War I years, but rather the new nationalist vision of the early Republic that framed the arguments in favor of the desired Bosporus Bridge. The strategic importance of the Bosporus straits was again highlighted by the Montreux Treaty, which was signed on July 20, 1936, giving Turkey sovereignty over the control of the international waters of the straits.[8] A bridge across the straits, visually and symbolically confirming this newly recognized sovereignty and marking Turkey's self-positioning literally as a "bridge between Europe and Asia," must have appealed to the nation-builders of the young republic. It was, however, not so much the central government in Ankara, but rather the business community and local leaders of Istanbul who advocated for specific infrastructural improvements, better port facilities and better connectivity to accelerate the economic recovery of their city.

The idea of a Bosporus bridge was seriously pursued between 1933 and 1938, largely through the efforts of a Turkish businessman Nuri Demirağ (later a politician) who lobbied the government for it. Having already built a strong reputation as Turkey's premier railroads contractor, Demirağ (whose last name means "iron network") proved to be a bold entrepreneur. Fascinated by contemporary bridge construction in the U.S., he sought preliminary agreements with a Bethlehem Steel subsidiary firm involved in the construction of the Golden Gate Bridge (1933–1937). Using some U.S.-based Turkish engineers as intermediaries, he then contacted the prominent engineering firm of Modjeski & Masters in New York. The firm was established in the late nineteenth century by the Polish engineer Ralph Modjeski, a legendary figure known as "America's urban bridge builder."[9] Its portfolio included such famous works as the Benjamin Franklin Bridge in Philadelphia (1921–1927) and the San Francisco–Oakland Bay Bridge (1931–1936), which was under construction when the Turkish project landed in the office.

The initial brief sent to Modjeski & Masters in November 1934 asked for a preliminary proposal, the drawing of which could be used to convince investors.[10] Archival material shows that using the little available information and photographs of the site, Modjeski engineers proposed a 2560m long steel truss bridge. Rising 53.34 meters above the water it was to carry both tram and bus lanes, combining a 701 meter long suspension section at deeper waters near the European shore with a lower, long cantilever bridge supported by piers in the shallower waters towards the Asian shore (Figure 14.2). Most significantly, it spanned from the Seraglio Point on the historic peninsula to the Salacak shore in Üsküdar on the Asian side. Although not the narrowest point of the straits, this particular location was significant for connecting the two major hubs of the city, while leaving the northern shores of the Bosporus untouched and picturesque.

Although what Modjeski sent was merely a preliminary idea largely derived from a very similar bridge that they were working on at the time (Iowa–Illinois Memorial Bridge over the Mississippi, 1935), it was extensively used for publicity in Turkish media as if the bridge, now named "Ataturk Bridge" after the founder of the republic and the first president, was a done deal. Several newspapers published enthusiastic accounts of the bridge "to be designed by the engineer of the Oakland Bay Bridge" the photographs of which were promptly included. Correspondence in the office of Modjeski & Masters shows that the firm repeatedly explained the need for further onsite studies and for a complete technical report at an additional cost of U.S.$35,000 separate from the U.S.$15 million estimated cost of the bridge, apparently to no avail. According to Demirağ's published memoirs, "in spite of Ataturk's personal enthusiasm," key figures in the government opposed the project

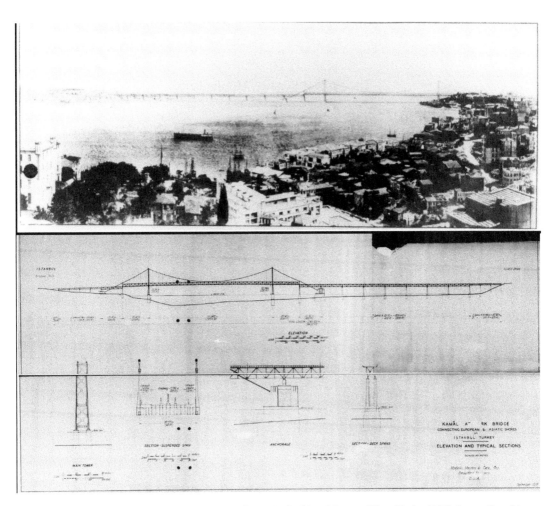

Figure 14.2 Early proposal by the engineering firm Modjeski & Masters (New York, 1935) for a railroad/motorway bridge connecting the historical peninsula with Salacak on the Asian shore.

Source: Modjeski & Masters Inc. Archives, Mechanicsburg, PA.

questioning its technical and economic feasibility. "[Their] ignorance of the progress in bridge construction and caisson systems …" he wrote, "… deprived Istanbul of a bridge that is destined to be constructed sooner or later."[11]

Although the project was clearly not going anywhere, Modjeski office continued to write to Turkish intermediaries and to the U.S. Commercial attaché in Istanbul, to reiterate that they were "very interested in foreign projects of this magnitude … even though the project may not become active for some time to come."[12] There are a number of plausible explanations as to why it proved difficult to convince the Turkish government and secure the necessary funding. Many bureaucrats in Ankara harbored serious qualms about a costly engineering project at a time when the regime's priority was developing Anatolian industries and enhancing the prominence of the new capital Ankara. Although Istanbul's master planning needs were acknowledged, with her population still below one million, the consensus was that ferries easily met the city's daily need for vehicular and pedestrian Bosporus crossings. This skepticism about the bridge's feasibility and necessity, coupled with Ataturk's death in 1938, the onset of World War II and the dire economic conditions of war years seem to have dealt the final blow to the

Modjeski project and to Demirağ's dream to make it a spectacular historical accomplishment for the early republican regime.

The Project Regains Momentum

The revival of the project in the 1950s corresponds with major historical shifts in Turkish national politics that brought Democrat Party (DP) to power and initiated the country's postwar global repositioning as NATO's easternmost bastion against communism. The nineteenth-century geopolitical role of sentinel assigned to Turkey was revived, this time in the context of the Cold War. Generous packages of U.S. economic cooperation aid financed Turkey's radical policy shift from railroads to highways as the country's primary mode of transportation, adding a renewed urgency to the idea of bridging the Bosporus. As distinct from earlier proposals however, it was now envisioned not as a rail bridge but as a motorway connection—a shift that largely accounts for the changes in design, scale, and overall conception along successive iterations of the project during the next two decades.

The revival of the project after a twelve-year hiatus needs to be understood in the context of Istanbul's unprecedented urban transformation under the new DP regime. For the first time since the turn of the century, the population of the city exceeded the one million mark and Istanbul regained its importance as the de facto capital of the country reversing the Ankara-centered policies of the early Republican period. Under the personal supervision of PM Adnan Menderes, the city received its American brand of modernist urbanism focused on highways and major arteries along the models set by Robert Moses in New York. Massive demolitions were carried out and new roads were cut through the historic fabric of the city. On the European side, a major north-south artery was built along the largely empty ridge overlooking the Bosporus and littoral roads along the shores were widened, effectively stretching the city from the new airport in the south to the Black Sea coast in the north. Collectively, these developments introduced a dramatic scalar shift in urban imaginary and marked the beginning of Istanbul's transformation from a historic shore city to a metropolis sprawling towards its hinterland. The only piece conspicuously missing to complete this new metropolitan scale was a bridge across the Bosporus.

As middle classes enthusiastically embraced the newly acquired sense of mobility and freedom afforded by the automobile, the demand for vehicular Bosporus crossings by ferries significantly increased. The real pressure came, however, from the hundreds of trucks that carried factory and farm products between Thrace and Anatolia every day, causing frequent bottlenecks in ferry traffic, not to mention full disruptions of ferry service in bad weather. Such scenes would be cited extensively to make a case for the necessity of the bridge, now a major government-sponsored project. More significantly, the long-awaited bridge was no longer conceived as just an engineering object in itself, but rather, as one component of a much larger, extensive highway system overseen by the General Directorate of Highways, the agency that became the primary interlocutor between the Turkish government and foreign expertise.[13] In 1957, the government's propaganda publication proudly announced its plans for the Bosporus Bridge, "a splendid monument to the love of construction and determination of the DP government, that will adorn the Bosporus like a jewel added to its historical beauty."[14]

The large volume of correspondence between Modjeski & Masters and the various officials in the Turkish General Directorate of Highways between 1951 and 1957 shows that the firm continued to be interested in the project and sought help from contacts in the U.S. Bureau of Public Roads, which was now working with their Turkish counterparts in the new highway-building program. Explaining the very different circumstances of the earlier project, they reiterated their willingness to revise the project for possible new Bosporus locations now under consideration and to rework the design for trucks and automobiles rather than the railway.[15] As the process dragged on however, without a clear commitment from Turkish officials who were now inclined to commission a feasibility study first and invite other engineering firms in some form of competition, Modjeski & Masters became increasingly skeptical and eventually declined to participate.

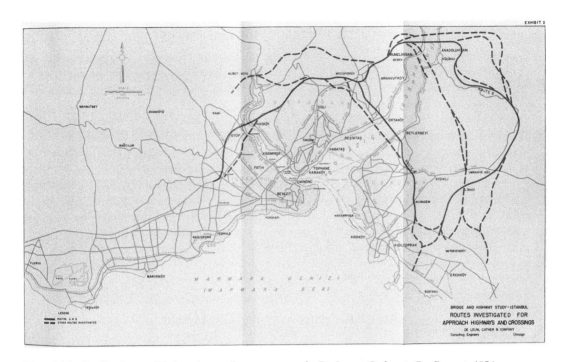

Figure 14.3 Studies for possible locations and connector roads, De Leuw, Cather & Co. Report, 1956.

Source: De Leuw, Cather & Co, *A Bosporus Straits Bridge and Connecting Highway System* (Chicago: 1956); courtesy of Parsons Corporation, copyright owner.

The breakthrough came in the mid-1950s, when the American consulting firm De Leuw, Cather & Co. of Chicago was commissioned, via the ICA (International Cooperation Administration of the U.S. government), to prepare a comprehensive report and a detailed feasibility study of possible locations for the bridge (Figure 14.3).[16] With its 174 pages of text, graphs, tables, statistics, maps, and drawings, featuring traffic origin-destination surveys, "desire lines," time-value analyses, user questionnaires, cost estimates and other such information, the report submitted to the Turkish Government in May 1956, is a classic example of the scientific discourse of expertise that informs postwar modernization theory: i.e. how data, charts, and numbers became the primary legitimation tools for large urban projects rendering them thoroughly rational, uncontestable, and inevitable in the eyes of authorities, stakeholders, and the general public.

Underscoring the inter-governmental nature and geopolitical premises of the project, the long list of contributors to the report included, on the Turkish side: General Directorate of Highways, the Navigation and Hydrological Office of the Turkish Navy, Istanbul Traffic and Metropolitan Planning Offices, and Maritime Bank of Turkey and on the US side, the International Cooperation Administration, US Bureau of Public Roads, and US Consulate in Istanbul. The 1956 report also sheds light on the complexities of such a trans-national, inter-agency undertakings and the asymmetries involved in the design process—mostly with Turkish engineers providing data and logistical help for the foreign technical know-how of European and American experts. For the bridge itself, a preliminary design by the structural engineering firm of David B. Steinmann was included in the report, featuring a steel truss suspension structure with two tower supports anchored in the water.

The report effectively turned what started as a Bosporus bridge project into a problem of comprehensive infrastructural planning at metropolitan scale. It recommended new zoning legislation, the creation of a "Regional Planning Agency" and the urgent construction of arterial highways connecting to the bridge "even if the bridge does not get built right away, in which case a new vehicular ferry service should be established at Ortakoy."¹⁷ In rather prophetic ways, it included forecasts on the demographic and urban impacts of the bridge, albeit seriously underestimating them and giving a positive spin to what would prove to be the onset of Istanbul's still contentious growth towards the natural forests and water sources of the north. Expected outward movement of population and commerce from the congested old city to the Bosporus hills and beyond was defined as one of the "invigorating effects of the bridge on the Turkish economy."[18]

Through the latter part of the 1950s, successive committees of experts from the General Directorate of Highways, Istanbul Municipality and Istanbul Technical University reviewed the 1956 report while many different proposals popped up along the way. For example, as an alternative to the suspension steel truss bridge project of Steinmann included in the report, a different type of concrete cantilever bridge by the German firm of Dyckerhoff and Widmann was also briefly considered but a committee of Turkish architects and planners rejected it on aesthetic grounds, arguing that a suspension bridge would look better on the Bosporus. Prominent German architect Paul Bonatz (who, after designing bridges for the *Reichsautobahnen* in Nazi Germany, had come to Turkey as educator and consultant) did propose a slender suspension bridge. Once again, however, the project would reach a dead end when the government that invested so heavily in it was dramatically toppled in May 1960 in what would be the first of a series of military coups. Among the many victims of the coup was the bridge project.

Revision, Controversy, and Completion

By 1968, when De Leuw, Cather & Co. produced a 212-page revision of their original study, a new Turkish government was in power. The revised report touches on what had already become evident in 1968: an enormous urban pressure on Istanbul as a result of massive migration from rural Anatolia and an unprecedented expansion of urban fringes in the form of squatter settlements built illegally on public land. Not surprisingly, these "informal settlements" were mushrooming around the proposed highway routes connecting to the bridge in anticipation of the speculative increases in the value of urban land. De Leuw, Cather & Co. suggested that the bridge and its connector road system could be an opportunity to address the larger question of informal settlements and the related planning challenges of a city now with a population close to 3 million. It recommended a "Joint Development of Urban Land" advising the government to clear land, combine with other parcels as necessary and either sell to private developers or retain for public use. In effect, this was a recommendation for the "establishment of a capitalist property regime" on urban land—something that successive governments had failed to enact in Turkey because of a symbiotic, clientelist relationship of authorities with squatter communities.[19]

With the ratification of Turkey's application to the European Economic Community in 1963, an international consortium of investment banks from EEC countries, UK and Japan pledged to finance the proposed bridge. By that time, Steinmann's 1956 design was criticized for placing the two towers in the water (rather than on land) and for its truss system being "obsolete in the light of new design techniques and higher strength steel."[20]

Modjeski & Masters were once again invited as consultants but they declined the invitation, having learned that the design contract was already given to the London firm of Freeman, Fox, and Partners.[21] Now to be built between Ortaköy and Beylerbeyi, about 3 km north of the original Modjeski & Masters proposal, the new Freeman & Fox project proposed an elegant structure 1,560m long, 33.40m wide and 165m high with minimal impact on the Bosporus silhouette. It not only placed the towers on land but also introduced two new concepts in suspension bridge design: a box type stiffening girder rather than the conventional truss type and inclined (rather than vertical) hanger cables.

Four consortiums bid for the tender to construct the bridge in six phases and the U.S.$22 million contract was signed in January 1970 with Hochtief Co. from Germany and the Cleveland Bridge and Engineering Co. from the UK. Its construction largely coincided with another period of turmoil in Turkish politics following the 1971 military coup but was nevertheless completed under two successive

Figure 14.4 Suspension bridge and connecting highway under construction, fall 1972.
Source: Image in Sibel Bozdoğan's collection; source unknown.

provisional governments between 1971 and 1973 (Figure 14.4). There is no question that the bridge generated great excitement in the collective consciousness of the country. Its image was everywhere: publicity material, stamps, banknotes, postcards, and—my personal favorite—in *mahyas* of mosques—electric illumination between minarets typically reserved for religious messages. The popularity, prestige, and, eventually, the heavy use and profitability of the "Ataturk Bridge" (as it was inaugurated) does not mean however, that a national consensus existed on the project. It was riddled with continuous controversy from the mid-1950s onwards reflecting the deep political divides in Turkey. While successive conservative governments embraced it as the centerpiece of an effective PR campaign of an active, energetic administrative style that prefers "doing rather than talking," professional associations, oppositional parties and media, secular elites, and left-wing circles were largely opposed to the project.

In a 36-page report in 1969, Turkish Chamber of Architects and Planners, the left leaning professional association, characterized it as a "bad decision"—a "political *fait accompli*"—that exaggerated the benefits of the bridge while suppressing any critical analysis.[22] It warned that the project would trigger urban growth towards the north and increased traffic would necessitate new bridges and connecting roads in a vicious circle or a "bridge trap." It complained that the project further encouraged private car ownership, which, in turn, would increase Turkey's dependency on foreign imports of cars and oil neither of which the country produced, depleting her foreign exchange reserves. Scarce resources could be better spent, it argued, on improving rail systems and maritime public transportation alternatives, and above all, jump-starting a subway system for Istanbul. It also criticized the project's exclusive dependency on foreign expertise and construction materials, without giving anything back to the country to advance Turkish engineering know-how or to develop domestic steel industries. Lastly, it lamented the bridge on aesthetic grounds that the size and scale of this technological object would destroy the unique panorama of Istanbul—something that would subsequently be disproved by the broad consensus regarding the beauty and iconic value of the slender structure.

What the Chamber of Architects report unequivocally shows is the rift between thinking in terms of national economic balances and equitable distribution of services and resources on the one hand, versus in terms of geopolitical benefits, international prestige and profitability for powerful groups on the other. This, in a nutshell, is Turkey's perennial rift between a secular-nationalist, largely impotent left and a far more effective populist-conservative right that has ruled the country since 1950. "If this bridge ends up being built" concluded the report,

> … it is still possible that a considerable majority of the population with limited awareness of economic and social matters will be mesmerized by this monument and say "how fortunate that it was built!" To impress people with the psychological weight of monumental structures to break their resistance to the hegemonic order is a well-known strategy since ancient Egypt.[23]

Nevertheless, when the bridge was opened on that sunny fall day in 1973 and government officials, celebrities and thousands of people walked from Asia to Europe for the first time, decades of controversy were briefly forgotten and a palpable national pride took over, vividly illustrating David Nye's argument that "technological sublime can be an element of social cohesion."[24]

The impact of the bridge on Istanbul's subsequent growth and spreading macro-form unfolded exactly as the Chamber of Architects feared. Phenomenal urban development to the north of the bridge, coupled with increased traffic crossing between Europe and Asia soon necessitated a second bridge (Fatih Sultan Mehmet Bridge, 1988), triggering the chain of the "bridge trap" that the authors of the 1969 report had warned about. None of it has been as controversial however, as the more recent Third Bridge (Yavuz Sultan Selim Bridge, 2016) and its connecting Northern Marmara Highway system, which has accelerated urban encroachment upon the northern forests and water basins of the city, unleashing what many experts agree to be an ecological catastrophe for Istanbul. In the end, what the Chamber of Architects and other critics of the first bridge considered to be a "bad decision" at the time would prove to be a powerful instrument of visual politics, boosting urban iconicity and national pride and seducing the electorate. Thereafter, the linking of infrastructural megaprojects with populist propaganda became a permanent feature of Turkish politics and has recently been carried to unprecedented new heights by the current AKP government of President Erdoğan.

Notes

1 For a brief history of Bosporus crossings, see İsmet İlter, *Boğaz ve Haliç Geçişlerinin Tarihçesi* (Ankara: Karayolları Genel Müdürlüğü Matbaası, 1973).
2 Richard Sennett, "The Hinge City" in *Living in the Endless City*, ed. Ricky Burdett and Deyan Sudjic (London: Phaidon Press, 2011), 221–222.

3 Drawing featured in *The Engineer* (September 13, 1867), 230.
4 "Suspension and Cantilever Bridges," *The Engineer* (July 11, 1884), 19.
5 James Garvie, C.E., "Bridging the Bosporus," *The Engineer* (March 3, 1893), 180.
6 Martin Wagner, "İstanbul'un Seyrüsefer Meselesi" *Arkitekt* 9 (1936): 252–256 and "Istanbul Havalisinin Planı" *Arkitekt* 10 (1936): 301–306.
7 Henri Prost, *Istanbul Hakkında Notlar* (İstanbul: Belediye Matbaası, 1938), 125–126.
8 James T. Shotwell and Francis Deak, *Turkey at the Straits: A Short History* (New York: The Macmillan Co, 1940), Appendix 3, 154–167.
9 See W.F. Durand, *Biographical Memoir of Ralph Modjeski 1861–1940* (National Academy of Sciences Publication, 1944) and the documentary film *Bridging Urban America* (2016).
10 I would like to thank Thomas Murphy of Modjeski & Masters Inc., Mechanicsburg, PA for making their archives available to me.
11 *Nuri Demirağ'ın Hayat ve Mücadeleleri* (Istanbul: Nu.D. Matbaası, 1957), 56–57.
12 Letter from Joseph H. Ehlers of Modjeski & Masters Engineers to Julian Gillespie, American Commercial Attaché in Istanbul, August 19, 1938.
13 See Begum Adalet, *Hotels and Highways: The Construction of Modernization Theory in Cold War Turkey* (Stanford, CA: Stanford University Press, 2018).
14 *İstanbul'un Kitabi* (İstanbul: Neşriyat Turizm Müdürlüğü, 1957), 111–112.
15 Letter from Modjeski & Masters to Vecdi Diker, 21 June 1951. Diker was an engineer who headed the General Directorate of Highways and worked with Harold Hilts during the Turkish and U.S. governmental cooperation for highway building.
16 De Leuw, Cather & Co., *A Bosporus Straits Bridge and Connecting Highway System* (report prepared for the General Directorate of Highways of the Republic of Turkey, Chicago: May 1956).
17 Ibid. 8.
18 Ibid. 155.
19 See Cağlar Keyder, "The housing market from informal to global" in *Istanbul between the Global and the Local* (Lanham: Rowman & Littlefield, 1999), 143–159.
20 De Leuw, Cather International Inc., *Updating of the Bosporus Bridge and Connecting Highways Feasibility Study* (Chicago: October 1968), 3.
21 Letter from Modjeski & Masters to Turkish General Directorate of Highways, May 14, 1968.
22 *Boğaz Köprüsü Üzerine Mimarlar Odası Görüşü* [Opinion of the Chamber of Architects on the Bosporus Bridge] (Ankara: TMMOB, 1969).
23 *Boğaz Köprüsü Üzerine Mimarlar Odası Görüşü*, 36.
24 David Nye, *American Technological Sublime* (Cambridge: MIT Press, 1994), xi–xx.

15
BRASILIA, A STORY SEEN FROM THE ROADSIDE

Narratives of Landscape Transformation and the Technological Sublime

Sued Ferreira da Silva

Images of a monumental concrete city arising over the vast and arid plains of central Brazil have exerted a powerful hold on the Brazilian national imagination since the construction on the New Capital began in 1956. Celebrated and condemned, the project of Brasilia may be placed within a wider project of nation-building and the collective desire to realize modernity's utopian potential. Despite the city's extensive historiography, however, the role of the capital in the colonization of the interior is less well known. However, many political leaders, journalists, and opinion-makers viewed the siting of the capital as a necessary step in the production of a national landscape and a new political identity grounded on progress and modernization. Through epic language and evocative visual representations, official discourses and mass media circulated narratives of the technological sublime common to many settler colonialist societies, from the United States to Australia and the Soviet Union. And nowhere was this national imaginary more condensed than in the figure of the road. By evoking the aesthetic of the sublime to extol the grandeur and power of technology, public discourses celebrated the national road network as a symbol of monumental force, splitting and knitting the territory together, and mostly, symbolizing the conquest of humans over nature, of civilization over underdevelopment. This chapter examines the narratives of nature, landscape, and technology surrounding road construction during Brasilia's inaugural years. Acting as a powerful political link, the emerging road network cleared the way for a radical transformation of the landscape by technology, making possible new readings and understandings of the territory while reframing the political and cultural project behind the construction of Brasilia.

"All roads lead to Brasilia"—announced *Machete* Magazine in April 1960, celebrating the soon-to-be inaugurated new national capital.[1] Recalling the widely known Roman maxim, the magazine highlighted the significant role given to mobility infrastructures in the context of the construction of Brasilia, conceived to be "organically connected, by arteries and nerves, to the whole country."[2] This analogy was not taken for granted. Situated on the ground zero of the highway system, Brasilia became the *umbilicus* from which all distances would be measured. Even more, it would be the symbolic measure separating the past of structural inequalities and underdevelopment from the promise of a social utopia.

Geographically located in the central highlands, the construction of the city mobilized discourses of territorial integration and socioeconomic development that demanded the conquest of a region seen as wild and deserted. The colonization of nature became a tool within the rhetoric of nation-building, a step necessary to the foundation of a modern landscape and a new political identity grounded on progress and modernization. And it was the road, and the construction of a road network, that most acutely condensed the national imaginary. By evoking the epic language of the sublime to express the grandeur and power of technology, public discourses celebrated the national road as a symbol of monumental force, breaking apart older relations of landscape and knitting the territory together into the Brazilian polity. Acting as a powerful political link, the road brought the possibility of connecting regions, communicating across vast distances, and bringing progress over underdevelopment, of humans over nature.

Centered on the national road system as the main actor, this chapter examines political discourses and narratives of nature, landscape, and technology mobilized during the construction of Brasilia and its inaugural years, based on foundational texts, visual reports, and news articles extracted from historical popular magazines engaged in the spread of governmental projects and discourses. For many observers, infrastructure transformed nature into an ordered landscape, introducing new meanings that can be illustrated to a greater extent through the rhetoric of technological sublime, the *leitmotiv* of the narratives here to be presented.

Brasilia, a Project of Modernity

In August 1883, the founder of the Salesian order and consecrated saint Dom Joao Bosco had a prophetic dream. "Between 15- and 20-degrees latitude," he foresaw,

> lays a very broad and very lengthy body of water that had its origins from the end of a lake. Then a voice kept repeating to me, "When the mines hidden in the midst of these mountains will eventually be dug out, here will appear the promised land flowing with milk and honey. Its wealth will defy belief!"[3]

Bosco's prophecy both reflected and catalyzed the imagination of Brazilians eager to change the capital from the coasts of Rio de Janeiro to the wild and vast central highlands. His words would echo far into the future, forming the basis of narratives of Brasilia's mythical foundation. Such a potent vision of a city in the wilderness full of riches fueled advocates for the construction of a New Capital of Brazil, a decision made official with the first republican Constitution of 1891.

At the same time, many argued for the transfer of the capital on more practical grounds, citing the question of national security in the event of foreign invasions. In any case, after decades of hesitation and false starts, Brasilia finally got its start in 1956 as the central component of President Juscelino Kubitschek's (1902–1976) plan for national integration and economic expansion. Marked by the motto "Fifty years of modernization in five," the construction of the new capital relied on Kubitschek's political power to promote a new national identity through the ideals of progress and development.[4] In this sense, Brasilia embodied the Brazil of the future.

To build this future, many argued, Brazil would have to dismantle the colonial order by introducing a new one marked by modernization, breaking with tradition, and rejecting the inheritances of the past.[5] Brasilia would serve these aspirations by providing a material locus for the instantiation of modernity and the display of its utopian potential through the control of nature, the promise of progress, and of a good society governed by reason.[6] In the words of president Kubitschek:

> The foundation of Brasilia is a political act whose reach cannot be ignored by anyone. It is the march to the interior in its fullness. It is the complete consummation taking ownership of the land. Let us build in the heart of our country a powerful center of irradiation of life and progress.[7]

As the "synthesis target" of Kubitschek's plans, Brasilia and the Central Highlands would serve as a pressure valve for the overcrowded cities of the coast through urbanization and migration. It would bring economic and social progress, supported by public works and industrialization, with special focus on the interstate highway system and automobile industry. These new machines and the speed they promised occupied the fever dreams of politicians, engineers, and architects, who envisioned automobility as a central feature of everyday life in the New Capital. Instantaneity, the annulment of distances, the ordering of flows, goods, and territories became part of the process of modernization required for the "conquest of the center" through the president's "Via Crucis" (crossroads):

> I had, then, a vision of what should be done. I would carve out a "Via Crucis," departing from the four cardinal points, having Brasilia as the foundation. One does not win a territory if one does not have access to it. And the road is a civilizing element par excellence. Therefore, I conceived the plane of the great longitudinal, cut almost perpendicularly by the great transversal. Brasilia would be at the center of the system, which would be a tower from which to contemplate Brazil.[8]

Opposing the longitudinal circulation model established during the colonial period following the coast lines, a multidirectional model was proposed (Figure 15.1).[9] As a result, it made possible the

Figure 15.1 Map showing the position of Brasília in the Central Highlands, marking the distances between the New National Capital from the Capitals of States and Territories in 1957.

Source: Brasilia magazine, 1957. Courtesy of The Public Archive of Brasilia (ArPDF).

establishment of a network of cities, the population of the so-called "demographic void," the exploitation of raw materials, and the expansion of agricultural frontiers and consumer markets.

The transport system based on highways guided the urbanization of Brazil's central regions, determining both a specific terrain of occupation and spatial remit for planning.[10] "For this scope to be achieved," utters president Kubitschek,

> several taboos would have to be broken; carrying out the exploitation of Brazil's immense natural resources; striving for the elimination of appalling social gaps through a consistent dissemination of progress; (…) and, finally, changing the seat of government, building this new Capital in the geographic center of the country.[11]

The president's "city for cars" took shape through the Pilot Plan of the architect and urbanist Lucio Costa, who won the design competition held between 1956 and 1957. The ground plan would later be activated by the iconic architecture of Oscar Niemeyer. The modernist principles of Costa's proposal aligned with the republic's broader political aspirations, reflecting the desire to build simultaneously the new city and the new nation. During his administration, Kubitschek oversaw construction of 14,970 km of new highways and paved another 6,202 km, connecting the capital with the main regional centers in all corners of the country. Most resources were allocated to the highways linking Brasilia to Belém (2,000 km), Fortaleza (1,500 km), Belo Horizonte (700 km) and Goiânia (200 km).[12] As announced in the *Brasilia* magazine,

> Both the Government and the people long for the materialization of the plans devised for this new *urbs*, the construction of which, at the heart of the national territory, shall profoundly change the economic, social, political and administrative landscape of the country … the nation watches the execution of the works with keen interest and confidence, knowing that Brasília constitutes a more correct and more opportune initiative so that Brazil may, in fact, progress.[13]

Having taken central stage, infrastructure remained in the electoral agendas of political actors in the years to come and fed the continuous reproduction of mobility-oriented urbanism.[14] Consequently, the governmental agencies linked to private transportation, contractors, and automobile industries began to act as promoters of modernization. Major daily newspapers such as the *Correio Braziliense* continuously highlighted the economic importance of regional roads and parkways, the "advanced road techniques" implemented, "the rhythm of Brasilia" (referring to the record 1,000 working days necessary to conclude the city's construction), the changes in the landscape's physiognomy, and its "images of progress."[15]

By the early 1960s, then, the urbanization of the Central Highlands had become a key objective of public policy, a fundamental issue of the nation's development. The national territory was regarded as identical to a city, ordered, and controlled as one, to paraphrase Foucault, by tracing a network of interstate highways and parkways.[16] The ultimate aim was the creation of a social–political order that would transform the national territory into a homogeneous and controlled polity.

Hope for the Forgotten Backlands: Enacting the Sublime of Infrastructure

The landscape of Cerrado, a savanna-like biome in Brazil, evokes the sublimity theorized by Edmund Burke in his seminal work *A Philosophical Inquiry into the Origin of Our Sublime and Beautiful*.[17] For Burke, the sublime emerges out of the perception of infinity brought by the horizon, the vastness of the arid plains that in our imagination finds no obstacle, the absolute solitude, deprivation, and the senses of death and life in the renewal of seasons. However, there were two forces that could tame the sublime: human reason and the machine. Nature has become an obstacle to the project of modernity that Brasilia represents, conceived as wilderness and, therefore, uncivilized. For this reason, the state viewed the interstate highway system as a civilizing project, one that would liberate the country from an undesired condition of poverty and underdevelopment. The march of progress was reinforced through political propaganda battles against a hostile nature, and the human spirit of expansion and conquest laid the foundation for the creation of a modern landscape.

Infrastructure, then, acquired the same status as the verticality of the mountain, the infinitude of the sky, and the abyssal sea exalted by the romantics for their sublimity. Advancing over forests, mountains, and lakes, infrastructure exceeded human ken and took possession of the senses of grandeur, magnitude, and power once associated with nature. The velocity of machines compressed space and time, overcoming the barriers of the physical world. Accessibility led the subject to the unknown and a promise of possibilities. To control the vastness of the natural environment with roads clearing forests, crossing rivers and valleys, "the umbilical cord that made a piece of land, now destined to change the country's future (…) the willingness to unite the fates of the nation."[18]

The rhetoric of progress through the colonization of nature set the tone for many depictions of the massive project. Journalist Eduardo Santamaria's review of the project for O Cruzeiro Magazine in its December 20, 1958, edition provides a case in point. Santamaria depicted the construction of the Belo Horizonte-Brasília Highway, extolling the cyclopean works carried out in record time and documenting the caravan of machines crossing wild regions, the intricacy of everyday logistics, including the acquisition of equipment and materials in the construction sites cut open in the middle of dense forests, only possible to be accessible by plane in most locations.[19] He cited the Belo Horizonte-Brasilia's design and monumentality, evincing concerns about safety, the smoothness of the route, paving, and fencing. "The highway connecting Rio and Belo Horizonte to Brasília," he wrote, "is, practically, a great straight line. It has been built in a way that allows drivers an average speed of 100 kilometers without any danger."[20] He contrasts the straight line as a symbol of modernity with the organicity and vicissitudes of nature. To rephrase Desportes, such relentless linearity satisfied technical, aesthetic, and philosophical considerations, denoting the power of art in face of a "fallen" nature, meant to be ordered, rectified.[21]

Santamaria's piece drew heavily on notions of "improvement" through modern infrastructure. He called attention to the hotels, parking lots, workshops, restaurants, and other commerce and services buildings that settled along the roadside. This vernacular landscape, made possible by the machine, reinforced the expectations of social and economic development that the increased flow of people and goods would bring to the neighboring states of Minas Gerais and Goiás. He also referred to the "extermination of the barber bug" and the recovery of poor and "unhealthy" locations that had long resisted human settlement. Thus, Belo Horizonte-Brasília Highway became "the redemption of a region practically wasted to Brazil … the hope of the forgotten backlands."[22]

During the presidency of Kubitschek, the highway solidified into a landscape-object, celebrated for its form, monumentality, and capacity to engineer nature, subjugating and ordering it. Beyond a surface to carry goods and people, it was elevated to the status of the bearer of the nation's prosperous future, and an exemplar of the benefits of modernization to counter underdevelopment. As historian Rômulo de Paula Andrade argues, Kubitschek resumed the "interior imperialism" pursued under the dictatorship of President Getulio Vargas from 1937 to 1945, in which the vast Central Highlands loomed as a frontier to be conquered.[23] And for Kubitschek, Brasilia and its connecting roadways were the key:

> The true greatness of the country will only be known on the day when we dominate the great interior voids, planting cities, tearing roads, bringing technical progress to remote corners and exploring their immense wealth. And Brasília is the big step for that future world.[24]

These narratives of conquest and material progress were not simply the province of Brazilian politicians and members of the economic elite; they resonated throughout Brazilian popular culture, as is the case in many settler colonialist societies, including the United States, Canada, South Africa, Australia, and the Soviet Union. It was the "rhetoric of the technological sublime" that proved particular resonant in both capitalist and socialist systems.[25] In Leo Marx's evocative formulation,

> the sensory attributes of the engine—iron, fire, steam, smoke, noise, speed—evoke the essence of industrial power and wealth, and when set against the attributes of a natural terrain—fecundity, beauty, serenity, an ineffable numinosity—the effect can be spine-tingling.[26]

The language reserved for contemplation and the celebration of nature was transferred to technology, exalting its capacity to transform a piece of uncultivated land into an orderly garden.[27] Building on Leo Marx, David Nye argues that the attribution of sublimity to human creations acquired a new meaning in which sublime objects manifested the staggering power of reason. The feelings of weakness and humiliation before nature was redirected to the machine, where "the superior imagination of an engineer or a technician … creates an object that overwhelms the imagination of ordinary men."[28] Since the technological sublime undermines the notion of limitation, it requires continuous innovation to transform the world and the idea of a reason in constant evolution.

These magazines employed an epic language, flowering the act of founding the city in a solitary landscape, and aligned public power with the images of efficiency, planning, industrialization, and modernization.[29] They acted as a propaganda tool for the presidency, spreading its developmental discourses, and pacifying conflicts by extolling solely the positive aspects of the construction and the narratives of interior colonization.[30] In this sense, the discourse of media converged with the official discourse, shaping the landscape imagination through their narratives and visual representations.[31]

As Andrade contends, the highway system materialized as an infrastructure of movement, legitimating the state and its discourses of integration, while occupying the central voids of the country.[32] The highway conforms a new political landscape in which the state becomes mobile.[33] It amplifies the dichotomies between humans and nature, civilization and underdevelopment in such a way that justifies the state as the heroic actor in the drama of conquest.

The Making of a Modern Arcadia

"Brasilia is built on the horizon.—Brasilia is artificial. As artificial as the world should have been when it was created."[34] In the introductory lines of the chronicle "Brasília" from 1962, Clarice Lispector expressed her first impressions when she came across the newly inaugurated city, drawing attention to the artificiality of the landscape. As illustrated in "The March of Brasilia Construction," a section of the magazine *Brasília* from 1957—a monthly report published by the Urbanization Company of the New Capital (NOVACAP)—the landscape is reinterpreted as a product of human technological creation. Earthworks, excavations, the trails left by trucks, tractors, backhoes, road rollers in the Cerrado revealed its red soil substrate and aridity, an artificiality that referred to a new world in formation. Nature was then shaped, transformed, and improved through these actions:

> Intense work by men and machines: this is what has characterized this initial phase of the construction of Brasília. The physiognomy of the region is rapidly changing, where more than three thousand workers and about two hundred powerful motorized devices carry out a disciplined and productive activity on a daily basis.[35]

With landscape understood as a product of labor and planning, engineers, architects, and technicians assumed themselves to be the central figures in the drama of transformation.[36] It was a triumph over nature qualified by its greatness and vastness, subdued by the technological power, as highlighted in the captions of the images: "a road being opened (…) Man and machine working together (…) men, machines, enthusiasm and action" (Figure 15.2).[37]

The photographs captured a process, a dramatic transformation of the landscape into a new phenomenon, not solely an object of contemplation, but also of construction.[38] In this new technological

Figure 15.2 "The March of the Construction of Brasilia" was a monthly report that aimed at the documentation of the New Capital's construction progress from January 1957 to May 1963.

Source: Brasilia magazine, 1957. Courtesy of The Public Archive of Brasilia (ArPDF).

landscape, different positions were assigned to the human and non-human actors involved in its construction: on one hand, human subjects appeared reduced before the scale of the machines, buildings, and the long extensions of the worked land. On the other hand, observers exalted humans' pioneering spirit, as the embodiment of the hero archetype. In this regard, the anthropologist James Holston attested the birth of two mythicized characters in the making of Brasilia: the pioneers and the *candangos*.[39] The pioneers were "the firsts," or high-ranking state officials carrying the mission to build the city, together with liberal professionals, merchants and cultivators. The *candangos* comprised skilled or non-skilled construction workers coming especially from the interior. As Holston points out, "while the term pioneer was used as an honorific, the term *candango* was derogatory, almost offensive. It signified a man without qualities, without culture, a vagabond lower-class lowbrow."[40] With the state's recruitment campaign, the adjective *candango* came to designate "new nation builders," central constituents in the pact of development. The redefinition of the *candango* represents the construction of new national identities for a mass of forgotten Brazilians, while eclipsing the subaltern position in which they were submitted during the construction of Brasilia.[41] As NOVACAP related in the *Brasilia* magazine,

> just over four months ago, there was nothing but wilderness. Large green meadows, with vast and subtle plateaus gently resting in the warm, secular quietness of their solitude. Now we have a very different picture. A great number of dedicated and active laborers, who are joined each day by other workers, carry out this grandiose plan that a patriotic and entrepreneurial Government has entrusted to them. There is no longer just the wilderness. There is no longer just the lonely, beautiful, and silent land lying there, abandoned, and drowned in melancholy. Today there is Brasilia; Brasilia, the new Capital of Brazil, throbbing with life, which is emerging from everywhere.[42]

During the construction of the highway connecting Brasilia to Belém, considered "the work of the century," the *Machete* magazine depicted an epic undertaking full of danger, loneliness, and deprivation, evoking "the idea of prodigious strength."[43] Into the wilderness, the *candangos* were submitted to extreme weather conditions, living in unhealthy construction camps, and in constant conflict with indigenous populations.[44] Moreover, the absence of and muted violence against indigenous populations is evident in all magazines. As subjects of colonization, they were either treated as barbarians to be civilized or as aliens in a pristine landscape devoid of human presence. Thus, socially constructed as the "new Bandeirantes"—explorers and fortune hunters from the colonial period—the *candangos* were classified in opposition to the indigenous, with their identity celebrated as well as their cyclopean task of carrying Brazil's great destiny by conquering the Brazilian wildlands, from the central savannahs to "the green Devil" or the Amazon jungle up in the north. This battle against the forest acquired national attention after the death of Bernardo Sayão, the lead engineer working on the construction of the new capital, whose tragic death on January 15, 1959 was theatricalized:

> When the first waves of workers left Belém with the purpose of opening a road in the middle of the Amazon Jungle, a tall and strong man centralized all operations. (…) One day, the unexpected fall of a gigantic tree buried him under its ancient branches. Today, this road, the construction of which seemed impossible, and which brought about the miracle of national integration, is named after its pioneer, who was murdered by the forest.[45]

The martyrdom of Bernardo Sayão, the *candangos*' journeys into the wilderness, the visit of politicians to construction sites, and the many inaugurations all celebrated the collective effort in the creation of Brazil's modern identity. As David Nye maintained, the category of sublime goes beyond a solitary communion with nature; rather, it is a shared and universal emotion, and an element of social cohesion.[46] Thus, the sublime of infrastructure becomes the shared belief of national grandeur through grand works, in which a victorious battle against the wilderness was only possible through the power of the machine and the achievements of its founding heroes.

With Brasilia, the notion of city reclaims its past association as the ultimate achievement of human society, civility, and order, and therefore demands a redesigned nature that reflects these ideals. Thereafter, in order to meet the demands of civil construction and to reduce the perception of aridity and artificiality of the newly built landscape, the central government commissioned the forestry services in a project of visual transformation. Beginning in 1959, millions of eucalyptus trees and other exotic species were planted alongside the parkways and regional roads in substitution for the native vegetation (Figures 15.3 and 15.4).[47] This program followed Lucio Costa's recommendations that a homogeneous and large stretch of vegetation should be planted alongside highways and parkways, serving as a protective barrier to urban areas.[48] Here, the assemblage of the picturesque and City Beautiful Movement aesthetic codes conceived the landscape as a bucolic space of leisure, harmony, and order—a space to ennoble citizens through aesthetic transformation. In the words of Telles, Costa's urban proposal sought to merge nature with culture, a representation of the true modern synthesis.[49]

Amid this profusion of grandeur, engineers still had to design and execute mundane projects, such as the countless bridges, viaducts, shoulders, and pavements. These presented opportunities for a design approach grounded in a simple suite of aesthetic choices that expressed beauty, harmony, and order through materials and functions. Rather than a direct evocation of the technological sublime, this was the more restrained beauty of the fault-tolerant curve, the functional bridge, the smooth pavement. The effect of these mundane artifacts would not be felt singularly, but in their sheer multiplication and repetition through the system. As Nye emphasizes, "every form of transportation is implicitly part of an idealized landscape (…) Each form of transportation has been used to define and construct a landscape, to embody a certain gaze."[50] In this sense, Brasilia and its road network emerged as a feat of modernist aesthetics both through domination of the machine over nature at scale, and through the relentless

Figure 15.3 Earthworks of the parkway connecting the Pilot Plan of Brasilia with the satellite town Taguatinga in 1965.

Source: Courtesy of The Public Archive of Brasilia (ArPDF).

rhythmic repetition of its elements. Elements of nature would be included, but only insofar as they supported the aesthetic and technical aspirations of a human-made landscape. This modern Arcadia, therefore, reflects the bourgeois ideal of landscape improvement by collapsing technology, aesthetics, and a lyrical sense and utilitarianism into narratives of national progress.[51]

The eagerness to beautify the roadside reveals an understanding of landscape as a product of aesthetic and technological control. Plantation schemes suggested a nature that is to be ordered, controlled, and harmonized for human contemplation. Beyond the belt of eucalyptus, the immeasurable vastness of nature as wilderness creates a constant feeling of "delightful horror" to be kept at bay through technological works. By recalibrating nature through the metaphor of the garden, a remade horizon appears, demarcated by aligned trees, cloverleaf exchange, bridges, and walkways. The emerging road network cleared the way for a radical transformation of the landscape by technology, making possible new readings and understandings of the territory while it framed the political and cultural conjecture in which the construction of Brasilia is placed. Through epic language and visual representation, mass media and political discourses linked infrastructure with utopia and made it the symbolic and material expression of humans' emancipation from nature. These discourses comprised the dominant themes

Figure 15.4 A new landscape is shaped with a stretch of eucalyptus trees along the Taguatinga Parkway as shown in 1974.

Source: Courtesy of The Public Archive of Brasilia (ArPDF).

of modernity and supplied the framework for the New Brazilian Capital. On that account, all roads leading to Brasilia became the synecdoche for the Brazil of the future.

Notes

1. Pedro Gomes, "Todos os caminhos levam a Brasília," *Revista Manchete* 417 (April 1960).
2. Ibid.
3. Dom João Bosco as translated by Robinson & Robinson, 2014.
4. Jeferson C. Tavares, *Projetos para Brasília e a cultura urbanística nacional* (PhD diss., University of São Paulo, 2004), 44.
5. Hilde Heynen, *Architecture and Modernity: A Critique* (Cambridge: MIT Press, 1999), 10.
6. Jürgen Habermas, "Modernity versus Postmodernity," *New German Critique*, no. 22 (Winter 1981): 9.
7. Juscelino Kubitschek, "A mudança da capital," *Revista Brasília* 1, no. 1 (January 1957): 1, translated by the author.
8. Juscelino Kubitschek, *Por que construí Brasília* (Brasília: Senado Federal, 1975), 84.
9. Jusselma Duarte de Brito, *De Plano Piloto a Metrópole: a mancha urbana de Brasília* (PhD diss., University of Brasilia, 2009), 24, 54.
10. Ibid. 73, 104.

11 Kubitschek, *Por que construi Brasília*, 12.
12 Vania Maria Losada Moreira, 1998 as cited in Tavares, *Projetos para Brasília e a cultura urbanística nacional*, 54.
13 Novacap, "A marcha da construção de Brasilia," *Revista Brasília* 1, no. 1 (January 1957), 5, translated by the author.
14 Benny Schvarsberg, "Quem disse que ia ser fácil?" in *Leituras da cidade*, ed. Ana Clara Torres Ribeiro (Rio de Janeiro: Letra Capital, 2012), 109.
15 *Correio Braziliense*, 1960–1974.
16 Foucault as cited in Jean-Marc Besse, *O gosto do mundo: exercícios de paisagem* (Rio de Janeiro: EdUERJ, 2014), 121.
17 Edmund Burke, *A Philosophical Enquiry into the Origin of Our Ideas of the Sublime and Beautiful* (London and New York: Penguin, 1998 [1757]).
18 Gomes, "Todos os caminhos levam a Brasília."
19 Eduardo Santamaria, "Esperança do sertão esquecido," *Revista O Cruzeiro* (December 1958).
20 Ibid.
21 Desports as cited in Jean-Marc Besse, *O gosto do mundo: exercícios de paisagem* (Rio de Janeiro: EdUERJ, 2014), 123.
22 Santamaria, "Esperança do sertão esquecido."
23 Rômulo de Paula Andrade, "Vencidas a distância e floresta! A Transbrasiliana e a Amazônia desenvolvimentista," *Tempo* 25, no. 2 (May–July 2019): 365–381.
24 Juscelino Kubitschek, "Nada obstará a marcha do país para a conquista de si mesmo, que é a ocupação efetiva de suas grandes áreas internas," *Revista Brasília* 1, no. 4 (April 1957), translated by the author.
25 Leo Marx, *The Machine in the Garden: Technology and the Pastoral Ideal in America* (Oxford: Oxford University Press, 1964), 375.
26 Ibid. 374.
27 Ibid.
28 David E. Nye, *American Technological Sublime* (Cambridge, London: MIT Press, 1994), 60.
29 Luisa Videsott, *Narrativas da construção de Brasília: mídia, fotografias, projetos e história* (PhD diss., University of São Paulo, 2009), 285.
30 Ibid. 238.
31 Andrade, "Vencidas a distância e floresta!"
32 Ibid.
33 Ibid.
34 Clarice Lispector, *Selected Crônicas* (New York: New Directions Publishing, 1996).
35 Novacap, "A marcha da construção de Brasilia," *Revista Brasília* 1, no. 2 (February 1957), 4, translated by the author.
36 Mari Hvattum, "The man who loved views: C. A. Pihl and the making of the modern landscape," in *Routes, Roads, and Landscapes*, ed. Mari Hvattum and others (London and New York: Routledge, 2011), 114.
37 Novacap, "A marcha da construção de Brasilia," *Revista Brasília* 1, no. 1 (January 1957), 4, translated by the author.
38 Hvattum, "The man who loved views."
39 James Holston, *The Modernist City: An Anthropological Critique of Brasilia* (Chicago and London: The University of Chicago Press, 1989).
40 Ibid.
41 Ibid.
42 Novacap, "A marcha da construção de Brasilia," *Revista Brasília* 1, no. 2 (February 1957), 4, translated by the author.
43 Burke, *A Philosophical Enquiry into the Origin of Our Ideas of the Sublime and Beautiful*.
44 *Manchete Magazine Historical Edition* (April 21, 1960).
45 Ibid 63.
46 Nye, *American Technological Sublime*.
47 Francisco Ozanan Correa Coelho Alencar and others, *Arborização urbana no Distrito Federal: história e espécies do cerrado* (Brasília: Novacap, 2008).
48 Lucio Costa, *Relatório do Plano Piloto de Brasília* (Brasília: GDF, 1991 [1957]).
49 Sophia S. Telles, "Lucio Costa: monumentalidade e intimismo," *Novos Estudos CEBRAP*, no. 25 (October 1989): 75–94.
50 Nye, *American Technological Sublime*, 99.
51 Costa, *Relatório do Plano Piloto de Brasília*.

16
MORE THAN A "CIRCULATION MACHINE"

Recasting the Geographies of Infrastructure in Modernist Urbanism

Mejrema Zatrić

In modernist urbanism, transport infrastructure bore one of the four essential urban functions and was described as a "circulation machine," in a well-known formulation by Le Corbusier. Yet the history of urban plans of Antwerp (1933) in Belgium and the twin-cities of Slavonski and Bosanski Brod (1945) in Yugoslavia open a valuable perspective on the ways in which modernist architects incorporated the geography and politics of infrastructure into city planning. Rather than urban highways being merely subsumed under the "fourth function" of "circulation," the city as a whole was understood as an infrastructural extension and an element in a functional relationship with its environment. This chapter describes how this "other" functionalism of modernist urbanism was prefigured by applied human geography in the first half of the twentieth century and how it unfolded both through direct references to the scholarship of human geography and through shared political-economic requirements defined by free trade and state security on an ever-larger scale. In the case of inter-war Antwerp, planners explicitly discussed infrastructure as a political technology, one that tied geographies, economies and imaginaries into harmonious global scenarios. Then, in the context of Cold War Brods, Yugoslav planners recalibrated infrastructure as a tool of economic growth through territorial development, taking advantage of that nation's geopolitical and geographic middle ground. In both cases, infrastructure emerged as more than a "circulation machine," even if both were emblematic examples of modernist urban planning.

A machine-like array of conductors sits inside a bight of a river meander. The geometry of the web is slightly adjusted to the organic shape at the edges, yet the juxtaposition of the two seems more like an uneasy truce than a unison (Figure 16.1). This drawing is part of the "40 meters of the most accurate plans" drafted in Le Corbusier's studio for the Belgian city of Antwerp in 1933.[1] The plan was one of several attempts to translate the general program of modernist urbanism, referred to as *Le Ville Radieuse*, into reality.

A little more than a decade later, a similar scheme appeared inside a meander of the Balkan river Sava, as an answer to the first urbanistic commission of the Socialist Yugoslav government (Figure 16.2). Architect and urbanist Juraj Neidhardt, a contributor to the Antwerp plan during his stint in Le Corbusier's office, referred to the infrastructural prototype of the Radiant City in his proposal for the planning of the twin cities called Bosanski Brod and Slavonski Brod. Both the Antwerp and the Brod plans relied on the neat pattern of a secondary road network, placed at 45 degrees relative to the two main highways that connected the cities to their hinterland. Yet beyond this apparent isomorphism, what related these plans even more significantly was the way in which their transportation infrastructure corresponded to the vast territorial developmental scenarios that reveal the often overlooked mid-twentieth century characteristic of modernist *urbanisme*: the consideration of cities on a large, national and ultimately world scale. Rather than infrastructure being merely subsumed under the "fourth function" of functionalist urbanism, namely "circulation," the city as a whole

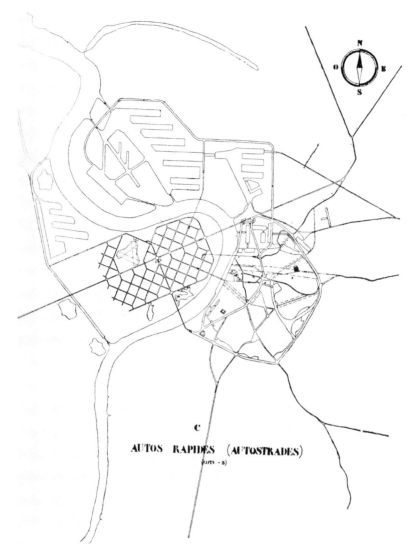

Figure 16.1 Urbanization of the Left Bank of the Scheldt in Antwerp: Circulation scheme, Le Corbusier, 1933.
Source: © F.L.C./ADAGP, Paris, 2021.

was understood as an infrastructural extension and an element in a functional relationship with its environment.

This "other" functionalism of modernist urbanism was prefigured by applied human geography in the first half of the twentieth century. In their effort to serve the economic and territorial ambitions of nascent modern nation states, human geographers projected functional relationships between infrastructures, landscape features, and cities. Guided by the assumption that movement and exchange conditioned the development of modern societies, they cast infrastructure as an essential fact of geography and means of world integration. However, the desire for the ever more open trade and traffic was inflected by the military-strategic concerns. The two world wars foregrounded the force of geographic expertise and infrastructure in both the prosecution of armed conflict and peacetime development.

Infrastructure in Modernist Urbanism

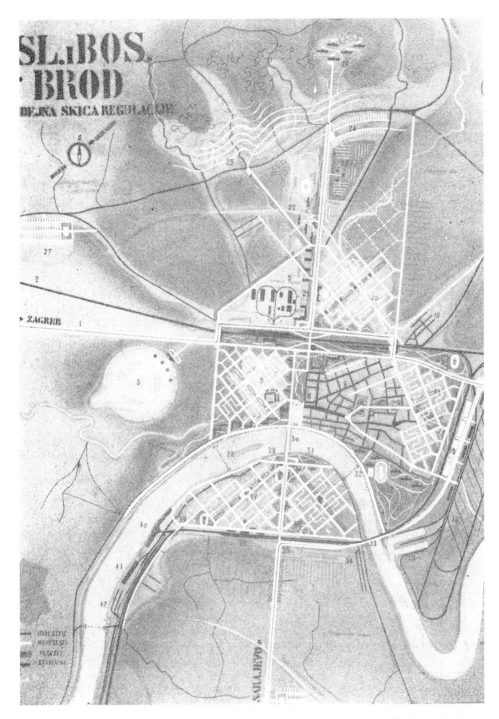

Figure 16.2 Conceptual sketch for the plan of Bosanski and Slavonski Brod, Juraj Neidhardt, 1945–1946.
Source: © Tatjana Neidhardt, 2021.

This chapter proposes that the geography of infrastructure was an important and politically charged concern of modernist urbanism. This concern unfolded both through direct references to the scholarship of human geography and through shared political-economic requirements defined by free trade and state security on an ever-larger scale. Modernist architects combined their proclivity for functionalism with the human geographic incorporation of infrastructure as a fact of landscape, definer of territory, and tool of governance. Although the Antwerp and Brod plans were never realized, they open a valuable perspective on the ways in which modernist urbanism incorporated the geography and politics of infrastructure into city planning. Le Corbusier's well known maxim that defined city streets as "machines for communication" elided the political charge of their strategic incorporation into trans-continental infrastructural networks. In the case of inter-war Antwerp, planners explicitly discussed infrastructure as a political technology, one that tied geographies, economies and imaginaries into harmonious global scenarios. Then, in the context of Cold War Brods, Yugoslav planners recalibrated infrastructure as a tool of economic growth through territorial development, taking advantage of that nation's geopolitical and geographic middle ground. In both cases, infrastructure emerged as more than a "circulation machine," even if both were emblematic examples of modernist urban planning.

Politics of Infrastructure in Human Geography

In most canonical early works of modern geography, infrastructure arose as a conditioning factor of both nation-building and world integration. The pioneering works of modern geographic scholarship already sought to account for the contents of land and sea as part of broader national and international political imaginaries. German geographer Albrecht Penck's 1871 initiative to produce the International Map of the World, for example, was inspired by the pursuit not only of international cooperation and peace, but also individual states' commercial interests and colonial enterprises.[2] In his 1905 work *L'Homme et la Terre*, French geographer Élisée Reclus complemented the regional descriptions with analysis of the agencies of "world powers."[3] Cloaked in the mantle of description and analysis, geography was simultaneously a worlding project implicated in the construction and reification of territorial imaginaries.

Fridrich Ratzel and Paul Vidal de la Blache, founders of modern geographic traditions in Germany and France, emphasized a switch from slow, gradual development of natural regions to the dynamics introduced by communication networks that provided for a superior order of territorial organization, characterizing the modern state.[4] Yet, both in the realm of science and international relations, the full force of infrastructure in modifying geographies became particularly apparent on the "meta-scale" of a "world system." At the same time, the visibility of the world as a system became possible only after the global communications network reached significant level of development. Already in the 1900s, Vidal de la Blache described the effect that the "welding" of continental transportation routes to maritime currents had as *bouclage du monde*.[5] Geographers of the nineteenth century hastened to describe emerging infrastructure such as transcontinental railroads, great inter-oceanic canals, network of shipping lines, and intercontinental telegraph lines.[6] What the integrated vision of the world made possible, however, was to understand infrastructural undertakings as interventions in a geopolitical "world game" where the various nations jostled for position relative to one another.[7]

By the early twentieth century, geographic analysis had already become established as a factor in efforts among nation-states to improve their prospects in this "world game." This was evident, for example, in the portioning of Africa among colonial powers. However, the possibilities of European co-operation through reciprocal recognition of national interests were fully expressed at the Paris Peace Conference of 1919. The United Sates and the European powers deployed geographic expertise to produce arguments in support of their territorial and political interests.[8] French human geography had a particularly pronounced geopolitical agency both before and at the Conference. Vidal de la Blache himself used "scientific" geography in the international political arena in defense of French colonial expansion, and a host of his followers applied a similar approach in support of the French cause in the Balkans.[9] One of the most prominent and effective expert voices at the Paris Peace Conference was the Serbian member of Vidal's scholarly circle, geographer Jovan Cvijić.[10]

In spite of his education being tied to the German idealist tradition through his doctoral studies with Penck, Cvijić's *oeuvre* aligns closely with French human geography in terms of its dual commitment to both empirical research and politically engaged, applied expertise. Just like his French colleagues, Cvijić dedicated his scholarly writings to developing a theoretical framework to rationalize the relationship between men and their environment. His pointed political discussions, however, were directed at advancing the Serbian national cause in the tumultuous decades surrounding World War I. Infrastructure was crucial to both enterprises.

Cvijić outlined his "bases of human geography" within the French intellectual framework, while drawing illustrations from his meticulous geological and ethnographic research in the Balkans.[11] His 1918 magnum opus *La Péninsule balkanique: géographie humaine* opened with analysis of the "main geographic characteristics" of the Balkan peninsula. These characteristics, he explained, were not merely geomorphological; rather, they comprised those features of the relief that had greatest impact on the life and development of the Balkan peoples.[12] In other words, Cvijić sought to generalize the mutual conditioning between geography and history. He argued that a set of longitudinal and transversal pathways (through an otherwise impenetrable relief) transformed the entire peninsula into a geographic bridge between Europe and Asia—a characteristic of decisive importance for the history of the Balkans.[13]

Some of Cvijić's best-known commentaries connected the geography of the Balkans to Euro-Asian politics. His bitter text "Annexation of Bosnia and Herzegovina" offered complex analysis of Austro-Hungarian railway construction policy in the Balkans as an element of the political-economic strategy against Serbia, and the campaign that anticipated eastward imperial expansion. In this sense, infrastructure unfolded as the connecting filament between geography and history, between the lay of the land and human affairs. As one of Vidal de la Blache's best known disciples, Jean Brunhes, claimed, in reference to the same geopolitical controversy between Austria-Hungary and Serbia: "Geography has its revenge on politics; it takes time because its life is longer, but it often has the last word."[14] Speaking in 1913, Brunhes had anticipated the magnitude of events to which Austrian domination of communication and trade routes in the Balkans could lead. The assassination of the Austrian prince next year in Sarajevo was a direct consequence of these tensions and it further sparked World War I.

When in his 1925 book *Géographie Humaine* Brunhes designated "roads" and "houses" as the first pair amongst the essential elements of geography, the human geographic outlook on infrastructural projects as "the most important events in the history of the world" and "true incarnations of Geography," had already moved into the purview of social reform and engineering alike.[15] In a world deeply shaken by the unprecedented scale of conflict, the apparent power of infrastructure to shape history underlay a growing number of projects and initiatives.

Canals and Skyscrapers in Antwerp

One of the most ambitious such initiatives was Belgian philosopher Paul Otlet's campaign to establish a "World City." His effort to implement it as a cluster of international institutions in Antwerp was not only illustrative of the way in which infrastructure enhanced the geographic determinants of geopolitics, but it also uncovered the importance that urbanism held in this regard, as a modifier of infrastructural networks.

When the municipality of Antwerp issued a planning competition for the left bank of the river Scheldt in 1933, Otlet seized the opportunity. His review of the competition's brief, "Anvers qui va a grandir," noted that the city wanted to be "the first port of a Continent of 350 million inhabitants," with 38 km of dockside facilities served by no less than 800 km of railway.[16] The competition focused on the 1000 ha swath of land across the river from the historic core of Antwerp, which had remained unbuilt because the heavy traffic of big ships through the Scheldt made bridging impractical. However, with the expected inauguration of two underwater tunnels, the prospects for the development of the site improved dramatically. The municipality asked the contestants to imagine there a new city of 100,000 inhabitants.

There were two ways, Otlet proposed, in which the problem posited by the competition brief could be tackled. The national solution relied on binding Antwerp tightly to the Belgian economy by making it a point of "exchange" between "lines" connecting it to Brussels, Charleroi, and Liege. The "international solution," on the other hand, could only be conceptualized by observing Antwerp "from without," as a part of a larger "World Plan."[17] It relied on the city's and the country's geography, their position "at the crossroads of the main roads, on the Scheldt which gives free access to the sea."[18] Otlet singled out those contestants taking the international approach, such as Le Corbusier, for presenting the "most interesting work."

For Le Corbusier, the competition provided an opportunity to popularize the general conception of modernist urbanism that he called the *Ville Radieuse*. Throughout the 1930s, Le Corbusier's "urbanisation" plans centered on the mobility afford through the automobile, concretizing its importance by separating it completely from the movement of pedestrians. His circulation scheme for the left bank in Antwerp featured a series of 400m × 400m superblocks served by "highways for rapid automobile traffic."[19] Elevated from the ground by means of *pilotis*, buildings were connected to surrounding parking lots, in turn attached to the so-called *redent* blocks. With its integral structure and focus on circulation, the Antwerp plan was consonant with Le Corbusier's urbanistic proposals from the 1920s. However, it also featured important differences.

Le Corbusier developed The Radiant City model amid intense exchanges with the regional syndicalist movement in France, as well as with his "discovery of geography."[20] The movement's focus on the geographic region, particularly the balance between regional character and regional economy, led to large-scale territorial projections and geopolitical speculation. Le Corbusier had studied geographic literature and attended Jean Brunhes' lectures at the Collège de France in the 1910s—engagements that will directly influence his books on territorial planning of the 1940s.[21] Already in the early 1930s, however, he increasingly understood cities as entangled in these geographic-economic constellations, and the infrastructural networks that came out of them. His syndicalist intellectual circle advocated international alliances based on geographic-historical dispositions and potentials for global economic coherence. If the world were politically organized in reference to these important axioms, the argument went, world peace would be insured. The regional syndicalists imagined territorial wholes as longitudinally divided geographic-economic and political entities, such as "Latin Federation" and "Oriental Federation," in order to provide them with a diversity of climates necessary for balanced production in agriculture and industry.[22]

In his 1934 text "Les graphiques expriment" (published in the syndicalist magazine *Prelude*), Le Corbusier explained how the success of such an ambitious organization would crucially depend on infrastructural development. The transportation and communication systems were functioning well but were not regulated: they forced together "contradictory potentials" and "embraced currents of different voltages."[23] The necessary "harmony" could be attained by the redevelopment on a "world scale," a daunting task that could only be accomplished gradually and by focusing on geography. To show how the "geographical configuration of the earth" was "extremely eloquent," Le Corbusier sketched a world map that illustrated the existing "regions of the machine-age industry" and marked prospective "lines of trade" that held the greatest potential, not only in terms of economic gains, but also in terms of achieving the world harmony (Figure 16.3).

Once situated inside this kind of a "world plan" determined by geography, infrastructure, and geopolitical projections, Le Corbusier's "radiant" urbanizations could be understood as infrastructural extensions accountable to this ambitious regionalist-syndicalist enterprise. The specific circumstances

Infrastructure in Modernist Urbanism

Figure 16.3 Sketch representing "lines of trade" that would secure "world harmony," Le Corbusier, 1934.
Source: © F.L.C./ADAGP, Paris, 2021.

of the Antwerp competition created a uniquely favorable occasion to rehearse this newly recognized meta-function of modernist urbanism, as both switch and amplifier. At the beginning of his description of the plan, published in the book *La Ville Radieuse*, Le Corbusier stated that "again and again we went beyond the verifiable present reality to the upper realm of the future reality, certain that this realm too could be checked with a maximum probability."[24] This intricate sentence alluded to the "probable future" on the basis of the project's close reading of Antwerp's geography in relation to the visionary concept of Paul Otlet's "World City."

One part of Le Corbusier's team's response was to imagine it as a cluster of monumental structures in the North-Eastern part of the left bank meander. Conspicuously apart from the rest of the generic Radiant City matrix, this World City quarter was connected to its "machine" by the avenue de la Gare Centrale, an elevated high speed highway that led towards the Belgian coast. Along with the avenue de la Cathédrale (the axis of which was determined by the Notre Dame cathedral in the historic core of Antwerp on the right bank), it was that key element that physically integrated the well-known modernist agenda of sun, air, and greenery to the wider strategic considerations of the plan. The avenue de la Gare Centrale serviced the residential quarters, acting as a central spine of the 400 x 400m street network, positioned at the angle of 45 degrees relative to its perfectly straight course. It also fed into the Central Station and five hotels situated inside five compact skyscrapers that (along with three segmented skyscrapers of the International Business City) formed an extension of the World City program.

Yet the smooth functioning of this vamped up *machine à habiter* also depended on the way in which the plan registered the "eloquence" of the earth's surface configuration in relation to the modern agenda of security. Indeed, when he exclaimed in the text that "a new city like the one planned for the left bank should have a reason for existing," Corbusier not only sought the justification for locating the World City in Antwerp, but also emphasized the fact that there were more necessary preconditions to achieve the desired international collaboration through the World City. Otlet's program of the "permanent Universal exhibition," would not be enough to justify the project. Rather, it was Antwerp's geographical position and infrastructures of communication that assured this instrumentality: "Antwerp dominates the Estuaries of Central Europe, it is fated to be the point of exchange between America, on the one hand, and Central and Eastern Europe on the other."[25] In the same vein, Le Corbusier relied on "the results to be expected from the Albert canal and various waterways which, in one way or another, will make of Antwerp the great Rhenish port, for which a provision was made in the Treaty of Versailles."[26]

Just like the World City, the perception of Antwerp as the "Rhenish port" in correlation with the treaty of Versailles, was closely linked to the project of assuring the world peace. The inter-war geopolitics of Europe revolved around the political-economic and strategic importance of the Ruhr region, the most extreme manifestation of which were arguments for founding the Rhineland-Westphalian state under the control of the League of Nations, which would neutralize the area and make it inoffensive.[27] Of primary concern here were the immense natural and infrastructural riches of the Ruhr: "mines, metallurgy, railways, canals, coastwise and overseas shipping lines etc.," as well as the imperial attitude that they aroused in the nation that controlled them.[28] By piercing a system of canals that would make Antwerp a coastal outlet of this vast and powerful territorial production system, and by attaching to it the center of world cooperation, this city became a veritable infrastructural extension that answered to the imperative of global security. Skyscrapers and canals, architecture and geography merged with infrastructure in response to the need to secure markets and lives in ways that countermanded the growing threat of war in Europe.

Railways and Highways in Brod

The basic tenets of modernist urbanism, proposed by the *Ville Radieuse* model, were endorsed by the Congrès Internationaux d'Architecture Moderne (CIAM), on the occasion of their fourth congress in 1933. Le Corbusier edited and published the original "Constatations" of CIAM 4 in 1943 as the *Athens Charter*. His version reformulated the original to emphasize an approach to urbanism "in accord with the harmonious destiny of the region" through continual reference to its geography.[29]

In Socialist Yugoslavia the Charter influenced the organization of cities and structured the first disciplinary conferences of architects and urbanists. However, in the post-war "urban regulations" and "general urban plans," the logic of functionalist segregation was deployed in parallel with the larger infrastructural logic defined by the state-led territorial development.

The first urban plan produced in Socialist Yugoslavia was for the border twin cities of Bosanski Brod and Slavonski Brod, situated on the Bosnian and Croatian side of the Sava river. The government commissioned the plan as part of an urgent effort to spur development and reconstruction after the war. Its completion in September of 1945, just four months after the Allied victory, underscored the urgency it held for the Bosnian and federal Yugoslav governments. Juraj Neidhardt, its author, was one of the most prominent proponents of modernist urbanism in Yugoslavia. Born in Zagreb, he studied with Peter Behrens at the Academy of Fine Arts in Vienna. After a brief and underwhelming professional experience in his native city, Neidhardt moved to Berlin, where he worked in Behrens' office between 1930 and 1932. In 1933 he transferred to Le Corbusier's office, where he stayed for three years, collaborating on a range of urbanization plans, as well as on the study *Le Ville Radieuse*. In 1938, he moved to Sarajevo, where he built a career in design, planning, and education.

Neidhardt's Bosnian oeuvre was marked by a profound interest in the Bosnian oriental vernacular, which inspired understanding of architecture and the city as a part of their geographic environment. The principle reference in this regard were "bases of human geography" elaborated in Jovan Cvijić's *La Péninsule balkanique*. Just like Cvijić and other human geographers, Neidhardt underlined the geographic-historical significance of houses, roads and other human interventions in the Earth's crust. However, the focus on geography of infrastructure in his urban planning was also influenced by his professional experience with Le Corbusier and a range of requirements from varied state institutions.

Neidhardt's plan for Bosanski Brod and Slavonski Brod featured a compact, introverted form (Figure 16.2). Its limits were defined by an orthogonal closed circuit of streets, while the only recognizable exchange with its surroundings were arrow-straight highways leading to the major Yugoslav cities of Sarajevo and Zagreb. The diagonal position of the secondary street network (relative to these two primary routes) and its rigid meeting with the curve of the river, were identical to the urbanization scheme developed for the left bank of the Scheldt in Antwerp. However, the infrastructural matrix of the Radiant City model and the formal similarities of the two river meanders were not the strongest associations between the two plans. Rather, it was their situation as nodes for important transport infrastructures connecting the mining regions of Bosnia and Rhineland with their consumers.

The connection of the Sava River Basin with more developed parts of Yugoslavia and Europe had been established by the Habsburg administration back in 1879, merely one year after Austria-Hungary occupied Bosnia and Herzegovina. The new regime sought both to modernize the country and to exploit its significant natural resources for imperial gain, particularly the rich coal and iron ore of the Middle Bosnian Mining Basin. Over the next half-century, coal refining and steel production facilities flourished in the towns of Zenica and Vareš. Neidhardt's plan would connect these towns to wider networks by providing a new crossing over the Sava river and links between the Bosnian narrow gauge railway and Croatian railway lines, leading to the Yugoslav capitals of Belgrade, Zagreb, and Ljubljana, and further into Central Europe.

In this sense, Neidhardt's title of the plan, "The Doors of Bosnia," referred not only to the passenger traffic, but also circulation of minerals from the Basin to the north. Neidhardt cooperated with numerous agencies and institutions in the plan's production, all of which corroborated the significance of Brod as both domestic and foreign trade outlet. Particularly important was re-establishment of traffic over the river Sava that all but stalled after the old bridge was destroyed by the Allies' military operations in 1944. The Ministry of Trade of the Bosnian Republic proposed various scenarios for resolving the communication crisis in the Brod cities. Its memo reviewed a range of likely infrastructural provisions, such as the bridge over Sava, the railway to Sarajevo and the river embankment.[30] The Ministry of Industry and Mining underlined the vital importance that the Brods plan held for the economy of Yugoslavia as a whole, as it permitted the supply of key raw materials to its industrially developed northern regions.[31]

In response to this extensive brief provided by a range of interested state institutions, Neidhardt produced a scheme that attached the Radiant City model to an intricate network of overland transportation, industry, and commerce. He described the plan as a "hoop in a chain" of economic operations, conditioned by an "industrial basin, rich in resources" that was, at the same time, a communication corridor, from the Sava to the sea.[32] Soon, however, the Brods plan was recalled by the decision of the Federal Yugoslav government to guide the railway over the Sava at a wholly different point—the city of Bosanski Šamac. The reason for this change can be found in its ongoing efforts to develop an integrated infrastructural network that could answer to the nonaligned geopolitical position of Yugoslavia in the circumstances of the Cold War.

Both Western powers and Yugoslav government used its infrastructures as strategic tools in enacting political goals, inflected by the Cold War international relations. The United Nations, for example, considered investment in Yugoslav roads as construction of a veritable bridge across the rift marked by the Iron Curtain.[33] Yugoslav ministries and planning institutions, in turn, channeled these investments in ways that helped them pursue their own political goals, through national infrastructural development. The definitions of railway and highway routes were results of complex cartographic calculations that involved economic and military strategies. The construction of advanced infrastructure in the Middle Bosnian Basin was abandoned early on because of its difficult relief, strategic importance as a military refuge and primary industries, sufficiently served by freight traffic. Caught up in the domestic and foreign techno-political affairs, the "communication machine" of the Brods plan was a part of the same "world game" that human geographers described as conditioned by infrastructure, that "incarnation of geography."

However, the way in which the post-World War II state played this game had changed significantly. In inter-war Antwerp, the joint agencies of the canals and modernist towers were employed in a grand avant-garde peacemaking vision of world cooperation. In post-war Brods, the railways and the highways responded to the increasingly complicated and oscillating political-economic priorities defined through exchange with international institutions pursuing economic growth as a means to global influence. Far from being reduced to the technocratic "circulation machine" (as much of the mainstream historical account would have it) the "radiant" infrastructure of the Antwerp and Brods plans was a techno-political tool, effective for the very reason of being "an essential fact of geography."

The "functionalist urbanism" of the Athens Charter was important in framing the post-World War II development of cities across Europe and beyond. Yet the onset of the Cold War brought new alignments, whereby state actors understood cities as functional elements in wide territorial constellations made up of geographies, infrastructures, and geopolitical agendas. In this sense, the 'infrastructure' of modern urbanism moved far beyond the boundaries of cities and metropolitan regions to encompass increasingly global scale projects of power, influence, and territorial control.

Notes

1 Charles-Édouard Jeanneret Le Corbusier, *The Radiant City* (New York: The Orion Press, 1964), 270.
2 Nick Megoran and Simon Dalby, "Geopolitics and Peace: A Century of Change in the Discipline of Geography," *Geopolitics* 23, no. 2 (2018): 253–257.
3 Michael Sivignon, "Le politique dans la géographie des Balkans: Reclus et ses successeurs, d'une géographie universelle à l'autre," *Hérodote*, no. 117 (2005): 155.
4 Guy Mercier, "La région et l'État selon Friedrich Ratzel et Paul Vidal de la Blache," *Annales de Géographie* 104, no. 583 (1995): 223.
5 Jean-Baptiste Arrault, "Une Géographie inattendue: le système mondial vu par Paul Vidal de la Blache," *L'Espace Géographique* 37, no. 1 (2008): 79.
6 Ibid. 78.
7 Ibid. 79.
8 Jeremy W. Crampton, "The cartographic calculation of space: race mapping and the Balkans at the Paris Peace Conference of 1919," *Social & Cultural Geography* 7, no. 5 (2006): 731–752.
9 See, for example, on Vidal's work in Peru: Guilherme Ribeiro, "La géographie vidalienne et la géopolitique," *Géographie et cultures* 75 (2010): 8 and Sivignon, "Le politique dans la géographie des Balkans," 153.
10 Crampton, "The Cartographic Calculation of Space," 747.
11 Jovan Cvijić, *La Péninsule Balkanique – Géohraphie humaine* (Paris: Libraire Armand Colin, 1918).
12 Cvijić, *La Péninsule Balkanique*, 11.
13 Ibid. 13–14.
14 Brunhes and E.S. Bates, "The specific characteristics and complex character of the subject-matter of human geography," *Scottish Geographical Magazine* 29, no. 6 (1913): 321.
15 Ibid. 309.
16 Paul Otlet, "Anvers qui va a grandir," *Le mouvement communal*, no. 150 (August 1933): 245.
17 Ibid. 248.
18 Ibid.
19 Le Corbusier, *The Radiant City*, 275.
20 See Mary C. McLeod, "Urbanism and Utopia: Le Corbusier from Regional Syndicalism to Vichy," (PhD diss., Princeton University, 1985), 236 and Hashim Sarkis, "Le Corbusier's 'Geo-Architecture' and the Emergence of Territorial Aesthetic," in *Re-Scaling the Environment: New Landscapes of Design (East West Central: Re-building Europe, 1950-1990)*, eds Akos Moravanszky and Karl R. Kegler (Birkhauser Architecture, 2016), 120.
21 Sarkis, "Le Corbusier's 'Geo-Architecture'," 121.
22 McLeod, "Urbanism and Utopia," 146.
23 Le Corbusier, "Les graphiques expriment," *Prelude*, no. 10 (March-April 1934): 7.
24 Le Corbusier, *The Radiant City*, 270.
25 Ibid. 277.
26 Ibid. 271.
27 See Royal J. Schmidt, *Versailles and the Ruhr: Seedbed of World War I* (The Hague: Springer Netherlands, 1968).
28 Ibid. 55.
29 Le Corbusier, *The Athens Charter* (New York: Grossman Publishers, 1973), 43–44.

30 Report issued by the Ministry of Trade of Bosnia and Herzegovina about the problem of the regulation of Slavonski and Bosanski Brod, 1945, 6044/45, Box 5, Ministry of Construction, Archive of Bosnia and Herzegovina, Sarajevo, Bosnia and Herzegovina.
31 Report issued by the Ministry of Industry and Mining about the problem of the regulation of Slavonski and Bosanski Brod, 1945, 1945 6044/45, Box 5, Ministry of Construction, Archive of Bosnia and Herzegovina, Sarajevo, Bosnia and Herzegovina.
32 Dušan Grabrijan and Juraj Neidhardt, *Arhitektura Bosne i put u savremeno* (Ljubljana: Državna založba Slovenije, 1957), 452.
33 Vincent Langendijk and Frank Schipper, "East, West, Home's Best: The Material Links of Cold War Yugoslavia, 1948-1980," *Icon* 22 (2016): 31–33.

17
INFRASTRUCTURE AS A POLITICAL TOOL OF REGIME LEGITIMIZATION IN DOHA, QATAR

Peter Chomowicz

Before a packed audience in Zurich in 2010, the Emir of Qatar, Sheikh Hamad bin Khalifa Al-Thani, and his second wife, Sheikha Moza, held high above their heads the trophy to host the FIFA World Cup soccer games in 2022. This pivotal moment recalls another one exactly sixty years prior that saw Qatar export its first drop of oil and forever change its future. Since 1950, successive emirs, awash with new found wealth from oil and natural gas exports, set about fashioning a modern city-state. Their varied efforts to modernize Qatar's capital, Doha, made it possible for the tiny state to host the world's largest sporting event, and all those years of struggle would pale in comparison to the massive infrastructure investment Hamad and Moza would undertake to fulfill the promise of a FIFA-hosting nation. This chapter describes how, since oil first began flowing, Qatari emirs have used the construction of urban infrastructure as a means of political legitimization, first among the national political class, then an international elite, and finally a global audience for the 2022 games.

Until the 1950s, Doha was a meagre coastal entrepôt, clinging precariously to the muddy shores of the Arabian Gulf. Its 12,000 souls made their living through fishing, pearl diving, and slave trading.[1] The little recorded history we have of the Qatar peninsula comes largely from foreign military and merchant sources, chronicling their invading, trading, and occupying of the region from the seventeenth to the twentieth centuries.[2] We know from these sources, and from recent archaeological investigations, that Doha and her sister city Al-Bidda were small but important trading hubs for traffic up and down the Arabian Gulf linking modern day Iraq and Iran with Oman and East Africa.[3] Trade east to west brought India and China into contact with nomadic Bedouin pastoralists in Eastern Arabia. Although clearly not "cosmopolitan" by today's standards, or even those of Doha's historic contemporaries, Eastern Arabian coastal cities enjoyed a high degree of foreign interaction throughout much of their history.[4] As a result, Qatari tribes over the last few centuries deftly balanced threats and opportunities from neighboring clans as well as foreign hegemons, a strategy we will see on a grand scale once oil is fully exploited after the 1950s.[5]

Qatar's tribal system comprises two distinctly different strands, the Hadar, settled coastal fisherman and traders, typically immigrants from Persia, usually practicing Shi'i Islam, and the Bedouin, pastoral nomads who roamed the desert expanses of Eastern Arabia and Qatar's southern peninsula, practicing a Wahhabi interpretation of Sunni Islam.[6] The two strands mutually supported, and at times warred, with each other in much the same way Ibn Khaldun describes the fluctuating relationship between urban centers of power and surrounding rural agrarian tribes.[7] The first step toward unifying Qatar's disparate tribal confederacy came in 1868 when the British Government installed Mohammed bin Thani (b. ? –1878, r. 1850–1876) as Qatar's first centralized political leader. Al-Thani heirs have since ruled over Qatar's local tribes of Bedouin pastoral nomads and settled merchant clans.

The interwar years were particularly hard on Doha. Japan's introduction of the cultured pearl, together with the Great Depression, collapsed the Arabian Gulf pearl industry, resulting in a mass migration and nearly halving Doha's population. Beginning in the early 1920s, the entire region was opening to oil exploration and extraction by foreign powers, with the Americans controlling much of the Arabian Peninsula, and Britain much of Mesopotamia. The newly established Petroleum Development Qatar (PDQ) company's early surveys showed favorable indications of large oil deposits off Qatar's west coast, but World War II suspended operations. Looking back, we see how in 1949 when the first oil tanker left Qatar, that it would also take with it an enduring social order rooted in Doha's dusty alleyways, meagre mudbrick huts, and muddy shores.

The Rise of the Petroleum State

With oil flowing out and dollars flowing in, Qatar's mid-century emir Sheikh Ali bin Abdulla Al-Thani (b.1895–1974, r.1949–1960) contended with two immediate threats to his throne: powerful merchant families, particularly the Al-Mana and the Darwish; and the voracious appetite for oil revenue constantly displayed by members of his own royal family, the Al-Thani. Once Sheik Ali devised a scheme to share oil revenue with those vying for power, he began to attract popular support from lower levels of Qatari society. Economic diversification, urban expansion, and state bureaucracy were Ali's goals in the 1950s, securing power for the Al-Thani line, enriching Qatari citizens, although at vastly different rates, and broadening the means to distribute oil revenue.

At first, oil revenue flowed only to the Al-Thani elite. In 1950, Sheikh Ali personally received 25 percent of all oil revenue, his family another sizeable portion, and what little remained supported various social projects. Looking to expand the capacity for production and export, the emir, British authorities, and the PDQ engaged in a give-and-take politics of development. In August of 1951, PDQ's general manager came to see the British Political Agent (PA) and the emir to "urge upon the Agent the need for development measures which would show the people of Qatar some tangible benefits from oil revenue."[8] During these early years of civic improvement the emir enjoyed a great swelling of popular support. And it is precisely because of the public nature of the state's spending that the elite class would increasingly side against the emir. Indeed, the following year the Foreign Office wrote

> the Ruler is afraid of his family and will always, I suppose, yield if they make enough noise. The family say: "How can you spend money on roads and hospitals and such like nonsense when we haven't even got a decent Cadillac to ride in?"[9]

Despite family demands, Doha had, by the end of the 1950s, made tremendous infrastructure investments. It now boasted city-wide electricity, an airport, the coastal road finally holding back the fêted harbor, a customs authority, deep water jetties, vegetable, fish and meat markets, police headquarters, water system, hospital, and dozens of primary schools.[10] As with other Gulf cities, British firms held many of Doha's design and engineering contracts. Foreseeing—and vigorously promoting—the emir's desire for sweeping changes to the city's urban and institutional order, the British foreign agent persuaded the emir to hire Hunting Aerosurvey to map Doha photogrammetrically in great detail, much as they had in Kuwait and Baghdad.[11] British architect John Harris, who drew up Dubai's first masterplan and designed what was, for many years, its tallest building, the World Trade Center, also designed Doha's first state hospital. A 250-bed, four story, precast concrete building, Harris' high modernist aesthetic and clever use of sun shading quickly became the model for nearly all government offices until the introduction of glass curtain walls in the 1980s. One cannot over emphasize how radically life was changing for all Doha residents. Modern medicine, automobiles, air-conditioning, desalinated water, jet transport, telephones, radio, and a steady diet of imported food far more diverse than the canned goods, rice, and fish many knew as their only meals, all became readily available in just a few short years.[12]

The Uneasy Politics of Growth

This spate of infrastructure building came at a time of, and in many ways resulted from, internecine political struggle within the ruling families. In 1949, when the emir, Shaikh Abdullah, was near death he abdicated the throne in favor of his eldest son Ali with the stipulation that the throne would later be occupied by Ali's nephew, Khalifa. This set in motion an internal power struggle between their descendants resulting in murder, attempted coups, successful coups, and constant political maneuvering.[13] It is important to recall that by 1868 the British, who desired a strategic foothold in the Gulf, grew tired of the constant warring between Gulf tribes and drew up the Trucial Agreement that installed Mohammad Al-Thani as the head of all the Qatar peninsula tribes.[14] Although Al-Thanis have ruled since, the capricious circumstances leave open the possibility that other clans and familial branches have just as much right to the throne. One way successive emirs have dealt with threats from other families and from their own kin is through infrastructure development. By using land purchases, construction contracts, cash allowances, and trips abroad, the emir deftly balanced interfamilial factionalism to constantly balance exchanging distributed oil wealth for absolute power.[15] As the state's coffers grew, so too did the size and appetite of the leading families; and so too did the abuses by the emir. The emir could not continue entertaining, in the words of the Political Agent, "the squawking of every hungry mouth," nor even his own mismanagement.[16] Qatar was quickly outgrowing itself and the emir needed a mechanism to dispel political claims, distribute allowances, and grow the city. He accomplished all three through the creation of a state bureaucracy.[17]

Britain's centuries of colonial rule in many parts of the world gave the Foreign Office and its political agents unparalleled expertise in state administration. For their part, Britain wanted a strategic foothold in the Gulf, access to oil, and lucrative engineering contracts for British firms. The emir wanted wealth beyond measure and political security for himself and his heir apparent. And the Qataris by and large wanted a share in the oil revenues. Of course they wished for luxuries, many having experienced first-hand the deprivations of the Great Depression. The common ground shared by these competing interests is, quite literally, "the ground," the architecture and infrastructure upon it.

Largely because of this emerging state apparatus, the 1960s enjoyed stunning rates of GDP growth and urban development. Sheikh Ahmed was, for the moment, still in power, and trying hard to diversify the industrial economy. No one knew how long oil would hold out, and it was impossible then to foresee that they were sitting upon the world's third largest proven natural gas reserves.[18] No official figures were ever published, but the emir's banker believed total state revenue in 1969 stood at £50 million of which £45 million was from oil revenue, half of which went to the extended royal family.[19]

The 1950s and 1960s were a time of constant monetary maneuvering. Though emirs Ali and Ahmed were advised by the British Foreign Office on matters of finance, state bureaucracy, and urban development, they had to balance foreign self-interest, the rapacious appetite of an enormous royal family who were often leading mercantile clans, the wishes of the Qatari people, and their own desire for luxuries. Both emirs were reportedly illiterate, but nonetheless well-schooled in the politics of popularity and court intrigue. Oil revenues provided material luxuries unimaginable to those who remembered the freshwater tanker that came to Doha every fortnight, the sweltering summers in adobe houses crammed with relatives in one or two tiny rooms, and the mud that invaded every inch of life during the winter rains. To bring a city from these humble origins to the very image of a modern, neo-liberal, late-capitalist skyscraper metropolis seen in Figure 17.2 was a constant balancing act between the powers closest to the emir. Unlike the founding years of the late nineteenth century that deftly pitted one empire against another – British, Ottoman, Wahhabi – the first oil emirs keenly perceived the internal dynamics that would either rip the country apart, or, if not unite the branches of the Al-Thani clan and leading merchant families, then at least bring them to agree to move in generally the same direction towards modernization.[20]

Defining Citizenship

Though still under the British Protectorate Treaty of 1916, Qatar began in the early 1960s to establish laws essential to its sovereignty and crucial to Doha's urban development. The first, and most basic, established who was a citizen. Law No.(1) of 1961 defined a Qatari as someone residing in Qatar before 1930.

The law had to navigate a number of complicated realities. Qatar had only officially ended slavery nine years earlier, and its long history of trans-Gulf migration from the east, nomadic herding from the west, and the various trade routes both north and south meant that determining citizenship among people with such divergent sojourns was difficult. Moreover, Bahrain maintained claims on portions of Qatar where large numbers of Bahrainian people had settled. But, as the window on citizenship closed with rising oil revenues, the state had to limit who was in the country, for what purpose, and most importantly who could own real property and thus benefit from the distribution of oil wealth. Passport-holding citizens were rewarded with new homes, government jobs, and luxuries unimaginable only a few years prior. Conversely, the imported workers required to build the modern capital had few rights and often suffered abuses. Currently, other forms of residence permit exist such as for those born in Qatar and who are long-term residents, which are not employer dependent. For all other foreign nationals, residence in Qatar is only possible through employer sponsorship in the *kafala* system, currently a highly contentious issue among human rights observers.[21] Given Qatar's long history of migration by neighboring Arab tribes and later by Iranian, Indian, and Palestinian migrants in the labor pool, the government further restricted its nationalism policies through Law No.(5) of 1963 that forbade foreigners from owning real property (immovable assets) or land.

Having restricted Qatari citizenship through Law No. 1 of 1961, Sheikh Ahmed turned his sights on internal threats. The next step was to break up Doha's enduring kin- and clan-based neighborhoods, called *al fereej* in Gulf dialect. Until oil extraction began in 1950, Doha's urban order was based upon the ancient and enduring *fereej* system. This archaic structure presented a direct obstacle to Sheikh Ahmed's political-urban calculus. The close-knit family structure often acted as a unified voice of potential opposition, while the corresponding residential architectural form, an inward oriented medina modified for coastal life, presented a bulwark against urban redevelopment plans. Removing the *fereej* as a fact and symbol would pave the way for urban renewal and with it political legitimization.

Controlling Doha

To gain control of the city, Sheikh Ahmed empowered the state's bureaucracy through Law No. 15 of 1963, which established the municipality of Doha with a government tasked to manage the building process for gardens (public green space), public health (hospitals/clinics) and accounts (capital improvements). This appeared to be a step towards democratization. Each citizen was in theory "freed" from the *fereej*'s tribal control and could instead act in their own self-interest to petition a neutral administrative bureaucracy. In reality, the municipality simply presented itself as neutral, while all decisions remained with the emir. A further complication is the employment of nationals through the bureaucratic distribution of jobs and contracts. Favoritism, nepotism and tribal conflict were rife in the early days of state administration, as older political and social interests recalibrated their loyalties and alignments with the new state. The growing bureaucracy continued to weaken the *fereej*'s power by enticing individuals into state jobs and away from family businesses in order to hold some degree of power over fellow citizens.

With the *fereej* now under government control, Ahmed needed a mechanism to both reclaim inner-city land and dismantle the remaining power blocks held by the extended clan *fereej*. Offering the *fereej* large tracts of land for relocation would not alone diminish their unity. He needed a way to dissolve the communicative ease and ideological unity made possible by the tight-knit *fereej* social-spatial structure. Law No.(1) of 1964, which established a land grant system, was the tool he needed.

To be sure, the land grant laws from 1964 were ingeniously designed. Land and low-interest loans were given to low-income or elderly citizens. This largesse on the emir's part had a deeper, less obvious motivation, one that would forever change the very social-spatial fabric of Doha society. The land-grant parcels were typically on the desert fringe outside the city, and the new free-standing houses, now called "villas," were the spatial inversion of the densely packed courtyard houses they left behind seen in Figure 17.1. These housing policies had several initial consequences.

Figure 17.1 Doha in late 1947: no paved roads, the entire "city" characterized by the courtyard dwelling.
Source: Source unknown, although likely British Royal Air Force.

First, families could leave their rather humble mud-brick or concrete courtyard dwelling for a three or four bedroom home complete with municipal utilities, central air-conditioning, and car ports. Equally important, they also had a rental stream from the vacated inner-city courtyard house that was being let to Indian and Pakistani laborers. Second, the emir now had control over Doha's real estate and could begin building a city commensurate with his country's new-found wealth. Lastly, the emir now also had a mechanism to selectively distribute wealth.

Ahmed's cousin and successor, Khalifa Al-Thani, further extended state control. As deputy minister in 1971, a year before he took power, Khalifa established a ministry structure termed the "Ministry of Municipal Affairs" that was responsible for all municipalities in the peninsula. As emir he formalized the process of eminent domain with Law No. 13 of 1988—the expropriation of property for public benefit. The law stipulates the creation of a property valuation board to compensate landowners. Then, as now, property claimed through eminent domain was another mechanism to handsomely compensate urban, land-owning citizens. Many who lived through this period describe how the law fueled land speculation.[22] If one had inside knowledge of a new road, or public building, for example, then one would buy the land only to have the Ministry of Municipality and Urban Planning (MMUP) take it over for many times the purchase price only a few months later. Having insider information on urban development and the finances to buy the land were possible only for leading mercantile families. The eminent domain law in many ways followed a path of dependencies of power, fueling already extant lines of wealth accumulation laid down over the last century.

Creating a Modern Capital

With power firmly consolidated, tight citizenship rules in place, and wealth beyond measure, Qatar's rulers set their sights on the creation of a modern capital city. Foreseeing the need for public support when he would forcibly take office in 1971, Sheikh Khalifa, while still Deputy Ruler and Prime Minister, went on national radio and TV to officially announce the state's budget. It was an historic first, to say the least, and demonstrated Khalifa's desire for popular support through political transparency. He did not mention the total national budget or the amounts to be spent on security or the armed forces—money used primarily for his own protection—but he did detail the capital budget to be spent on public works.

Khalifa claimed the budget had three main aims: 1) increase the income of the individual Qatari; 2) improve both the quality and quantity of public services; and 3) encourage the industrial sector, independent of oil. He described how the budget provided for new schools, medical laboratories, and funds to send Qataris overseas for university education. Additionally, it provided for an expanded road network, sewage treatment plant, electric grid, water piping and desalinization, land grants and housing loans for those with low incomes, television and radio broadcasting, labor housing, and oil pipeline enhancements. He concluded by expressing pleasure at the continual increase in the budget for the state's development projects, "which shows that the State is exerting fruitful energy to supplement the elements of progress of Qatar and to raise the standard of living of its people in all walks of life."[23] By calling attention to specific public works, most notably housing and land compensation, Khalifa was laying the groundwork for his palace coup by appealing to public support largely through infrastructure, development, and urban transformation.

Khalifa's palace coup was, in part, a maneuver to reclaim what he felt was rightly his. Ever since his grandfather, Sheikh Abdullah, put in writing some twenty-four years earlier his decree for Khalifa to follow Ahmed as emir, Khalifa must have grown impatient. No doubt his impatience was brought to a new level when Abdullah's son reneged on his father's wishes and installed his own son as emir. But revenge and honor were not the only motivations. Khalifa had a vision for Qatar as a modern nation, and a genuine interest in public works that would raise the quality of life for all citizens.

On February 22, 1972, Khalifa took control of the country while Sheikh Ahmed was on a hunting trip in Iran. In his first public address, the new emir recounted that since becoming heir apparent and prime minister he had "tried in vain to dissuade by advice and counsel those irresponsible elements who had been indulging in profiteering and accumulation of fortune at the expense of the people." He told the audience that all his previous efforts had "been met with deaf ears by those elements' self-indulgence and disrespect for public interest" and the country had "revolved in a vicious circle and our hopes and high aspirations for Qatar after independence withered away and were lost."[24] In this way, he sought to appeal directly to the people for broad support of his coup. He promised sweeping reform and massive urban change including: the establishment of municipal councils, consumers' cooperative societies to help control inflation through price controls, a new state university, and the re-planning of Doha city.[25]

Sheikh Khalifa's inaugural speech highlights several pivotal moments in Qatar's development. First, Qatar now had independence, unimaginable wealth, and the desire to plan and administrate a fully autonomous state, with Doha as its capital. Second, Khalifa's plans strongly emphasized the physical creation of things and places. He was giving Qataris money, jobs, houses, roads, universities, and hospitals. What he was not giving them was democratic freedom and the ability to take part in the planning of the nation's physical development. While Doha's modern, Western-styled city may seem to embody neo-liberal freedom and individuality, it holds the population hostage to the regime's control over sovereign wealth, its capricious decisions, and its desire for unquestioned obedience. Ironically, the image of freedom embodied in the modern road and skyscraper replaced the shared involvements and reciprocal social relations found in the *fereej*; a long-established system of architectural and communicative forms that most threatened the monarchy's ambitions for modern development.

Khalifa's speech promises a new life for the Qatari people built upon their complete dependence on the state. His "family" is now all of Qatar. Government jobs, government building contracts, government education, housing: every situation puts Khalifa as the *paterfamilias* par excellence. This is a position that his son, Hamad (b. 1952–present, r. 1995–2013), the current emir's father, would take to new heights, and his grandson Tamim (b. 1980–present, r. 2013–present) would, like many of his mid-twentieth century predecessors, struggle with as he seeks to balance the competing demands of state revenue, urban development, the pace of social and institutional change, and the interests of foreign powers.

Despite Khalifa's rapid urban transformation program, his son Hamad deposed him in a "bloodless" coup in 1995, based on claims that Khalifa's projects were not moving ahead rapidly enough. Khalifa had in hand the first and only officially adopted master plan for Doha drawn up in 1972 by the British firm Llewelyn-Davies, Weeks, Forestier-Walker and Bor. And he had commissioned three other master plans by renowned firms detailing Doha's urban development. Khalifa also had mobilized the various ministries, municipalities, and armies of foreign engineering and management professionals to enact the plans. But apart from the Llewelyn-Davies plan, none of the others would be formally adopted and all were only partially implemented by the time his son took control.

In an eerily familiar pattern, Sheikh Hamad bin Khalifa, second son of Sheikh Khalifa, took the throne while his father was out of the country. Officially, Hamad succeeded his father in a "handover of power." From birth Hamad had been groomed as heir apparent. Attending Sandhurst, Britain's premier military academy, prepared Hamad as both the official heir and as commander of Qatar's Armed Forces. Like his father, one of Hamad's first acts was to proclaim the unmet potential of Qatar and commission one of the world's largest architecture and planning firms, Hellmuth, Obata & Kassabaum (HOK) to prepare a twenty-year master plan for the entire country, with particular focus on the urban development of Doha. It seems that internecine politics and large-scale planning ambitions had once again contributed to the changing fortunes of the country.

Hamad, and his second wife, Sheikha Moza bint Nasser Al-Misned, would take Doha's development to an entirely different level. The royal couple wasted no time in enacting major reforms. Looking back over twenty years of rule it seems he had one, overarching goal for his country: international recognition. Recognizing that out of desire or necessity the world will eventually wean itself from oil and natural gas, Hamad drew up the "2030 Vision," a short pamphlet meant to guide all aspects of Qatar's future development with a focus on creating a "knowledge-based economy."[26] Hamad immediately set up Qatar Foundation for Education, Research, and Community Development (QF) as the main vehicle to build a high-tech, knowledge intensive industries. In 1996, with Sheikha Moza at the helm, QF broke ground on a sprawling 12 square kilometer campus hosting branch campuses of six renowned US universities, a 40,000 stadium, billion-dollar research centers, a state of the art medical and biomedical research hospital, museums, public art, convention center, light rail intermodal transit, and an eighteen-hole golf course. In and around Doha, Hamad's massive projects abound, some bearing his moniker, for example, Hamad Medical Corporation, the national healthcare system with hospitals throughout the country; and Hamad International Airport, a U.S.$15 billion passenger and freight terminal built on an artificial peninsula in the Arabian Gulf. But all of these projects pale in comparison to the promise Hamad and Moza made in 2010 when they won the bid to host the 2022 FIFA world cup games. Stadiums, an entirely new elevated and subterranean metro system linking all of Doha which at the time of its construction set the world's record for employing the most boring machines at one time, bridges, road interchanges, aluminum smelting plants, enormous expansion of liquified natural gas capacity, an entirely new shipping hub carved from the desert coast, experimental farms, and a new desalinization system suppling fresh water to the entire country.[27] As in the early years of oil production, the massive state projects further enriched the royal and mercantile class who now own massive conglomerates that hold the contracts to build and run all these projects.

Conclusion

The central theme of this essay is the use of infrastructure - architecture and urban planning - as a political tool of regime legitimization and socio-economic development. We have seen how successive emirs since the mid-twentieth century deftly balanced competing demands from within their own family, from the Qatari population, and now increasingly from the international community. In this way, they have carved out a political pathway in defiance of Western interests. From the vantage of Western policy analysts such as Walt Rostow, the ruling class of oil-rich Middle Eastern nations had to make a stark choice in order to climb the "ladder of development" —a choice between maintaining a feudal theocracy and embracing Western-style capitalist democracy. But in each decade since 1950, emirs have turned neither fully towards Mecca nor Washington, but rather carved out their own path. Indeed, Doha's rapid socio-architectural transformation is an ongoing synthesis of many facets of Qatari life, not simply bound to the reductionist categories of tradition and modernity, feudalism and capitalism, past and future, free markets and command economies.

Until recently this synthesis looked as if it has thrown off its Islamic-Wahhabi roots and embraced late capitalist, neo-liberal economic policies as embodied in the modernist skyscraper skyline of Doha's central business district in West Bay (Figure 17.2). The rise of West Bay's high-rises coincided with Sheikh Hamad's *2030 Vision* to turn all of Qatar away from its reliance on petrochemicals and re-established its

Figure 17.2 The West Bay business district seen behind traditional Arabian *dhow* sailboats.

Source: Photograph by Peter Chomowicz, 2015.

economic and cultural foundation upon so-called "knowledge-based industries" of education, science, engineering, and medicine, the basics of modern institutions and infrastructure to be sure.

Perhaps, then, it is not altogether surprising that the compass would in a few short years pivot toward the opposite pole as Hamad's son Tamim, upon ascending the throne in 2013 through Hamad's abdication, began seeking a closer connection to Qatari heritage.[28] This reorientation is expressed in recent years through cultural exhibitions and building schemes aimed toward resuscitating narratives of ancient social, cosmic, and natural conditions as embodied in the themes of pearl diving, camel racing, falcon hunting, and the vernacular architecture of the *fereej*; themes directly underlying the ancestral mystique of sea, sand, and air. Even, or perhaps especially, many of the FIFA 2022 stadiums are aggrandizements of humble Qatari heritage such as Bedouin tents and *dhow* boats. Overwhelmingly, these constructs show Qatari heritage and identity as intimately connected to nature's hardships, and all are enabled by a highly technical infrastructure.[29] But with the city casting a shadow over every aspect of Qatari life for the last seventy years it is impossible to ignore the modern, imported quality of Doha. By depicting buildings, roads, and stadiums in much the same light as Bedouin tribesmen—characters of fierce individuality proudly standing tall against harsh elements—Qatari elites hope to counter international criticism that it remains a backward vassal of Saudi Arabia, or as a perpetrator of human rights abuses, or funder of terror networks.[30] Tamim's building schemes evince a new dimension of the socio-political importance of infrastructure, in that infrastructure is not solely physical constructs, but also a deeper interpretation of history that undergirds society and enables its future development.

In early 2017, Tamim's development goals seemed thwarted when U.S. President Donald Trump delivered a speech in Riyadh asking the region's leaders to take greater steps toward curbing Islamist terrorism. Saudi Arabia and the United Arab Emirates responded by announcing their economic boycott of Qatar on the grounds its leaders fund and support such networks. Despite Tamim's ardent denial, Qatar's neighbors closed air routes and the land border, which immediately halted the importation of vital food and building material.

The embargo's pain was only made more acute by Hamad's unprecedented commitment to urban transformation in order to host the FIFA World Cup in 2022, an estimated U.S.$300 billion or roughly 150 percent of annual GDP.[31] In addition to the massive infrastructure projects associated with the games, other investments in education, research, and defense are only getting more expensive the longer the embargo lasts. Add to this the precipitous drop in crude oil prices since 2015, and one might think the emir would eagerly settle the economic blockade. And yet, despite these difficulties, Tamim has never been more popular. His image graces everything from cappuccino foam to building facades; from bumper stickers to unrelentingly recirculated social media posts all proclaiming an unflinching faith in their leader.

Upon an urban backdrop of massive construction schemes drawn from Qatari heritage, the nation seems galvanized in the young emir's ability to fulfill his father's ambition of achieving international recognition, national sovereignty, and technological modernity embodied in the ever-developing metropolis of Doha. The blockade has only rallied Qataris to stand behind the emir, entwining his image with the city's and thereby blurring the distinction between the political and the architectural and proudly proclaiming that both emir and city will stand firm as did their ancestors in the face of hardship. Such effusive popular support suggests that the canny deployment of infrastructure as the prime lever of regime legitimization has been a success for the ruling elite of Qatar.

Notes

1 The first population survey of Qatar is found in J.G. Lorimer, *Gazetteer of the Persian Gulf, Oman and Central Arabia* (Calcutta, India: Superintendent Government Printing, 1915, republished by Gregg International, Westmead: United Kingdom, 1970).

2 For an extensive account of ancient Arabian Gulf history see Alvin J. Cottrell, *The Persian Gulf States A General Survey* (Baltimore: The Johns Hopkins University Press, 1980). See also Ali Ajjat, "Social Development of the Pirate Coast," *Middle East Forum* 38 (1962): 75–80. For works focusing on Qatar history from the late

eighteenth century to the mid-twentieth century, see Habibur Rahman, *The Emergence of Qatar* (London: Kegan Paul, 2005); and Rosemarie Zahlan, *The Creation of Qatar* (London: Croom Helm, 1979).

3   Robert Carter, who has led significant archaeological expeditions in Doha, provides a vital understanding of the city's early history and trade. See Robert Carter, "Globalizing Interactions in the Arabian Neolithic and 'Ubaid," in *Globalization in Prehistory: Contact, Exchange and the "People Without History"*, eds Nicole Boivin and Michael D. Frachetti (Cambridge: Cambridge University Press, 2018); and Robert Carter, "Mapping the Growth of an Arabian Gulf Town: The Case of Qatar," *Journal of the Economic and Social History of the Orient* 60 (2017): 420–487.

4   Robert Carter, *Sea of Pearls: Seven Thousand Years of the Industry that Shaped the Gulf* (London: Arabian Publishing Ltd., 2012).

5   See James Onley, "Britain and Gulf Shaikhdoms, 1820-1971: The Politics of Protection," Occasional Paper No. 4, Center for International and Regional Studies, Georgetown University in Qatar, 2009.

6   Sharon Nagy, "Making Room for Migrants, Making Sense of Difference: Spatial and Ideological Expressions of Social Diversity in Urban Qatar," *Urban Studies*, 43, no. 1 (2006): 119–137; David Commins, *The Wahhabi Mission and Saudi Arabia* (London: I.B. Tauris, 2006).

7   Ibn Khaldun, *The Muqaddimah An Introduction to History*, trans. Franz Rosenthal (Princeton, New Jersey: Princeton University Press, [1967] 2005). For extensive descriptions of nineteenth century Gulf States see William Gifford Palgrave, *Personal Narrative of a Year's Journey through Central and Eastern Arabia 1862-1863* (New York: Macmillan and Co. 1868).

8   British Foreign Office 1016/162.

9   British Foreign Office 1016/184.

10   British Foreign Office 371/148915; Shaikha Al-Misnad, *The Development of Modern Education in the Gulf* (London: Ithaca Press, 2008).

11   FO 1016/164.

12   Sir Rupert Hay, "The Impact of the Oil Industry on the Persian Gulf Shaykhdoms," *The Middle East Journal* 9, no. 4 (1955): 361–372.

13   Dr. Mohammed El-Katiri and Cdr Steve Tatham RN, "Qatar: A Little Local Difficulty?" Working Paper UK Defence Academy Research & Assessment Branch (August, 2009).

14   Details of the Treaty can be found in Zahlan 1979:143; Lorimer 1970; and FO 171/817.

15   The use of unearned rents, oil, and gas receipts In Qatar's case, in exchange for political participation, is described in the literature as Rentier State Theory (RST). Late Rentierism is when mercantile families have established their well-functioning business conglomerates. For a full discussion of Qatar's RST, see Jill Crystal, *Oil and Politic in the Gulf* (Cambridge: Cambridge University Press, 1995); Matthew Gray, "A Theory of 'Late Rentierism' in the Arab States of the Gulf," Center For International and Regional Studies, Occasional Paper No. 7, Doha: Georgetown University, 2011; Mehran Kamrava, *Qatar: Small State, Big Politics* (Ithaca: Cornell University Press, 2013).

16   The Eastern Bank, now Standard Chartered Bank, held the emir's personal and state account through the 1950s and 1960s and its Qatar branch president frequently wrote to his superiors in London of how the emir spent wildly on extravagances and running up enormous debts to the bank and leading Qatari merchant families.

17   British Foreign Office 1016/184.

18   www.bp.com/en/global/corporate/energy-economics/statistical-review-of-world-energy/natural-gas.html.html#natural-gas-reserves (accessed April 22, 2021).

19   Eastern Bank Letter No. 60/2, December 30, 1969, Deasy to Winton.

20   J.E. Peterson, "Tribes and Politics in Eastern Arabia," *Middle East Journal* 31 no. 3 (1977): 297–312.

21   A. Anthony, "Sheikha Mozah: The (Un)acceptable Face of Qatar's Global Expansion," *The Guardian*, December 14, 2014, Zahra R. Babar, "The Cost of Belonging: Citizenship Construction in the State of Qatar," *Middle East Journal* 68, no. 3 (2014): 403–420.

22   Research participants include: a male retired government employee born in Qatar in 1949; a retired Qatari petroleum executive born in Qatar in 1952; and a civil engineer born in Qatar in 1955.

23   Eastern Bank Letter P&C 62/60 pp.i–ii, March 22, 1971, D.B. McKay to London.

24   British Foreign and Commonwealth Office 8/1891, letter from Frank O'Shanohun.

25   FCO 8/1890.

26   2030 Vision document: www.gco.gov.qa/en/about-qatar/national-vision2030/ (accessed 10 May 2021).

27   www.theconstructionindex.co.uk/news/view/qatar-tbms-take-guinness-world-record (accessed April 27, 2021).

28   Mehran Kamrava, "Royal Factionalism and Political Liberalization in Qatar," *Middle East Journal* 63, no. 3 (2009): 401–420.

29   See Nasser Mohammad Al Othman, *With Their Bare Hands: The Story of the Oil Industry in Qatar* (London: Longman Group, 1984); John Moorhead, *In Defiance of the Elements* (London: Quartet Books Ltd., 1977).

30   E. Dickinson, "The Case Against Qatar," *Foreign Policy* 30 (September 2014): 1.

31   MEED Digest 2015.

PART VI

The Long Road

18

THE GLOBAL SPREAD OF STREET PAVEMENT MATERIALS AND TECHNOLOGY, 1820–1920

Robin B. Williams

Long before the automobile, municipal leaders around the world sought to modernize city streets to improve public hygiene, safety and transportation. Issues of resource availability made trade networks, often global in scope, a defining factor in how municipal engineers and city politicians selected street pavements. From the early nineteenth century until the 1920s, when horse-drawn vehicles dominated, cities experimented with a wide range of materials to solve the problem of a durable and effective street pavement, balancing cost, availability, and performance. A succession of pavement types spread around the industrializing world resulting from technological innovations and increased access to natural resources. The earliest modern pavement employed in many cities during the nineteenth century were naturally rounded cobblestones that arrived in port towns as discarded ship ballast – the detritus of global trade networks. Affordable Telford and Macadam pavements involving layers of gravel, invented in the United Kingdom in the early nineteenth century, quickly spread worldwide. But durability and dust problems demanded more solid pavements. While cut stone pavements like granite Belgian blocks were strongest, the deafening noise caused by metal horse hooves clattering on such surfaces popularized wood as a silent, though less permanent alternative. Plank roads, introduced in Russia, spread to Canada by the 1830s and to the United States a decade later. Wood blocks from Australia, Canada, and Scandinavia supplied cities often half a world away. Smooth, durable, and relatively quiet asphalt, first used in Paris in the 1850s, offered great promise, but was very expensive, relying on natural material collected by hand from Trinidad. Worse, like wood, it absorbed horse urine. Vitrified bricks would predominate in North America after 1880, but prohibitive shipping costs and noise pollution presented challenges. Such trade-offs defined pavement decisions until the 1920s, when petroleum-based asphalt prevailed.

From the early nineteenth century until the 1920s, cities around the world struggled to find a solution to the street pavement problem. From noise pollution created by metal-rimmed wheels and horses' hooves clattering on hard stone surfaces to public health concerns over animal waste littering roadways and the problem of getting stuck in the mud of dirt streets, the challenges posed by the growth of cities and their street networks became a defining by-product of modernization. Although some cities embraced affordable local solutions, such as the use of oyster shells as a street pavement in the American South, many modern pavements relied on a global trade network of resources and technical knowledge. Cobblestones, macadam, wood blocks, granite Belgian blocks (or setts), and natural asphalt each took their turn as pavement types that directly benefited from international trade. But not every modern pavement solution lent itself to global trade. Vitrified brick, for example, could be produced anywhere suitable clay existed, but as a very dense and heavy product, its weight discouraged long distance shipments.

Although street pavement has a long history going back to antiquity, the growth of cities due to industrialization magnified problems of hygiene and noise pollution that had existed for centuries. Citizens and public officials alike complained about the deplorable conditions of streets that threatened the health, safety and efficiency of life in the modern city. Some European cities had installed stone pavement on major streets by the sixteenth century, and a few American cities following suit in the seventeenth century. But the dramatic increase in the number of horse-drawn vehicles and pedestrians by the early nineteenth century compelled cities across the globe to find suitable street pavements for broader application. In most cities, the majority of streets were dirt, which could generate clouds of dust when dry and present impassable quagmires when wet, making transportation difficult. The importance of moving fire-fighting equipment rapidly through the city, for example, explains why Sanborn Fire Insurance maps indicated whether a street was "paved" or "unpaved."

Stone pavements had an earned reputation as a durable pavement, but frequently became uneven, and presented a problem of deafening noise as metal-rimmed wheels and iron horseshoes clattered in increasing numbers. The irregularity of stone pavements also made the clearing of mud and horse manure challenging. Smoother street surfaces, such as macadam and wood blocks, solved those problems, but lacked durability, requiring expensive repairs or replacement within five or so years, and could possibly worsen the hygiene problem by absorbing feces and urine. The introduction of natural asphalt during the second half of the century offered a smooth, quiet, and durable surface, yet the harvesting and processing costs made it the most expensive of pavement types. Cost often trumped other attributes in how decision-makers—from municipal engineers to residents—selected a material. Maintenance and cleaning also proved significant considerations (Figure 18.1); planners and street engineers had to calculate not only the cost of materials, but the amount of machinery and labor needed to keep streets clean.

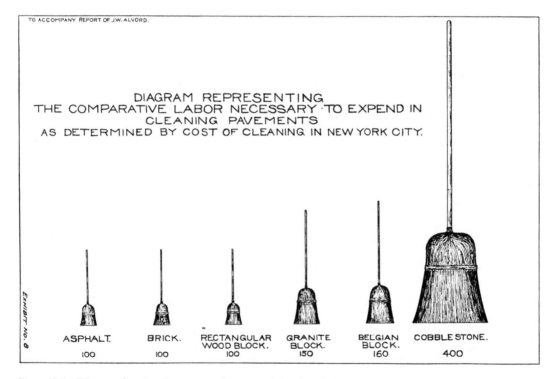

Figure 18.1 Diagram showing the comparative costs of cleaning different pavement types.

Source: Alvord, "A Report to the Street Paving Committee of the Commercial Club on the Street Paving Problem of Chicago," 1904.

Over time, the development and expansion of commercial trade networks played a key role in helping municipalities balance cost with performance of street paving materials.

Cobblestones

While most European cities had adopted some form of stone block pavement before the modern era, most North American cities had dirt streets well into the nineteenth century. An exception were the older port cities on the east coast, such as New York and Boston, which began making use of naturally rounded and irregular cobblestones as early as 1656 and certainly by 1700.[1] The stones arrived in port towns as discarded ship ballast—the detritus of global trade networks reflected by their geological diversity. Using rock to improve the stability of ships had been a common practice for centuries. To make room for the heavy loads of raw materials for export, the ballast stones were manually removed from the ships and typically deposited on a wharf, where they became a ready resource for affordable, though crude street pavement. Even the labor force occasionally reflected these global networks: in Alexandria, Virginia, in the 1790s, city officials employed Hessians, decommissioned German soldiers who fought for the British in the revolution, to install cobblestones on Princess Street.[2]

By the beginning of the twentieth century, the use of cobblestone pavement in the United States had spread inland to cities on major waterways, including Albany and Buffalo, New York, through the Erie Canal system, and Pittsburgh and Cincinnati along the Ohio River. Among the historic east coast port cities that had once paved most of their streets with cobblestones, only Baltimore retained a significant number by the dawn of the twentieth century, with 84.6 percent of its streets so paved, compared to 8.6 percent in New York, 2.8 percent in Philadelphia and 0.1 percent in Boston, according to a 1904 report.[3] This rapid and extensive replacement of cobblestone pavement owed no doubt to its crude and bumpy nature, which William Gillespie, a professor of civil engineering at Union College in Schenectady, New York, criticized in 1847 as a "common but very inferior pavement which disgraces the streets of nearly all our cities."[4] Although not included in the 1904 report, Savannah, Georgia, retains more historic cobblestone pavement than any other American city. City officials began paving Savannah's streets with cobblestones by 1843, and acquired between 1,700 and 3,250 tons of this material each year, which cost only a "wharfage" fee (since the wharfs were privately owned). All or parts of thirteen streets were paved with cobblestones before the ready supply diminished in the early 1880s following a new requirement for ballast to be unloaded outside the city.[5]

A unique cobblestone etched with Chinese characters in Savannah testifies to the global scale of trade networks in the nineteenth century (Figure 18.2). The smaller characters tell us that it was carved in the third year of the reign of Emperor Jiaqing of the Qing dynasty (1796–1820), hence 1798. The three larger characters identify a name—Zhang Lin'an. The combination of a name and a date indicates that this stone was used as a tombstone. At some point during the first half of the nineteenth century, the tombstone was removed and became a piece of rubble placed in a ship's hold as ballast. In Savannah, it became a pavement stone in Whitaker Ramp, one of the narrow roadways that descend forty feet from the downtown area to the waterfront, where it remained until 2011 when the cobblestones in that ramp were replaced with stamped concrete. Fortunately, the Chinese cobblestone was saved and is now displayed in the rotunda of Savannah City Hall.

Macadam

The challenge of creating serviceable roadbeds beyond port areas resulted in experiments by Pierre-Marie-Jérôme Trésaguet in the 1760s in France and Thomas Telford in Wales in the early 1800s. Their respective methods were labor intensive and expensive, involving substantial foundations and additional layers of broken stones and pronounced cambering of the roadbed. Trésaguet's method spread to central Europe, Switzerland and Sweden after 1760, and a variation on it was initially used on the first major

Figure 18.2 Chinese cobblestone in situ in Whitaker Ramp, Savannah, ca. 2010.

Source: Image courtesy of David Anderson.

road project in America, the National Road, for the first completed section, between Cumberland, Maryland, and Wheeling, Virginia (now West Virginia), between 1808 and 1821.[6]

A contemporary of Telford, Scottish inventor John Loudon McAdam developed a simpler method of road building that utilized the native ground as the foundation and two thinner layers of consistently sized hand-broken stones: a lower layer roughly eight inches thick and comprising stones no larger than three inches across and an upper layer two inches thick and with stones less than an inch (2 cm). The size of the stones was regulated by passing them through a ring. McAdam developed his road-building techniques as a trustee of the Ayrshire Turnpike in the Scottish Lowlands beginning in 1783 and after 1804 as the general surveyor for the local governing body of Bristol, England. In 1816, McAdam was made surveyor of the Bristol Turnpike Trust and published his first of two treatises, *Remarks on the Present System of Road-Making* (1816; with eight subsequent editions through 1827) and *Practical Essay on the Scientific Repair and Preservation of Roads* (1819). These works helped disseminate his ideas to a global audience. First introduced in London in 1820 by McAdam, "macadamized" pavement technology spread to Australia by 1822 and a year later to the United States.[7]

The American use of macadam, according to Clay McShane, "bore little resemblance to the original" due to the utilization of gravel that was "too large, too small, or not laid to sufficient thickness" as a result of the "high American wages [that] made it prohibitively expensive to crush rock by hand." The use of blasting powder to break stones to the proper sizes allowed Frederick Law Olmsted and Calvert Vaux to lay out "the first technically correct macadam pavements in the U.S. in Central Park in 1858."[8] Macadam eventually enjoyed widespread and extensive use in the United States in the nineteenth century and even into the first decades of the twentieth century due to its relative ease of installation and affordability. As of 1904, macadam remained the most common type of pavement in some major cities, including Boston, New York, and St. Louis (Figure 18.3).[9] Yet macadam was far from permanent and generated complaints about dust, pressuring municipal engineers to experiment after 1840 with more expensive pavements of wood, stone, asphalt, and vitrified brick to solve the pavement problem.

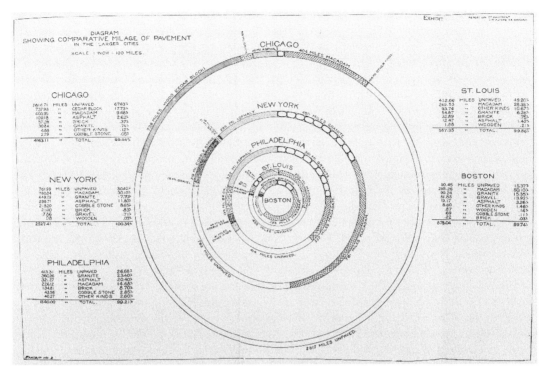

Figure 18.3 Diagram showing comparative mileage of different pavement types in larger U.S. cities.

Source: Alvord, "A Report to the Street Paving Committee of the Commercial Club on the Street Paving Problem of Chicago," 1904.

Plank Roads

A short-lived but widely popular alternative to macadam were plank roads. In North America, the first plank road was constructed leading east from Toronto, Canada West, in 1835–1836, with the idea being attributed to D'Arcy Boulton, a Toronto merchant and land speculator.[10] One source at the time claimed the idea of plank roads had begun in Russia and "was introduced into Canada by Lord Sydenham," but this is unlikely since Sydenham arrived in Canada as its new Governor General in 1839.[11] The twelve-foot-wide road led to the construction of over 200 miles of plank roads in Canada West (now Ontario) by 1839. Having learned of these new roads, George Geddes, an engineer and agriculturalist from Fairmont, near Syracuse, and later a New York state senator, made two visits to Canada to study their construction and financing. Through his advocacy the first plank road in the United States was constructed in 1846 in the village of Cicero north of Syracuse, inaugurating the "plank road boom" of over 10,000 miles of plank roads constructed in the U.S. over the next eleven years by more than one thousand private companies.[12] But costly repairs and insufficient maintenance brought an abrupt end to their use.

Wood Blocks

Wood blocks emerged as the first pavement material to rely for its success on marketing and trade—and, for some countries, on international trade. The idea of using wood blocks as a street surface appears to have been introduced in St. Petersburg, Russia, between 1820 and 1832 with the hexagonal "Guryev Pavement," named after its inventor V.P. Guryev.[13] The idea spread quickly. By the end of the 1830s, Manchester and London in the United Kingdom and New York in the United States had begun experimenting with this type of pavement. But these early experiments were with untreated wood that promptly decayed. In the United States, the development of Nicolson blocks, patented in 1859 by Samuel Nicolson and first used in 1856 in Boston, involved laying the blocks end-grain up on a concrete foundation and filling the joints with tar.[14] His product inspired imitators, including the Stafford Pavement, DeGolyer Patent Improved Wood Pavement, Paul National Wood Paving, and Stow's Foundation Pavement.[15] In North America, a continent amply endowed with trees, a wide range of wood species were utilized and varied by region—including cedar in the Midwest, yellow pine in the Southeast, and mesquite in Texas. But even the Nicolson Blocks and their many imitators suffered from multiple problems, including being slippery when wet, offering poor traction for horses on steep grades, absorbing horse urine and excrement and rotting almost as quickly as their predecessors.[16] Despite these drawbacks, supporters of wood blocks in later decades would advocate the use of harder woods or stronger preservatives to promote this quietest of pavements.

The use of wood blocks in London illustrated the international nature of this pavement type and the challenges such trade networks posed. The first wood blocks were installed in 1839 on the Old Bailey, which ran past Newgate Prison.[17] By the 1840s the importation of Swedish softwoods, particularly yellow deal (pine), for paving in London led to a trade deficit with the Baltic region.[18] These early blocks decayed quickly, prompting the Commissioners of Woods and Forests in 1844 to call on the government "to lay down no more wood pavement in the metropolis."[19] After returning to the use of pine blocks in the 1870s, following the improved techniques involving tar and better foundation materials, Australian hardwoods became the material of choice during the last decade of the nineteenth century in the British cities. Beginning with Jarrah on Westminster Bridge Road in 1889 and Karri a year later, these first woods came from Western Australia.[20] In 1894 and 1895, preference shifted to hardwoods from New South Wales in eastern Australia, including tallow wood, black butt, blue gum and red gum.

In an ongoing effort to find the most effective material for pavement, wood types from other parts of the world, including

> White oak and gum wood from South Carolina and Mora wood from Demerara [Dutch Guiana] are also being introduced; and as these are of a tough and fibrous nature, and considerably lighter than Jarrah, it is considered they will be less noisy and slippery than the other hard woods mentioned.[21]

This variety of materials was partly due to the responsibility for public works decisions being left to the individual districts of the capital, called vestries. According to a news report in *The Brisbane Courier*,

> Mr. T.J. Mackle, a member of the Paddington Vestry, fought hard, and against bitter opposition, to introduce Australian hardwoods into his parish, and after years of unremitting toil he has succeeded, and now Paddington is as `hot' on these woods as can well be.

The report also noted how English importers blamed a shortage of wood blocks in England on mismanagement by "unbusinesslike" Australian exporters.[22]

A decade later, municipal engineers throughout England preferred Swedish or Russian "redwood (Pinus sylvestris)," otherwise known as red pine in Europe and Scotch pine in the U.S. According to a report in the journal *Municipal Engineering*, the redwood was preferred because its "price was satisfactory, its life was definitely known, and the paving companies handled it."[23] As the report noted, when issuing pavement contracts, municipal authorities

> specified redwood in nearly every case, and the paving companies did not handle any other kind of wood. The influence of the paving companies was all powerful in most of the municipalities when a change of wood was to be considered.

Yet, by 1915, Canadian wood imports—Douglas fir, white spruce, jack pine, and red pine—offered the possibility of cheaper prices. The report enthused about the extent of Canadian forests: "The supply along the line of the Grand Trunk Railway is unlimited, there being enough still uncut to pave every street, not only in Europe, but in the world," but reflecting the realities of trade and economics, "they can find a sale only on condition that the normal price c.i.f. [cost, insurance, freight] is less than $53.50 per standard for well manufactured sound grade."[24]

As noted by David O. Whitten in his study of wood block pavement, the issue of wood preservatives, particularly tar-based creosote, dominated engineering literature.[25] The question of what chemical would be most effective had years earlier even interested Edgar Allan Poe, who addressed the issue of "Street Paving" on the front page of his publication *The Broadway Journal* in April 1845. To address the problem of decay, which he believed caused "injury to the public health from miasmata arising from the wood," he proposed as a preservative agent the use of a corrosive sublimate, mercuric chloride. Interestingly, he framed the issue in terms of economics and trade:

> The cost of the Bi-chloride of Mercury is we presume, at present, something less than one dollar per pound—but the cost would be greatly reduced should the mineralizing process occasion an unusual demand. The South American quicksilver mines, now unworked, would be put into operation, and we should get the article, perhaps, for forty or even thirty cents per pound.[26]

His rumination on the topic illustrates how yet another component of street pavement was impacted by international trade.

Natural Asphalt

The use of bituminous materials has a surprisingly long history, dating back to antiquity, but it was not until the nineteenth century that coal tar, rock asphalt, and natural asphalt found applications, in turn, on road surfaces. Macadam roads faced the continual challenge of loosening gravel and copious dust. Filling the gaps with dust from the construction of a macadam road mixed with water created a fairly successful simple and inexpensive result called water-bound macadam, but it lacked durability. The use of coal tar mixed with macadam gravel, first employed on a road in England in 1840, led to the widely employed material called tar-macadam, from which the frequently misused term "tarmac" comes.[27] The exploitation of two large rock asphalt deposits in Europe—the Seyssel deposit in the Rhone Valley in France and the Val de Travers deposit in the Neuchatel region of Switzerland—led to the use of the material in a mastic form for footpaths in the 1830s. But it wasn't until rock asphalt was ground, heated, and compressed with a roller, a method discovered by Swiss engineer André Merian in 1849 and applied to the Rue Bergere in Paris in 1854, that the first true application of sheet asphalt took place, revolutionizing street pavement technology.[28] Compressed Val de Travers rock asphalt was used in London on Threadneedle Street in 1869, in New York around Union Square in 1872, and on Pennsylvania Avenue in Washington, D.C. in 1876; however, the rock asphalt method proved unsuccessful in the United States.[29]

More revolutionary, and more consequential to the global trade of asphalt, was the method patented in the United States in 1870 by Belgian born chemist Edmund J. DeSmedt, involving natural asphalt from Trinidad, part of the British West Indies at the time. Compared to the rock asphalt used mainly in Europe, natural asphalt has a higher percentage of bitumen. DeSmedt demonstrated his method, which involved "using Trinidad asphalt softened by heavy petroleum oil and mixed with sand and powdered carbonate of lime," on a street in front of City Hall in Newark, New Jersey, in 1870—the first successful asphalt street pavement in the United States.[30] Notably, "he was the first to heat the asphalt before mixing it with sand and placing it on the surface of the roadway, creating what is known today as hot-mix asphalt."[31] Based on his success in New Jersey, DeSmedt was involved in the formation of several asphalt

EXPORTS OF LAND ASPHALT FROM TRINIDAD. (*a*) (IN TONS OF 2,240 LB.)

Year.	To United States.			To Europe.			To Other Countries.			Grand Total of Exports in Crude Equivalent.
	Crude.	Épuré.	Total Equivalent in Crude.	Crude.	Épuré.	Total Equivalent in Crude.	Crude.	Épuré.	Total Equivalent in Crude.	
	Tons.	Tons.	Tons.	Tons.	Tons.	Tons.	Tons.	Tons.	Tons.	Tons.
1897....	19,243	*Nil.*	19,243	293	700	1,343	415	178	682	21,268
1898....	18,160	*Nil.*	18,160	700	258	1,087	404	312	872	20,119
1899....	25,613	345	26,130	275	280	695	....	100	150	26,975
1900....	34,796	(*b*)	34,796	251	(*b*)	251	197	(*b*)	197	35,244
1901....	31,767	11	31,767	1,704	(*b*)	1,704	1,446	(*b*)	1,446	34,917

EXPORTS OF PITCH-LAKE ASPHALT FROM TRINIDAD. (*a*) (IN TONS OF 2,240 LB.)

Year.	To United States.			To Europe.			To Other Countries.			Grand Total of Exports in Crude Equivalent.
	Crude.	Dried.	Total Equivalent in Crude.	Crude.	Épuré and Dried.	Total Equivalent in Crude.	Crude.	Épuré and Dried.	Total Equivalent in Crude.	
	Tons.	Tons.	Tons.	Tons.	Tons.	Tons.	Tons.	Tons.	Tons.	Tons.
1897....	71,969	1,769	74,407	14,629	13,510	34,856	....	500	680	109,943
1898....	46,089	1,692	48,424	15,703	13,228	35,537	693	1,646	2,999	86,960
1899....	70,111	480	70,777	21,337	13,749	41,956	....	1,699	2,359	115,092
1900....	67,758	3,160	70,938	23,386	16,114	47,352	1,422	2,420	4,453	122,743
1901....	80,449	*Nil.*	80,449	31,213	15,815	54,761	....	586	844	136,054

(*a*) The exports prior to 1897 will be found in THE MINERAL INDUSTRY, Vol. VII. (*b*) Included in the shipments of crude.

Figure 18.4 Table showing exports of asphalt from Trinidad, 1897–1901.

Source: "Asphaltum," in *The Mineral Industry, Its Statistics, Technology and Trade in the United States and Other Countries to the End of 1901*, ed. Joseph Struthers, Vol. 10 [New York and London: *The Engineering and Mining Journal*, 1903], 49.

and asphalt paving companies.[32] His method received a major boost in 1876, when a Congressionally appointed commission organized a demonstration project on Pennsylvania Avenue, pitting the Val de Travers rock asphalt against natural sheet asphalt; DeSmedt's process proved the most viable.[33]

In short order, Trinidad became the leading source of natural asphalt for street pavement, with smaller amounts coming from France, Germany, Hungary, Spain, the United States and Venezuela.[34] Much of the asphalt excavated in Trinidad, both from Pitch Lake and the surrounding land-based operations, was exported to the United States, but significant amounts also went to Europe and some "to other countries" (Figure 18.4). The use of natural sheet asphalt in the United States grew from 300,000 square yards in 1880 to 38,000,000 square yards in 1900, by which time over 85 percent of that was from the Pitch Lake deposit in Trinidad, and roughly half of that installed by the Barber Asphalt Paving Company.[35] A promotional booklet from that company gives a detailed description of Pitch Lake. Approximately half a mile in diameter and covering 114 acres, the lake is located about three-quarters of a mile from the shore of the island, providing convenient accessibility to ships. Comprising mostly asphalt,

> The surface is hard enough, except in irregular patches in the center, to bear the weight of carts and mules. It is necessary, however, for one to keep moving, otherwise he soon sinks in the material, which under the hot rays of the sun becomes quite mobile, although not sticky, owing to the large amount of water which it contains. When asphalt is dug from any portion of the deposit, in the course of a few days the hole is filled by new material coming from below.[36]

Street Pavement Technology

Figure 18.5 Workers collecting natural asphalt by hand, Pitch Lake, Trinidad, ca. 1915.

Source: Courtesy of the George Grantham Bain Collection, No. LC-B2-3971-11, Library of Congress, Washington, D.C.

Given the relatively soft surface of the lake, collection had to be done by hand, instead of using heavy equipment (Figure 18.5). Even the time of day mattered when working on the lake: "The asphalt is dug by means of picks or mattocks just before dawn, when the asphalt is comparatively brittle."[37] The crude asphalt would then need to be refined, either in the United States, where it was cheaper to refine and then use domestically, or in Trinidad, if being shipped to any other country.

Despite being the most expensive form of pavement in the late nineteenth century, natural sheet asphalt quickly gained appeal for its smoothness and superior durability over wood, as well as its presumed cheaper maintenance and cleaning costs, according to New York City Street Cleaning Commissioner, George Waring.[38] Yet, that experience was not universal. In Savannah, asphalt had *higher* maintenance costs than any other form of pavement. As noted in 1896 by the city's Public Works Commissioner Harry Willink:

> It will be seen that the cost of cleaning asphalt streets is about five times that of cleaning shell, cobble or granite. Asphalt, while a pretty pavement, and as claimed by some the most sanitary of all pavements, unless kept absolutely clean speedily becomes the most unsanitary and injurious to the public's health as well as offensive to its eyes. It accordingly requires more attention than any other class of pavements. The method of cleaning also makes it especially expensive.[39]

Thus, asphalt faced ongoing challenges, including high initial costs, absorption of horse excrement, vulnerability to water, and difficulty in cleaning by machine. Municipal engineers and planners around the world were obliged to continue the quest for the most durable pavement available at the lowest cost.

Conclusion

By the early twentieth century, the development of cheaper and more predictable artificial asphalt pavements resulting from advances in asphalt chemistry made synthetic asphalt significantly cheaper than its natural predecessor.[40] This development brought an end to the global trade of natural asphalt, to be replaced by the global trade of petroleum products with which each locality could manufacture its own asphalt. Combined with the supplanting of horse-drawn vehicles and their noisy metal rims and horseshoes with rubber-tired automobiles, synthetic asphalt also resolved the pavement problem with a smooth, affordable, sufficiently durable and non-absorbent surface. The pervasive adoption of synthetic asphalt across the world also resulted in a homogenization of street character, as the highly individualistic pavement identity of each city—defined for so long by local responses to the materials available through global trade—sought the benefits of this most eminently modern material.

Notes

1 For the year 1656, see George W. Tillson, "The Development of Street Pavements," *Journal of the Franklin Institute* 163, no. 6 (June 1907): 438; and for the more cautious estimate of by 1700, see Clay McShane, *Down the Asphalt Path* (New York: Columbia University Press, 1994), 11.
2 As noted on a historic marker located in the middle of Princess Street at North St. Asaph Street.
3 John W. Alvord, "A Report to the Street Paving Committee of the Commercial Club on the Street Paving Problem of Chicago" (Chicago: R. R. Donnelley & Sons Company, Printers, 1904), exhibits 2, 9–14.
4 W.M. Gillespie, *A Manual of the Principles and Practice of Road-Making: Comprising the Location, Construction, and Improvement of Roads (Common, Macadam, Paved, Plank, etc.); and Railroads* (New York: A.S. Barnes & Co., 1848), 216–217.
5 Gamble, 419.
6 Billy Joe Peyton, "Surveying and Building the Road," in *The National Road*, ed. Karl Raitz (Baltimore: The Johns Hopkins University Press, 1996), 140–142.
7 Regarding Australia, see J.B. Metcalf and G.S. Donald, "Road Pavements in Australia," *Proceedings of the 14th ARRB [Australian Road Research Board] Conference*, Part 1 (1988): 50; regarding the United States, see Peyton, "Surveying and Building the Road," 150.
8 McShane, *Down the Asphalt Path*, 56.
9 Alvord, "A Report to the Street Paving Committee of the Commercial Club on the Street Paving Problem of Chicago," exhibit no. 2. Macadam represented 50.1, 30.1 and 28.35 percent of all street surfaces in Boston, New York, and St. Louis, respectively, where unpaved was still the largest percentage.
10 W. Kingsford, *History, Structure, and Statistics of Plank Roads, in the United States and Canada* (Philadelphia: A. Hart, Late Carey & Hart, 1851), 5.
11 "The First Plank Road Movement," *Hunt's Merchants' Magazine and Commercial Review* 24 (January–June 1851): 65. The assertion was repeated with more detail by Remley J. Glass, "Early Transportation and the Plank Road," *The Annals of Iowa* 21 (1939): 513.
12 "The First Plank Road Movement," 64. Regarding the statistics on total miles of plank roads constructed and the number of companies, see Daniel B. Klein and John Majewski, "Turnpikes and Toll Roads in Nineteenth-Century America," *EH Net Encyclopedia*, http://eh.net/encyclopedia/turnpikes-and-toll-roads-in-nineteenth-century-america/.
13 Y.N. Kruzhnov, "Pavements," *Saint Petersburg Encyclopedia*, www.encspb.ru/object/2804025714?lc=en. In some nineteenth-century sources, his name is spelt Gourieff.
14 Nicolson patented his wood block pavement in 1859 and in that same year published *The Nicolson Pavement, Invented by Samuel Nicolson, of Boston, Mass.* (Boston: Henry W. Dutton & Son, 1859).
15 For a promotional brochure for each of these products, see the Chicago History Museum for DeGolyer Patent Improved Wood Pavement and the Stafford Pavement; Lincoln, Nebraska, City Archives for Paul National Wood Paving Company; and the City of Savannah Municipal Archives for the Stow's Foundation Pavement.
16 Carl Abbott, "Plank Roads and Wood-Block Pavements," *Journal of Forest History* 25, no. 4 (October 1981): 218.
17 "London Pavements," *The Manufacturer and Builder* [New York] 10, no. 9 (September 1878): 199.
18 Carlton Reid, "Sherlock Holmes and the Mystery of London's Forgotten Australian Timber Roads," Roads Were Not Built For Cars blog, June 26, 2013, www.roadswerenotbuiltforcars.com/wood/.
19 "Epitome of News," *The Illustrated London News* 4 (April 1844): 275.
20 Thomas Aitken, *Road Making and Maintenance: A Practical Treatise for Engineers, Surveyors, and Others. With an Historical Sketch of Ancient and Modern Practice* (London: C. Griffin and Company, Ltd., 1900), 331, 340.
21 Ibid.
22 "Wood-Paving in London," *The Brisbane Courier*, May 27, 1898, p. 6. The same news report noted that there were forty different kinds of deal [pine] wood coming from Norway.
23 "Canadian Wood Blocks for Paving in Great Britain," *Municipal Engineering* [Indianapolis] 49 (July–December 1915): 225.

24 Ibid.
25 David O. Whitten, "A Century of Parquet Pavements: Wood as a Paving Material in the United States and Abroad, 1840-1940; Part 2, Twentieth Century Decline: Geography, Technology, History," *Essays in Economic and Business History* 16 (1998), unpaginated online copy, http://kaswell.com/wp-content/uploads/2012/06/Article-by-David-O.-Whitten.docx.
26 Edgar Allan Poe, "Street Paving," *The Broadway Journal* 1, no. 16 (April 19, 1845), 242.
27 Don Clow, "From Macadam to Asphalt: The Paving of the Streets of London in the Victorian Era. Part 1: From Macadam To Stone Sett," Greater London Industrial Archaeology Society, 2004. www.glias.org.uk/journals/8-a.html.
28 "French Asphalt Roads, and American Attempts to Imitate Them," *Scientific American* (February 12, 1870): 107.
29 See "London Pavements," *The Manufacturer and Builder* [New York], 10, no. 9 (September 1878): 199; and T. Hugh Boorman, *Asphalts, Their Sources and Utilizations* (New York: William T. Comstock, 1908), 11.
30 A.W. Dow, "The History of the Asphalt Industry to 1901, Inclusive," in *The Mineral Industry, Its Statistics, Technology and Trade in the United States and Other Countries to the End of 1901*, Vol. 10, ed. Joseph Struthers (New York and London: The Engineering and Mining Journal, 1903), 51.
31 Jeff L. Brown, "Rocky Road: The Story of Asphalt Pavement," *Civil Engineering* 83, no. 5 (2013): 40.
32 The American Asphalt Paving Co., The Grahamite Asphalt Co., The Grahamite Asphalt Paving Co., and The Grahamite & Trinidad Asphalt Paving Co. See Dow, "The History of the Asphalt Industry to 1901, Inclusive," 51–52.
33 "The Barber Asphalt Pavements," (Washington, D.C.: Barber Asphalt Paving Company, c1901), 7. The commission comprised Generals H.G. Wright and Q.A. Gilmore of the Corps of Engineers and Edward Clark, Architect of the Capitol.
34 "Asphaltum," *The Mineral Industry, Its Statistics, Technology and Trade in the United States and Other Countries to the End of 1901*, Vol. 10, ed. Joseph Struthers (New York and London: The Engineering and Mining Journal, 1903), 46.
35 "The Barber Asphalt Pavements,"10–11, 30.
36 Ibid. 12.
37 Ibid. 17.
38 Quoted in Clay McShane, "Transforming the Use of Urban Space: A Look at the Revolution in Street Pavements, 1880–1924," *Journal of Urban History* 5, no. 3 (1979): 295.
39 *Annual Report of Herman Myers, Mayor of the City of Savannah, for the Year Ending December 31, 1896*, 156–157.
40 McShane, *Down the Asphalt Path*, 59.

19
PARALLEL LINES
Urban Expressways in the United States
Romina Canna

This chapter focuses on urban expressways in American cities, as distinct from the system of which they are part. The passage of the Federal Aid Highway Act of 1956 marked the culmination of a long process to establish what would become the Interstate Highway System. Starting in the nineteenth century, a series of events outlined the need for and scope of a potential network, while the technological, financial, and social developments starting at the dawn of the twentieth century transformed the underlying logic and objectives of a national road system. Originally intended to operate on the abstract grid of territory, the system instead became a network of connections between urban centers. Understood in this context, the development of the urban expressway followed two parallel lines. One line was drawn by governmental institutions, civic associations, and private capital, beginning in the nineteenth century, as a reaction to a changing urban environment. The other was constructed through a series of government documents produced in the first half of the twentieth century, debating the proper form and institutional frame of a modern national road system and its relation to the city. From this perspective, the urban expressway was the result of the convergence of these once-parallel lines, radically transforming the postwar American city and the meaning of the urban itself.

The political, financial, and jurisdictional maneuvering that ultimately led to the construction of the Interstate Highway System in the United States is a well-known episode. Much of the existing literature focuses on the apparently orderly sequence of decisions and realizations of the network.[1] There is also a growing body of literature dealing with the impact of the Interstate on urban fabric, particularly through the destruction of neighborhoods, the amplification of racial segregation, and the urban revolts against the highway system itself.[2] Largely absent from the literature, however, is analysis of how the national scale and territorial ambition of the Interstate Highway System came to include, incorporate, and ultimately transform the very notion of the "urban." In this chapter, I argue that there exists a distinct history of urban expressways that reflects the intertwined evolution of two parallel lines of development: one drawn by the efforts from governmental institutions, civic associations, and private capital since the nineteenth century to envision a changing urban environment and the role of intra-urban thoroughfares; and the other, constructed through a series of documents in the first half of the twentieth century over the proper form and institutional frame of a modern national road system and its relation to the city. From this perspective, the urban expressway was the result of the convergence of these once-parallel lines, radically transforming the postwar American city and the meaning of the urban itself.

Congestion and Efficiency

Beginning in the early twentieth century, traffic congestion became a visible symptom of the inadequacy of existing urban infrastructure in a new era of mobility. Congestion therefore became central to the discussion about city planning: the gradual strangulation of cities by traffic, population growth, commercial exchange, and production shifted the primary focus of urban planning toward efficiency.[3] The "City Efficient" movement emerged in this context as an effort to control and strengthen the functional, economic, and infrastructural capacities of the city, eschewing the civic and scenographic considerations of the earlier "City Beautiful" movement.[4] In a 1912 conference at the Engineers Club of Philadelphia, engineer and urban planner Nelson P. Lewis defined limited objectives for city planning: "It is," he argued,

> simply the exercise of such foresight as will promote the orderly and sightly development of a city and its environs along rational lines … The object should be to reduce to a minimum the resistance to both intraurban and interurban traffic. A city cannot live, much less grow, without them.[5]

Street specialization, parkways, limited-access highways, and other roadway typologies were rapidly becoming key elements of a vocabulary for a new era of planning based on efficiency.

These efforts culminated at the 1939 New York World's Fair, where General Motors presented a pavilion entitled *Futurama: Highways and Horizons*. Designed by stage and industrial designer Norman Bel Geddes, the pavilion featured a colossal model of the American landscape set twenty years in the future around which observers rotated in slow-moving booths. The model projected a vision of a modern society catalyzed around infrastructure, technology, and the private automobile structured around "express boulevards" crossing the city (Figure 19.1). At the exit door, a small pin was given to each visitor of the exhibition, reading, "I have seen the future." The message paved the way, at least temporarily, for widespread acceptance of a highway system and a promising new urban element: the expressway.

In the same year, Franklin D. Roosevelt's Work Projects Administration published its annual "Report on Progress" with data about the use of federal funding for public works.[6] Of the 31,140 annual projects realized in 1939, more than 25% were devoted to highways, roads and streets, corresponding to a total of 111,000 miles of new or improved roads.[7] Although part of this mileage was in rural areas, a significant effort was put into strengthening mobility within cities, funding bridges, paving and widening roads, culverts, eliminating grade crossings, and installing roadside landscaping and street signs. The development of new urban thoroughfares as a sign of efficient and modern planning signaled the dawn of a city to come.

Defense and Territory

On July 7, 1919, U.S. Secretary of War Newton Baker declared that "(t)his is the beginning of a new era. The World War was a war of motor transport. It was a war of movement …"[8] Baker's comments were made at a ceremony marking the departure of the Transcontinental Motor Convoy, a war game organized to test the U.S. Army's ability to move from coast to coast. The arduous crossing unveiled the inadequacy of existing roadways when faced with the threat of contemporary combat scenarios: the American terrain would have to be re-imagined as a defense project on an unprecedented scale. This lesson was not lost on one of the convoy's observation officers, the young lieutenant colonel Dwight D. Eisenhower, who as President would later secure the construction of the Interstate Highways System.[9]

The notion of building modern roads already had a civic-commercial precedent in the Good Roads Movement. Initiated in the late nineteenth century to lobby for road improvements for bicycles, and later for enhanced connections among towns, the growing movement pressured national politicians to act. In response to the growing demand for good roads, the Office of Road Inquiry, a predecessor of the Bureau of Public Roads, was established in 1893. This agency was the first to deal with better roads at federal level, although it lacked sufficient legislative or financial support to accomplish its objectives. In this context, in 1912, Carl Fisher, businessman and member of the Good

Romina Canna

Figure 19.1 Norman Bel Geddes, Express boulevards at the "City of Tomorrow," Futurama model, 1939.
Source: The Edith Lutyens and Norman Bel Geddes Foundation, Inc.

Figure 19.2 The Transcontinental Motor Convoy of 1919 passing through Utah.

Source: Edward Mantel Archives, National Archives, Eisenhower Presidential Library, Abilene, Kansas.

Roads Movement, started campaigning for the so-called "Lincoln Highway." Fisher, among others, was displeased with the role of government in fulfilling the needs of the growing mobility: "(t)he feds were building scattered demonstration roads but left the real work to states and localities, most of which … didn't know what they were doing."[10] Supported by companies such as Goodyear and Packard, the road was meant to be not only an example of modern infrastructure but also a critique of the slow action of government in this field.[11] Seven years later, with segments that were still nothing more than mud and stones, the coast to coast "Lincoln" would provide the extensively documented route of the Transcontinental Motor Convoy (Figure 19.2).

In 1921, Congress approved the first Federal Aid Highway Act for the creation of a federally funded national road system. Based on the less far-reaching Federal Aid Road Act of 1916, the law included the recommendations of Thomas MacDonald, Chief of the Bureau of Public Roads (BPR), which revolved around establishing institutional roles, assigning to the states the responsibility of producing highway plans and positioning the federal government as enforcer of quality and standards, and the principle that highways, besides their defense-related role, would also be instruments of economic expansion and growth of urban areas. In response, U.S. Army General John Pershing released a selection of roadways intended to serve military interests. The so-called "Pershing Map" is the first graphic registry of a territorial system of "highways" connecting strategic points: bases, industrial centers and urban areas with high military value (Figure 19.3).

Until the 1930s, research around a national road system in the U.S. focused on two aspects: the morphology and materiality of the roadways, and the definition and hierarchy of routes. Underlying these two factors was a third, focused on the uncertain meaning and reach of a system that would serve both military and civil use. This last consideration was the most complex of the three, given its relation to urban logics as a tool for growth. Planners and engineers thus faced a challenge: the new roads were simultaneously understood to be part of a territorial, transcontinental system, motivated

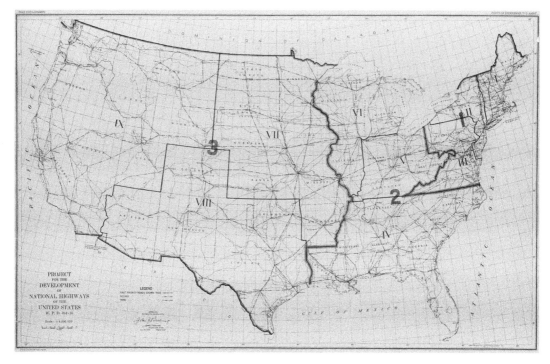

Figure 19.3 The *Pershing Map*, Records of the Bureau of Public Roads, 1892–1972.

Source: National Archives and Records Administration, College Park, Maryland.

by defense considerations, while they were also understood to be anchored in cities. This apparent contradiction would not only create a challenging task for planners and engineers, but it would also, and perhaps more importantly, challenge the notion of "the urban" for the rapidly changing American city.

Metropolitan Expansion

Starting with the expansion of steam railroads in the middle of the nineteenth century, mass transportation opened a new chapter in the spatial and functional role of infrastructure and its potential to shape urban-suburban territories. As historian Kenneth T. Jackson has observed: "The steam locomotive became an accepted part of the urban landscape … (t)he locomotive came to be regarded as a positive force for good as a means for enabling families to escape the congestion of the crowded city."[12] The modern streetcar continued the work of expanding inhabitable territory, cheaply and quickly. Country-wide streetcar rides increased from two billion in 1890 to five billion in 1905, consolidating the growth of the American metropolis.[13] In Boston, for example, the extension of the city grew from 2.5 miles from City Hall to six miles in ten years.[14] Transit development became an essential element in the changing nature of cities, triggering speculative land consumption and reinforcing existing patterns of social division and racial segregation.

Thus, when Geddes set about designing *Futurama*, he did so in the context of an American metropolitan territory that had already undergone rapid transformation over the first three decades of the twentieth century. Much of this territorial expansion was made possible first by the evolution of mass transportation, and far more potently, the widespread adoption of the private automobile as a major mode of transportation. Automobile registrations grew from 8,000 in 1905 to over 22 million in 1925.[15] And as Americans sought new horizons outside of central cities, public policies and private actors made homes—and home ownership—possible for the burgeoning white middle class, notably excluding and isolating people of color.

The need for "express" streets connecting the central city with its fringes started at the beginning of the 1900s. Although some thoroughfares connecting the city and the suburbs existed, these were often dusty roads with dangerous crossings and precarious construction. The first "expressway" was built by private capital to meet the vision of its racing-enthusiast sponsor. Starting in 1906, the William K. Vanderbilt Long Island Parkway Motor Parkway was built as an interrupted, pristine asphalt ribbon with limited, toll access and the most modern standards to grant "automobilists" a specialized thoroughfare.[16] Soon, express-traffic thoroughfares would bloom in many major cities, and New York—through the implacable determination of Robert Moses—would provide a blueprint for expressways within urban fabrics, expediting the involvement of all levels of government in the financing and creation of a national system. By the 1930s, there was substantial public approval for specialized, modern roads. This support, combined with the growing involvement of the federal government and the lobbying power of the auto industry, secured the way for a new expressway network.

Building the Case

Between the policies and agencies of the New Deal in the 1930s, and postwar recovery in the 1950s, government and trade associations produced numerous studies, reports, and ultimately legislative acts in support of a national road system, while corporations such as General Motors, Uniroyal, Chrysler, and Standard Oil established powerful lobbies in Washington, D.C. Two reports—*Toll and Free Roads*, of 1939; the *Interregional Highway Report* of 1944 later transformed into the 1944 Federal-Aid Highway Act, and the 1956 Federal-Aid Highway Act—are central documents to understanding the ideological, morphological, and material evolution of the urban expressway.

Toll and Free Roads, 1939

In 1938, in a meeting with Bureau of Public Roads (BPR) Chief Thomas MacDonald, President Roosevelt drew three thick blue lines running east to west, and three north to south across the continental United States. This so-called "Roosevelt Map" evinced a desire to operate on a new territorial scale, while its diagrammatic nature also made it clear that the urban implications of the plan had not yet been discovered (Figure 19.4). Following Roosevelt's lead, the Federal-Aid Highway Act of 1938 proposed an initial feasibility study "to investigate and make a report … with respect to the feasibility of funding, and cost of, superhighways … and the feasibility of a toll system on such roads."[17] The "superhighways" were intended to be built according to the most modern engineering standards. Taking the German *Reichsautobahn* as a model, the American system aimed to be, fundamentally, a system of territorial crossings.

Released in 1939, the BPR report *Toll and Free Roads* addressed several clear objectives, including "(t)he need of a special system of direct interregional highways, with all necessary connections through and around cities, designed to meet the requirements of the national defense and the needs of growing peacetime traffic of longer range."[18] The report demonstrated that traffic levels justified the creation of a system, however, traffic had a precise location and unexpected patterns of behavior, thus complicating the idea of financing it through a toll system. Under the title "Highway Trips are Predominantly Short," the report revealed that a high percentage of trips taken on the nation's early system of highways were of less than twenty miles, and were not, in fact, engaging the scale of the broader territory.[19] Of the total trips taken in the U.S., 25.7% were of about five miles and took place in and around urban areas, where mutations in city form and population distribution were rapidly occurring.[20] The original conception of a highway system, born in the service of defense objectives in 1919, had proven excessively narrow when assessed through the lens of data, the system could no longer be considered a mere military tool.

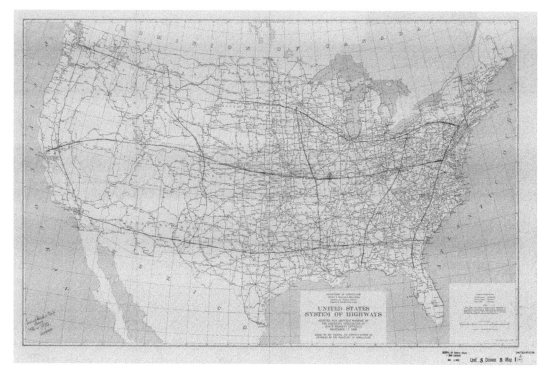

Figure 19.4 The *Roosevelt Map*, Records of the Bureau of Public Roads, 1892–1972.
Source: National Archives and Records Administration, College Park, Maryland.

The network could instead become an indispensable support for the evolving logistics of the city, an evolution driven by increasing mobility and new settlement patterns.

Furthermore, and in contrast to the initial assumption that the growing congestion was triggered by traffic crossing through the city, the study stated that only a small percentage of traffic behaved in that way. Using Washington D.C. as a case study, the statistics revealed that out of 20,500 vehicles entering the city daily, an overwhelming 89% stopped in the city, rather than passing through.[21] The city was a destination, and as such it required an infrastructure that could move people in and out rapidly and efficiently. In a document intended to study infrastructure on a continental, territorial scale, the revelation that high-velocity roads might be rooted within the city proved a surprise. The Bureau of Public Roads had inadvertently produced statistical data in support of a fundamentally urban-related system.

Exceeding the objective of the report as a mere feasibility study, and under the title of "A Master Plan for Free Highway Development" the document focuses on a case study to display its findings and to propose an idea for their implementation. Entitled "Baltimore as an Example," the report uses traffic data to offer an action plan considering existing elements of the city:

> The new street plan … contemplates the construction of modern express arteries along the approximate lines of several of the existing radial streets, running to suitable design intersections and distributing squares, located at the east and west sides of the central business section.[22]

The "tentative study," consisting on a diagrammatic map of Baltimore along with a picture of a projected image of an expressway in the city, is a first attempt to place the urban branches of a system that had originally been conceived to serve the territorial scale (Figure 19.5).

Urban Expressways in the U.S.

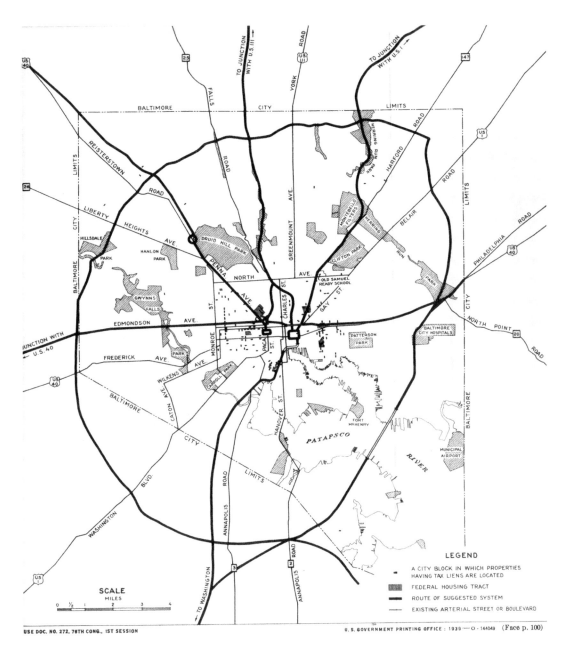

Figure 19.5 Tentative study for the city of Baltimore, *Toll and Free Roads*, Bureau of Public Roads, 1939.
Source: Northwestern University Transportation Library, Evanston, Illinois.

From 1939 until his retirement in 1953, the chief of the BPR, Thomas MacDonald, would insist on the need to establish policies for a comprehensive reconstruction of the American city. Few, however, seemed to notice his urgent call for an approach that would view large-scale urban redevelopment and a national road system as a joint project. Through much of the interwar period, the idea of a national road system remained, for most advocates, a territorial element of infrastructure, separate from the concerns of city planning.

The Interregional Highway Report, 1944

In 1941, Roosevelt established a national committee to produce a master plan based on the *Toll and Free Roads* report. The committee assembled a multidisciplinary team intended to cover a wide range of interests and expertise: Thomas MacDonald and Herbert Fairbank from the BPR; Highway officials Donald Kennedy and Charles Purcell; urban planners Harland Bartholomew and Rexford Tugwell; former Alabama Governor Bibb Graves; and the President's uncle and Chairman of the National Resources Planning Board, Frederic Delano. Delano and Bartholomew's participation was particularly noteworthy, given their experience in producing the 1929 Regional Plan for New York and its Environs. The Regional Plan was one of the first to place a major city within a metropolitan context, activated predominantly by a nationally interconnected road system. For the Regional Plan Committee, this national road system would transect the city through highly diagrammatic radial and belt lines.

Roosevelt's committee issued its Interregional Highway Report in 1944, proposing the construction of a network of 33,920 miles of expressways of which an overwhelming 15% were dedicated to urban areas.[23] Confirming the 1939 projections, the report concluded that cities, as quantifiable entities, would become the origin of and primary justification for the entire system, and the factor that would determine its configuration. And, much like the Regional Plan of New York, the report's authors envisioned the intersection of the national and the urban road system through the diagram, where national roads moved through cities in the form of limited-access, high-speed urban expressways. Under the title "Relation to Urban Planning," the report insists on the need to consider the expressway as part of the future city, compatible with existing plans and those in preparation: "(T)he interregional routes ... should be located so as to promote a desirable development or at least to support a natural development rather than to retard or to distort the evolution of the city."[24] Careful attention to the placement of urban expressways would be crucial to their success, but, the committee warned, "if improperly located, they will become more and more of an encumbrance to the city's functions and an all too durable reminder of planning that was bad."[25]

The report recognized that the city center would continue to be a hub of activity, and that suburban growth seemed to suggest an even larger future shift in the organization of the city. The expressway would likely intensify this trend, unless planning decisions were made to try to stem the tide, arguing that land use planning should precede the siting of the new urban expressways. MacDonald and Bartholomew were the two key figures in the land use approach. Both believed it was necessary to superimpose the urban plan on the interstate expressway system to reconcile scales and requirements. If this harmonizing of scales were achieved, they argued, then the expressway would be purely beneficial for the city.

On December 20, 1944, Roosevelt signed the Federal-Aid Highway Act for an "Interstate" system of highways, based on the "Interregional" Highway Report.

The subtle replacement of the term "interregional" with "interstate" signaled a change in how the system would be executed. A system that had originally been conceived at the regional and urban level, and which responded to measurable local conditions, was, for bureaucratic and political reasons, replaced with one that necessarily involved the states as key actors in a federal system. In this sense, regions and cities were treated with a systematic logic that prioritized the scale of the territory, and which was fundamentally determined by technical, typological, and juridical factors. Even with enabling legislation, the effort to construct a national highway system stalled. The Korean conflict, the inadequate financial structure, and the lack of coordination between federal and state agencies would delay the construction of the system for over a decade.

The Federal-Aid Highway Act 1956

When Dwight D. Eisenhower became president in 1953, he was already a supporter of the establishment of an interstate highway system, having participated in the arduous 1919 Transcontinental Motor Convoy, and having seen the German *Autobahn* in person during World War II. By 1956, two additional factors led an already enthusiastic Eisenhower to press ahead. First, emerging statistical evidence captured what had been the trend for years, an increase in private and commercial traffic and a concomitant decrease in public transit. Second, the Cold War converted the territory into a potential target, making relevant some of the martial justifications laid out in 1919. The threat of a nuclear attack called for an efficient system to contemplate mass urban evacuations. The United States was building its defense capabilities from within, and the highway system, especially in its urban segments, was an urgent part of this project.

In the years after World War II, there was little controversy over the need for a national highway system, only over the financial structure necessary for its execution. In 1955, Congress received the so-called Fallon Bill, named after George Fallon, president of the Congressional Subcommittee on Roads, part of the Committee on Public Works. The financial plan proposed the "pay-as-you-go" formula, consisting of an increase in taxes on fuel, tires, and cargo trucks. The funds would be invested directly into the Interstate system, elevating federal participation to an overwhelming 90% to guarantee construction. The bill seemed to shape a well-rounded argument: the Federal budget would cover most of its cost and no debts would be incurred, while future maintenance would be guaranteed. Nevertheless, the strong opposition from the Teamsters Union and the oil and tire industries would ultimately block the bill, and it was rejected, on July 27, 1955, with 292 votes against and 123 in favor.[26]

However, since the defeat of the bill, the increasingly influential Teamsters Union had begun to reconsider their position based on a simple conclusion; without expressways, the cargo industry would not be able to continue to grow. For many years, cargo trucks had been gaining market share from the railroads, given the efficiency and flexibility they offered and its ability to penetrate urban centers. The equation was simple: the failure to extend the system would act as a break on business growth. Paradoxically, paying taxes could grant better access to cities and, therefore, could ultimately prove profitable. Over a few months, between July and January, the political atmosphere had changed significantly, and the bill passed the House of Representatives by a margin of 388 to nineteen and the Senate by an 89 to one.[27] The law established 41,000 miles of Interstate highways, intended to cross the entire American territory, directly connecting 90% of cities with 50,000 inhabitants or more. The objective was to do what had been intended for nearly twenty years: to connect the entire country to a high-speed road network radiating from and connecting the major cities.

The signing of the bill only affirmed the operative structure in which traffic as a quantitative measure determined the form and position of the system, without regard to the specifics of each urban reality. The 1939 and 1944 recommendations on the linkage of the program with policies related to urban planning were left out of the final law; its main objective was to serve as a financial catalyst for the execution of an infrastructure program.

Within the ambit of the national road system, the urban expressway had undergone a complex evolution: once considered as a possible trigger for a new era of urban planning and the birth of a new city, it was largely reduced to a project of highway engineering, one which saw the system primarily through the lens of quantifiable traffic conditions and projections able to meet its financing foundations. Except for the intrusion of some municipal leaders with racial segregation agendas, highway engineers had an almost complete hegemony over the planning and construction of the expressway system, with scarce involvement of planning agencies or policies. As historian Mark Rose points out:

> Because construction was financed by motorists and truckers through gasoline taxes collected in the Highway Trust Fund and returned to the states for highway building, cost-benefit ratios appeared crucial in fixing each corridor. Management of planning and construction were matters of engineers; not even senior members of the U.S. Senate could secure a mile or a routing not warranted by other than traffic volume and direction.[28]

After years of debate about the reach or inherent capacities of the system, the project would ultimately take shape as a tool for economic development, strongly related to private capital and growth. The destiny of the urban order combined with the potential of the expressway, would become an economic formula for the production and circulation of values in the form of statistics and traffic projections. The American city, conceptually and physically, would shift from being a civic space, to a space for economic exchange welded to a diagrammatic overlay of transecting high speed roads. The 1956 law brought much optimism, as local and state officials could dust off the plans that had filed away for years. The drawings were now beginning to be transformed into impeccable ribbons of asphalt, and they began to shape what the law had promised: "coast-to-coast without a stoplight."[29]

Urban Expressway

The urban expressway is more than the terminal branch of a broader system. I suggest that the urban expressway has its own history, distinct from the network of which it is part. This history began long before the system itself was realized, and is based in a complex web of economic and logistic considerations, territorial development, land extension and speculation, and population growth and segregation. Therefore, while its systematic design and construction do respond to the logics of the Interstate system, its "urban" qualification is a clear reflection of an object born out of the financial, spatial, and social conflicts of the American city in the first half of the twentieth century. Its two parallel lines of development—one focused on solutions for a new urban era, and another focused on the logistics of territorial mobility—will collide in the material translation of the Interstate in its urban segments.

The collision of these two logics is evident in the conflictive nature of its name: "urban expressway." The term "expressway" refers to an infrastructural element with a specific function: an efficient conduit for traffic. This element, in turn, only assumes its full functionality when it applies standards and is linked to a broader network. The adjective "urban," meanwhile, refers to a specific place or fabric, a collective construction that reaches its richest expression in diversity. Beyond this semantic distinction, these two conditions—one specific and diverse, the other general and standardized—were opposed, intertwined, and awkwardly synthesized over the period I study here. Understood in this way, the urban expressway is more than a mere instance of autonomous infrastructure in the city. It is, rather, the physical register of a conflict between the urban and the territory, the specific and the general. The American city of the twentieth century would in part be defined by these intertwined terms, and these uncomfortable hybrid elements.

Notes

1 See Mark H. Rose, *Interstate: Express Highway Politics, 1939-1989* (Knoxville: University of Tennessee Press, 1990); Earl Swift, *The Big Roads: The Untold Story of the Engineers, Visionaries, and Trailblazers Who Created the American Superhighways* (New York: Houghton Mifflin Harcourt, 2011); Tom Lewis, *Divided Highways. Building the Interstate Highways, Transforming American Life* (Ithaca: Cornell University Press, 2013).
2 See Raymond A. Mohl, "Planned Destruction: The Interstates and Central City Housing," in *From Tenements to the Taylor Homes: In Search of an Urban Housing Policy in Twentieth-Century America*, eds John F. Bauman, Roger Biles, and Kristin Szylvian (University Park: The Pennsylvania University Press, 2000); Eric Avila, *The Folklore of the Freeway. Race and Revolts in the Modernist City* (Minneapolis: University of Minnesota Press, 2014).
3 See M. Christine Boyer, *Dreaming the Rational City* (Cambridge: MIT Press, 1983).
4 See Mel Scott, *American City Planning since 1890* (Berkeley, University of California Press, 1969); John D. Fairfield, *The Mysteries of the Great City. The Politics of Urban Design, 1877-1937* (Columbus: Ohio State University Press, 1993).
5 Nelson Lewis, "The Engineer in His Relation to City Plan," *Proceedings of the Engineers' Club of Philadelphia 29* (Philadelphia: The Engineers' Club of Philadelphia: 1912): 198. See also M. Christine Boyer, *Dreaming the Rational City* (Cambridge: MIT Press, 1983), 84.
6 United States Federal Works Agency, Work Projects Administration, *Report on Progress of the WPA Program*, June 1939.
7 Ibid. 16.
8 Richard Weingroff, "Zero Milestone: Washington, DC," U.S. Department of Transportation/Federal Highway Administration, June 27, 2017, www.fhwa.dot.gov/infrastructure/zero.cfm.

9. Dwight Eisenhower, *At Ease. Stories I Tell to Friends* (Garden City: Doubleday and Company, 1967).
10. Swift, *The Big Roads*, 31.
11. Ibid.
12. Kenneth T. Jackson, *Crabgrass Frontier: The Suburbanization of the United States* (New York: Oxford University Press, 1987).
13. Jay Young, "Infrastructure: Mass Transit in 19th- and 20th-Century Urban America," Oxford Research Encyclopedia of American History, March 2015.
14. Sam Bass Warner, *Streetcar Suburbs: The Process of Growth in Boston, 1870–1900* (Cambridge: Harvard University Press, 1962).
15. Jackson, *Crabgrass Frontier*, 162.
16. Ibid.
17. United States Bureau of Public Roads, *Toll and Free Roads*. 76th Congress, 1st Session, House Document No. 272. Washington: Government Printing Office, 1939, 1.
18. Ibid. Letter of Transmittal, VII.
19. Ibid. 7.
20. Ibid. 11.
21. Ibid. 91.
22. Ibid. 100.
23. United States Bureau of Public Roads, *Interregional Highways Report*, 78th Congress, 2nd Session, House Document No. 379, Washington, D.C.: Government Printing Office, 1944, 6.
24. Ibid. 70.
25. Ibid.
26. Rose, *Interstate*, 82.
27. Ibid. 88.
28. Ibid. 103.
29. Richard Thruelsen, "Coast to Coast Without a Stoplight," *Saturday Evening Post* 229, no. 16 (October 1956): 23.

20
GOOD NEIGHBORS AND *AUTOMOVILISTAS*

Imaginaries of Hemispheric Travel along the Pan-American Highway, 1936–1942

Dicle Taskin

The Pan-American Highway is a hemispheric infrastructure project which extends from Alaska to Patagonia, with an incomplete section called the Darién Gap between Panama and Colombia. It embodied the Pan-American promise of hemispheric connectivity and integration. This promise was unstable, mutable, and contested, and its meanings shifted throughout the twentieth century in tune with the changing power dynamics within Pan-Americanism. Between the 1930s and the World War II years, this promise became entwined with the narratives, representations, and practices of automobility and hemispheric travel. The scale of the Pan-American Highway, which is commonly referred to as the longest road in the world, was a powerful metaphor for unification. During these years, the highway embodied a future where one could drive across the Americas from one end to the other, and cross the borders with Pan-American passports and hemispheric tourist cards. In this chapter, I trace these travel narratives, representations, and practices between 1936 and 1942 to question how this travel imaginary shaped the Pan-American Highway project, its promise of integration, and its imprint on the built environment. I compare the travelogues of the U.S. American drivers who embarked on expeditions to Latin America during the Good Neighbor Policy years, with the advocacy efforts of Automóvil Club Argentino, which organized international car races, expeditions, and caravans to promote the Pan-American Highway project. Through this comparison, I highlight how long-distance travel assumed different roles in relation to the Pan-American Highway project, performing ideological, representational, and logistical functions.

In 1941, Automóvil Club Argentino (ACA) published *Caracas Buenos Aires*, a tourist guide that was adapted from an official manual prepared for an international car race scheduled to take place in 1942.[1] The guide was prepared for public, for those who might be interested in following the itinerary of this much anticipated race, which was going to span 11,050 kilometers following the Pan-American Highway route from Caracas to Buenos Aires through Colombia, Ecuador, Peru, and Bolivia. The first couple of pages of the guide provide practical information such as custom formalities, immigration offices, important traffic rules and other regulations. This brief introduction is followed by two hundred and ten pages of road directions in Spanish and English, which are compiled in two columns and divided into seven chapters (Figure 20.1). Each line of the manual corresponds to a road turn, a landmark, a place name, or a description of an infrastructural component, such as a steel bridge or a masonry culvert. A third column correlates each of these directions with distance, measured both from the starting point and the destination of each chapter. Photographs of paved road surfaces, bridges, and tunnels blend with other images more akin to conventional tourist guides, depicting towns, churches, and landscape. Folding route maps placed between each chapter provide some visual navigation guidance, with zoomed-in details that show more complicated inner-city directions. Reading this tourist guide in today's context is a strikingly monotonous and yet thought-provoking experience, which gives the glimpse of a time

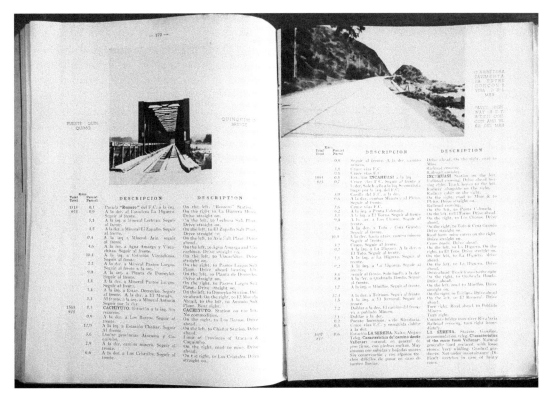

Figure 20.1 A spread from Caracas Buenos Aires tourist guide. Images of bridges and paved road surfaces with 200-page long road directions. Automóvil Club Argentino, *Caracas Buenos Aires*, 1941.

Source: Courtesy of the Automóvil Club Argentino Library, Buenos Aires.

when the Pan-American Highway embodied an imagined future where one would drive across the Americas from one end to the other, and cross the borders with Pan-American passports and hemispheric tourist cards. In this chapter, I will question how long-distance, automobile-based, transcontinental travel shaped the scalar and spatial imaginary of the Pan-American Highway system and its promise of integration.

Pan-Americanism was first conceptualized by Simón Bolívar in the 1820s, as a political movement to unite Latin American nations, fighting to gain their independence from the European empires. The concept was later misappropriated by the United States, which sought to increase its geopolitical and economic influence in Latin America. The idea of building a transcontinental infrastructure first emerged in this context, in the 1870s, with the writer Hinton Rowan Helper's proposal of the Three-Americas Railway. Over the next fifty years, a range of difficulties beset the project, including disagreements on possible routes, geographical constraints, the uneven distribution of engineering expertise, and rivaling interests of nations, investors, and other stakeholders.[2] During the same period, a paradigm shift in transportation towards automobile based travel took hold, influenced by the Good Roads movement in the United States and the emergence of automobile and touring clubs in urban centers across the Americas. By 1923, with the acceptance of the Pan-American Highway proposal at the Fifth Pan-American Conference, the promise of hemispheric integration was already entangled with a rich imaginary of travel. During the Good Neighbor Policy in the 1930s and 40s, many U.S. American travelers embarked on long expeditions to Latin America and produced travelogues, maps, films, guides, and other publications. These years were also marked by the growing automobile ownership across Latin America and the advocacy of touring and automobile clubs for road-building efforts. In 1936, Automóvil Club Argentino started organizing international road races across South America to promote the Pan-American Highway and asserted itself as a powerful advocate for the project. In this chapter, I will compare these narratives and events to argue that the imaginaries of hemispheric travel assumed different ideological, representational, and logistical functions within the Pan-American Highway project, not only shaping its promise of integration but also its infrastructural imprint in the built environment. I will mainly focus on the timeline between 1936 and 1942, to highlight how the discourses around automobility, modernization, and the Good Neighbor Policy shaped these travel imaginaries while debates around the Pan-American Highway's potential role in the defense of the Western Hemisphere were emerging.

Good Neighbors along the "Long Tough Trail"

In 1941, Sullivan C. Richardson, a journalist for the Detroit News, and Arthur Whitaker started an expedition along the Pan-American Highway from Detroit to Cape Horn in Chile. The map of their itinerary was placed on the side of their 1941 model Chrysler Plymouth car, together with the flags of all the member countries of the Pan-American Union, and the phrase "Viva el Panamericanismo!" A year later, Richardson published a travelogue based on their experience on the road, with the title *Adventure South: Three Men and a Lone Car Blaze the Pan-American Highway Route Down Two Continents to Cape Horn!*. The keyword of "adventure" was essential to the travelogue because, by 1941, the highway remained largely unfinished through Central America. In the first few pages, Richardson framed the highway as central to the development of mutual understanding between the United Stated and Latin America, but until that day, it was "a long tough trail to Cape Horn."[3] The book carried many details about the people that the expedition team met along the road, where each anecdote stood as a representation of some basic characteristics that Richardson attributed to Latin Americans, whether it was hospitality, indifference, or resilience. The emphasis, however, was on the "long tough trail" and the many hardships that the team faced during their trip. While the book included photographs of landscapes, monuments, and Inca architecture, the real protagonist was the 1941 Plymouth, captured as it was being dragged by mules across rivers, floating on rafts built on rowboats, getting stuck in the mud, and being hauled up hills by villagers. At the end of this "adventure," Richardson and Whitaker christened the car as "Miss Pan-America," using water from the Magellan Strait collected in an old can carried all the way from Detroit specifically for this purpose.[4]

These narratives, which mostly featured English speaking travelers from North America driving south across the continent, were consonant with the Good Neighbor policy and its emphatic promotion of tourism, Pan-Americanism, and regional collaboration. The Good Neighbor Policy was adopted in 1933 by Franklin D. Roosevelt's administration, and it marked a departure from U.S. military interventions in Latin America to non-interventionist policies and discourses of regional collaboration.[5] According to cultural anthropologist Rosa E. Ficek, the Good Neighbor Policy was "a geopolitical imaginary which emphasized cooperation, responsibility, and cultural understanding within a homogenous, bounded hemispheric community under U.S. control."[6] This geopolitical imaginary fit into the framework of Pan-Americanism and it was essential for the maintenance of the U.S. hegemony across Latin America. Ficek argues that the Pan-American Highway project, especially its Central American section, the Inter-American Highway, was a symbol of the Good Neighbor Policy. In this context, driving across Latin America became a "neighborly practice."[7] According to architect Robert Alexander González, these travel narratives were essential to the creation of this Pan-American imaginary, which appealed to distinct groups of people for different reasons. Travel, in this context, was a way of claiming a Pan-American identity, which was "rooted in an imagined state of coexistence with all the peoples of the Western Hemisphere."[8] Historian Ricardo Salvatore agrees that the Pan-American Highway played an important role in the creation of Pan-American as a "non-place." His analysis of the Good Neighbor Policy travel narratives, however, centers on the uneven power dynamics of Pan-Americanism, seen through the lens of "imperial mechanics."[9]

In "Imperial Mechanics: South America's Hemispheric Integration in the Machine Age," Salvatore explains how infrastructure projects such as the Pan-American Highway and the Panama Canal underpinned notions of United States superiority through engineering, technology, and construction expertise.[10] Within this framework, the Pan-American Highway presented a "transportation utopia" built on "dreamscapes about commercial integration, the extension of U.S. tourism, the exportation of U.S. culture, and the possibility of apprehending the regions' realities and problems."[11] From Salvatore's perspective, travel stories not only played a role in the construction of Pan-America but also revealed the patterns of uneven development and inequality. Their most important function was to create a "fiction of a united hemisphere in moments in which the countries of Latin America lagged behind in transportation development."[12] To prove this argument, he analyzes the 1942 Paul Pleiss and Herbert Lanks expedition sponsored by the American Automobile Association, focusing on juxtapositions of the "modern" and the "unmodern."

According to Salvatore, Pleiss and Lanks observed that the roads were much better along the coastlines, in agricultural export areas, near oil extraction sites, around industrial towns, and in certain countries where the automobile culture is already established. These observations established a contrast with other passages about areas with poor road conditions and visible signs of indigenous culture. According to Salvatore, these juxtapositions were sometimes more implicit within lengthy observations about Andean markets or "primitive technologies" that determined agricultural methods. At other times, however, they were more pronounced, as in the case of motorists stopping at Pachacamac to witness the "amazing spectacle" of "cars speeding past the prehistoric ruins" which made the automobiles look like "small dots."[13] Such observations were not uncommon during the Good Neighbor Policy era, when the covers of general interest magazines could feature portraits of indigenous people in their traditional clothing alongside captions such as "Indian from Pisac Peru: You can now motor through his country on the Pan-American Highway."[14] For Salvatore, however, the unevenness and inequality captured in these narratives would ultimately lead the project's incompletion, as they proved that "the Pan-American Highway existed only in the minds of statesmen and in the blueprints of road builders, as something to be realized in the future."[15] As a "transportation utopia," the project still fulfilled its purpose, regardless of the fact the physical infrastructure was never completed. As Salvatore explained, "… their chief role in the making of U.S. Foreign policy was symbolic: to sustain the fiction of a homogenous landscape (Latin America) ready 'to be connected' to a superior technological civilization (United States)."[16]

Like Pleiss and Lanks, the Richardson expedition also captured the unevenness of development. However, the latter group also reveals included details which emphasized the hardships and difficulties they experienced on the road as a way to convey a sense of "adventure." Even though the highway was mostly paved through South America, the Richardson travelogue focused disproportionately on the incomplete sections where the highway consists of bull-cart and donkey trails. There were also instances when the expedition team chose to follow alternative routes, instead of the completed section of the highway, a decision that was legitimized in terms of gaining practice before reaching the difficult sections of the road.[17] These decisions further emphasize the adventure framework of "long tough trail" and draw attention to some of the inconsistencies between the imaginary of travel and the promise of integration. But more importantly, they contradict with other South America travel narratives from the same time, where long-distance travel functioned as an advocacy tool for the Pan-American Highway project. These travel narratives celebrate the paved surfaces, bridges, intersections, and road signage in order to emphasize the smooth flow of the highway, rather than dramatic frictions of adventure.

Travel as Advocacy: *Raides*, Road Races, and Automobile Caravans

In 1938, Carlos P. Anesi, the president of Automóvil Club Argentino (ACA), urged completion of the Pan-American Highway by 1942 to commemorate the 450th anniversary of Columbus's arrival. The club would celebrate this landmark with a transcontinental road race from Buenos Aires to New York.[18] The race, which was referred to as *Gran Premio de las Americas*, was going to be organized synchronously with two automobile caravans departing from New York and Buenos Aires to meet at the halfway point in Bogotá, Colombia (Figure 20.2). The race from Caracas to Buenos Aires, which led to the publication of the race manual as a tourist guide, was a prelude for *Gran Premio de las Americas*.

Through 1940 and 1941, preparations for the Caracas–Buenos Aires race continued at full speed despite the looming threats of world war. For Anesi and the other officials at ACA, the war would not be not an obstacle but an added justification: The Pan-American Highway was now more necessary than ever in order to provide an overland connection through the Western Hemisphere, act as a guide for military aircraft, and function as a landing strip if the need arose.[19] The road race to Caracas was an important step toward completing the Pan-American Highway, and it was no longer about proving the capabilities of men and machines. Instead, it was about uniting the nations across Latin America, a task that was even more crucial at a time when Europe was in disarray.[20] Then, only four days before competitors were set to begin, the race was postponed—not because of the war in Europe, but because the border conflict between Ecuador and Peru had escalated into a war.

Road races, automobile caravans, and formally organized expeditions, usually referred to as *raides*, were strong advocacy tools for road building efforts, which had become synonymous with national progress and integration by the end of the 1920s. With the Great Depression, the case for road building grew even stronger. South American countries needed to reduce the time and cost of transporting agricultural products for export markets, and sought to make up for lost revenues through increased tourism.[21] Thus, the long-distance national road races in the 1920s became even more popular in the 1930s when the promotion of tourism became a main focal point. The camping trips and automobile caravans organized by ACA to remote locations with few passable roads heavily influenced the creation of new routes and touristic destinations.[22] This emphasis on tourism also changed the nature of automobile races. In 1937, Argentina prohibited the organization of sports-car races on national roads since the high rate of accidents reflected poorly on the road-building efforts. In response, the Argentinian highway administration established *Turismo Carretera*, the new category for long-distance road races, which required the competing cars to be unmodified, widely accessible, and suitable for tourism.[23] According to historian Anahí Ballent, this change enhanced the popularity of the long-distance road races and made them central to the regional and international integration efforts. In 1936, ACA organized its first international *Gran Premio* from Buenos Aires to Santiago de Chile. Each subsequent road race was going to cover a more extensive territory, linking Buenos Aires to Lima, then to Caracas, and eventually to New York. These races also inspired many drivers who ventured into solo or group expeditions. These drivers featured frequently on the pages of *Automovilismo* magazine and often remarked on how Anesi's plans for a *Gran Premio* to New York made the idea of driving the Americas plausible.[24]

In terms of representational and discursive construction of Pan-America, these international road races, automobile caravans, and *raides* performed a similar function to Good Neighbor Policy narratives. There was still a very strong emphasis on integration and unification corresponding to different territorial scales. The 1936 international road race to Santiago de Chile, for example, was broadcasted live on the radio for fourteen days. According to Anahí Ballent, transnational media coverage was an important symbol of integration, as the broadcasts introduced the element of simultaneity, allowing listeners to visualize the route and to hear about unfamiliar villages, towns, and landscapes along the way.[25] Not only did this create a shared cognitive map of the region, but it also enabled a Pan-American spatial imaginary linked through infrastructure.

The Pan-American Highway

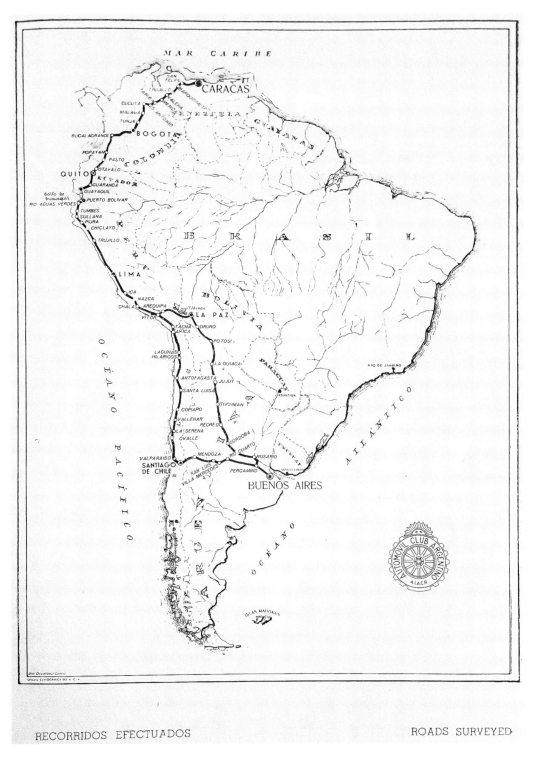

Figure 20.2 Map showing the itinerary of Gran Premio de la América del Sur, the international automobile race from Caracas to Buenos Aires, Automóvil Club Argentino, *Caracas Buenos Aires*, 1941.

Source: Courtesy of the Automóvil Club Argentino Library, Buenos Aires.

Beyond these symbolic and representational aspects, these road races and expeditions functioned as effective tools for road building campaigns that operated on a different logistical and institutional scale. In terms of advocacy and promotion, their main function was to prove the passability of the roads. In contrast to the travel narratives of the Good Neighbor Policy, they did not use descriptions or adjectives that emphasized the difficulty or the incompleteness of the road. Even with solo expeditions, which were often undertaken on routes that included incomplete roads, the travelers did not produce lengthy travelogues. Instead, they compiled maps, diagrams, road directions, and other documents for the general public who may want to follow the same itinerary. The articles in *Automovilismo* still celebrated these drivers for their courage, but the message always remained the same: as it was once again proved by this particular expedition, the road in question was passable. In many cases, these expeditions also functioned as the preliminary step for road races, which were then followed by automobile caravans consisting of regular drivers and travelers. This sequence was an essential part of the advocacy campaign. As historian Melina Piglia suggests, these efforts "fixed" the roads in public imagination and created a "tourism of movement," rather than of destination.[26]

This act of "fixing" also referred to physical and administrative components of the Pan-American Highway project. In many cases, the preparations for a road race included detailed topographical studies, production of maps and sections, and placement of landmarks and road signage.[27] For the international road races along the Pan-American Highway, this process also included meetings with participating countries where the construction progress was discussed and disagreements about missing links along the border zones were resolved. The preparations for the 1941 road race between Buenos Aires and Caracas, for example, included construction of roads along the Guayaquil Gulf in Ecuador and repairs of certain sections in Bolivia (Figure 20.3).[28] When the race was ultimately postponed to 1942, *Automovilismo* magazine announced the news with a detailed report on the damaged roads that were in need of repairs, rather than dwelling on the nature of the 1941 Ecuadorian-Peruvian war itself.[29]

The race from Caracas to Buenos Aires finally took place in 1948, but it was not going to be a prologue for *Gran Premio de las Americas* as previously envisioned. Instead, it proved that a road race from Buenos Aires to New York was going to be too costly and too complicated, and Anesi's plan was soon abandoned.[30] These races, nevertheless, enabled ACA to emerge as a leader and a strong advocate for the Pan-American Highway in a way that challenged the U.S. hegemony associated with the project. The *Caracas Buenos Aires* guide published in 1941 remained as a relic from this specific time frame when the imaginary of integration was heavily shaped by scalar discourses of automobile-based travel, which would soon become irrelevant with the shift to air travel.

Enduring Imaginaries of Travel

During the groundbreaking ceremony of the Central American Pavilion for the 1964-1965 New York World's Fair, Robert Moses emphasized his "long-standing interest" in the Pan-American Highway, which he saw as a "symbol and physical evidence of the growing closeness between North and South America." Indeed, if hemispheric travel was increasingly the province of the air, infrastructure builders such as Moses were drawn to the unfulfilled promise of the Pan-American Highway. He expressed his desire to have a separate pavilion dedicated to this grand project, and envisioned a future with "not thousands, but millions of people who find their way down from the United States, through Central America, to South America, upon this highway which passes through some extraordinary country."[31] During its first year, the Fair hosted the Pan-American Highway gardens to celebrate the completion of the Inter-American Highway, the portion of the Pan-American highway system which extends from Mexico to the Panama Canal.[32] In 1965, the second year of the Fair, the gardens were replaced with the Pan-American Highway Rides, sponsored by the car rental company Avis. The ride provided a simulation of hemispheric travel at the scale of a circuit surrounded with the tropical plants and statues deemed to be representative of Central America.[33]

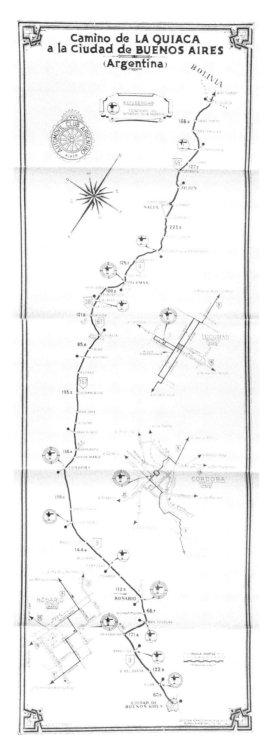

Figure 20.3 A folding route map showing the itinerary of the race between the Bolivian border and Buenos Aires. Icons indicate the Automóvil Club Argentino service stations along the path. Automóvil Club Argentino, *Caracas Buenos Aires*, 1941.

Source: Courtesy of the Automóvil Club Argentino Library, Buenos Aires.

The travel imaginary captured by these installations was typical of the Good Neighbor Policy years, but the context of the Pan-American Highway and the discourses about integration had drastically changed since the early post-war period. With the move to Alliance for Progress, the highway had become embedded in Cold War discourses of developmentalism and was reframed as a "freedom road" for its "stabilizing effect" in the region and its role in the fight against communism.[34] The importance of travel within the imaginary of hemispheric integration had faded with this new geopolitical and ideological shift. Meanwhile, the emergence of air travel as the new "transportation utopia" had made the previously celebrated transcontinental automobile trips increasingly impractical and irrelevant. Even at the World's Fair, the Pan-American Highway ride was sponsored by a car rental company, which suggested a future where one would simply fly to a desired location and rent an automobile to see the surroundings, instead of driving from one end of the continent to another with a camper in tow. Hemispheric travel, in this new utopia, was more selective and fragmented, and a "tourism of destination" had prevailed over a "tourism of movement."

In the following decades, the travel imaginaries became more focused on the Darién Gap, the 250 mile-long stretch between Panama and Colombia, which still remains incomplete today. For automobile companies, the Darién Gap was the ultimate test, and it was an appealing prospect to produce the first car to cross the gap. In the 1960s and early 1970s, many companies organized expeditions to the region, which featured on the pages of popular magazines and newspapers. As incompleteness became one of the defining features of the Pan-American Highway, countries across South America continued building infrastructures as extensions of the Pan-American Highway system. Rosa E. Ficek argues that these regional integration efforts in South America challenged the original imperial design of the Pan-American Highway, imagined as a road extending along the North-South axis for longitudinal communication, and turned it into a complex infrastructural system which fostered integration among Latin American countries "under less asymmetrical terms."[35] The scale of the highway still remained an ubiquitous reference, keeping alive the project's utopian origins. Today, these scalar references continue to stimulate the imagination of many travelers who decide to drive across the Americas along the Pan-American Highway. Ficek argues that these contemporary U.S. American travelers differ from those of the Good Neighbor Policy years. Instead of looking at Latin America to see the "signs of modernity-in-the-making or yet-to-come," they see the journey as an escape from the modern life, a route for self-realization, while drawing from U.S. cultural references.[36] Ficek reflects on this comparison to understand the different contexts of north-to-south travel along the Pan-American Highway, while reminding us that south-to-north travel also shaped this infrastructure project in the process of "remaking Pan-America."

In this chapter, I built on with this north-south duality to highlight how the travel imaginaries of the Pan-American Highway were shaped by different subject positions and modes of organization. The narratives of "Good Neighbors" driving south across the continent offer historians a representation of Pan-America which is captured from the vantage point of empire, while the collective events of Automóvil Club Argentino present travel as a means for infrastructure building and regional integration. Focusing on these different narratives and modes of travel provide some nuance to "imperial mechanics," which acts as a useful framework to analyze the uneven power dynamics at the root of the Pan-American Highway project while risking becoming overly deterministic. Through these comparisons, we can have a better understanding of how the Pan-American Highway functioned as an imperial design, as well as a medium through which different aspirations about regional integration were articulated. These comparisons also illustrate the agency of these travel imaginaries beyond their ideological and representational functions. Through the international and trans-continental automobile races, Automóvil Club Argentina could present itself as a leader for the project, organize international meetings to resolve the disputes over border connections, and effectively influence the route planning and decisions. The preparations for the races provided impetus for infrastructural improvements, ranging from extensive road repairs and construction to the standardization and installation of road signage. These histories tell us that the travel imaginaries also assumed logistical and material functions in the process of "remaking Pan-America," shaping the Pan-American Highway and its infrastructural imprint in the built environment.

Notes

1. Automóvil Club Argentino, *Caracas Buenos Aires*, 1941.
2. Eric Rutkow, *The Longest Line on the Map: The United States, the Pan-American Highway, and the Quest to Link the Americas* (New York: Scribner, 2018).
3. Sullivan C. Richardson, *Adventure South: Three Men and a Lone Car Blaze the Pan American Highway Route Down Two Continents to Cape Horn!* (Detroit: Arnold-Powers Inc., 1942), 7.
4. Ibid. 286.
5. Rosa E. Ficek, "Imperial Routes, National Networks and Regional Projects in the Pan-American Highway, 1884–1977," *The Journal of Transport History* 37, no. 2 (December 1, 2016): 129–154.
6. Ibid. 140.
7. Rosa E. Ficek, "Driving the Pan American Highway from North to South: International Association for the History of Transport, Traffic and Mobility," *Mobility History Blog*, accessed May 31, 2021, https://t2m.org/driving-the-pan-american-highway-from-north-to-south/.
8. Robert Alexander Gonzalez, *Designing Pan-America: U.S. Architectural Visions for the Western Hemisphere*, 1st edn (Austin: University of Texas Press, 2011), 9.
9. Ricardo D. Salvatore, "Imperial Mechanics: South America's Hemispheric Integration in the Machine Age," *American Quarterly* 58, no. 3 (September 2006): 663–691.
10. Ibid. 670.
11. Ibid. 676.
12. Ibid. 665.
13. Ibid. 683.
14. Magazine Cover, *Américas*, January 1953.
15. Salvatore, 682.
16. Ibid. 686.
17. Richardson, 17.
18. Carlos Pedro Anesi, *La carretera panamericana; su inauguración en el 9o cincuentenario del descubrimiento de América, 1492–12 de octubre–1942*, "El gran premio de las Américas" (Buenos Aires: Talleres gráficos de la Compañía general fabril financiera, 1938).
19. "La Vinculación Americana a Través del 'Gran Premio de la America del Sur'," *Automovilismo*, November 1940.
20. "Las Grandes Pruebas del ACA Depararon Siempre Magníficas Jornadas," *Automovilismo*, September 1940.
21. Anahí Ballent, "Kilómetro Cero: La Construcción del Universo Simbólico del Camino en la Argentina de los Años Treinta," *Boletín del Instituto de Historia Argentina y Americana Dr. Emilio Ravignani*, no. 27 (2005): 107–137.
22. Melina Piglia, *Autos, Rutas y Turismo: El Automóvil Club Argentino y El Estado*, Historia y Cultura (Buenos Aires: Siglo Veintiuno Editores, 2014).
23. Ballent, 125.
24. Driver, "Raids Constructivos : Aportes Estimables en Favor del Proyectado Gran Premio de las Americas," *Automovilismo*, February 1940.
25. Ballent, 121.
26. Piglia, 84.
27. Ibid. 82.
28. "Fue Postergado el Gran Premio de la America del Sur," *Automovilismo*, August 1941. and "Extraordinario Entusiasmo Despierta el Gran Premio de la America del Sur," *Automovilismo*, June 1941.
29. "Fue Postergado el Gran Premio de la America del Sur," *Automovilismo*, August 1941.
30. Piglia, 80.
31. "Groundbreaking at the New York World's Fair 1964-1965 Central American Pavilion," 1963, F128 T791.L4, New York Historical Society.
32. *Official Guide: New York World's Fair 1964–1965* (Time, Inc., 1964).
33. *Official Guide: New York World's Fair 1964–1965* (Time, Inc., 1965).
34. Rutkow, 284.
35. Ficek, "Imperial Routes, National Networks and Regional Projects in the Pan-American Highway, 1884–1977," 144.
36. Ficek, "Driving the Pan American Highway from North to South: International Association for the History of Transport, Traffic and Mobility."

PART VII

Power Fields

21
NUCLEAR POWER STATIONS IN POST-WAR BRITAIN

Picturesque Landscapes for the Masses

Laura Coucill and Luca Csepely-Knorr

Power generation in post-war Britain was an exercise in nation building. Significant advancements in technology and engineering led to infrastructure of unprecedented size and scale. Larger power generating stations began to occupy new locations beyond urban perimeters and, in the case of nuclear power generation, to the extent of purposeful isolation from populated areas. Equivalent expansion of transmission networks spread across the country, culminating in new typologies now widely recognized. The manifestation of power generation and distribution in areas of protected land, such as coastlines and national parks required the reappraisal of the relationship between rural and urban space. With a core duty to protect visual amenity, under the auspices of the newly nationalized Central Electricity Generating Board (CEGB), architects and landscape architects were responsible for envisaging the new aesthetics of power generation and transmission. This chapter explores the aesthetics of power generation in the post-war period through the study of the interdisciplinary cooperation and organizational structures which engendered working relations among the various design professions. Special attention is paid to the last power station and largest reactors to be built as part of the UK's first commercial nuclear program, located at Wylfa, Anglesey in Wales, where the input of landscape architect Sylvia Crowe and the industrial expertise of architects Farmer and Dark were integral to its design success.

After six years of total war, Britain was ready to rebuild. Fresh approaches to urban planning, such as the New Towns Act 1946, reimagined cities and regions as well as proposing brand new settlements. The government invested heavily in the development of infrastructure, which officials saw as critical to delivering improved welfare and living standards. And it was the expansion of power generation that would be the key to moving this large-scale nation-building project forward. After all, the rebuilding of bombed cities and the construction of New Towns, motorways, hospitals, schools, and factories required tremendous amounts of power, leading to a rapid increase in the demand for electricity and stable networks for its distribution.

The introduction of the National Grid in 1935 made national electricity distribution possible and enabled power stations to be relocated out of urban centers to peripheral locations. However, the advent of war put the expansion of the electric system on hold. Meanwhile, advancements in nuclear science towards the end of the war promised a new power source with significantly greater yield, but came with specific, technical requirements, such as siting in areas removed from population centers – areas that would also become key recreational resources for a newly mobilized, modern society. As a result, a variety of tower arrays, step-down transformers, and substations emerged, becoming landmarks of the post-war society. Formal differences in architectural typologies distinguish different modes of engineering and technology, for example, the absence of cooling towers set apart nuclear reactors from conventional power stations. Other signatures of the period include new cladding solutions, which produced buildings that exhibited inner functionality, a marked contrast to monumental, brick clad forms of urban, pre-war generators.

In this chapter, we study the interdisciplinary cooperation and organizational structures that enabled architects and landscape architects to work together after World War II. We argue that this high level of cooperation allowed them to bring infrastructure and landscape into a techno-aesthetic dialogue, and thereby to establish a broadly social approach to the design of power plant. We pay special attention to the work of Sylvia Crowe in the creation of Wylfa Power Station in Ynys Mon, North Wales in the late 1960s. Her work both encapsulated and catalyzed the emerging state of the art of infrastructure design around power generation and transmission.

The Changing Aesthetics of Power Generation

In the decades following World War II, design collaboration in the electricity sector gained currency across the disciplines of power engineering, architecture, and landscape architecture. The nationalization of the electricity sector in 1948 sparked increased interest in the economics and efficiency of electricity generation and transmission, leading to a series of developments that resulted in the early appointment of architects and landscape architects in the design process for power stations, and ultimately to a paradigmatic shift in the aesthetic approach to design.

For architects and landscape architects, the UK's first commercial nuclear energy program in the 1950s was a new design challenge which required locating new technology in remote contexts. Some sites held protected status as Areas of Outstanding Natural Beauty (AONB) or National Parks and part of the challenge for designers would be to reconcile invasive and extensive industrial sites with existing ecologies. Although the work of Capability Brown and Humphry Repton in the eighteenth and nineteenth centuries demonstrated the capacity of landscape to absorb large industrial structures, the beneficiaries of their carefully curated views were limited to their patrons. Part of the design challenge was that the new landscapes of nuclear power would be for the masses; while learning from historic examples, designers had to work for new audiences and uses.

Immediately after World War II, secrecy surrounding Calder Hall may have initially limited the scope for architectural and landscape input. However, marked contrasts between designs for the first and last stations in the initial nuclear program, Calder Hall (1956) and Wylfa (1969), reflect the advancements in engineering and design that took place (Figure 21.1). Christopher Hinton, nuclear engineer and Chairman of the Central Generating Electricity Board (CEGB) between 1957 and 1964, acknowledged this by describing Windscale in Cumbria (now Sellafield) as "monuments to our original ignorance."[1] The Electricity Act (1957) played a fundamental role in driving these advancements by including a clause which outlined the requirement to minimize the visual impact of generating and transmission sites on their surroundings.[2] This unique requirement of a major nationalized industry to balance "the twin objectives of cheap electricity efficiently produced and respect for the environment" prompted changes within the structure of the electricity authorities to produce the necessary conditions for design innovation.[3] Design firms were appointed during the site selection stages of electricity generating projects, for the purposes of whole site design and coordination.[4]

The reorganization of the electricity authorities offered the opportunity to dispel skepticism from engineers concerned that "intellectuals, ignorant of the complicated techniques of electricity generation and supply, [would] demand that they make their machines look pretty."[5] Such misunderstandings of architectural and landscape disciplines were challenged by the multidisciplinary team appointed to lead the newly formed CEGB (1958). Christopher Hinton and advisory board members keenly publicized a positive attitude to multidisciplinary teams and an integrated approach to power station design. Site coordination, design delivery and construction were overseen by the newly formed CEGB Architect's Section, headed by Michael Shepheard, and assisted by landscape architect John Herbert. This team advised William Holford, Professor of Town Planning at University College London, who held a special responsibility as part time member of the CEGB for architecture and the conservation of amenity. Holford and Hinton worked closely together to improve coordination between design and engineering disciplines, stating that it is "too seldom considered that industrial buildings or plant might have aesthetic qualities."[6]

Power Stations in Post-War Britain

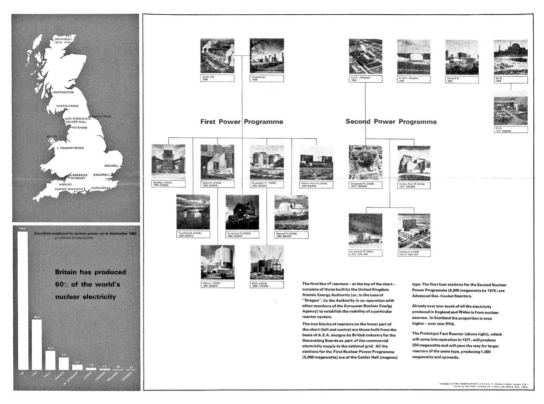

Figure 21.1 Poster published by UKAEA in 1969 to publicize and promote the near completion of the MAGNOX program and present the advances made in reactor output in the second program.

Source: UKAEA, British Nuclear Power. London: UKAEA, 1969 © Nuclear Decommissioning Authority (NDA).

In the following sections, we examine three separate economic drivers that led to the expansion of interest in environment and visual amenity in the production of electricity. These changing economic and environmental considerations informed several approaches to multidisciplinary design which informed the appearance of power generating sites. First, during the early years of nationalization, officials encouraged design input to make use of new materials developed during the war, with a view to maximize the cost efficiency of power station construction. Second, a desire to meet future demand for electricity catalyzed technological advancements in generating capacity and hence plant footprint, location, and design. Third, the introduction of an Architect's Section to the CEGB enabled architects and landscape architects to be involved in projects from the site selection stages.[7]

Economies of Construction

Power station architecture in the post-war period made a radical shift from the monumental brick cathedral, epitomized by Sir Gilbert Scott's treatment of Battersea Power Station, to "a more open, honest and integrated approach," which expressed the technical and engineering functions of electricity generating plant.[8] The monumentality of early power station typologies symbolized power in urban centers, which was dispersed by the introduction of the National Grid.

Following WWII, the electricity supply system was nationalized, and the British Electrical Authority (BEA) was made responsible for the generation and transmission of electricity across 12 geographically defined generating divisions. Initially, the organization was not associated with any significant developments in architectural style, which aligned with the conservative approach of the BEA Chief Engineer at the time and the traditionalist mindset of the Royal Fine Art Commission, by whom all new designs were reviewed.[9]

One of the most influential documents driving the shift in architectural style was the *Enquiry into Economy in the Construction of Power Stations*.[10] Commissioned by the Ministry of Fuel and Power, the report recommended that the BEA should "encourage the experiment of new building techniques in the interests of economy" in addition to the integration of "architects as equal partners in the design team of each new power station."[11] One of the earliest firms to rethink their approach in the wake of the *Enquiry* was Farmer and Dark Architects. Renowned for their brick clad contributions to power station design, Farmer and Dark received significant attention for their new direction. Described by the *Architectural Review* as "a suitable skin drawn over [...] mechanical parts," stations at Willington (1954 – 60), Marchwood (1954 - 59) and Belvedere (1954 – 60) made use of steel frames with brightly colored aluminum cladding and patent glazing.[12] With this new style, the monumentality of former "brick cathedrals" was broken down to allow clear expression of aggregate engineering elements, with the turbine hall as centerpiece.[13] Specialist architectural input was not unprecedented prior to this, but under the BEA and the subsequent Central Electricity Authority (CEA), it became significantly more common.

Economies of Technology

Several factors propelled officials to involve architects and landscape architects more centrally in the design of energy infrastructure. Increasing demands for power production during and after World War II required larger and more boilers, turbines, control rooms, and switch housing, which in turn led to an expansion of the footprints of conventional coal, oil, and gas generating stations. Meanwhile, the development and implementation of atomic energy was gaining pace as the United Kingdom Atomic Energy Authority (UKAEA) commissioned its first 50 MWe prototype reactor at Calder Hall in 1956.[14] Civil authorities sought the input of design professionals who could navigate between limited available space, difficult terrain for siting and construction, and demands for larger and more complex facilities.

Designs for initial nuclear reactors, known as MAGNOX, after the magnesium alloy used in the fuel rods, followed a gas-cooled, graphite moderated typology.[15] From this prototype, the UK's first civil nuclear program expanded to include nine stations, with further reactors exported internationally to sites in Tōkai, Japan and Latina, Italy.[16] Initially, reactor designs were developed competitively between four industry consortia.[17] First tender packages from design teams were required to offer a proposal for a complete twin-reactor power station which could be constructed at either Berkeley, Bradwell, or Hunterston (Scotland). Reports from an engineering perspective suggest that for the first tenders the electricity authorities "had little influence on the designs [...], perhaps because their nuclear engineering and project management organizations were still being established."[18]

To develop its projects, UKAEA issued turnkey contracts that required close coordination of the various firms involved. Arguably, this tight administrative structure made the engineering context for nuclear power station design less complicated, as fewer contractors were involved. Finding a unified approach to engineering plant, built form, and landscape, however, proved challenging. Sylvia Crowe, one of the country's leading landscape architects and critics, reported that the government's established procedure invited competing practices to "present projects for a reactor on an unknown site."[19]

However, she worried that such abstraction ignored the unique environmental, geological, and topographical qualities of individual sites. "Although [the reactors] have the same technical requirements," she argued, "[each] is in a quite different type of landscape, which must affect they type of building which will best fit into it."[20]

It was clear that the newness of nuclear energy demanded a different approach to those adopted for conventional power stations. Proximity to cooling water was necessary, bedrock footings were highly desirable and distance from dense populations all pointed to remote, largely undeveloped areas of the countryside. Previously, conventional power stations with lower outputs had been located close to areas of distribution for reasons of transmission efficiency. Whilst increases in output had seen conventional plants located further from populated centers, MAGNOX issued bold proposals to site future plants in National Parks and on un-spoilt headlands. These more remote settings drew attention from the design professions; new infrastructural typologies, such as cooling towers, set in vast open landscapes, presented a significant shift from designing for urban territories and the human scale.[21] Nuclear power stations received particular attention, with *The Architectural Review* reporting that the siting of atomic plants has been "has been vigorously discussed" because "they have usually gone to spectacular areas in unspoiled country."[22]

More broadly, the expansion of industrial infrastructure had led to increased calls to preserve the British countryside from a broad range of professionals and activists. As Sylva Crowe recalled: "There was a missionary optimism mingled with anxiety that you could not overcome the destruction and invasion of the English countryside in time."[23] Professional bodies, such as the Institute of Landscape Architects, the Town Planning Institute or the Royal Institute of British Architects recognized that broad and long-term solutions needed collaboration between the design professions including planning, architecture, landscape as well as key decision makers in policy-making.

Economies of Organization

By today's standards, legislation and administrative reorganization would be unexpected drivers for design innovation. However, for electricity in the post-war period, rather than introducing restrictive red tape, policy and economics proved to be a catalyst for design innovation via the reorganization of the industry and its administrators. In 1956, the Ministry of Fuel and Power convened the Herbert Committee, an independent panel of experts, to assess the efficiency of the Central Electricity Authority. The committee concluded that the industry was not "inefficient" in its current state, however, it warned that imminent changes in the industry risked "losing efficiency."[24] The imminent changes the report referred to include the surge in demand for electricity supply and the inability of existing organizational and administrative structures to cope with the growth of the industry. The commission's work culminated in the passage of the Electricity Act of 1957. Two key moves set out by this law were the introduction of the Central Generating Electricity Board (CEGB) as the owner and operator of electricity transmission and operating systems in England and Wales, and the requirement to protect visual amenity in the spaces occupied by new electricity infrastructure.

Commonly known as the "Amenity Clause," Section 37 of the Electricity Act 1957, required the minimization of the impact of generating and transmission sites on scenery, flora and fauna.[25] It required the newly nationalized industry was to work within

> ... statutory guidelines which required it *not* simply to produce electricity as cheaply as possible, with a little cosmetic landscaping tacked on as a gesture; but consciously to balance in each project the twin objectives of cheap electricity efficiently produced and respect for the environment.[26]

Twelve area boards operated electricity supply in their designated regions under the auspices of the CEGB, but new power stations, regardless of location, were centrally coordinated and it was the statutory duty of the CEGB to deliver the objectives of the "Amenity Clause." The gravity with which the government treated the new statutory duties was reflected by the appointment of William Holford as part time member of the board to provide advice on design matters. As the lead author of the Town and Country Planning Act 1947, Holford was a major advocate for the inclusion of landscape design in post-war planning and played a lead role in introducing the discipline of landscape architecture into official circles.[27] Holford was not new to the energy sector, as he had already provided advice in various capacities leading up to the formation of the CEGB. As a part-time member, his objective was to counter the treatment of design as a token cosmetic gesture and through his fellowship at the Institute of Landscape Architects he supported a conference titled *The Landscape of Industry* (March 1957).[28] In November 1957, he sought recommendations of landscape architects for power station projects from Sylvia Crowe (as president of the Institute of Landscape Architects).[29] His paper with Christopher Hinton titled *Power Production and Transmission in the Countryside: Preserving Amenities*, served as a benchmark for the early appointment of landscape architects in the design of power stations.[30]

In addition to Holford, the government appointed Michael Shepheard as Chief Architect. Acting from Head Office and initially supported by a team of three, Shepheard's role was to brief and advise Holford and coordinate three project groups relating to geographical regions. During his tenure from 1959 to 1970, Shepheard's team grew to thirty-two designers. Their role being to coordinate the work of appointed "architects and landscape architects for each project with the requirements of project engineers on a continuing basis during the design process, and by preparing design memoranda for the guidance of those responsible for the building work."[31] The first landscape architect in the team was John Herbert, who was responsible for preparatory work and research outside the scope of the consultant landscape architects.[32]

With this leadership in place, landscape became a central feature in the siting and design of new power stations across the country. Every tender required a landscape scheme as part of the proposal, which would be reviewed by the local planning authority and landscape architects were commonly called upon as "expert witness" to give evidence at public inquiries.[33]

The appointment of design consultants at the very outset of projects meant that the responsibilities of each team had to be clarified. Both architects and landscape architects were to advise on site the main visual components of the site, including layout, orientation, building massing and materiality.[34] Landscape proposals extended beyond the immediate design and construction phases to consider long term maintenance, the planting conservation, ground contouring and screening. This applied within site boundaries and in agreed strategic positions beyond the ownership boundaries of the CEGB.[35] Landscape consultants were often assisted by the CEGB's own landscape team in issues relating to siting the stations. Ronald Hebblethwaite led the landscape team within the CEGB's Development and Construction Division which housed its own landscape team. This division was responsible for pioneering techniques across conventional and nuclear schemes, including the development of computational and photogrammetry techniques for analyzing visual impact on sites, researching various techniques for establishing trees in pulverized fuel ash, and in the especially difficult conditions of draw-down areas at hydro-electric schemes.[36]

Wylfa: A Case Study

Crowe's involvement with Trawsfynydd (1965), set in the Snowdonia National Park, is much better documented than Wylfa (1969) because of its setting and eminent architect, Basil Spence (Figure 21.2). However, designs for Wylfa are notable for several reasons. As the last station to be built as part of the MAGNOX program, Wylfa was arguably the most considered ensemble of engineering and landscape design and can be viewed as the culmination of experience gained since the start of the commercial

Figure 21.2 Trawsfynydd Power Station. Planting was used at Trawsfynydd to screen ancillary accommodation and accentuate the reactor buildings.

Source: © L. Coucill, 2015.

nuclear program – a clear product of the organizational arrangement propagated by the 1957 Electricity Act, and also the zenith of Crowe's work and theory in *The Landscape of Power*.[37]

Wylfa also exhibited some of the most advanced engineering in the reactor series and Crowe's influence on the building position, massing and materiality captures the essence of the multidisciplinary working practices adopted to respond to economies of technology and construction. The generating capacity at Wylfa was 1180 MW from two reactor cores, which was almost double that of any other facility in the program. This, together with the reactor and generator engineering solutions employed at Wylfa, influenced the appearance and arrangement of built form on the site.

Alongside Farmer and Dark Architects, Crowe leveraged her renown and experience to push for design cooperation throughout the project to skillfully adorn the exposed headland location – an Area of Outstanding Natural Beauty (AONB) recognized for the diversity of its geology, flora, and fauna – with the reactor housing.[38] Wylfa was only the second station to have the reactors and steam generators contained in pre-stressed concrete construction, characterized by cylindrical vessels. Together with the architects, Crowe took care to emphasize these formal qualities to showcase the geometry of the reactor housing to optimal effect.

In her 1962 *Wylfa Landscape Report* for the CEGB, Crowe considers the appearance of the site from all vantage points, including views in the immediate surroundings and more distant vistas form populated areas (Figure 21.3).[39] She explains how the view from Wylfa headland should "be dominated by the station, and the drama of its scale should be given full play."[40] To achieve this,

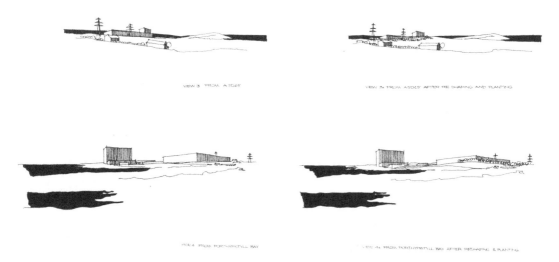

Figure 21.3 Crowe's sketches of Wylfa from a range of vantage points to explore the massing and composition of forms in the landscape.

Source: S. Corwe, *Wylfa Landscape Report*, 1962 © Sylvia Crowe Collection at the MERL Archives, Reading: AR CRO PF/A/14.

careful consideration was given to minimize the visibility of roads and perimeter fencing from these viewpoints which continue to be accessible by coastal paths that predate the station. Crowe also took the opportunity to extend coastal paths to offer further views of the reactor housing; an approach in line with Edmund Burke's philosophies on the sublime and the beautiful.[41] The position of the reactors on the headland allowed Crowe to make use of the coastline as a natural perimeter. Rather than introducing visually obtrusive fencing, these invisible boundaries continue to offer an uninterrupted display of the reactors.[42]

To heighten the prominence of the reactors, Crowe's report documents further consideration of the exposure and visibility of the site in relation to public access and use in surrounding areas through sketches from populated areas including nearby Cemaes Bay, a popular tourist spot. This work has a particular emphasis on downplaying less impressive structures needed on site, such as substations and ancillary accommodation in contrast to the reactor buildings. This objective correlates with her resistance to allow these smaller scattered structures to occupy large areas of the site.[43] Her approach to this at Wylfa was twofold; positioning these on the landside of the site and shielding them in existing and exaggerated landforms sculpted from 500 cubic years of spoil generated by the construction process.[44] However, these buildings were not entirely concealed in close range as Crowe consciously created a foreground from which the buildings emerge in other views (Figure 21.4).[45]

These approaches reflect Crowe's ideas about how landscape can play a major role in the drama of a site, both revealing and screening for visual effect. With subtle alterations, the pattern of the landscape was restored after the construction period in a way that integrally frames the power station. Rather than the geometry of the station dominating the landscape, the landscape, and the building work as one design conceit; something described by Crowe as "knitting the landscape back together."[46]

Conclusions

As national stature became increasingly entwined with economic prosperity during the Cold War period in Britain, infrastructure programs took on new importance and building power stations can therefore be seen as an exercise in nation building. Responsibility for the design of them, however, was an open question in the years just after the war. Would engineers and contractors hold sway, or would there be a

Figure 21.4 Wylfa Power Station. View from Wylfa Headland, demonstrating Crowe's use of natural barriers to avoid visually obtrusive perimeter security fencing.

Source: © L. Coucill, 2020.

role for architects and landscape architects? With the emergence of the first civil nuclear program in post-war Britain, three economic drivers played a central role in generating the conditions for the increased role of architects and landscape architects: the search for cost-effective new materials to satisfy budget conscious ministries; the need for engineers to concentrate on the highly technical aspects of reactor construction, opening up professional space for site and elevation design and the challenges posed by siting new plants outside of cities amid difficult and cherished landscapes. The "Amenity Clause" of the Electricity Act of 1957 placed the interests of society and environment front and center, leading to a dramatic expansion of landscape architecture, a discipline formerly associated with smaller scale, mostly private commissions.

Landscape architecture burgeoned as a profession during the first wave of the civil atomic program, and it is worth mentioning that this was driven in a large part by a small number of prominent female practitioners. They demonstrated the skillful capability to work with and across the design disciplines as evident in the work of Sylvia Crowe at Wylfa; a project which not only drew together critical ideas developed throughout her career, but in doing so managed to position a bold, modern infrastructure as an "eye-catcher" within a newly created landscape, that at the same time was "knitted back" to a more natural appearance. Her work interpreted the historic methodologies of the English landscape garden to celebrate a landmark building in a period of national modernization. Crowe's contemporary, Brenda Colvin, proposed that the infrastructures of modern society, including power stations, oil refineries, factories, reservoirs, and motorways are analogous to historic typologies, such as castles, temples and pyramids and drew attention as such, perhaps most notably in the photography of Bernd and Hilla Becher.[47]

One of the differences between historic monuments and the relatively new infrastructures of national modernization is their expected lifespan and future. North Wales is also home to a suite of castles built by Edward I, and although both power stations and castles were built to withstand attack, the technology of the former has a predefined lifespan which determines a temporary presence in the landscape. After 44 years of operation, Wylfa Reactor 1 was shut down in 2015. Castles too were superseded by technology but remain as legacies of their time in the landscape. In contrast, Wylfa will eventually be carefully decommissioned and demolished. Rather than the monumental forms coordinated around the reactor technology and clad in materials complementing the rocky headland, it's legacy will likely be two dome-shaped coverings signposting and containing the former reactor cores.

Each power generation site in the first nuclear program was distinct, with geographic context and topography taken as central factors. Moreover, all exhibit forward and collaborative thinking about the manifestation of infrastructure in the landscape, as well as its acceptance as a symbol of modernity in previously undeveloped areas. Equally, alongside landscape setting, each station reveals the legal, economic, and technical conditions that underpin its construction. From the cooling towers at Calder Hall to the manicured views of Wylfa, interventions range in distribution and footprint, from those so vast they are imperceptible, to those prominently condensed, coordinated, and celebrated as landmarks.

Access to and the preservation of the countryside from the extension of suburban housing as well as the intrusion of infrastructure were key concerns in post-war planning discourse in Britain. Nuclear power stations built in remote areas of outstanding natural quality, needed careful consideration as well as strong arguments to withhold the public enquiries and public opposition. Collaboration between the design professions was key in the success of making these acceptable. The CEGB's communication declaring themselves "the modern patron of landscaping art" and comparing their consultant designers to Capability Brown and Humphrey Repton positioned the new landscapes of infrastructure equal to the highly popular and internationally hailed and followed picturesque English landscape gardens and their vision of "Arcadia."[48] Economic drivers, institutional considerations, national ownership, public responsibility and statutory duties created infrastructural ensembles in post-war Britain that were ecologically, environmentally and aesthetically comparable to one of the most well-known and nostalgically referenced British art form: the picturesque garden.

Notes

1 M. Gowing, "Lord Hinton of Bankside, O. M., F. Eng. 12 May 1901-22 June 1983," *Biographical Memoirs of Fellows of the Royal Society* 36 (1990): 219–239.
2 A.H. Hanson, "Electricity Reviewed: The Herbert Report," *Public Administration* 34, no. 2 (1956): 211–214.
3 T. Aldous, and B. Clouston, *Landscape by Design* (London: Heinemann,, 1979), 53–54.
4 C. Hinton and W. Holford, "Power Production and Transmission in the Countryside: Preserving Amenities," *Journal of the Royal Society of Arts* 108, no. 5043 (1960): 180–210.
5 D. Wainwright, "Designing for Power," *Design Journal* 224 (1964): 40–47.
6 Ibid.
7 Hanson, "Electricity Reviewed," 211–214.
8 *Architectural Review* 127 (1960): 389.
9 J. Clarke, *High Merit: Existing English Post-War Coal and Oil-Fired Power Stations in Context* (London: Historic England, 2013).
10 Ibid. 11.
11 Ibid. 11.
12 *Architectural Review* 127 (1960): 389.
13 Ibid.
14 HM Government, *A Programme of Nuclear Power* (London: HMSO, 1955).
15 UKAEA, *British Nuclear Power* (London: UKAEA, 1969).

16 UKAEA, *The Nuclear Energy Industry of the United Kingdom* (London: Charles Ronser & Associates, 1961); S.H. Wearne and R.H. Bird, *UK Experience of Consortia Engineering for Nuclear Power Stations* (Manchester: University of Manchester Press, 2017), 5.
17 UKAEA, *The Nuclear Energy Industry of the United Kingdom*, 35.
18 Wearne and Bird, *UK Experience of Consortia Engineering for Nuclear Power Stations*, 5.
19 S. Crowe, *The Landscape of Power* (London: Architectural Press, 1958: 63.
20 Ibid.
21 T. Sharp, "Societies and Institutions: ILA: Thomas Sharp: Christmas Tree Landscape," *The Architects' Journal* 110 (October 1949): 458.
22 *Architectural Review* 127 (1960): 389.
23 S. Harvey (ed.), *Reflections on Landscape. The Lives and Work of Six British Landscape Architects* (London: Gower Technical Press 1987), 34.
24 Ibid.
25 J. Clarke, *High Merit: Existing English Post-War Coal and Oil-Fired Power Stations in Context* (London: Historic England, 2013), 12.
26 Aldous and Clouston, *Landscape by Design*, 53–54.
27 Ibid 54; A. Powers, "Landscape in Britain," in *The Architecture of Landscape 1940–1960*, ed. M. Treib (Philadelphia: University of Pennsylvania Press, 2002), 62.
28 C. Hinton and W. Holford, "Power Production and Transmission in the Countryside: Preserving Amenities," *Journal of the Royal Society of Arts* 108, 5043 (1960): 180–210; Landscape Institute Archives at the Museum of English Rural Life, Reading. LI membership application files (MERL SRI AD2/2/3/8 SURNAME H).
29 Holford Archives, University of Liverpool: D147/GB/18.
30 Hinton and Holford, "Power Production and Transmission in the Countryside," 180–210.
31 D. Wainwright, "Designing for Power," *Design Journal* 224 (1964): 40–47.
32 Aldous and Clouston, *Landscape by Design*, 53–54.
33 Ibid. 54–55.
34 Ibid.
35 Ibid.
36 Ibid. 56.
37 Crowe, *The Landscape of Power*.
38 H. Grove-White, "The Landscape of Power, Sylvia Crowe at Wylfa," in *Landmarks*, ed. B. Spence (Cardiff: Design Commission for Wales, 2015).
39 S. Crowe, *Wylfa Landscape Report*, Sylvia Crowe Collection at the MERL Archives, Reading: AR CRO PF/A/14, 1962.
40 Ibid.
41 E. Burke, *A Philosophical Enquiry into the Origin of Our Ideas of the Sublime and Beautiful* (Oxford: Oxford University Press, 2008).
42 Ibid.
43 S. Crowe, "Power and the Landscape," *Journal of the Institute of Landscape Architects* 52 (November 1960): 3–7.
44 Crowe, *Wylfa Landscape Report*, 4.
45 Crowe, "Power and the Landscape," 3–7.
46 S. Crowe, *The Landscape of Power* (London: Architectural Press, 1958) and S. Crowe, *The Landscape of Roads* (London: Architectural Press, 1960).
47 B. Colvin, *Land and Landscape* (London: John Murray, 1970), 344; B. Becher and H. Becher, *Basic Forms of Industrial Buildings* (London: Thames & Hudson, 2005).
48 CEGB, *Power and the Countryside* (London: CEGB, 1965).

22
TVA IN THE DESERT
U.S. Development Projects in the Hashemite Kingdom of Jordan, 1951–1961

Dalal Musaed Alsayer

On February 27, 1951, the Hashemite Kingdom of Jordan entered into the first of a series of Point Four technical assistance agreements with the United States to carry out water development projects in the Jordan River Valley. This resulted in the "Unified Development of the Water Resources of the Jordan Valley Region" (Unified Plan), developed by Charles T. Main, Inc., which proposed a series of dams and levees along the river. It was designed upon an entirely constructed environmental imaginary for the study's team never visited Jordan, but instead drew heavily from their experiences in Tennessee with the Tennessee Valley Authority (TVA) to devise their plan. Much like the New Deal's Tennessee River Valley Authority (TVA) in scale and scope, the Unified Plan was an inherently socio-technological project that dismissed political boundaries and remade the Jordan Valley into an image of U.S. engineering prowess. The TVA in Jordan brought with it rural housing to settle bedouins *(nomadic tribespeople), home economic programs for women, and "masculine" activities for men that superimposed New Deal U.S. beliefs unto an inherently Arab, predominantly Muslim society. This allowed the U.S. to package its New Deal arsenal of man-in-nature, woman-at-home, urban/rural divide, and scientific farming in its Cold War battles. This blanketing of natural, political, and social environments with a superimposed system, along with the myriad objects and architecture it produced, restructured social, spatial, and ideological systems. This chapter examines the ramifications of the TVA model, developed under the New Deal and exported as a one-size-fits-all model under the overseas developmental aid programs of Presidents Harry S. Truman and Dwight D. Eisenhower in Jordan. This chapter traces what happens after the TVA landed in the desert and the dust settled: a landscape and its people reorganized with the intent of bringing Jordan into the U.S. sphere of influence.*

Five men sit atop a bridge as water gushes below them. Their demeanor evokes a triumph over the river: engineered and made to be productive (Figure 22.1). The photograph that captures the moment looks like countless representations of U.S. New Deal era construction projects. But it was actually taken along the Jordan River Valley in 1961 as part of the U.S. postwar technical assistance programs. While separated by three decades and 6,000 miles, the rhetoric, the ideals, and the infrastructure are the same. Taken as part of the documentation process of postwar U.S. development aid programs, the bridge and its engineered river are but one small part of the U.S. global sweep against communism under the guise of "development."

The Hashemite Kingdom of Jordan entered into the first of a series of agreements with the United States (U.S.) on February 27, 1951, and four months later, the U.S. engineering firm of Knappen, Tippetts, and Abbott was contracted to carry out water development projects.[1] The U.S. State Department described this initial "Point Four" agreement and subsequent iterations as an "interchange of technical knowledge and skills and in related activities designed to contribute to the balanced and integrated development of the economic resources and productive capacities of Jordan."[2] The Point

Figure 22.1 Construction workers sitting atop a bridge as water flows through the East Ghor Canal, ca. 1961.

Source: Courtesy of Folder 28, Box 1, Photographs Relating to U.S. Aid to Jordan 1953–1962, RG 469-J Records of U.S. Foreign Assistance Agencies, 1948–1961, National Archives and Records Administration (NARA), College Park, MD, U.S.A.

Four agreement expanded from water management to include laboratories, schools, housing, home economics programs, and community development programs.[3]

The initial Point Four investment in water resources culminated with the "Unified Development of the Water Resources of the Jordan Valley Region" (Unified Plan), developed by Charles T. Main, Inc., which proposed a series of dams and levees along the river.[4] Much like the New Deal's Tennessee River Valley Authority (TVA) in scale and scope, the Unified Plan was an inherently socio-technological project that dismissed political boundaries and remade the Jordan Valley into an image of U.S. engineering success. This blanketing of natural, political, and social environments with a superimposed system, along with the myriad objects and architecture it produced, restructured social, spatial, and ideological systems.

This chapter examines the ramifications of the TVA model, developed under the New Deal and exported as a one-size-fits-all model under the overseas developmental aid programs of Presidents Harry S. Truman and Dwight D. Eisenhower in Jordan. As a techno-social apparatus, U.S. postwar aid programs introduced new architectures, body politics, identities, and an understanding of space.

The TVA in Jordan brought with it rural housing to settle *bedouins* (nomadic tribespeople), home economics programs targeting women, and masculinized activities for men that superimposed U.S. cultural attitudes onto an Arab, predominantly Muslim society. This allowed the U.S. to package its New Deal arsenal—man-in-nature, woman-at-home, urban versus rural divide, and scientific farming—for export in its Cold War battles. This chapter traces what happened after the TVA landed in the desert and the dust settled: a landscape and its people reorganized with the intent of bringing Jordan into the U.S. sphere of influence.

To understand the U.S. presence in Jordan it is useful to briefly recount the program that guided it, namely, Point Four. Announced during his second inaugural address on January 20, 1949, President Truman's Point Four promoted extension-based farming and home economic programs which was grounded in the sheer belief in U.S. technological prowess, all of which were direct outgrowths of the 1930s-era New Deal.[5] Although short-lived, Point Four paved the way for rural, agricultural, and extension programs that placed the rural village at the center of U.S.'s global campaign against communism under the banner of "development."[6] The Hashemite Kingdom of Jordan became one of those nations in 1952, receiving $400,000 as part of a Title III, Voluntary Relief Agencies Public Law 480 grant (PL480 grant) that allowed the revenues of U.S. agricultural surplus sold in Jordan to be used for aid programs.[7] This grant, along with subsequent Point Four grants, was used to develop a "rural" housing typology that was to be low cost, easy-to-build, and (critically) "suitable" for the Jordanian landscape. The experimental house was made of adobe bricks and finished with white cement stucco. It boasted two rooms, a kitchen, modern bathroom, a porch, and was complete with electricity and plumbing. Yet, it was to be topped with a vaulted dome and was constructed using traditional adobe, for it needed to appear local despite its modern amenities (Figure 22.2).[8] The house was estimated to cost JD 300, which was equivalent to U.S.$45 in 1952 and U.S.$420 in 2018, of which only "15 percent was for material," and according to the aid agency in charge, it was deemed to be suitable as cheap housing for desert habitation.[9]

These PL480 houses were to be built in the newly irrigated swaths of lands in the East Ghor along the Jordan River, near those bridges seen in Figure 22.1. The East Ghor Canal along the Jordan River was conceived in the U.S. aid workers' imaginary as a rural landscape that needed to be modernized. These PL480-funded homes are central to an understanding of how a specific—that is, U.S.—form of modernization that was exported to budding nations in the early part of the 1950s; however, the home is best understood within the larger, complex network of actors, architecture, infrastructure, and paraphernalia it ushered into the Arabian desert. A close reading of the parallels drawn between the New Deal and postwar aid programs, the form taken by modernization, and what it enabled will offer a way to understand how the "modern world" was envisioned, deployed, and sustained by the U.S. in the postwar years.

Constructing the "Third World"

Following World War II, the U.S. extended development aid to nations in Latin America, East and South Asia, and Sub-Saharan Africa, and the Middle East. This aid was part of a much broader Cold War struggle for ideological, military, and economic influence. As part of this struggle, the U.S. and Europe articulated a new order where countries were divided into "First," "Second," and "Third" Worlds. The latter, the so-called "Third World," which belonged neither to the capitalist "First World" nor to the socialist "Second World," is central to the discussion of modernization and development in the Cold War context. One of the key agencies in the formulation of a postwar order was the International Development Advisory Board (IDAB). Chaired by Eric Johnston, head of the American Motion Pictures Association, the IDAB was interested in both the political, economic rationale for extending foreign aid, as well as the optics and cultural forms by which such aid would be channeled. Through the actions of the IDAB and other bodies, the U.S. invented the "Third World" as a region

TVA in the Desert

Figure 22.2 Construction of the PL-480-funded demonstration home using adobe bricks, Wadi Fara', Jordan, ca. 1954.

Source: Courtesy of Folder 10, Box 1, Photographs Relating to U.S. Aid to Jordan 1953–1962, Record Group 469-J Records of U.S. Foreign Assistance Agencies, 1948–1961, US National Archives and Records Administration (NARA), College Park, MD, U.S.A.

that was geographically "South," ideologically up for grabs, and physically incapable of developing its landscape (Figure 22.3).[10]

IDAB developed and disseminated booklets to national and international bodies active on the ground as a way to communicate, introduce, and reinvent "the language of development," giving new and precise meanings to terms such as "peasant," "village," and "farmer" to local tribespeople. In Jordan, aid agencies such as UNICEF, CARE, and IDAB visually transformed the tribesman into a farmer by repackaging the Arabic word, "*Fellah*," (m. farmer) and demonstrating what said *fellah* had to do (Figure 22.4). It was through these translations and representations that the "rural" and "urban" were packaged as a solution to a perceived need for modernization.

This story of modernization in the Jordan is not a novel one, but what is compelling is the way in which U.S. experts actively manufactured parallels between the environment they knew and the one with which they were confronted. This confrontation—in essence "the constellation of ideas that groups of humans develop about a given landscape, usually local or regional, that commonly includes assessments about that environment as well as how it came to be in its current state"—is what environmental historian Diana K. Davis calls an "environmental imaginary."[11] The U.S.'s environmental imaginary of the Arabia was actively manufactured in the first half of the twentieth century through cartographic

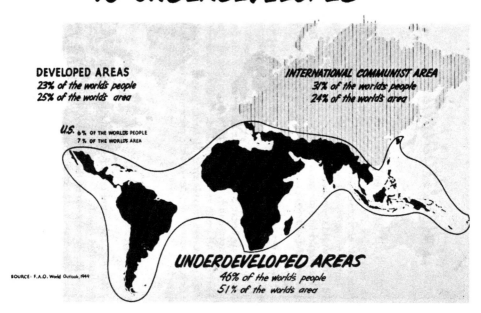

Figure 22.3 The construction of the "Third World," 1951.

Source: *Partners in Progress: A Report to President Truman by the International Development Advisory Board* (New York: Simon & Schuster, 1951), 12. Image courtesy of the International Development Advisory Board.

representations that were produced for oil exploration, which conceptually distanced the region from the "West" by drawing Arabia apart from Europe and other familiar geographies. This cartographic move paved the way for future [mis]conceptions of the Arabian environmental imaginary by doing two things: first, it replaced local depictions of the territory, and second, in their representations, these maps began to define regions according to U.S. understandings of territories such as urban and rural. By projecting the parallel between the rural U.S. landscape and native environments, postwar aid programs attempted to thwart the spread of communism by providing need-based technical know-how supplied by U.S. expertise.

U.S. Engineering and Exporting Infrastructure

Under Point Four, the earlier nationwide mobilization of expertise in the New Deal era that harnessed the power of U.S. engineers, experts and volunteers to transform the rural landscape of the Southern United States, was exported globally.[12] The alphabet soup of agencies developed under President Franklin D. Roosevelt enabled the federal government to act at the national scale and provided a model of tried and tested modernization of both society and landscape.[13] This New Deal ambition to harness science into applied knowledge that can be deployed elsewhere, or what is called "portable knowledge," is central to the subsequent story of U.S. development aid in foreign lands.[14] One of the New Deal's largest achievements, carried out by the Tennessee River Valley Authority (TVA), brought with it electrification, industrialization, and conservation to the rural mountainous region of the upland South. The TVA served as a place of experimentation and eventual optimization of knowledge applied to the construction of infrastructure and the reorganization of landscape.

Figure 22.4 "Dear Farmer" Poster describing when to "pick," how to "transport," and "box" tomatoes, ca. 1958.

Source: Courtesy of Folder 5, Box 2, Photographs Relating to U.S. Aid to Jordan 1953–1962, Record Group 469-J Records of U.S. Foreign Assistance Agencies, 1948–1961, US National Archives and Records Administration (NARA), College Park, MD, U.S.A.

Point Four experts working overseas deployed the "TVA model" to the Jordan River Valley in the form of the Jordan River Valley Authority (JVA) through "displacement" and "translation."[15] The JVA displaced preexisting social and spatial systems in the Jordan River Valley and translated the TVA system from the scale of the Southern U.S. to the scale of the world. Experience with rural electrification in the mountains left U.S. planners and engineers with the conviction that landscape was no impediment to development, and that technology could overcome any obstacle. Put briefly, U.S. "resources policy might have become influential overseas not because of its managerial roots in a vast, empty continent, but because it appeared to offer a road-tested solution for rural modernization."[16]

When Point Four entered Jordan in 1951, the country was riddled with political instabilities and resentment towards the U.S. The sudden influx of Palestinian refugees, the early beginnings of Arab nationalism, the renewed interest of Christian missionaries, and the general antipathy towards Western powers, meant that the U.S. had to address several conflicting interests. Point Four agreements with the Kingdom focused on two intertwined objectives: first, large scale infrastructure projects that would provide not only new services, but also an advertisement for modernity; and second, social engineering projects that sought to remake a society from the ground up based on a U.S. cultural model.

The first objective took hold in 1953, when the TVA was invited to draw up a unified plan for development of the Jordan Valley Region upon the request of the United Nations Relief and Works Agency for Palestine Refugees in the Near East (UNRWA).[17] The driving force behind this decision was UNRWA's director John Blandford Jr., who had served in the TVA as Assistant Chairman, Coordinator and Secretary of the Board, and General Manager. Undertaken by Charles T. Main, Inc. of Boston, Massachusetts, the study and development was to be funded by Point Four, the United Nations, and the governments of the two nations. The plan came to be known as the "Unified Development of the Water Resources of the Jordan Valley Region" (or simply Unified Plan).[18] It was built upon the premise of an entirely constructed environmental imaginary. The study's authors never visited Jordan, instead, the entire study was "based upon materials, reports and data made available to TVA and was made without field investigations."[19] When confronted with differing environmental and social constructs, U.S. experts made the foreign familiar by making it seem more like the U.S.

The sheer belief in both U.S. expertise and the "universality" of the TVA model is on full display in the Unified Plan. The plan's recommendations ranged from irrigation methods and canals to technical expert training. The Plan dismissed the political boundaries by arguing that

> [m]any of the earlier plans were prepared when the present political boundaries did not exist. Partly for this reason, but principally in the interest of sound engineering practice, the TVA was invited to disregard political boundaries, and to prepare a report indicating the most efficient method of utilizing the whole of the watershed in the best interest of the area.[20]

Ultimately, the Unified Plan devised the Greater Yarmouk project, which included two canals, the East and West Ghor, two large storage dams, and a slew of smaller dams along the Jordan River. Of these, only the East Ghor Canal was realized during this period. The JVA came to symbolize an environment engineered, a nation united, and a landscape made productive. The JVA as a symbol of political economic power is especially potent when seen as a techno-social apparatus that dislocates existing social contracts and spatial configurations. The JVA's role in modernizing the country is so profound because "[f]or many postcolonial governments, this ability to rearrange the natural and social environment became a means to demonstrate the strength of the modern state as a techno-economic power."[21]

Of Environments and Homes: Exporting Domesticity

Where the Jordanian "environment" was seen as something that could be harnessed by mass industrialization, its "society" could equally be transformed. Part of this effort involved the introduction of single-family living into the Jordanian landscape through model homes that came with a clear narrative that located "man-in-nature" and "woman-at-home."[22] These clearly designated roles for each gender were the building block of U.S. foreign aid in the Cold War. Model homes focused on women while agriculture sites were geared towards men, a thread that can be traced to the U.S. Department of Agriculture (USDA) and New Deal agricultural extension services.[23] Envisioned as a part of both physical and intangible infrastructures, these model homes were to be connected through U.S.-funded roads, were to be part of the U.S.-affiliated American University of Beirut (AUB), and were to be staffed with U.S. experts.

The years after World War II saw the restructuring of the U.S. society with the return of soldiers and the "refeminization" of women to their prewar domestic role. The overarching goal was the construction of what historian Elizabeth Cohen has called "the consumer republic," an American way grounded in a vast economy of good and services provided to growing families and expanding suburbs.[24] The home in general, and the single-family home in particular, was central to the reconfiguring of the U.S. economy. To realize this ideal, federal, state, and local governments invested billions of dollars in the construction of new highways, water and sewer lines, electricity grids, and other infrastructure. All of this would fundamentally reshape U.S. households, gender roles, and identities during the postwar years.[25]

As the U.S. looked to extend its influence abroad, the "good life" emerged as a soft power export product. As historian Robert Fishman observes, "the export of American ideas, goods and customs was inseparable from the suburban dream."[26] The famous "Kitchen Debate" between Richard Nixon and Nikita Krushchev at the American Exposition in Moscow in 1959 brought the domestic sphere into sharp relief as a Cold War ideological project. Because the home was the site in which the "American way of life" was actualized, it only seemed right to take this tried and tested cultural form to the so-called "Third World" in order to cultivate allegiance to the capitalist system. Largely funded by Ford Foundation, Point Four, and PL480 grants, this effort at soft diplomacy spread across many countries in the world, including Jordan.

The environmental imaginary that was established through the International Development Advisory Board helped pave the way for the distinct "types" of home that were built, and replaced the local "nomadic" and "sedentary" conceptions of space with Western concepts of "rural" and "urban."[27] U.S. Point Four experts bolstered the place of the tribal *bedouin* (nomadic tribespeople) in a "rural" landscape.[28] The *bedouin*, which etymologically refers to a nomadic lifestyle, differs from the *fellah*, or farmer, however, they were both homogenized and assimilated into one large grouping, called "*qaraweyoun*," or villagers. The Point Four program established *Community Development Programs* in Jordan with demonstration farms as its centerpiece and village cooperatives that were deemed "an instrument of democracy."[29] Located along the East Ghor Canal, these demonstration farms romanticized the role of the virile man in a rugged landscape, echoing the U.S. "man-in-nature" ideal under the New Deal's Civilian Conservation Corps (CCC).[30]

Beyond the distinction made linguistically, a formal architectural language was adopted to distinguish between the two. The so-called "rural" typology comprised a house made of adobe bricks, sand, and wood local to the region, drawing on orientalist imaginaries with their white walls and dark wood finishes (See Figure 22.2). The "urban" homes, on the other hand, deployed a modern aesthetic, with austere brick facades, industrial finishes, a flat roof, and large windows. In both cases, the homes defined a domestic sphere within which women were exposed to entirely Western ways of life, effectively constructing a modern companionate nuclear family.[31] "Urban" women were taught a slew of hands-on techniques that demonstrated female "modernity" through a woman's appearance, hygienic practices, and home economy skills. They were taught that their hair should be brushed and styled, their shoes polished, and their teeth brushed. They were also taught the importance of a "well-balanced breakfast" and to prepare meals made from produce now available to Jordan through the irrigation of large swaths of land in the rural landscape, thanks to the JVA and imported seeds and livestock.

Under Point Four, U.S. instructors train Jordanian women in cooking and nutrition in the imported U.S. kitchens, equipped with modern appliances that were making their way into the Jordanian consumer market. These imported appliances would have a ready-made consumer base, composed of women who knew how to use them, were primed to purchase them, and supposedly eager to consume this new "way of life." As nominal household heads, men were trained in technical schools to manufacture furniture, products, and items that were used to furnish model homes, community projects, and institutional buildings.

Meanwhile, unlike their "urban" counterparts, "rural" women received limited attention and training from Point Four. While "urban" women were taught by U.S. experts and went to study for workshops at the American University of Beirut (AUB), "rural" women were trained by "urban" Jordanian women.[32] Point Four experts envisioned the "rural" landscape as the place for agriculture and using imported seeds cultivated large swaths of lands creating farms, such as Deir Alla and Wadi Fara, to produce a productive landscape along the Jordan River Valley. As part of its expanded program, Point Four deployed large-scale demonstration farms in 155 villages in cooperation with the Near East Foundation (NEF) in 1954.[33] With a focus on both agriculture and animal husbandry, Point Four and NEF undertook experimentation in the "countryside" to develop stronger animals and plants by importing in livestock and crossbreeding.

This dichotomy between the "rural" and "urban" context was a result of the imported binary made possible by the environmental imaginary, which coupled modernization with social and environmental transformations. Critically, these "rural" homes and demonstration sites were connected to "urban" centers in Jordan and beyond to neighboring Arab countries through large-scale U.S.-funded road infrastructure. The canal, the house, the farm, and the road worked in unison to create an infrastructure of U.S.-funded capitalism across Jordan and beyond.

Conclusions: Rising Arab Sentiments and Changing U.S. Tactics

By the mid-1950s, and with the rise of the pan-Arab movement spurred on by Egyptian President Gamal Abdel Nasser, U.S. projects in the region became targets for protest. Agency offices and projects were burglarized, vandalized, and burnt down in early 1956 as part of the larger anti-Western movement that was sweeping the region. While U.S. agencies continued to work in Jordan into the late 1950s, they shifted from large-scale interventions to localized interactions with individuals, established cooperatives, and ministries. Moreover, more "global" entities such as the World Bank and the United Nations Development Programme (UNDP) took over the role of Point Four and other aid agencies.

Equally, there was also backlash in the U.S. with regards to the types and costs of aid projects, with many in Congress questioning the actual effectiveness of such programs. In a 1958 report to the House Foreign Affairs Committee, several aspects of foreign aid were called into question, including the building of a Jordanian Highway, which was said to be superfluous and unnecessary in a country that had "less than 9,000 automobiles."[34] The rapid political changes in the region and in the U.S. meant that all U.S. overseas aid programs were consolidated and replaced by the newly established United States Agency for International Development (USAID) in 1961, and the Jordanian Government entered into new agreements with U.S. companies in which locals had to be hired to fill positions.[35]

While the name Point Four is relatively unknown in Jordan, its profound impact in the nation remains to this day. In 1987, the East Ghor Canal was renamed the King Abdullah Canal and, by the 2000s, the dams envisioned by the Unified Plan were constructed. The current national library of Jordan is filled with books that ponder what it means to be Jordanian and how to reconcile the *bedouin* and the *fellah* with a national identity.[36] The importation of U.S. model homes and the superimposition of rural and urban conceptions of space has greatly impacted the social, political, and cultural understanding of the Jordanian landscape and its people. The environmental imaginary that came with U.S. aid workers and the construction of large-scale infrastructure allowed for the politicizing of space and the re-appropriation of architecture to suit an idealized, one-size-fits-all model of development that attempted to displace socio-spatial understandings. Postwar U.S. aid to Jordan was an ideologically driven effort to reengineer the country's landscapes and ecologies in ways that furthered the global fight against Soviet communism. In the end, this intervention disrupted social and spatial relations that had long been present in the landscape, leaving in its wake a fragmented society and a nation undefined.

Notes

1 "American Engineering Company Undertakes Point 4 Water Development in Jordan," No. 481, June 6, 1951, State Department Circular for Press, Clippings Folder, Box 62, George M. Elsey Papers, Harry S. Truman Library, Independence, OH, USA (HSTL).
2 "Point 4" General Agreement for Technical Cooperation Between the United States of American and the Hashemite Kingdom of Jordan, Point 4 Agreement, Country: Jordan, Social and Technical Assistance Government Folder, Foreign Service 1951 Box, American Friends Service Committee Archives, Philadelphia, PA, U.S.A.
3 "Point 4 Project Agreement with Jordan," No. 120, February 16, 1952, State Department Circular for Press, Clippings Folder, Box 62, George M. Elsey Papers, HSTL.

4 For a detailed history of the different proposals and how the Unified Plan was developed, see Dalal Musaed Alsayer, "Architecture, Environment, Development: The United States and the Making of Modern Arabia, 1949-1961" (PhD Dissertation, Philadelphia, PA, University of Pennsylvania, 2019), Ch. 4.
5 On the relationship between the New Deal and Point Four, see David Ekbladh, *The Great American Mission: Modernization and the Construction of an American World Order* (Princeton, NJ: Princeton University Press, 2011); Kiran Klaus Patel, *The New Deal: A Global History* (Princeton, NJ: Princeton University Press, 2017); Sarah Lorenzini, *Global Development: A Cold War History*, America in the World (Princeton, NJ: Princeton University Press, 2019).
6 For Point Four rhetoric, see Sergei Y. Shenin, *The United States and the Third World: The Origins of Postwar Relations and the Point Four Program* (Huntington, NY: Nova Science Publishers, Inc, 2000).
7 History of Aid, Box 1, Albert Huntington, HSTL.
8 Point IV Project Authorization, Project No. (1)1627731, Project Authorization by Country I-J Folder, Box 1, TCA Documents Compiled for use of the IDAB, 1951, Office of the Administrator, Technical Cooperation Administration, RG 469 Records of the Agency for International Development and Predecessor Agencies (hereafter RG 469), National Archives and Records Administration (NARA), College Park, MD (NARA).
9 Picture Captions, Folder 10, Box 1, Photographs Relating to U.S. Aid to Jordan 1953-1962, RG 469-J Records of U.S. Foreign Assistance Agencies, 1948–1961 (RG 469-J), NARA.
10 See, for example, International Development Advisory Board, *Partners in Progress: A Report to President Truman by the International Development Advisory Board* (New York, NY: Simon and Schuster, 1951).
11 Diana K. Davis, "Imperialism, Orientalism, and the Environment in the Middle East: History, Policy, Power and Practice," in *Environmental Imaginaries of the Middle East and North Africa*, Ecology and History (Athens, OH: Ohio University Press, 2011), 3.
12 See Deborah Fitzgerald, *Every Farm a Factory: The Industrial Ideal in American Agriculture*, Yale Agrarian Studies Series (New Haven, CT: Yale University Press, 2003); Daniel Immerwahr, *Thinking Small: The United States and the Lure of Community Development* (Cambridge, MA: Harvard University Press, 2015).
13 Sarah T. Phillips, *This Land, This Nation: Conservation, Rural America, and the New Deal* (Cambridge, UK: Cambridge University Press, 2007).
14 Donna C. Mehos and Suzanne M. Moon, "The Uses of Portability: Circulating Experts in the Technopolitics of Cold War and Decolonization," in *Entangled Geographies: Empire and Technopolitics in the Global Cold War*, ed. Gabrielle Hecht (Cambridge, MA: MIT Press, 2011), 43–74.
15 Bruno Latour, "Give Me a Laboratory and I Will Raise the World," in *Science Observed: Perspectives on the Social Study of Science* (London, UK: Sage Publications, 1983), 153–155.
16 Phillips, *This Land, This Nation: Conservation, Rural America, and the New Deal*, 19.
17 For a detailed analysis of the different proposals, see Alsayer, "Architecture, Environment, Development: The United States and the Making of Modern Arabia, 1949–1961," 253–64.
18 Chas. T. Main, "The Unified Development of the Water Resources of the Jordan Valley Region" (Boston, MA: United Nations, 1953).
19 Ibid. i.
20 Ibid. Introductory Remarks.
21 Timothy Mitchell, *Rule of Experts: Egypt, Techno-Politics, Modernity* (Berkeley, CA: University of California Press, 2002), 21.
22 On the role of gender and environment as it relates to the New Deal, see Neil M. Maher, *Nature's New Deal: The Civilian Conservation Corps and the Roots of the American Environmental Movement* (Oxford, New York: Oxford University Press, 2008); Francesca Russello Ammon, *Bulldozer: Demolition and Clearance of the Postwar Landscape* (New Haven, CT: Yale University Press, 2016).
23 On the export of the American Way via housing, see Fitzgerald, *Every Farm a Factory*.
24 See Lizabeth Cohen, *A Consumers' Republic: The Politics of Mass Consumption in Postwar America* (New York, NY: Vintage Books, 2004), Ch. 3.
25 Elaine Tyler May, *Homeward Bound: American Families in the Cold War Era*, 20th Anniversary Edition (New York, NY: Basic Books, 2008).
26 Robert A. Beauregard, *When America Became Suburban* (Minneapolis, MN: University of Minnesota Press, 2006), 165.
27 For more explanation on the sedentary and nomadic Arab lifestyle, see Farah Al-Nakib, "Revisiting Hadar and Badu in Kuwait: Citizenship, Housing, and the Construction of a Dichotomy," *International Journal of Middle Eastern Studies*, Urban and Rural Spaces 46, no. 1 (2014): 5–30.
28 Toby Dodge, *Inventing Iraq: The Failure of Nation-Building and a History Denied* (New York, NY: Columbia University Press, 2005), Ch. 5.
29 "Cooperatives as an Instrument of Democracy," Talk by Stanley Andrews, Administrator of the Technical Cooperative Administration, before the Biennial Congress of the Cooperative League, Chicago, Illinois, November 6, 1952, 11/6 Coop League of USA, Chicago, IL Folder, Box 7, Stanley Andrews Papers, HSTL.

30 Maher, *Nature's New Deal: The Civilian Conservation Corps and the Roots of the American Environmental Movement*.
31 See May, *Homeward Bound*.
32 Near East Foundation Annual Report of the Educational Director, October 1946, Box 6, RG 2, Near East Foundation (NEF), Rockefeller Archive Center, Sleepy Hollow, NY, U.S.A. (RAC), 9.
33 A Study of Community Development Opportunities in Jordan Including Community Loans, December 29, 1954, Jordan Reports: A Study of Community Development Opportunities in Jordan Folder, Box 72, Series 1: Project Files, Record Group 1, NEF, RAC.
34 Responses to Questions Compiled by the House Foreign Affairs Committee Relating to Criticisms of the Mutual Security Program, Response to Questions Compiled by the House Foreign Affairs Committee Folder, Box 3, Albert H. Huntington, Jr. Papers, HSTL.
35 Letter from the Vice President of the Municipality to the Person in Charge at Aqaba, April 6, 1961, Document No. 106/29/10/21; and Letter from Person in Charge at Aqaba to District Leader in Aqaba, May 30, 1961, Document No. 136/29/10/21/ف, Jordanian National Archives.
36 Betty S. Anderson, "Writing the Nation: Textbooks of the Hashemite Kingdom of Jordan," *Comparative Studies of South Asia, Africa and the Middle East* 21, nos 1–2 (2001): 5–14.

23
SHAPED FROM ABOVE
Cartographic Domination and U.S. Military Infrastructure in 1950s Spain

José Vela Castillo

During the 1950s the U.S. established an impressive set of military bases in Spain. Following a mutual defense agreement signed in 1953 that sealed a strategic alliance between the two countries, the formerly excluded from the community of western nations Francoist Spain became part of the new strategic board of the Cold War. The U.S. "Empire" expanded across the globe, encircling the USSR and its allies with a net of military installations in foreign "friend" countries. A distinct cartographic power that emerged after the extensive air bombing experiences of WWII based in aerial photography was deployed in the form of infrastructural control of the territory. This power had its material incarnation in Spain in the construction of four main bases (three for the USAF and one for the Navy) plus secondary facilities linked by a dense network of communications systems and an underground pipeline. This chapter examines the cartographic studies of the 1940s and the subsequent development of military infrastructure in the 1950s in order to trace the extent of global spatial domination established by the U.S. in Spain following the end of World War II.

On March 29, 1958 the honorable Katharine St. George, member of the Armed Services Committee of the U.S. House of the Representatives, a Republican and, incidentally, cousin of Franklin Delano Roosevelt, landed in Madrid, Spain. She was about to start a detailed inspection of the military bases that the U.S. was building in the country. In a little more than a week she visited the five main installations under construction—Torrejón, Zaragoza, Rota, Morón, and San Pablo—returning home on April 7 to deliver a detailed report to the Congressional Committee. After declaring that "there is no better place for European bases than Spain," she offered the following remark:

> Spain is ideally suited [for housing the U.S. military bases], protected by the Pyrenees and the waters of the Atlantic and the Mediterranean. Her vast plains are well suited to runways, because there is room for what we need at the present and room for enlargement and lengthening of runways, if necessary, in the future.[1]

That a Congresswoman in a supervising capacity and in such a quick visit to Spain was so clear in her understanding of the primarily geographical and infrastructural dimension of the military bases' construction program seems telling. That she spoke about Spain, a sovereign foreign country, as if it were empty land ready to be used at will, disturbing. Her report, in any case, clearly demonstrates how ingrained was the U.S. presumption of the right to "cartographic domination" of space.[2] Given Spain's geopolitical importance as well as its own infrastructural deficiencies, the development of the postwar military bases perfectly demonstrates how the Cold War expansionist ideology of the United States dovetailed with national development goals of a European country that had suffered much over the last two decades.

In 1953, the U.S. and Spain signed the *Pactos de Madrid*, an agreement that sealed a strategic alliance between the two countries. From this pact, the U.S. established four main military bases along a diagonal line that crossed Spain from Southwest to Northeast. One base served the Navy and three served the USAF. All boasted long runways and extensive auxiliary facilities, secondary installations, and a communications network. The vast infrastructure project was expanded and deepened over the following decades, and much of it continues to be used today. However, the military bases program of the 1950s was not the start but the culmination of a broader interest in the Iberian Peninsula that began with the revision of the whole cartography of Spain during the war years, and followed with the project of a full aerial photogrammetric coverage for the production of detailed mapping of the country.

This chapter examines the cartographic studies of the 1940s and the subsequent development of military infrastructure in the 1950s in order to trace the extent of global spatial domination established by the U.S. in Spain following the end of World War II. I argue that, building upon an incremental, transnational, and geopolitical understandings of infrastructure, the U.S. Spanish Bases program greatly expanded the deployment of the "from above" power paradigm, now based in aerial photography, that re-shaped the world. In this sense, the base program constitutes one of the most complete and overarching incarnations of an imperial power shaping global territory from above.

Mapping Spain

The sound of the four cyclone engines of the B17f aircraft roared over the deserted landscape of Spain 20,000 feet below. The day was clear and especially cold toward the end of February 1946 (Figure 23.1).

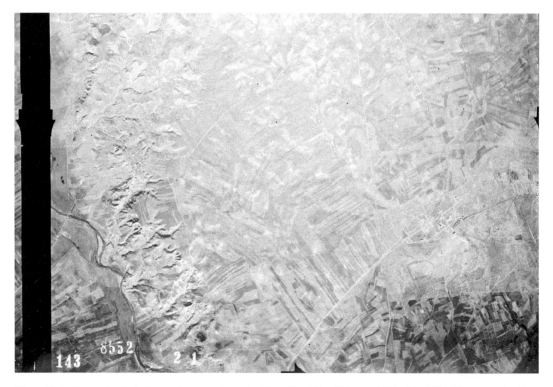

Figure 23.1 Torrejón de Ardoz landscape, where the Torrejón AB will be established in 1954. Photograph taken February 25, 1946, "Vuelo Americano serie A."

Source: Centro Nacional de Información Geográfica, Instituto Geográfico Nacional. CC-BY 4.0.

The plane was part of the U.S. 306th Bombardment Group, but its mission was quite different this time. The gunner, cramped in the small compartment with his gaze fixed on the intervalometer while the plane kept the given line of flight, could barely hear the continuous click of the Fairchild K-17B aircraft camera. He was shooting images and not dropping bombs, the targets not to be destroyed but preserved.[3] Yet the close connection between the military view and aerial photography remains.[4]

Mapping, cartography, and surveying have always been instruments of control and power, since the clay tablets used in Babylonia (like the Nippur map of around 1500 BCE). Every empire, from the Persians and the Romans to the Spanish and the British have created detailed instruments of land description tied to infrastructure and domination. The postwar U.S. global expansion was no exception, and the U.S. military deployed mapping and cartography on an unprecedented scale to facilitate this expansion even if, as Neil Smith points out, "[T]he emerging American Empire defined its power in the first place through the more abstract geography of the world market rather than through direct political control of territory."[5]

The U.S. Army Map Service was formed at the beginning of World War II as a reorganization of existing services under the command of the U.S. Army Corps of Engineers. The Map Service produced an extensive cartographic survey of Europe between 1941 and 1945, mainly by compiling and redrawing existing maps. Even if Spain did not enter the war, its strategic position led to the urgent effort by the British and the Americans to build up a detailed cartography of the country. The Army Map Service started to work in Spain in 1941, and between 1943 and 1945 its staff compiled, redrew, and published up to 253 topographic maps at 1:50,000 scale, focusing on the Southern Atlantic, the Mediterranean, and the Balearic Islands.[6] The planimetry of some of the coastal areas was revised with the aid of aerial photography, taken during 1941 and 1942 by the British Royal Air Force (Figure 23.2).[7]

With the war in Europe approaching its end, the need for accurate cartography of Western Europe continued as part of the post-war reconfiguration of forces. If by 1940 both the State Department and the Council of Foreign Relations were already planning the postwar political geography of the world, as well as the new transnational institutions that would regulate it (United Nations, World Bank, International Monetary Fund), the end of the hostilities marked the moment when these strategies could be implemented. The key strategic challenge, from the U.S. point of view, was to contain the spread of communism without having to hold vast territories militarily, as European empires had done.[8] For some at the State Department it was clear that the transformations in war technology, especially the generalization of air power and the advances in communications, would render obsolete the old notions of holding territory. Instead, command and control could be effected at range over distance through naval and air power, thereby securing sovereign borders, ensuring free markets, and spreading American democratic ideals.[9]

As part of this strategic endeavor, the U.S. military launched Project Casey Jones in June 1945 with the aim to produce a comprehensive cartographic survey of Western Europe using aerial photogrammetry. This required agreements with the various European governments to continue allowing American military aircraft to fly over their territories.

To this end, U.S. ambassador Carlton J.H. Hayes and Spanish Foreign Affairs Minister José Félix de Lequerica signed an agreement on air transport services on December 2, 1944.[10] At first the agreement only allowed commercial U.S. aircraft to operate in Spain. However, an additional protocol signed in February 1945 allowed the U.S. Air Transport Command to conduct "non-military" flights over Spain, which was a neutral country.[11] Under this cover, the U.S. gained informal permission to do an aerial photographic survey of Spain with the intention to produce detailed new cartography. The flights took place mainly in 1945 and 1946, with occasional follow-up runs through 1949.[12]

The Army Map Service was in charge of the cartographic work that followed, and in 1953 produced a new updated version of the Spanish topographic map (scale=1:50,000) which remained classified for U.S. military use. However, the quality of the photographs taken in the 1945–1946 flights over Spain were suboptimal, and the need for more accurate maps grew as the U.S. military presence expanded.

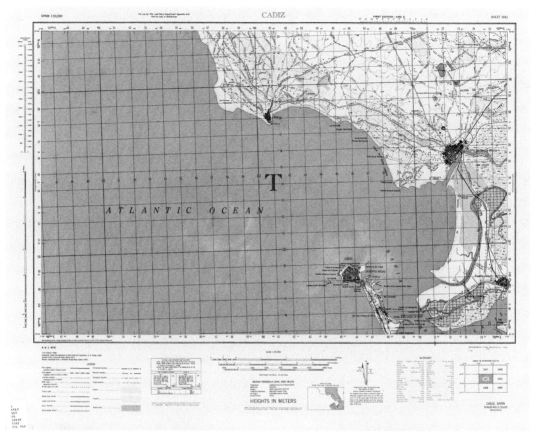

Figure 23.2 Sheet 1061, "Cadiz." Map of Spain at 1:50,000 produced by the Army Map Service. The small village of Rota, where the US Naval Station was to be established in 1954, is seen in the upper center.

Source: University of Texas Libraries.

To this end, the U.S. and Spain reached new agreements in 1953 and 1955 that enabled a new comprehensive aerial photographic survey. This time, the project would be overseen by the United States Air Forces in Europe, and conducted by the AMS with the participation of the Spanish military. Flight took place between March 1956 and September 1957.[13] In the following years the AMS produced an updated version of the Spanish cartographic chart, much more precise and detailed that any previous Spanish map. AMS staff shared the photographs with their Spanish counterparts at the moment they were taken.

The AMS used a suite of cartographic elements for mapmaking, including planimetry, altimetry, UTM coordinates, and geodetic vertices; together these comprised the basis for subsequent maps made by the Spaniards for the next 20 years. The first photogrammetric flight that Spain realized independently was not undertaken until 1975. In this sense, the "cartographic domination of space," as architectural theorist Mark L. Gillem argues, "rather than actual control of large swaths of foreign land became the American model. Once the United States could map and measure independent nations, officials could then watch over these nations, which may require economic, political, or military control."[14]

Negotiating Power through Infrastructure after World War II

Cartographic power, of course, was never enough; it needed people and materials in motion to activate it. If the U.S. was to control markets and allegiances without holding territory, it would need infrastructure to mobilize its force strength. U.S. Bases in Spain, then, were crucial for supporting this overall strategy of planning and domination from above—not of a given territory, but as part of a broader world-building strategy. The bases constituted one element of a comprehensive global program of military infrastructure to be built from scratch and almost without limitations of territory, money, or sovereignty. Spain had remained nominally neutral during the war and was never occupied, but in the Cold War geopolitical landscape the country took full advantage of U.S. funding and expertise as a bulwark against Soviet influence.

Beginning in the early 1950s, the U.S. government sent military and technical missions to Spain to study the country's geographic, logistical, and infrastructural conditions as part of base pre-planning. The missions had access to the full aerial photography coverage produced by the AMS, which retained better cartographical and territorial information than the Spanish themselves. The U.S. did not have any interest in the control of Spanish territory *per se*, but in taking advantage of its geopolitical and strategic value. The usual nostrums about expanding democracy and freedom were also clearly undermined by their willingness to bargain with the last fascist regime in Europe as part of the effort to contain communism.

The fact remained that Spain offered a strong logistical choice for the establishment of U.S. air and naval outposts at the beginning of the 1950s. From there, the U.S. could exert both a deterrent and retaliatory force in keeping with the policy of "containment" of Soviet ambitions, and in the process, it could secure U.S. global access to the markets of the world. The Spanish bases would be, accordingly, part of a bigger design to deploy massive infrastructural networks across Europe and the Mediterranean, transcending the borders of the various nations.[15] A big part of this broad project of defense of the West was implemented by means of the North Atlantic Organization Treaty (NATO). However, owing to the mistrust if not direct contempt of the Franco regime from most of the European countries, especially Britain and France, Spain did not enter NATO (although it eventually would in 1982 after Franco's death and in the democratic period), which meant that a different type of agreement was necessary.

It is in the cauldron of postwar rebuilding and remilitarization that the term "infrastructure" comes into common parlance in military, logistical, and diplomatic circles. The use of the term in English was limited during the early twentieth century to engineers discussing translational projects with their French (and also Spanish) counterparts. It is only after World War II that the word starts to acquire its contemporary meaning, particularly with the creation of the NATO "Common Infrastructure Program" in 1949.[16] In a 1953 report for the U.S. Congress after a Special Study Mission to Europe, the Representatives felt the obligation to provide a definition, putting the word inside quotation marks:

> The term "infrastructure" means the fixed installations in support of military forces. It is a French word, ordinarily used to refer to the roadbed of a railway, which has been adopted by NATO. Included in the infrastructure program are airfields, jet fuel distribution and storage installations, signal communications, and war headquarters.[17]

The shift that the use of the word introduces goes in two directions: to the distributed and additive integration of different parts that should work within a system, and to the supranational implementation and regulation of them since they will spread, materially and operationally, across different states.[18] This concept of infrastructure fully permeated the postwar U.S. bases program.

After securing bases in the Portuguese Azores Islands (a new agreement with Portugal was reached in 1951) and Libya (Wheelus Air Base), the U.S. designed a set of bases in the French Protectorate of Morocco (1950–1953). Spain came next to reinforce the Southeast flank of Europe and the entrance to the Mediterranean. Tentative diplomatic approaches between Spain and the U.S. commenced in 1947, but negotiations started in earnest after Admiral Forrest P. Sherman, the Chief of Naval Operations visited Franco on July 16, 1951. From the beginning, the interest of the U.S. was two-fold: first, to establish naval bases to control de Gibraltar straits (beyond the British outpost) and provide a safe haven for the Sixth Fleet patrolling the Mediterranean; and second, to establish air bases that could be integrated into the USAF Strategic Air Command (SAC).[19] Even if the U.S. already had British and Moroccan bases assigned to it (plus the Greek and Turkish installations), Spain offered a perfect complementary location. For Spain, the objective was also two-fold: political backing from the main Western power to the internationally isolated Franco regime, and urgent economic aid for her derelict economy after years of autarky and stagnation.

Planning the U.S. Bases in Cold War Spain

On August 22nd, 1951, the U.S. government sent two study missions to Spain, one military and one civil, to conduct an in-depth survey of the real situation of the country and the best options and sites for the intended bases. Led by Major General James W. Spry, the Joint Survey Team comprised six additional officers, two from each military branch, and up to 30 technicians. Over the course of two months, the team visited and reviewed multiple locations and existing military and logistical facilities to evaluate their suitability for U.S. needs. Using the extensive and detailed topographic maps developed in the 1940s, they focused on the Mediterranean and North Atlantic coast for the Navy and the three main inner plateaus better suited for airfield operations in the Mediterranean eastern flank: the river Ebro valley, the plateau of La Mancha, and the Guadalquivir depression. These areas were aligned in a Southwest to Northeast diagonal with the Moroccan bases with Moscow as the ultimate destination.

The team broke into several subunits to consider various aspects of Spanish geography and society. The Temporary Economy Survey Group, for example, was led by Sidney C. Suffrin of the Economic Cooperation Administration. Suffrin's group examined the (precarious) situation of the Spanish economy to know the extent of economic aid that the U.S. might need to be in exchange for the bases.[20] Per the group's recommendation, the U.S. devoted a portion of the aid package for investment in basic Spanish infrastructure, such as the railroad system, road transportation, and ports, all to facilitate the construction of the bases and to assure their operability. The military proposed a set of tentative locations specifying the use of the installations and evaluating the necessary investments to meet the U.S. standards in already existing facilities.

Negotiations were not easy. The fundamental positions were clear, but there was a lot of bargaining: the U.S. wanted the maximum freedom in the disposition and use of the bases, with minimum commitments to economic help or to military assistance in the defense of Spain. The Spaniards wanted maximum international recognition, expanded economic aid, and modern military equipment. While the U.S. made some concessions in the process, scholars have noted that in the end, American negotiators prevailed in their overarching aims, likely more a sign of Spanish desperation than Yankee bargaining skills.[21] Finally, on September 26 1953, the state parties signed the bilateral Pact of Madrid covering a term of ten years, after which they could be revised and extended for two additional periods of five years. The Pact consisted in three main agreements; a Defense Agreement, an Economic Aid Agreement, and a Mutual Defense Assistance Agreement, plus some additional protocols.[22] They also included additional agreements that remained secret at the moment of signature. One of them was the Technical Agreement that details how the bases would be implemented.

The first Annex of the Technical Agreement provides a detailed description of the intended bases and secondary installations, plus their military expected use (Figure 23.3).[23] The backbone of the design was a set of air bases that supported the operations of the Strategic Air Command, including two main bases for long range B-47 heavy bombers (that could reach the heartland of the Soviet Union). These would be located in the southeast of the Peninsula in Los Llanos, Albacete and in Morón, Seville, and would be protected by fighter and reconnaissance bases towards the northeast and center of the Peninsula in Zaragoza, Reus, and Torrejón.

Cartographic Domination

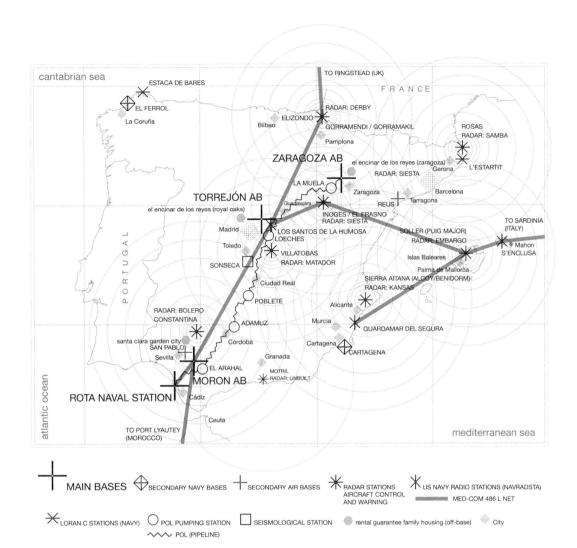

Figure 23.3 Distribution of the U.S. bases in Spain, ca. 1959.

Source: José Vela Castillo.

The system's headquarters would be built near Madrid (Figure 23.4). Meanwhile, secondary air bases were planned in El Copero and Los Palacios, and additional bases in Alcalá and San Pablo. To supply the oil and lubricants needed for the aircrafts, the various installations were to be linked by a 485-mile pipeline running from its terminal on the southwest Atlantic coast, in Rota (Cádiz) to Zaragoza. The terminal, in turn, would be protected by the Navy's main base, which included a runaway for Navy air operations. Two secondary bases for the Navy were also planned for storage of fuel and ammunition, and for technical installations.

The Technical Agreement also granted the rights to build the necessary aircraft control and warning stations as well as the network of communications that linked them. This network would grow in complexity over the next several decades to include a range of elements: a microwave communication system connected to the European USAF system via tropospheric antennae (ten stations); a long-distance radio system (three stations); two Loran-C stations for the Navy connected with U.S.

Figure 23.4 Torrejón AFB in construction, ca. 1957.

Source: U.S. Embassy Photographic Collection. Universidad de Alcalá de Henares, Madrid. CC-BY-NC-ND 4.0.

and NATO; and a group of seven radar stations. Not all of the sites mentioned in the agreements were actually used, but the extension of the intervention remained of vast in scale, covering a significant amount of the territory, with focus on the Mediterranean coast and emphasis in supranational connectivity.

The design started shortly after signing the Madrid Pact, and initial construction began by late 1954, with most bases fully operational in 1958 and 1959. A complex bureaucratic framework supported the design, with the Navy Bureau of Yards and Docks as the office in charge, Architects and Engineers Spanish Bases (AESB) as the design office and Brown-Raymond-Walsh as the main contractor.[24] AESB was a joint venture formed by two engineering firms, Frederic R. Harris, Inc. from New York and Metcalf & Eddy from Boston and by two architectural firms, Pereira and Luckman from Los Angeles and Shaw, Metz & Dolio from Chicago. AESB acted in Spain as a modern architecture and engineering consultancy firm, coordinating an important group of technicians, engineers, and architects from his offices in Madrid. Frederick Lothian Langhorst, an architect with a substantial career (he had been a Taliesin fellow from 1931 to 1936), working at this moment in Paris for Daniel, Mann, Johnson, and Mendenhall, was hired as chief designer. Prominent Spanish architects also worked both within AESB, such as Luis Vazquez de Castro, or as external collaborators, such as Francisco de Asís Cabrero, Damian Galmés, or Fernando Moreno Barberá.[25]

Figure 23.5 Rota Naval Station in the 1960s.

Source: U.S. Embassy Photographic Collection. Universidad de Alcalá de Henares, Madrid. CC-BY-NC-ND 4.0.

The resulting architecture designs followed post-war International Style models, producing functional and almost standardized designs for the different installations. The construction systems were, however, adapted to the local materials and building capacities, since in the Agreements it was stated that the Spanish construction industry should be in charge of the construction whereas possible. The use of exposed brick (plastered in the Southern bases), or the absence of American prefabricated systems and wood construction was the norm, in a soft power effort to integrate the constructions in the local environment (Figure 23.5).

Through the process of design and construction, the U.S. defense strategy evolved and reoriented. The new B52 long range bombers (8,800 miles against the 3,500 of the B47) became operational in 1955, which meant that the Spanish bases were not as necessary to station the planes, but more for maintenance, recovery, and refueling. In addition, operations in the Middle East grew increasingly important to U.S. geopolitical interests. Perhaps most importantly, by the mid-1960s, the U.S. had established its intercontinental ballistic missile and submarine-launched ballistic missile systems, changing the scope and scale of logistical operations forever. None of this rendered the bases in Spain obsolete as much as it involved them in an ever-changing set of technological, logistical, and diplomatic entanglements, requiring continual adjustment over the course of the Cold War.

Conclusion

The U.S. bases program reveals some of the key social, spatial, and political dimensions embedded in the concept of infrastructure. Materially, the bases comprised a grand ensemble of airfields, living quarters, antennae arrays, ports, roads, rail lines, concrete underground ammunition silos, a subterranean pipeline, and all the associated hardware. Yet contrary to civilian infrastructures, the bases produced only very indirect revenues in the sites where they were located, demanding on the contrary a constant influx of dollars to keep them operative. At the same time, the bases catalyzed a vastly expanded immaterial network of high frequency microwaves, long wave radio signals, radar pulses, codes, protocols, and routines. All the while, this network of material and immaterial elements underpinned a global ideological conflict, reshaping the geopolitical order of things. The bases supported the movement of ships, planes, persons, and weapons as much as information across their tight communication network.

In the end, what they actually circulated is power itself—power as a distributed entity, which flows across the bases as military might, economic investment, and ideological influence, and that is transferred through the intercommunicated network to distant places. The bases overcame the power of the state where they were deployed, practically imposing a domination that is realized from the air, and is articulated as a network of non-sovereign power as applied to a given and circumscribed territory. Inside the bases only their own local (i.e. American) rules applied, effectively creating a state of exception within the Spanish territory.

As instruments of incredible and potentially devastating power, the U.S. bases in Spain subverted traditional notions of local dominion by locating power extra-territorially as part of a broader network of interests whose aim was fundamentally ideological (the process of Americanization), however keeping the old disadvantages of located power. As Ashley Carse puts it, they need to be considered as "both abstractions and material assemblages."[26] Yet they are also material representations of a power that, definitely, has gone global. The U.S. bases construct an infrastructural network for a territory that *does not exist* as such, that is located elsewhere, or that exist only as an effect of the infrastructural deployment itself. In that sense, they seem to be the perfect example of an ultimately successful project of deterritorialization of power that still lasts today.

Notes

1 Katharine St. George, *Report on Inspection of Spanish Bases of Torrejon, Zaragoza, San Pablo, Moron, and Rota* (Washington, DC: United States Government Printing Office, 1958), 1.
2 "Cartographic domination" is a term used by Mark L. Gillem in *America Town: Building the Outposts of Empire* (Minneapolis, MN: University of Minnesota Press, 2007), 285 note 4.
3 As the Swiss author and architect Max Frisch wrote: "Flying over a small town that looks like one of our architecture models, I involuntarily discover that I would be able to drop bombs on it." Max Frisch, "Nach einem Flug," in *Tagebuch 1946–1949*. Translated by the author. Thanks to Sıla Karataş for this quote.
4 See Paul Virilio, *War and Cinema: The Logistics of Perception* (New York: Verso, 1989); see also Caren Kaplan, *Aerial Aftermaths: Wartime from Above* (Durham, NC: Duke University Press, 2018), who provides a more critical view.
5 Neil Smith, *American Empire. Roosevelt's Geographer and the Prelude to Globalization* (Berkeley, CA: University of California Press, 2003), 19.
6 Luis Urteaga, Francesc Nadal, and José Ignacio Muro, "Los mapas de España del Army Map Service," *Eria* 51 (2000): 31–43.
7 Felipe Fernández García, "Un vuelo del litoral andaluz de 1942-43," *Ería* 87 (2012): 39–49.
8 Smith, *American Empire*, 353.
9 Ibid. 344.
10 Air Transportation Agreement signed at Madrid, December 2, 1944 in Department of State Executive Agreement Series No. 432, or 58 Stat. (pt. 2) 1473.
11 *Foreign Relations of the United States: Diplomatic Papers 1945, Volume V, Europe* (Washington, DC: United States Government Printing Office, 1967), 724.

12 Felipe Fernández García and Francisco Quirós Linares, "El vuelo fotográfico de la 'Serie A'," *Eria* 43 (1997): 190–198.
13 Anexo número 1 al Acuerdo Técnico. Adquisición y desarrollo de las zonas, servidumbres e instalaciones convenidas. Acuerdo Técnico Anejo al Convenio defensivo, Madrid 26 de septiembre de 1953 (Secreto). Archivo General de la Administración, Alcalá de Henares. Sig 82/21130.
14 Gillem, *America Town*, 285 note 4.
15 For example, the U.S. had nuclear weapons deployed in non-nuclear NATO countries, yet the decision of triggering them was only in the hands of the president of the U.S.
16 See Ashley Carse, "Keyword: Infrastructure. How a humble French engineering term shaped the modern world," in *Infrastructures and Social Complexity. A Companion*, ed. Penny Harvey, Casper Bruun Jensen, and Atsuro Morita (New York: Routledge, 2017), 27–39.
17 *Report. Special Study Mission to Europe: April 3–16, 1953* (Washington, DC: United States Government Printing Office, 1953), 1.
18 Like, for example, pipelines. See Jost Delbrück, "International Law and Military Forces Abroad: U.S. Military Presence in Europe, 1945-1965" in *US Military Forces in Europe: The Early Years 1945–1970*, ed. S. Duke and W. Krieger (Boulder, CO: Westview, 1993), 101.
19 The mission of the SAC was of nuclear deterrence against the Soviet Union, assuring to retaliate immediately any attack with overwhelming capacity.
20 *Foreign Relations of the United States, 1951. Europe: Political and Economic Developments*, Volume IV, Part 1 (Washington, DC: U.S. Government Printing Office, 1951), 838.
21 See B.N. Liedtke, *Embracing Dictatorship. United States Relations with Spain, 1945–1953* (New York: Macmillan, 1997) and Ángel Viñas, *En las garras del águila. Los pactos con Estados Unidos, de Francisco Franco a Felipe González, 1945-1995* (Barcelona: Crítica, 2003).
22 See *Boletín Oficial del Estado*, 2 October 1953.
23 Acuerdo Técnico Anejo al Convenio defensivo, Madrid, 26 September 1953 (Secreto). Archivo General de la Administración, Alcalá de Henares, Sig 82/21130.
24 See *US Navy Civil Engineering Corps Bulletin* 8, no. 10 (October 1954): 6–9; 9, no. 10 (October 1955): 8–9 and 11, no. 7 (July 1957).
25 Luis Bilbao Larrondo, "El debate en torno a la Influencia de la arquitectura estadounidense en España: Los arquitectos Luis Vázquez de Castro, Valentín Picatoste y las Memorias de los técnicos españoles en EE. UU.," in *La arquitectura norteamericana, motor y espejo de la arquitectura española en el arranque de la modernidad (1940–1965)* (Pamplona: T6 Ediciones, 2006) and Pilar Salazar Lozano, "Un impulso transatlantico. Canales de influencia de la arquitectura estadounidense en España. 1945-1960," PhD diss. (Universidad de Navarra, Pamplona, 2018). Pilar Salazar devoted a well-documented chapter of her doctoral dissertation to the design and construction of the U.S. bases in Spain.
26 Carse, "Keyword: Infrastructure. How a Humble French Engineering Term Shaped the Modern World," 35.

PART VIII

Liquid Worlds

24
WATER AND INFRASTRUCTURE IN LATE COLONIAL GUANAJUATO

Luis Gordo Peláez

On the evening of July 27, 1780, a major rainstorm overflowed Guanajuato's river, inundating the city's center and resulting in numerous fatalities and damage. This type of environmental adversity was not unknown to residents; powerful floods had often ravaged the central districts of Guanajuato, a city that had originated as a mining camp in the mid-sixteenth century. Situated in El Bajío, an extraordinary economic hub for colonial Mexico and one of the most developed areas in eighteenth-century Spanish America, Guanajuato's silver bonanza was not without its drawbacks. Its location amid the slopes of a mountain range proved to be a continuous challenge for the shaping of its urban space and built fabric, evolving in a pattern of steep and irregular streets. Likewise, the city's mining industry directed the urban expansion along the course of the Guanajuato River and influenced the design of public infrastructures to ameliorate the living conditions of its population. Although the city had recently embarked on a number of projects (including the completion of two dams); by the late eighteenth century, Guanajuato was facing increasing difficulties in water and food supply, sanitation, and public health. The latest flood deepened its infrastructure problems, as well as the precarious existence of Guanajuato's residents in this urban environment. News soon reached the colonial government in Mexico City demanding urgent attention, funds, and expertise to reshape Guanajuato's unfit infrastructures, a move that mirrors urban and built initiatives in other Spanish American dominions. This chapter presents an account of proposed and designed water-related infrastructures for Guanajuato (dams, bridges, river channeling) and how they reflected contemporary urban ideals and building practices, notions of utility and good governance, and discourses of spatial rationality, public health, sanitation, and civic order.

Four days on horseback north of Mexico City, the Real de Minas de Santa Fe de Guanajuato lies nestled in the mountains of the silver-rich Bajío region. The city emerged in the eighteenth century as an economic hub for colonial Mexico. Large mansions and new religious foundations were added to the original urban core of the Plaza Mayor and the Plaza de San Diego, where the parish church and the convent of the barefoot Franciscans had been erected in the previous century. Soon afterward, the Jesuits opened a school and the Bethlehemites established a hospital, a much-needed medical facility for the growing population of mine workers in the city and its nearby communities. By 1800, Guanajuato ranked among the most urbanized areas of Spanish America.

The city's silver bonanza was not without drawbacks. Its location, on the hillside of a ridge of mountains, proved to be a continuous challenge for the shaping of its urban space and built fabric, evolving in a pattern of irregular and sloping streets. In 1764, Francisco de Ajofrín described Guanajuato as "a city of confusion, surrounded by craggy peaks, some high, others low … denying its residents plains and flatlands to form their houses." For this Spanish friar, Guanajuato had "neither land for farming, nor any comfort for living, since nature was so scarce that even water, that abounds in any other land, was denied [here]."[1] Also, the city's mining industry dictated urban expansion along the river course, which came with its own set of problems. Therefore, much of the public infrastructures and urban initiatives in late colonial Guanajuato were designed to tackle adverse conditions, particularly those regarding water supply and water management. This chapter traces the development of the city's water-related infrastructures and how they reflected contemporary urban ideals and building practices, discourses of utility and good governance, and notions of spatial rationality, public health, sanitation, and order.

Water Supply

Reading through the city council minutes from the eighteenth century, one quickly discerns the two main preoccupations of Guanajuato's authorities: the supply of drinking water and the recurrence of flash floods. In 1788, alderman José Hernández Chico praised the abundance of nearby springs that supplemented the wells and *aljibes* (tanks) in the houses of the local elite.[2] Also, the Guanajuato River and other small waterways flowed through the city. And yet water supply would be a pressing problem throughout the 1700s. As Spanish naval officer and scientist Antonio de Ulloa noted in 1777, Guanajuato, with its semi-arid climate, bore the dual misfortune of torrential downpours and floods in the rainy season (June-September) and terrible droughts in the dry season (October-May).[3]

In 1738, three years before being chartered as a city, Guanajuato's *cabildo* (town council) appointed *peritos* (experts) Leopoldo Eugenio Palacios, Juan Esteban Zerrato, and Tiburcio Manuel Subías to inspect the area's natural qualities. In a mountainous location, nine leguas (23 miles) north of the city, they identified four springs that would be sufficient to supply Guanajuato with drinking water.[4] The project to carry that water to the city, however, would be monumental. It would include a pool on site to collect it and a masonry *atarjea* (canal) for its conduction, in some stretches supported by arches and piers to traverse the steep topography. Its completion time was estimated to be five years; its cost, an exorbitant amount ranging from 140,000 to 200,000 pesos.[5] The proposal for this massive water infrastructure was timely. That same year, the city of Querétaro saw the completion of its monumental aqueduct, a celebrated infrastructure whose fame soon spread across New Spain.[6] However, Guanajuato's project remained on the drawing board, despite obtaining viceregal support, presumably because the cost and the technological challenges were too great.[7]

By mid-century, Guanajuato's population was steadily growing and the limited access to water was becoming a major problem. Several years of droughts prompted the *cabildo* to investigate other alternatives closer to the city. After eight years of work and funding delays, the municipal government completed La Olla Dam or *Presa Grande* in 1749 at the more reasonable cost of 24,000 pesos.[8] (Figure 24.1) Its masonry-buttressed wall topped by statues would be replicated in two more public dams three decades later. Referring to the city's water scarcity, Ajofrín stated, "a large dam was necessary to build in one of the small valleys to the east [of the city center]." This was, he concluded, "a magnificent and useful work, and although the water is not the best, it supplies the city by being carried in loads."[9]

Discussions of a second dam began soon. In 1756, architect Felipe de Ureña, and masons Paulino Gabriel Suárez and Salvador Cayetano Yáñez submitted the budget and design of a new structure in the Olla Chica, a site located just above the first dam.[10] Ureña estimated a cost of nearly 50,000 pesos for construction of the dam and a 1.3-mile atarjea carrying freshwater to four basins in different parts of the city.[11] However, the proposal to fund it through new taxes on tobacco, wines, and liquors prompted local merchants to oppose the idea, questioning the expertise and credentials of its designer. As Fátima Halcón has shown, the protests reached Mexico City, where some renowned surveyors and architects experienced in hydraulic infrastructures (Felipe de Zúñiga Ontiveros, Lorenzo Rodríguez, Manuel Álvarez) rejected the project, challenging its underestimated cost, incorrect measurements, and faulty design.[12] This negative response also evinced the tension and competition between guild masters and between creole and European builders in the viceregal

Water in Late Colonial Guanajuato

Figure 24.1 Vista de la Presa Grande (Guanajuato). In *Album mexicano: colección de paisajes, monumentos, costumbres y ciudades principales de la república/litografiadas por C. Castro, A. Gallice, M. Mohar, E. Perez y J. Alvarez*. Mexico: Antigua litografía Debray Sucs., C. Montauriol, [1875-1885].

Source: Agencia Española de Cooperación Internacional para el Desarrollo. Biblioteca (3RC-398).

capital. Ultimately the scheme went unrealized, and the plans have been lost, but the same location would be chosen for the nineteenth-century San Renovato Dam. Ureña himself remained active in Guanajuato for the next two decades, but his peripatetic career also led him to work in disparate regions, from Mexico City to Zacatecas to Oaxaca. Indeed, given their experience working in such rough terrain, engineers, surveyors, and architects working in the Bajío region found themselves in demand for mining and agricultural commissions, land and watercourse surveys, and infrastructure projects throughout the country.

In the 1770s, water remained in insufficient supply for the rapidly expanding Guanajuato mining district. Discussions to pipe it from La Olla Dam using the natural incline of the landscape had continued for two decades, but nothing materialized. Even while Guanajuato's colonial aldermen held out hope for a water atarjea, they moved ahead with a second dam as a more practical solution to the immediate crisis. From the new chosen site, Los Pozuelos, water could be carried to the city's western barrios beyond the San Ignacio Bridge (San Roque, Belén, Venado, and the mines), allowing the first dam to be emptied and cleaned without interrupting Guanajuato's water supply. Work at Los Pozuelos Dam proceeded slowly and officials had to adjust its underestimated costs (9,000 pesos) during construction. Designed by Anastasio Miguel Urrutia in 1790, the dam's fabric consisted of a buttressed wall topped by four statues, seen as protectors of this waterwork and emblems of the city's identity and piety: Santa Fe, Nuestra Señora de Guanajuato, Saint Peter of Alcántara, and Saint

Figure 24.2 Anastasio Miguel de Urrutia, Los Pozuelos Dam, 1790.

Source: Archivo Histórico de la Universidad de Guanajuato, Guanajuato, Fondo Ayuntamiento, Aguas, Caja 1, Exp. 6.

Ignatius of Loyola (Figure 24.2). The municipal government submitted Urrutia's design to the viceroy in Mexico City, along with the petition for additional funds for the dam's completion. Urrutia's colored drawing evoke the late Mexican baroque, with voluptuous ornamentation and intricate repeating forms, just a few years before a reformist aesthetic agenda of sober, classical motifs swept the country. The extra cost was approved, and the dam finally completed in July 1791.[13]

By the late eighteenth century, the two dams at Guanajuato, along with a third one (Los Santos), built in 1778 by *maestro mayor* (chief architect) José Alejandro Durán in the nearby refining town of Marfil, supplied water to these populous mining settlements. However, without piping, water from the reservoirs still had to be carried by a legion of *aguadores* (water sellers) on mules or by foot. Thus, freshwater scarcity remained a vivid problem for many residents, particularly for those living in small dwellings without cisterns or the means to afford its purchase. In 1777, *procurador general* (the city's attorney representing the public interest) Francisco de Azpilcueta alluded to this when advocating for Los Pozuelos Dam, for it would reduce by half the purchase price of water in the western barrios.[14] Equally clarifying is a 1786 petition to Guanajuato's *cabildo* against a project to remove gutters from the city's buildings and replace them with pipes embedded in their fabrics. As the petitioner argued, the proposed interior conduits were costly to build, fragile to maintain, and vulnerable to blockages. Furthermore, the water pouring from the existent external channels was used for laundering and drinking, particularly by the poor who often were seen, "after the rains, collecting the water carried off by the gutters in their barrels and pots, and with it bathing and supplying their homes." The function of these gutters was of the utmost importance for a place where water was scarce, expensive, and even unhealthy, given that the public dam often turned muddy and dirty during the rainy season. Appealing to the good judgement of the city officials in keeping "those gutters that were always used in Guanajuato, in the entire kingdom [of New Spain] and even in Spain," the petitioner inquired: "would it not be harmful and detrimental to deprive the residents from [both] this abundant assistance that they take from the public gutters, and from their delight in an essential nourishment that comes down from heaven?"[15]

Water Management

In its effort to capture and control water, colonial Guanajuato faced similar challenges to other urbanized regions, including the capital. Both cities were regularly exposed to seasonal floods, and their inhabitants worked to establish dominion over water. In both locations, surveyors, architects, and engineers mapped and inspected lakes, rivers, and aquifers in an ongoing quest to control their flows with infrastructure. However, Mexico City emerged from a lacustrine setting, superimposed over a pre-Hispanic metropolis that had thrived in its aquatic environment prior to the conquest. Spanish Guanajuato, instead, originated as a small garrison and mining camp in the sparsely populated hills enclosing the Guanajuato River basin, territory of the semi-nomadic Chichimeca peoples. In its first 100 years, colonial Guanajuato was a minor settlement, but its mining operations increasingly threatened the relationship of the town with the waters. By the mid-1700s, this industry of extraction and its subsequent effects in the natural environment (deforestation, soil erosion, water pollution, mine waste) ruined the ecological balance of the area, and Guanajuato's residents were doomed to endure an unpredictable and often destructive relationship with water.[16]

Guanajuato's prosperity and new dams did not prevent episodes of tragedy. In the second half of the eighteenth century six major floods ravaged Guanajuato, washing away buildings, goods, and lives; forcing local authorities to confront the challenges of the city's location, and the financial and technological cost of securing a foothold in this environment. One of the most vulnerable areas was the Calle Alonso, a busy street at the back of the city hall alongside Guanajuato's tempestuous river. On many occasions, with the impending rains looming over Guanajuato, residents alerted the city officials to the problems of garbage and debris filling the river and blocking the bridges, endangering those living nearby and their properties.

Since the early 1700s, the municipality had engaged in periodic clean-ups of the Guanajuato River, yet a more efficient solution proved elusive. After 1750, the number of proposals and *peritos* for riverine projects increased dramatically. That year, Spanish engineer José Rozuela de Ledesma, a still largely unknown figure, proposed his "complete remedy and conservation of the reconditioning of the said river, indicating all the needed circumstances not to cause damage during its swelling."[17] The report included a topographic map of Guanajuato rendered in oblique perspective from the San Miguel Hill (Figure 24.3). This panoramic view remains the most complete image (albeit partly distorted) of the colonial city, with its streets, built fabric, mountains, and waterways. Ledesma was certainly familiar with the concerns of residents regarding the river, such as its multiple bridges, the confluence of several streams, the *cañadas* (ravines) running into the city, and a number of *embovedados* (vaults) over the watercourse. He would also have been acquainted with the earlier inspections conducted by the *maestro mayor* Felipe de Santiago Balona and mason Anastasio Franco, who concluded that to keep the river clean and the city safe from future floods would require a costly operation to channel the entire river, and rebuild deteriorated bridges and vulnerable fabric. He called for a ban on the discarding of rubble in the river, and for the inspection of ongoing constructions along the riverbanks. The multiple and poorly fenced garbage dumps near the water were also to be removed and disposed of in new locations, away from the city center. Balona and Franco also prepared a map, the whereabouts of which are unknown, that presumaby outlined those critical areas to ensure Guanajuato's health and safety for the future.[18]

With little action forthcoming from these prevention plans, the river continued to inundate the city. A powerful flash flood in 1760 wiped out most of the city center, with more than 250 houses

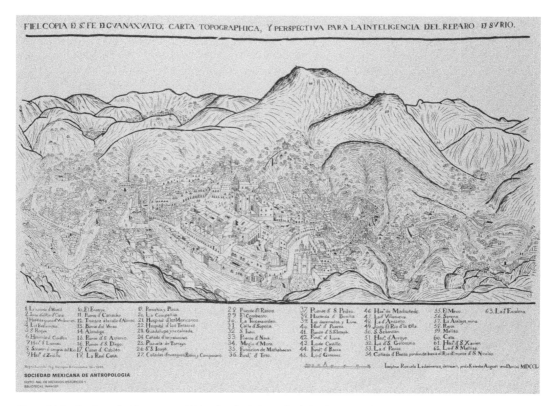

Figure 24.3 Enrique A. Cervantes, 1943, after José Rozuela de Ledesma, Fiel copia de Sta. Fe de Guanaxuato; carta topografica, y perspectiva para la inteligencia de el reparo de su rio, 1750.

Source: Colección Histórica de Mapas de México. Biblioteca Nacional de Antropología e Historia, Mexico. Reproduction authorized by the Instituto Nacional de Antropología e Historia.

ruined and buried in a sea of mud.[19] Father Ajofrín recalled how the swollen river "ruined houses, drowned people, destroyed riches, and caused endless harm."[20] The municipal government submitted an assessment of damages and a request for funds to the viceroy in Mexico City, yet no new plans for flood prevention followed. Clearing the streets, assessing the damage, repairing, and cleaning the river remained the overwhelming focus of the government's efforts. New excise taxes imposed following the 1766 visit of Spanish inspector general José de Gálvez provided additional income for the city to finance a required militia regiment and some public works and infrastructures.[21] The surplus was to be invested in building bridges, cleaning the river, and opening a new road to Marfil. In the following decade, the city pushed forward its public works agenda in those areas.

In the 1770s, a new generation of local *maestros*, Francisco Bruno de Ureña and Manuel Ventura de la Cerda, meticulously inspected the river through the city center, walking downstream from the east to the west end, and annotating their observations. They recommended replacing some bridges due to the poor state of their masonry, the small span of their arches, and their inadequate design. But eliminating the flood threat in Guanajuato was, they concluded, an almost insurmountable ambition. Particularly detrimental were the small dikes built by hacienda-owners to divert waters for mineral processing. Ideally, they argued, the river needed to be widened to 33 feet and completely embanked with stone walls along its course. The cost of this engineering project, which would require demolishing buildings and redrawing streets, was prohibitive. Alternatively, the same masters proposed a drainage gallery under the southeastern hills surrounding the city, departing near the Hacienda of San José de Gracia (Parque Embajadoras today).[22] Although never initiated during the colonial period, the project was revisited after Mexico's independence and built as the new Cuajín Tunnel by local engineer Ponciano Aguilar more than a century after its conception.

The rain raged Guanajuato again in July 1780. The downpour and subsequent flood deepened the city's infrastructure problems and exposed the precarious existence of its residents. News soon reached Mexico City demanding urgent attention, funds, and expertise to reshape the vulnerable city. This time the news followed another recent and tragic event: the collapse and flooding of La Valenciana, one of the most profitable silver mines in colonial Spanish America, taking 250 lives.[23] The havoc caused by these events aroused concern at the center of colonial power. The economic and personal loss, as well as the threat of future tragedies, incited a prompt viceregal response by dispatching Joaquín Velázquez de León, a mathematician and scientist experienced in the largest Novohispanic engineering project: the Valley of Mexico's drainage or Desagüe. The arrival of Velázquez in Guanajuato coincided with a period of increasing attention to public infrastructure in Spain and its colonies. The monarchy's program of reforms to stop the decline of the Spanish empire and accelerate its economic growth went hand in hand with an architectural and engineering agenda aimed at improving living conditions and bolstering the construction of infrastructure essential for public wellbeing, industrial productivity, and reliable transportation.

For five months (from December 1780 to May 1781), Velázquez observed, evaluated, and obtained periodic measurements of water quantity and height in hopes of providing solutions to the floods. He reiterated the urgency of enclosing the refining mills with solid walls preventing the frequent debris discharge into the river, one of the main causes of the inundations. He also recommended the demolition of a number of small foundries and sheds on the riverbanks that threatened to hamper the streamflow and clog bridges, though he stopped short of calling for a complete removal of the houses along the river. The excessive cost and legal consequence of such operation swayed his recommendation, instead, to repair the houses in bad shape and to shore up all their openings, no higher than 16 feet, facing the river.[24] Finally, he identified one of the areas most vulnerable to rainstorm surge: the confluence of the Guanajuato and Cata rivers, to the west of the city center. While the city followed through on some of Velázquez's proposals, this partial approach inevitably met with limited success, leaving the same problems for the city leaders at the end of the century.

Water Infrastructure and Urban Growth

Guanajuato expanded from its original settlement as a mining camp, adapting to the ravines of the surrounding hills, and developing as an irregular site along the riverbank.[25] Subsequent mining booms increased the occupation of and construction in the lands adjacent to the river, profoundly affecting the city's relation with its environment, and constantly exposing people to water polluted from the use of mercury in the silver extraction process. The use of water for amalgamation and refining accounts for the increasing number of *haciendas de beneficio* (refining mills) that proliferated in Guanajuato. By 1780 there were 50 haciendas and 300 *zangarros* (small metalworking factories) operating in Marfil and Guanajuato, most of them in the Desterrados and Belén barrios, and alongside the Pastita River.[26] Likewise, mine workers often settled near the haciendas, initially in wooden and adobe cabins (*jacales*), later replaced by more durable constructions. The propagation of these modest buildings, prone to water damage, posed additional challenges to the city's inundation and sanitation problems.

By 1792, with a population of about 51,000 for the city and over 100,000 for the district, Guanajuato had become one of the most dynamic urban centers of New Spain. Its public works agenda was further propelled by the new *intendente* Juan Antonio Riaño. Intendentes were government officials appointed by the Spanish monarchs to the newly created *intendencias* (provinces) as part of their efforts to improve the colonial administration and economy, and expand royal power. They were instrumental in the implementation of the Bourbon reforms, overseeing tax collection, promoting agricultural production, improving mining, and developing public works programs.

Well-connected with the spheres of colonial power, Riaño's awareness of the debates on rationalism and the modernization of urban environments shaped his contribution to the well-being of Guanajuato's residents. His talent was not in proposing new ideas, but in placing a new emphasis on urban policies, making tangible improvements to the city, and prioritizing specific projects for street paving, water and food supply, and reshaping of public spaces. In doing so, Riaño was adhering to the 1786 Royal Ordinances of Intendancies that required these officials to work diligently in the implementation of public works, but also to the *bandos* (edicts) on civic order, sanitation, and infrastructures issued in Mexico City.[27] Riaño's earlier appointment as intendente of Michoacán might have also affected his performance. There, he made himself well-acquainted with the fabric of a new aqueduct and other works in its capital, Valladolid, confronting issues of the city's living environment, water and food supply; the same problems Guanajuato was facing by the late eighteenth-century.

One of the first items on Riaño's agenda was the appropriate design and fabric for the city's eleven bridges. Some were simple wooden structures, others masonry constructions of one or two arches spanning the river and adorned with sculptures. Throughout the 1790s, Rina directed the renovation or replacement of unsound bridges with solid works that facilitated the fluid circulation of people and goods across the city. For instance, Riana ordered the Camacho and San Pedro bridges cleared, repaired, and enlarged, as both were main crossings linking the city center with its eastern and western barrios, and needed to withstand a swollen river. Furthermore, as Riaño argued, deteriorated bridges, missing parapets, and rails could jeopardize the lives of children and inebriated people.[28] This interest in wellbeing and efficiency also guided Riaño's oversight of the construction of the Laja River Bridge in nearby Celaya "for the perpetual utility of travelers," as two classicizing stone markers announce. Designed by Francisco Eduardo Tresguerras and completed in 1809, the new crossing received national attention from the periodical *Diario de México*. The article celebrated the city's munificence and the viceroy's support for public works in pursuit of the common good, concluding that "a bridge, a road, and other such works are preferable to works of piety due to their general benefit to both souls and bodies."[29]

Amid this variety of projects, two engineering schemes resurfaced often in the plans to save Guanajuato from its waters. The first one, proposed by Velázquez in 1780, advocated for the construction of a large masonry wall (*murallón*) with a diamond-shaped profile at the junction of the Guanajuato and the Cata rivers.[30] A decade later, Riaño revived the project and added it to the list of infrastructure priorities, describing it as "an embankment in-between two robust walls, in the shape of a diamond point" which would prevent "the currents from reversing or flowing backwards" and the devastation this caused to western barrios and streets.[31] The intended location for this infrastructure in an undeveloped headland can be inferred from several 1780s maps (Figure 24.4).[32] The urgency of the *murallón* was reiterated in 1795 and its project finally approved by the viceroy a year later. However, bids for its construction were not received and the *murallón* never made it beyond the drafting table.[33] Ongoing budgetary challenges as well as attention to other urgent repairs and projects, such as the new granary of Granaditas, relegated the river channeling to the realm of dreams.[34]

The second project involved the Socavón, a tunnel-like structure near the Camacho Bridge and the Casa del Real Ensaye (office of Guanajuato's royal metal assayer). There were debates at the municipal level whether to keep the existing tunnel or to modify its design. Since at least 1780, city officials had considered demolishing the buildings above this underground gallery and replacing it with a wide, open trench (*tajo*) that would help to straighten the meandering river.[35] The idea of a tajo was then in the making in Mexico City, a project with which Velázquez and the Guanajuato elite were familiar, and to which local residents could add their own experience in the construction of shafts and underground tunnels for the mining industry.[36] Indeed, local miner and *alcalde mayor* (district governor) Antonio de Obregón y Alcocer, Count of Valenciana, had proposed to fund the new trench entirely in exchange for the urban space left by the altered river course. In 1796, his son-in-law, the Count of Pérez Gálvez, still advocated for the same project.[37]

Water in Late Colonial Guanajuato

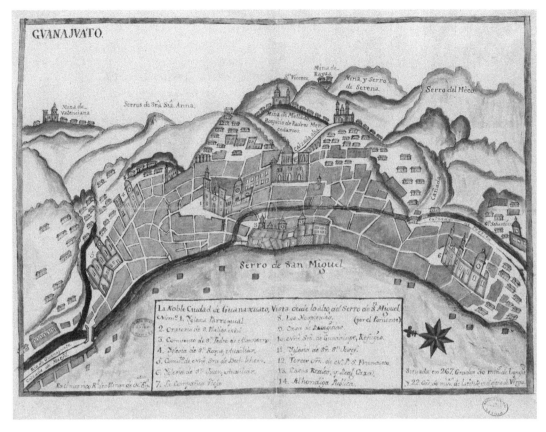

Figure 24.4 "Plano de la ciudad de Guanajuato," ca. 1783.
Source: Ministerio de Cultura y Deportes, Archivo General de Indias, MP-MEXICO,601.

Despite these ambitious plans, few would be realized before the Mexican Insurgency of 1810, which halted all major projects during the last decade of colonial rule. Some water infrastructure projects were revisited in early post-colonial Guanajuato. For instance, in 1832 local entrepreneur Marcelino Rocha revived the project to pipe the water from La Olla Dam to fountains in the city center.[38] But floods would continue through the nineteenth and early twentieth centuries. In 1905, a devastating flash flood with over 900 victims caught the attention of national and international newspapers, including *The New York Times*. Photographs of ruined or shored up buildings and muddy streets captured what had been a persistent problem throughout late colonial Guanajuato. It would not be until well after then that Guanajuato would get its water infrastructure in place.

Epilogue

Local colonial administrators, merchants, and mine owners had long sought to advance Bourbon reform ideals through public works projects in ways that would transform Guanajuato into a model for other Novohispanic provinces. However, their ambitions were hindered by a number of obstacles, including lack of funds, bureaucratic delays, inadequate waste disposal, and hacienda owners who neglected to clean the river stretches bordering their properties. Despite new tax revenues introduced in the 1760s, financing infrastructure proved challenging. Viceregal scrutiny and oversight added to the delays. Indeed, since the 1780s, Guanajuato's cabildo was required to petition the viceroy's approval annually with an explanation of the estimated cost for river cleaning. On several occasions, either the request was submitted too late or the response from Mexico City did not arrive on time before the rainy season. This delay often prompted local authorities to take matters into their own hands, which led to further censure from the viceregal authorities.[39]

The attempt to shape Guanajuato's water infrastructure went hand in hand with other late colonial public works, urban regulations, and architectural projects that aimed to enhance and modernize the city in Spanish America. This program reflected the urban ideals of contemporary architects, military engineers, and city planners, but it also spoke to the belief of the Spanish monarchy and its reformers that modern architecture and engineering projects, particularly new public works and infrastructures, and a restrictive urban policy would benefit the common good, assist in social control, propel economic progress, and, ultimately, transmit the image of good government in action. In the end, however, realities on the ground frustrated their ambitions, and Guanajuato's urgent water challenges would have to wait for another century for a solution.

Notes

1 Francisco de Ajofrín, *Diario del viaje que por orden de la Sagrada Congregación de Propaganda Fide hizo a la América Septentrional en el siglo XVIII el P. Fray Francisco de Ajofrín, Capuchino,* ed. Vicente Castañeda y Alcover (Madrid: Real Academia de la Historia, 1958), I, 263–265.
2 José Hernández Chico, "Descripción de la Ciudad y Real de Minas de Guanajuato (1788)," in *Descripciones económicas regionales de Nueva España. Provincias del Centro, Sureste y Sur, 1766-1827,* eds Enrique Florescano and Isabel Gil Sánchez (Mexico City: Instituto Nacional de Antropología e Historia, 1976), 22.
3 Isauro Rionda Arreguín, ed., *Testimonios sobre Guanajuato* (Guanajuato: Gobierno del Estado de Guanajuato, 1989), 70.
4 One legua equals 2.6 miles, and one vara roughly 33 inches.
5 Enrique Marco Dorta, *Estudios y documentos de Arte Hispanoamericano* (Madrid: Real Academia de la Historia, 1981), 13–14, 91–92.
6 Luis J. Gordo Peláez, "Fábrica y fama de los acueductos novohispanos: De la peregrina 'Targea' y 'Arcos' de Santiago de Querétaro," in *Actas del Séptimo Congreso Nacional de Historia de la Construcción,* ed. Santiago Huerta Fernández (Madrid: Instituto Juan de Herrera, 2011), I, 623–632.
7 Archivo Histórico, Universidad de Guanajuato [AHUG], Guanajuato, Fondo Ayuntamiento, Aguas, Caja 1, Exp. 3
8 Lucio Marmolejo, *Efemérides Guanajuatenses, o datos para formar la historia de la ciudad de Guanajuato: obra escrita con presencia de los más auténticos e interesantes documentos* (Guanajuato: Imprenta del Colegio de Artes y Oficios, 1883-1884), II, 48–49, 74–75.
9 Ajofrín, *Diario,* I, 264–265.
10 AHUG, Aguas, Caja 1, Exp. 3.
11 Marco Dorta, 92–101.
12 Fátima Halcón, *La difusión del estípite en Nueva España. La obra de Felipe de Ureña* (Seville: Universidad de Sevilla, 2012), 102–105.
13 AHUG, Aguas, Caja 1, Exp. 5, ff. 4r.–15v., and Exp. 6.
14 Ibid. 1r.–3v.
15 AHUG, Ramo Citadino, Caja 7, ca. 1786. 2 f., in Alma Linda Reza, *Guanajuato y sus miasmas. Higiene y salud pública, 1792-1804* (Guanajuato: Presidencia Municipal, 2001), 80–81.
16 Daviken Studnicki-Gizbert and David Schecter, "The Environmental Dynamics of a Colonial Fuel-Rush: Silver Mining and Deforestation in New Spain, 1522 to 1810," *Environmental History* 15, no. 1 (2010): 94–119.
17 AHUG, Limpieza, desasolve y explotación del río, 1749-1772, Caja 4, ff. 1r.–2v., 42r–46r.
18 Ibid. ff. 20r., 28r., 37v.–41v.
19 Ibid. ff. 2r.–3r.; Marmolejo, *Efemérides,* II, 92–93, 99–101.
20 Ajofrín, *Diario,* I, 267.
21 David Brading, *Miners and Merchants in Bourbon Mexico, 1763-1810* (Cambridge: Cambridge University Press, 1971), 235.
22 AHUG, Limpieza, 1749-1772, Caja 4, expediente 4, f. 1r.–6v.
23 Marmolejo, *Efemérides,* II, 247–249.
24 AHUG, Limpieza, 1780-1789, Caja 4.

25 José Luis Lara Valdés, *La ciudad de Guanajuato en el siglo XVIII. Estudio urbanístico y arquitectónico* (Guanajuato: Presidencia Municipal, 2001), 16.
26 Brading, *Miners*, 282.
27 Sharon Bailey Glasco, *Constructing Mexico City. Colonial Conflicts over Culture, Space, and Authority* (New York: Palgrave Macmillan, 2010).
28 AHUG, Limpieza, 1791-1792, Caja 4.
29 *Diario de México* ([Mexico City]: Imprenta de la calle de Santo Domingo los Diarios, 1807), 5 (February 27, 1807): 223–224.
30 AHUG, Limpieza, 1780-1789, Caja 4.
31 AHUG, Ramo Protocolo, 1792-1803, f. 26r. See Jorge A. Castro Rivas and Matilde Rangel López, *Relación histórica de la Intendencia de Guanajuato durante el período de 1787 a 1809* (Guanajuato: Universidad de Guanajuato, 1998), 61.
32 AGN, Historia, Vol. 279, exp. 1; Mapas, Planos e Ilustraciones (280): "Ignografía horizontal de Guanajuato," "Ciudad de Guanajuato."
33 AHUG, Limpieza, 1794-1795, Caja 4; Puente de Camacho, 1795-1820, Caja 5.
34 Luis Gordo Peláez, "'A Palace for the Maize': The Granary of Granaditas in Guanajuato and Neoclassical Civic Architecture in Colonial Mexico," *RACAR: Revue D'Art Canadienne* 38, no. 2 (2013): 71–89.
35 AHUG, Limpieza, 1780-1789, Caja 4.
36 Vera Candiani, *Dreaming of Dry Land: Environmental Transformation in Colonial Mexico City* (Stanford: Stanford University Press, 2014).
37 AHUG, Puente de Camacho, 1795-1820, Caja 5.
38 Marmolejo, *Efemérides*, III, 220.
39 AHUG, Limpieza, 1780-1789, Caja 4.

25
LAND RECLAMATION IN THE MAKING OF HONG KONG[1]

Charlie Qiuli Xue and Cong Sun

Hong Kong has long faced the prospect of limited land for development, as the only available flat land lies in narrow coastal strips between the mountains of the islands and the sea. Since 1840, when the first group of colonists arrived, they have continuously reclaimed land from the sea. To date, among the 1,106 sq km of land area within the Hong Kong territory, 70 sq km have been reclaimed from the sea. The coastline winds for 1,100 km along more than 200 islands and islets. However, the public only has access to one-fifth of this waterfront space, as the remainder is blocked by container terminals or other industrial facilities. In the twentieth century, officials directed the extension of the shoreline along Victoria Harbor 1,000 meters toward the water in order to acquire valuable land for urban development. Because of this land scarcity, high density and high-rise buildings along the harbor have come to define the urban landscape of Hong Kong. This chapter examines two aspects of waterfront development in Hong Kong: the ecological and social problems caused by land reclamation, and the historical evolution of waterfront architecture and planning from colonial to global periods. We study varied types and uses of newly reclaimed waterfront space, including leisure, commercial, and residential. The chapter aims to reveal the design challenges related to waterfront reclamation and spatial production amid calls for increased attention to place-making and public space for active civic life.

Since the first group of British colonists arrived in Hong Kong in 1840, the territory has continuously reclaimed land from the sea for urban infrastructure and basic survival. To date, over six percent of the territory is built on reclaimed land along the 1,100 km coastline, including some of the most densely inhabited districts. From a colonial entrepôt in the early twentieth century to an industrial base in the 1950s to the emergence as an international financial center in the 1980s, Hong Kong is constantly under pressure to accommodate its seven million residents, the 45 million tourists who visit annually, and diverse work, trade, and living activities within its limited land area.[2]

Throughout the past 180 years, the development of Hong Kong has required the acquisition of land from water, and making waterfront space suitable for living and working. The skyline along the harbor has gradually become the symbol of Hong Kong (Figure 25.1). This chapter describes the relationship between reclamation and urban development in Hong Kong and how waterfront space has been shaped by the surge of infrastructure upgrades and construction. The chapter first provides a general reclamation history and then focuses on three case studies to illustrate how advancing infrastructure has led to the production of new waterfront space. In this ongoing drama of water and land, a story emerges of how a coastal village transformed itself into a global city.

Figure 25.1 Both sides of Victoria Harbor comprise land reclaimed from the sea.

Source: Photographs courtesy of Charlie Xue.

Building a City on Reclaimed Land

The City of Victoria began on the northern shore of Hong Kong Island across from Kowloon Peninsula, on a rare spit of flat land between the sea and a steeply rising mountain. The Hong Kong Island and Kowloon Peninsula form the Victoria Harbor, with an average water depth of 16 meters, suitable for ship harboring and wharfing. In 1842, colonists built three roads on the mountain edges of Hong Kong Island: Queen's Road, Hollywood Road along the contour, and the perpendicular Wyndham Street to connect the two roads. These early roads are at least 30 meters above sea level. The land on the south (mountain) side of Queen's Road was developed as a residential area and on the north side as a business district. A "government hill" was zoned for the erection of governmental department buildings. The main cathedral, post office, and supreme court are scattered in the area. Sand and stone generated during construction were poured into the harbor to expand a large stretch of flat land. Admiral Sir Charles Elliot (1801–1875), the then diplomat and colonial administrator, divided the land into forty sections, each with 100 feet of frontage, and sold them to merchants. Most of these land plots were used for building piers, docks, warehouses, and trade offices, usually four stories high. The southern part of Hong Kong Island faces the ocean of the South China Sea, so it was not included in the early blueprint of Victoria City.

From 1860 to 1930, the government and private organizations reclaimed land along the Hong Kong Island waterfront from Kennedy City to Causeway Bay for governmental, port, and commercial use. East–west thoroughfares were continuously added from Queen's Road, Bonham Strand to Des Voeux Road and Connaught Road in Central, on average 300 meters northward away from the early Queen's Road. In the early twentieth century, the population of the territory was around 160,000. More than half lived in the Victoria City. On Kowloon Peninsula, land was reclaimed from the harbor for the Canton-Kowloon railway, a train station, an airport, and the expansion of private businesses and a typhoon shelter. The government saw the frequent necessity of reclamation, and set up a Praya Reclamation Office within the Public Works Department in 1891. In the 100 years' of city construction prior to World War II, the total reclaimed land amounted to approximately 5 km^2, a fraction of the eventual total of 70 km^2. However, this patch-by-patch progression provided decision-makers with land sales money, opportunities to learn, build confidence, and hope for obtaining future land (Figure 25.2).[3]

When Japanese troop surrendered in September 1945, the population in Hong Kong was 600,000. After the war, many people came back to Hong Kong. With the founding of the People's Republic of China in 1949, a large number of refugees arrived in Hong Kong and the population rose to three million. With abundant manpower and funding, the old entrepôt rapidly became an industrial center. In order to disperse people and industry from city proper to suburb, the satellite towns of Kwun Tong, Tsuen Wan, Shatin, and Tuen Mun were established between the 1950s and the 1980s. To meet industrial and residential needs, these new towns were formed either by reclaiming land or by altering the shape of water bodies. Thus, some bays and inlets became narrow "rivers," along which large tracts of industrial and residential land were created, leased, and built up. The seawall of Hong Kong Island was continuously pushed forward toward the harbor, opening space for the creation of Victoria Park in 1955, and the Island Eastern Corridor traffic bypass in the 1980s. To increase land in city area, Kowloon was pushed 600 meters westward, and acquired 340 hectares. To provide adequate land for manufacturing, Tai Po Industrial Park was planned on reclaimed land of the To Lo Harbor in the 1970s. It was part of the Tai Po new town. To accommodate the emerging science and technology sector, Hong Kong Science Park and Cyberport were opened on the new seaside in 2001 and 2004, respectively.

As tourism in Hong Kong grew, Ocean Park and Disneyland were conceived and built upon separate areas of reclaimed land in southern Hong Kong Island in 1976 and Lantau Island in 2005, respectively. For such theme parks, the seaside is the ideal location. Up to 2016, 70 km^2 land was obtained from the sea, which is equivalent to the area of Hong Kong Island.[4] From colonial to global times, Hong Kong's development has been highly dependent on the creation of new land and waterfront.[5] Before 1997, reclamation was a top-down administrative decision from the government, and local reclamation by the private sector was also encouraged. Through land auctions, the government gained considerable revenue. Filling the sea received little resistance, as the Legislative Council members were appointed by the governor and different voices were rarely heard.

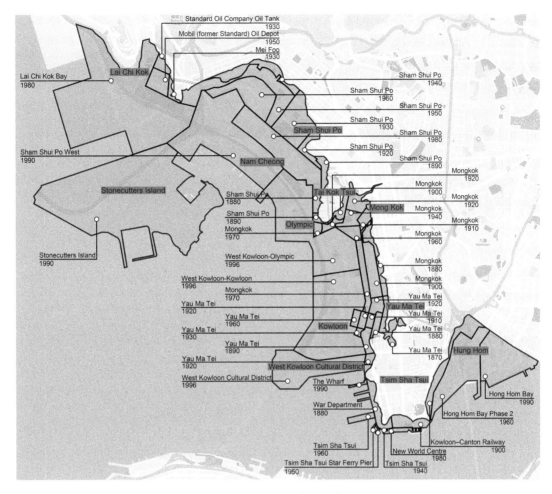

Figure 25.2 A century and a half of land reclamation along the Kowloon coast.

Source: Drawing by Charlie Qiuli Xue and Cong Sun.

Infrastructure-Led "Core Programme"

In 1984, the British and Chinese governments issued a joint declaration on returning the sovereignty of Hong Kong to China, with the handover set for 1997. Amid fears of Communist rule and the specter of the Tiananmen Square Massacre in 1989, many middle-class residents in Hong Kong emigrated (mostly to Canada and Australia). To boost confidence, the British government in Hong Kong proposed a series of large-scale infrastructure projects to enable relocation of the airport from the city center to Lantau Island. Kai Tak Airport was built on the Kowloon peninsula in 1946 and enlarged in 1958. Its location in the center of Kowloon City meant that the airport presented one of the most challenging locations for commercial pilots from all over the world. Airplanes soared over the city, mere hundreds of meters above the ground, and both passengers and pedestrians on the streets could see each other. The 3,000m runway projected out onto the sea and pilots needed to be vigilant during landing and take-off, as their airplane could otherwise crash into the water or mountains. This airport located in the city struggled to cope with the increasing number of passengers in the 1980s, and after many rounds of debate, feasibility reports, and consultations, the Hong Kong government declared it would move the airport to Chek Lap Kok in the northwest of the territory.

The new airport was located in a lagoon outside Lantau Island. Chek Lap Kok was a reef, and most of the airport land, around 900 hectares, was obtained by reclamation. The third runway, which is planned to be completed in 2023, adds another 650 hectares of land from the sea. To support this relocation, new roads and railways had to be extended to reach the site, which was originally a remote island. For this purpose, the Hong Kong government launched the "Hong Kong Airport Core Programme," or "Rose Garden Plan," in 1990, comprising the Chek Lap Kok International Airport, the Airport Express railway line, a new town of Tung Chung, the North Lantau Highway, the Lantau Link, Route 3, the West Kowloon Highway, the West Kowloon reclamation area, the West Cross Harbor Tunnel, and the central reclamation plan. These infrastructure projects were aimed to link the old city of Hong Kong Island and Kowloon Peninsula to the airport in a smooth and rapid manner. The government devoted portions of the reclaimed land to a new cultural district, cruise pier, and civic center. The following sections examine three such new sites to illustrate how infrastructure-led developments have shaped the culture, economy, and politics of Hong Kong.

West Kowloon Cultural District

In the late 1990s, many Chinese cities launched grand cultural projects in new towns, and Hong Kong felt pressure from its rivals.[6] The city had built a Cultural Center on the Tsim Sha Tsui waterfront in 1989, but the buildings proved inadequate to meet growing demands. Not to be outdone by Mainland China, the government announced plans to build the "West Kowloon Cultural District" in 1996. When planners laid out the Tung Chung and Airport Express lines in the early 1990s, they reclaimed a 60-ha parcel of land on the western side of Kowloon Peninsula. The land supported the new Kowloon Station building, with the train lines underground, a bus terminal at ground level topped by a two-story shopping mall, and thirteen residential and commercial skyscrapers.[7] In front of the Kowloon station complex, forty-two ha of reclaimed land were dedicated to the new cultural district.

In 2001, the Hong Kong government solicited design schemes for its West Kowloon Cultural District. Up to that point, most public buildings had been designed by government architects, and by the Architectural Services Department after 1986. Design competitions for important corporation headquarters, such as those of Hong Kong Bank, were held in the private sector. However, Beijing and Shanghai had already opened similar landmark building designs to international competition. Now, to compete with neighboring cities, Hong Kong followed suit, and in a competition with 250 entries, Foster & Partners from the UK won first prize. The winning design involved the installation of a sky canopy above the buildings and public space, which the authorities envisioned as an effective symbol of the city. A canopy can easily be seen and perceived as a symbol.

To raise capital for the project, the Hong Kong government tried to introduce private funding. With the Foster & Partners designs in hand, the government issued an invitation to develop the West Kowloon Cultural District in September 2003. The tenderer was expected to have experience in development, sales, and management of large-scale building groups, and to inject HK$30 billion into the project (Since 1983, the Hong Kong dollar has been pegged to the U.S. dollar, where U.S.$1 = HK$7.8). In April 2004, the government received five tenders. In November 2004, three entries were confirmed. An exhibition of three plans was displayed to the public for fifteen weeks from December 2004 to March 2005. The tenderers included major property developers Cheung Kong, Sun Hung Kai, Henderson Land, and Sino.

The developers brought in international architects, engineers, and various consultants. Each tenderer spent HK$10 million on models, display halls, lighting, and brochures for their plan. The consortiums which bid to gain the site invested large amounts of money into "promoting" culture and expected the sum to be recouped through the development of commercial properties. However, many observers questioned whether the property developers had sufficient experience to manage the cultural facilities.[8] Under increased pressure, the government gave up the single-operator plan, sending ten years of governmental, consortium, and public efforts down the drain. In

Figure 25.3 West Kowloon Cultural District.

Source: Photographs courtesy of Charlie Xue.

2008, the government established the authority of the West Kowloon Cultural District and applied for funding of HK$21.6 billion from the Legislative Council. In 2009, an invitation for a master plan competition was sent to international designers. Master plans of three companies, namely Foster & Partners, OMA, and Rocco Design were displayed to the public for three months from August 2010 (Figure 25.3).

For their entry, Foster & Partners demonstrated the theme of a "park in the city," according to which a park would be featured prominently in West Kowloon and all vehicular traffic diverted underground. In this new master plan, lawn and forest are highlighted. The design made West Kowloon appear as an attractive leisure landscape. Rocco Design, meanwhile, focused on pedestrian and vehicular circulation. Local factors such as a market and stone-paved streets were integrated into the site plan. Artistic rafts were floated on the sea as metaphors of Hong Kong's fishing rafts. Finally, OMA designed three clusters of buildings, namely the "East Arts," "West Performance," and "Central Market" clusters. The most surprising design element was a suspension bridge linking Jordan and Austin roads, extending the project beyond the site boundary. The bridge strengthened the celebratory atmosphere and connected the cultural district to the old city.

Foster & Partners ultimately won the bid for the master plan of West Kowloon Cultural District. The southwest portion of the district is now a large park positioned on a gentle slope. Most of the district's performance and exhibition buildings are located close to Canton Road, with vehicular traffic hidden underground.

The cultural district will eventually include fifteen buildings. Since 2013, the design and construction of several buildings have been confirmed, including the Xiqu (Chinese Opera) Center designed by Bing Thom of Vancouver and Ronald Lu of Hong Kong, the M+ Museum designed by Herzog & de Meuron from Switzerland, TFP Farrells, and Arup & Partners HK, a theater designed by UN Studio from the Netherlands and AD + RG of Hong Kong, and a branch of the Beijing Palace Museum designed by Rocco Design. With the generosity of the Hong Kong government, infrastructure construction of the site began in 2013 and the estimated cost has already escalated to HK$47 billion, which is double the government's 2008 estimation.

Kai Tak Airport Redevelopment

On July 6, 1998, the Hong Kong International Airport moved from Kai Tak to Chek Lap Kok in one night. The roaring sky of Kowloon Peninsula was left quiet. The old airport, terminal, maintenance buildings, and runway, which had served Hong Kong for fifty years, were deserted. In 1998, the government proposed to create additional land in Kai Tak by filling the ditches and part of Kowloon Bay. The water in the long channel between the runway and To Kwa Wan is basically static and locals voiced concerns regarding its pollution. By filling the channel, the area would become a complete piece of usable land. However, by this time concerns about sustainability were growing, making reclamation an increasingly sensitive topic. The plan to fill the sea area at Kai Tak met with fierce opposition from the public, and the government published a "zero reclamation" scheme in 2006. The outline zoning plan for the new Kai Tak development would leave the sea area intact.

While airports around the world are expanding, very few have been discarded like Kai Tak, which now awaited the long chain of approvals for its new life. Compared with mainland China, redevelopment in Hong Kong is exceptionally slow because of many stages of public hearings, engagement, consultation, and budget approval (for the public sector) in the Legislative Council. The public consultation meetings frequently occur in government buildings or local districts on weekdays but more commonly on weekends. Demonstrations at the Town Planning Board occur at almost every meeting because rezoning and changes of use are closely linked with residents' interests. However, the opinions of various parties are absorbed in longer processes that help to avoid creating "white elephant" or "ghost" cities. Finally, after fifteen years of discussion and consultation, Kai Tak found its new use.

Under the new Kai Tak outline zoning plan, planners designated sites for a new stadium, metro station, and public housing (Figure 25.4). Additionally, Foster & Partners designed a cruise terminal which opened in 2013 at the end of the airport runway, which proved perfect for use as a pier. The cruise business has since been active and brought many tourists to Hong Kong and other Asian ports. The land plots of the old runway and airport were leased to private developers for extremely high prices. The land premium on such leases is the main source of the Hong Kong government's income.

Contention over Central Reclamation

The development of Hong Kong has long been tied to land reclamation out of sheer necessity. Since the 1980s, large-scale road, transit, and airport infrastructure projects had taken shape across the metropolis by filling in the bay with new landform. However, as democratic participation increased in Hong Kong in the 1990s, people expressed concern that the vast Victoria Harbor was quickly dwindling in size, and that the estuarine ecology had deteriorated and would eventually disappear. The Society for Protection of the Harbor was founded in November 1995 and obtained 170,000 signatures from citizens to support

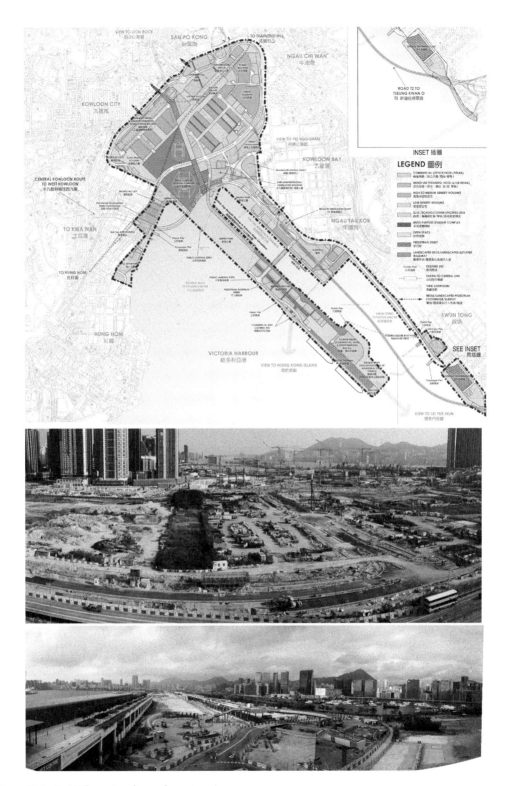

Figure 25.4 Kai Tak master plan and construction.

Source: Map courtesy of Planning Department, HKSAR, second photograph courtesy of Raymond Wong.

relevant protection legislation. On June 27, 1996, the Protection of the Harbor Ordinance proposed by civil activists and Legislative Council member Christine Loh was passed in the Legislative Council three days before the sovereignty handover, and later became Chapter 531 of the Hong Kong Law. The motion stated that the harbor, as a special public asset and part of the natural heritage of the Hong Kong people, was subject to the "presumption against reclamation" principle.

However, without new land for expansion, the transportation infrastructure became ever more stressed. Traffic into and out of Central increased rapidly after 1997 because of more business visitors and tourists from China and all over the world, and the roads could no longer bear the load. At the end of 2002, the Executive Council approved Phase III of the 23-ha Central Reclamation Plan. However, the Society for Protection of the Harbor asked for a judicial review, and the court sided against the Town Planning Board. The High Court judgment of July 8, 2003 stated that three requirements of "compelling, overriding, and present need," "no viable alternative," and "minimum impairment to the harbor" had to be met before the presumption against reclamation could be rebutted.

Nevertheless, the government initialized the project despite the court's decision, under the premise that stopping work would result in huge compensation claims from the contractors. This prompted a protracted legal battle between the Society and government; the latter maintained that it actively reviewed its projects according to the three requirements as stated by the court, and continued to express the urgency of the Central-Wan Chai Bypass to citizens.

At the end of 2003, the High Court decided that the central reclamation largely conformed to the three requirements, and the Society for Protection of the Harbor lost the case.[9] Undeterred by the findings, grass roots actions and protests continue the effort to protect the harbor. These actions have aimed to educate both the government and citizens. Perhaps as an effort to mitigate conflicts, construction of the central waterfront greensward began after the legal battle, and the waterfront promenade and Tamar Park were created upon the completion of the government headquarters building in 2011. This land accommodates citizens, has a lawn frequented by tourists, and, somewhat ironically, provides space for demonstrations outside the government building. The shortage of buildable land has challenged Hong Kong for sixty years, and the issue becomes increasingly acute and politicized when various groups with vested interests wrestle in the public forum.[10]

After the battle over the Central Reclamation Plan, the government became more cautious about building out into other parts of the sea. However, in the twenty-first century, several such projects have moved forward. According to the newly approved reclamation plan and after public consultation with few adverse opinions, the government demolished the Star Ferry Pier in December 2006. Built in 1958 after central reclamation in the early 1950s, the Star Ferry Pier was a functional structure with a thin floor, roof slabs, whitewashed external walls, and a clock tower. Although a relatively modest structure, the pier faithfully reflected its structure and material. The large clock on the pier was the last mechanical timepiece on a Hong Kong building. Before its demolition, hundreds of citizens went on hunger strikes to protect the pier. Their main demand was the "protection of collective memory." Police arrested protestors and formed a human shield to ensure the completion of the demolition work.[11]

Just six months later, the same scenario occurred a few hundred yards to the east of the old Star Ferry Pier at Queen's Pier. Built in 1953, Queen's Pier was aligned with the front entrance of City Hall. If the Star Ferry Pier was considered "architecture," Queen's Pier was at most a "building" or a simple "sheltering" structure. During the colonial era, when royal family members and new governors arrived in Hong Kong, they usually took a boat to Queen's Pier, where they participated in a welcoming ritual, during which red carpet was extended to the front gate of City Hall. Citizens were not permitted to attend these ceremonies. From the end of 2006 to July 2007, a series of protests erupted to save Queen's Pier, including candlelight vigils, overnight sit-ins, and hunger strikes that often resulted in confrontations with the police.[12] The government finally demolished Queen's Pier and stored its components in a warehouse. Several schemes were suggested by the private sector, such as rebuilding the pier in the same place or reassembling the components in a new location. The original location of

Queen's Pier is now the center of an expressway, and the new location is positioned far from City Hall. Neither scheme does much to preserve the memory of the original pier.

The opposition and protesting of demolition of the two piers were motivated by "collective memory" from the members of public. But what memory? Whose memory? How many groups' memory? The voice from the public can be noisy but inchoate. People often link their memory to some elapsed "golden" era—especially the 1970s and 1980s when Hong Kong rose to prominence as an "Asian Dragon"—a global economic powerhouse—to rival Tokyo. In the economic high tide of the 1970s, too many old buildings with historic values were demolished to yield land for higher and denser development. The demolition and protesting events educate the public to treasure the past vestige. The society becomes more alerted in protecting the heritage. In 2016, when New World Development purchased an old block in North Point for redevelopment, there was a State Cinema with a unique roof structure built in 1952. The society strongly urged that it should remain in place. This enabled the Antiquity Advisory Board to label it Class I heritage, and the developer promised to protect and reuse it. In 2021, the residents stopped bulldozers from destroying a district reservoir tank built in 1904, which used a structure similar to a Roman cistern. The protection of the State Cinema and other heritage buildings in the past ten years can be partly attributed to the rise of a heritage consciousness following the protests against the demolition of the Starr Ferry and Queen's Piers.

The Central Reclamation provides ample waterfront space of around 40 ha (Figure 25.5). This may be an insignificant area for some cities, but for dense urban Hong Kong, it is a rare waterfront place in the city center for people to breathe, stroll, play, and meet. Many uses were proposed. Finally, a building complex with a gross floor area of 136,000 m^2, containing the HKSAR government headquarters, the Legislative Council, and the Chief Executive office was built, and the space between the buildings and the harbor became Tamar Park. The building itself serves as an example of sustainability and being open to society and nature. The lawn in front of the building provides a comfortable vantage point overlooking the harbor. Government officials and citizens are learning how to use the space, which has come to serve as a symbol of civic society.

Conclusion

This chapter briefly reviews the evolution of reclamation in Hong Kong and particularly three cases around the "airport core programme" since 1990. For a small territory like Hong Kong, land acquisition is always imperative. Waterfront land is extremely valuable because it can be used as high-value residential buildings, offices, hotels, retail complexes, and much-enjoyed leisure space. The struggle around land use, demolition, and building represents a conflict of development versus preservation.

The West Kowloon Cultural District was generated by Hong Kong's quest for cultural capital in the region. The cross-harbor tunnel, subway, airport express, and nearby high-speed railway merge with the master plan of cultural facilities. The traffic infrastructure and public transportation encourages people to visit the museums and attend performances. The site supports Hong Kong's commitment to high culture. The waterfront cultural mega-structures delineate an exciting urban profile. However, they are far from the areas where majority of people live, and intensify the gentrification.

The Kai Tak redevelopment showcases how a deserted airport can have a new life and serve the economy. Before the cruise ship pier was built, cruise ships had to berth in Tsim Sha Tsui, whose space was far from adequate. The former runway provides sufficient length for several cruise ships to berth at the same time. The land plots on the runway are leased at high premiums and contribute to government income. Under pressure from the public, the "zero filling" scheme created a seemingly "sustainable" solution, although it is costly to treat water in the narrow channel. It also provides mostly sea views for future building users. The old airport helps to form a new sub-center.

The frustration and fulfillment of central reclamation demonstrates the democratic conflicts between parties with vested interests. The importance of "collective memory" increased in civic society, but ultimately it was defeated by the economic reasons (e.g. Central-Wanchai Bypass). Tamar Park was a

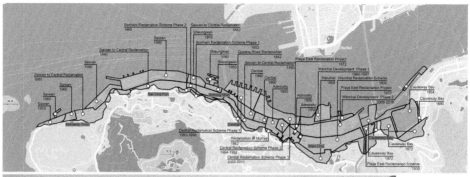

Figure 25.5 Central Reclamation and Tamar Park.

Source: Second picture of construction, courtesy of Raymond Wong.

military base in colonial times and is now the government headquarters of the Special Administrative Region. Even such a "Central Park" is partly encroached upon by the entrance of an underground expressway. Nevertheless, Hong Kong residents now have one more park for leisure, exercise, exhibition, political assembly, and demonstration. It has become a key location in recent years for social events and political gatherings.

The three cases above do not represent piecemeal growth over a long period of historical evolution, but growth generated by infrastructural updates and construction. They are the results of top-down policies with little bottom-up feedback. They quickly and dramatically changed the townscape and seascape of the city.

In Hong Kong, the acquisition of old buildings is a method for obtaining land and re-building at a higher density. However, this depends on the collection of property rights from many different owners, which is costly and time-consuming. Collecting land in the New Territories is also difficult because it requires dealing with old laws and rural landlords. In comparison, there were fewer legal problems and resistance to reclaiming land from the sea in the colonial era. Following this path of least resistance, the government repeatedly harvested land from the harbor and thereby created today's Hong Kong. Once residents found that the vast harbor had become a ditch, alarm regarding sustainability and a societal interest in collective memory arose. The population is increasing and land demands are always acute. The government feels it must propose an immense plan of reclamation in east Lantau Island but is meeting tremendous opposition from Hong Kong society. It is clear that the fierce struggle for new development versus the equally strident demands for preservation will continue to see-saw for a long time.

Notes

1. The authors heartily thank Professor Joseph Heathcott for his valuable advice and editing.
2. Data of Hong Kong is from the Hong Kong Government, *Hong Kong Annual Book* (Hong Kong: Government Printer, 2018).
3. Charlie Q.L. Xue and others, "The shaping of early Hong Kong: Transplantation and adaptation by the British professions, 1841–1941," *Planning Perspective* 27, no. 4 (December 2012): 549–568.
4. The figure is from "Oriental pearl from 1.5 century's reclamation," *Wen Wei Po* (October 18, 2018).
5. Charlie Q.L. Xue, *Hong Kong Architecture 1945-2015: From Colonial to Global* (Singapore: Springer, 2016). The reclamation part to reference of He Peiran, *Dihuan Shanyi: Changing Land and Moving Mountains: 160 Years of Port and Land Development in Hong Kong* (Hong Kong: Commercial Press, 2004).
6. Charlie Xue, Ka Chuen Hui, and Peng Zang, "Public Buildings in Hong Kong: A short account of evolution since the 1960s," *Habitat International* 38, no. 1 (2013): 57–69.
7. Charlie Q.L. Xue, Hailin Zhai, and Joshua Roberts, "An urban island floating on the MTR station: a case study of the West Kowloon development in Hong Kong," *Urban Design International* 15, no. 4 (October 2010): 191–207.
8. On people's doubt and debate on private developers' ability in West Kowloon, see Legislative Council Secretariat, "Excerpts of debates: building West Kowloon Cultural District by public participation," RN08/10-11 (2011).
9. Protection of Victoria Harbour; see (Harbourprotection.org 2015), see also Winston Chu, Court of Final Appeal Judgment Meaning of "Overriding Public Need" Proposed Proportionality Principle on Reclamation of Victoria Harbour (1st edn) (Hong Kong: Society of Protection of the Harbour, 2011).
10. The debate on buildable land in Hong Kong usually includes voices from many different groups (e.g., the government planning department, local citizens, and politicians). See report "Getting every inch of land for building," *Ta Kung Pao* (February 13, 2015).
11. For more information about the Star Ferry Pier, see *Cultural Research*, Lingnan, No.4 (March 2007).
12. For more information about the Queen's Pier demolition, see information from *Ming Pao Daily News* and *Singtao Daily*, July 30–August 1, 2007. Also see C Lai, "Heritage: Last resistance," *South China Morning Post* (May 13, 2007), A12.

26
BOMBAY/MUMBAI WATERFRONTS IN THE HINDI FILM *DEEWAAR* [*THE WALL*] (1975)[1]

Vandana Baweja

This paper analyzes the representation of Bombay's waterfronts in the Hindi movie Deewaar [The Wall] *(1975) in the context of India's three foundational ideals—socialism, secularism, and modernist urbanism. The film depicts waterfronts as sites of historic globalization processes that have shaped the city's urban culture. The waterfronts in the film—Marine Drive, Malabar Hill, and Versova Beach on the west; and the docks and Ballard Estate on the east—comprise spaces of globalization that represent a tension between globalization; and the three ideals of socialism, secularism, and modernist urbanism. The narrative ends with upholding the state's economic ideology that was geared at deglobalization. The film celebrates the docks as a site of Bombay's secular cosmopolitanism, but also depicts the docks as a symbol of the failure of the state's promise to build an equitable society. In* Deewaar, *the glitzy waterfronts of Marine Drive and Nariman Point represent aspirational urban icons of planned urbanism, which nevertheless failed the modernist promise of an equitable society. Viewed through the lens of urban histories,* Deewaar's *depiction of waterfronts as spaces of globalization in Bombay illuminates the contradictions of Nehruvian statecraft with respect to globalization to represent social mobility and cosmopolitanism in the city in the 1970s.*

The city of Mumbai (formerly known as Bombay) occupies a narrow peninsula on the western coast of India, with its southern tip in the Arabian Sea and mainland the to the north. To the west lies the Arabian Sea, while the eastern shore forms a natural deep-water harbor with the adjacent Konkan coast. The city developed on a south to north peninsular axis, with its western and eastern waterfronts forming a historic palimpsest of the city's changing relationship with transoceanic networks of trade, culture contact, and political control. Thus, these waterfronts and the infrastructure that supports them are chronotropes of the city's urban history within the broader ambit of globalization.

This chapter considers representation of Bombay's waterfronts in the Hindi movie *Deewaar* [*The Wall*] (1975) in the context of the three foundational ideals of the Indian state—socialism, secularism, and urban modernity.[2] I use the toponym Bombay to indicate the city as it was officially known prior to 1995. I argue that the film frames waterfronts as key sites in the formation of the city's urban culture, and that the specific spaces constituting the *mis-en-scène*—Marine Drive, Malabar Hill, and Versova Beach on the west; and the docks and Ballard Estate on the east—represent a tension between an economic and urban cultural cosmopolitan and the nation-building project. I show how the narrative of the film attempts closure around the state's strategy of developing a formal national command economy, independent of foreign control. While the film celebrates the docks as a site of Bombay's secular cosmopolitanism on the one hand, it simultaneously depicts them on the other hand as a symbol of the failure of the state's ability to police its economic borders and its promise to build an equitable society. Throughout *Deewaar*, the glitzy waterfronts of Marine Drive and Nariman Point represent aspirational urban icons of planned urbanism that were made possible through global expertise and modern infrastructure, which nevertheless failed the modernist promise of an equitable society. In the end, *Deewaar*'s depiction of waterfronts as infrastructural spaces of globalization illuminates the paradoxes of Nehruvian statecraft. The film uses affective relations to waterfronts as globalized spaces of modern infrastructure and liminal spaces between the nation-state and Indian ocean networks to represent the contradictions of post-independence Indian political economy with respect to developmental modernization and globalization.

The Struggle to Control Bombay/Mumbai

Following the Great Indian Rebellion in 1857, the Bombay Presidency came under direct British control when the Crown seized the Subcontinent from the East India Company. The city continued to serve as the financial center of India, both under colonial rule and independence in 1947. In 1960, the former Bombay Presidency was divided between the states of Gujarat and Maharashtra on linguistic basis, and Bombay city became the capital of Maharashtra. Jawahar Lal Nehru, India's first prime minister, advanced a foundational ideology of modernization that included political democracy, a socialist economy, a state sponsored development agenda, urbanization, and secularism.[3] The nation-state was formed through the union of numerous ethno-linguistic provinces, which were further fragmented along religious and caste fault lines. Thus, ideals of citizenship were forged through privileging the individual's allegiance to the Indian nation over loyalty to caste, religion, or linguistic-ethnicity. The Nehruvian promise of the utopian state was geared toward the creation of a classless society and the repudiation of provincial and historic registers of identity, which attracted Nehru to the social program of modernist urbanism, architecture, and infrastructure development.[4] To move this agenda forward, Congress party leaders legislated a socialist economy wherein the state owned the majority of the industrial sector, and after 1969 acquired the banking sector too.

As part of the British Empire, the Indian economy had long been part of global trade and finance networks, with Bombay as India's chief entrepôt after the mid-nineteenth century. As India embraced socialism, however, it withdrew from the global economy, which was synonymous with colonialism. But the state continued to embrace modernist urbanism, infrastructure, and architecture for its allure of universalism, although in actuality these were rooted in the very globalizing logics and colonial spheres of influence that India sought to escape. As part of a developmental modernization project, the Indian state became a patron of New Towns, modern architecture, and large infrastructure projects of which Chandigarh and the Bhakra Nangal dam are prime examples. Nehru famously called dams as the new temples of India. Nehru's attraction to modern architecture, modernist planning, and large infrastructure projects as nation-building missions was embedded in modernization's utopian promise to create cosmopolitan urban environments that transcended provincial loyalties and parochial identities. However, these modernization projects represent an ideological contradiction. On the one hand, they were embedded in global hegemonic flows of expertise and paradigms of progress through development. On the other hand, planners and state officials conceived development as a nation-building project, using infrastructure to expand the state's role in society. Thus, in the Nehruvian world, cultural, urban, and infrastructural development would be intellectually and ideologically compartmentalized from economic globalization.

Bombay: From an Archipelago to a City

Prior to the mid-nineteenth century, Bombay developed around a fortified colonial factory called the Bombay Castle, which was built on the eastern coast of the Bombay island to take advantage of its natural harbor.[5] The castle was eventually engulfed within a much larger walled settlement called the Bombay Fort.[6] On the western coast of the fort was an open area called the esplanade or *Maidan*, which was a strategic space for a clear line of fire.⁷ After 1803, organic settlements that housed Indian laborers, merchants, and the indigenous population sprawled outside the northern edge of the fort's walls.⁸ This pattern continued to shape colonial Bombay's class divide, with elite colonial spaces in the south and west; and a mosaic of ethno-linguistic, religious, and caste-based enclaves in the north and east. Thus, in the eighteenth-century Bombay's waterfronts comprised the eastern fortified settlement with maritime access to the harbor and the western esplanade on the Arabian Sea. This east–west geography shaped the future functional and class divide of Bombay's seafronts with eastern dockyards as spaces of low-end globalization and western leisure waterfronts as spaces of high-end globalization. This east–west geography forms the basis of *Deewaar*'s spatial narrative.

Bombay's eastern seafront contains a natural deep-water harbor, which made it an ideal site for docks, quays, *bunders* (piers), and other shipping infrastructure. The dockyards on the east comprise an area of 730 hectares along a waterfront seventeen miles long, stretching from Colaba in the south to Wadala in the north.⁹ Sassoon Dock (1878–1893, rebuilt 1995), the city's first wet dock is just north of Colaba.¹⁰ Built through the Apollo Reclamation project (1865–1897), to the north of the Sassoon dock is the Apollo *bunder*, which contains the Gateway of India (1924) designed by the Scottish architect George Wittet (1878–1926). The Ballard Estate and the Ballard Pier (1908–1914), located north of the Apollo *bunder*, were built on Bombay Port Trust's reclaimed land next to the docks. Wittet planned the Ballard estate as a commercial district for businesses that operated at the docks.¹¹ To the north of Ballard Pier are dockyards—Prince's Dock (1880), Victoria Dock (1888), and Alexandra Dock (1914, renamed Indira Dock in 1972).¹² Many of these waterfront spaces form the *mis-en-scène* as part of the urban milieu for the film *Deewaar* (see Figure 26.1). The western seafront comprises promenades such as Marine Drive and Worli Sea face. In addition to these civic spaces, the west coast has public beaches such as Chowpatty, Dadar, Juhu, and Versova, which are punctuated by a series of *Koliwada* communities.

Shifting Economies on the Waterfront

Until the mid-nineteenth century, Bombay grew in a south to north axis along the peninsula and around Fort George, constructed by the British East India Company in 1769. In addition to this colonial trade, there was also an indigenous economy via Indian oceanic networks that predated the European colonial rule in the regions of the Red Sea, the Persian Gulf, and the Swahili coast—with the caveat that Bombay was the new entrepôt in the Indian ocean economy on the western coast.¹³ The city's status in global trade networks changed dramatically after the Suez Canal opened in 1869, which established a much faster trade route between Europe, the Middle East, and the Subcontinent. Bombay's proximity to the Suez Canal, and the city's growing strategic importance in British colonialism, ensured its gateway status, and the facilities of the waterfront expanded to accommodate increased transoceanic trade.¹⁴ Meanwhile, the American civil war disrupted the cotton supply chain to the British textile mills, and Bombay became the *cottonopolis* of India—the hub of cotton export to mills in Manchester and Lancashire. Macroeconomic trade via Bombay, which comprises high-end globalization, including: Malwa opium smuggled into China; cotton yarn exported into China; raw cotton supplied from the Indian Deccan region to Lancashire mills; exports of mineral ores, grains, and animal hides; imports of manufactured goods from England; and Arabian imports via Muscat, Ormuz, and Basra generated capital for high-end urban, infrastructural, and industrial development of Bombay in the nineteenth century.¹⁵ These high-end trade flows resulted in what I call spaces and infrastructures of high-end globalization. Along with these high-end projects, mercantile districts known as *Bazaar* enclaves emerged that were the result of indigenous trade in the Indian Ocean. Known as the *Bazaar* economy, these trade flows were either completely independent of the colonial economy or collaborative enterprises, in which Indian agents acted as intermediaries between Indian oceanic indigenous agents and the British. The *Bazaar* economy constitutes low-end globalization, which comprises movement of people and goods across borders, in which individual agents act as autonomous agents either outside, or somewhat

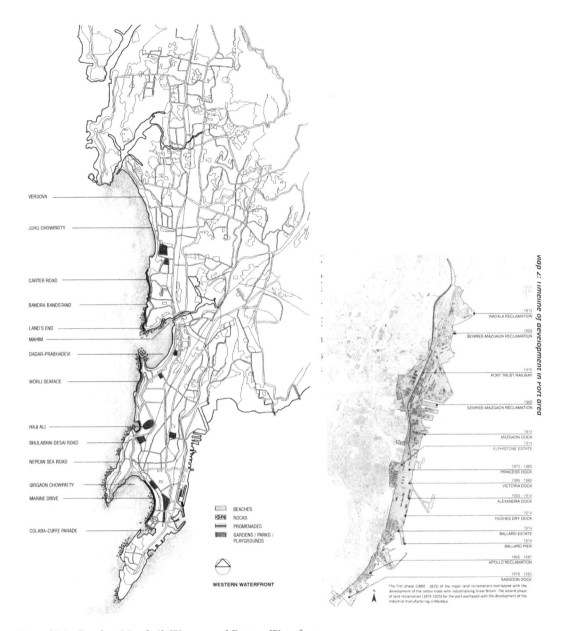

Figure 26.1 Bombay/Mumbai's Western and Eastern Waterfronts.

Source: Map drawn by the Vandana Baweja.

outside, legal and formal trade apparatuses. The construction of infrastructural, industrial, and urban projects demanded a large migrant workforce that led to the rapid expansion of informal settlements in the city. These spaces of low-end globalization—namely *Bazaar* enclaves and informal settlements—in colonial Bombay grew on the basis of indigenous architecture and urbanism of the émigré merchants and laborers.

Profits from the cotton trade inaugurated large-scale urban design and infrastructural projects in Bombay. Lord Elphinstone, Governor of Bombay (1853–1860), which opened up land for the eventual construction of an ensemble of Victorian Gothic buildings along the *Maidan*.[16] This ensemble included the Public Works Department Offices (1872), the Central Telegraph Office (1872), the Secretariat building (1874), the University Library and Convocation Hall (1874), the High Court (1878), and finally the pièce de resistance, the Victoria Terminus (1888).[17] Until the first quarter of the twentieth century, this Gothic collection dominated Bombay's western waterfront. By the 1930s, Marine Drive began to eclipse this Gothic waterfront. The Back Bay reclamation project, which commenced in the 1920s and concluded in the 1970s with the construction of the Nariman Point business district, extended the western waterfront further into the Arabian Sea. Marine Drive (also known as Queen's Necklace) is a C-shaped waterfront animated by a promenade and a boulevard. Between the promenade and the Arabian Sea, a retaining wall lined with concrete tetrapods forms the coastal edge of Marine Drive (Figure 26.1). On the landside of the boulevard, a row of Art Deco buildings faces the ocean. Nariman Point, a business district constructed after independence, defines the southern extent of Marine Drive, while Chowpatty beach forms its northern end. Malabar Hill, the most elite residential area in the city, defines Back Bay's northwestern extent.

The economic stratifications of colonial Bombay were mapped spatially on the city to create an urban geography of formal and informal urbanism, which corresponds to spaces of high-end and low-end globalization. The elite colonial spaces such as the Gothic ensemble, Elphinstone Circle, Flora Fountain, and Marine Drive were built in South Bombay. These spaces of high-end globalization are the product of international technological, capital, and cultural flows.

Conflicts between Economic and Cultural Cosmopolitanism after Independence

In the Nehruvian calculus, the city of Bombay had a peculiar position. On the one hand, until the 1990s it was India's most cosmopolitan city and, thus, emblematic of Nehruvian secularism. Numerous ethno-linguistic, religious, and caste-based population clusters in close proximity make Bombay a rich urban mosaic of provincial factions, which made it a site of cultural cosmopolitanism. This made the city a microcosm of the Indian state, with the caveat that many of these communities continue to inhabit unplanned settlements, slums, and waterfront villages—all of which were Nehru's bane in the arena of modern urbanism and infrastructure. On the other hand, in the 1970s Bombay was a site of tension between the socialist and globalist economies, as it became the principal entrepôt of gold smuggling from Dubai into India. The tension between indigenous mercantile capitalism and a global economy, which I call economic cosmopolitanism, is a recurring phenomenon in the city's history. This triumvirate of conflicts between cultural versus economic cosmopolitanism, informal versus formal infrastructure and urbanism, and high-end versus low-end globalization forms the basis of the waterfronts as the *mise-en-scène* in *Deewaar*.

The Bombay of *Deewaar*

From the 1950s to the 1970s, through successive regulations the Nehruvian economy became insular in an attempt to become self-sufficient and, thus, withdrew from global free market capitalism. The Nehruvian promise of an equitable society relied on distributive measures—such as high corporate and individual taxes, foreign exchange controls, limitations on the free import of goods, nationalization of banks, state monopoly on the industrial sector, and labor participation in industrial enterprises—which despite being well-intentioned failed due to depressed growth and corruption.[18] By the 1970s, in the context of the OPEC crises the attempt to become a self-sufficient closed economy had the opposite effect of scarcities of fossil fuels, construction materials, food, housing, and job opportunities. This led to even wider class differences, labor unrest, and an illegal economy. The legal economy in India operates with "white money," on which people pay taxes, while the illegal "black money" economy runs on a range of activities that include high-end organized crime, petty crime, and tax evasion via underreported legal transactions. Here, it is important to distinguish between the illegal economy and the informal economy. The informal economy comprises acts of tax-evasion via low-end small cash transactions for legal services provided by the urban poor, such as street vending and manual labor, which are illegal from a taxation purpose but tolerated by the state, as opposed to the illegal economy that comprises big cash transactions through both licit and illicit activities.

In the 1970s in Bombay, the illegal economy comprised a spectrum of activities that included white-collar, petty, and organized crime. White-collar crimes comprise underreporting of corporate profits to evade taxes, wage theft, underpayment of import duties and levies, and real estate transactions via untaxed cash.[19] Petty crime includes violations on a small scale, such as theft, pickpocketing, and shoplifting, in which individuals act independently. Such offenders are not professional hardcore criminals, and often turn to crime due to poverty-induced desperation. Organized crime includes a range of activities, such as: black-market sale of commodities, fuel, and construction materials, particularly cement; murder; extortion; kidnapping; smuggling of gold, diamonds, and foreign luxury goods; and money laundering.[20] Gold smuggling from Dubai along the historic Indian ocean routes became a key component of organized crime. After the 1962 Chinese attack, India imposed Gold Control Rules to restrict gold trade and the 1965 Gold Control Act prohibited the ownership of bullion, which led to the illegal import of gold.[21] With an exponential rise in black money and the devaluation of the Indian rupee, gold smuggling increased dramatically.[22] During the late 1960s and 1970s, at the height of socialism Bombay became a hub of illegal global trade, comprised principally of the smuggling of luxury goods and gold.

Deewaar: The Narrative

The smuggling of gold into Bombay in the 1970s and 1980s was a key theme in a number of films such as *Deewaar* [*The Wall*] (1975), *Don* (1978), and *Shaan* [*Prestige*] (1980).[23] *Deewaar*'s narrative centers on the political and economic breakdowns of the Nehruvian state along with the unfulfilled dream of rationally planned and well-ordered cities. The film revolves around a mother's account of her two sons and their efforts to navigate the failures of the nation-state. Through a flashback of her life story, the mother Sumitra Devi (Nirupa Roy) narrates how her older son Vijay (Amitabh Bachchan) became a gold smuggler who betrays the nation, and how her younger son Ravi (Shashi Kapoor) became a law-enforcing police officer.

The film begins in a provincial mill town, where Sumitra's husband, Anand Verma (Satyen Kappoo), a union leader, demands better working conditions and wages for laborers. However, the mill-owner kidnaps Sumitra and their two sons in order to strong-arm Anand into signing a union contract that betrays the workers. Faced with an ethical dilemma—a choice between his family and the interests of the union—Anand opts to protect his family. Subsequently, he flees the town out of shame. Sumitra and her two sons, at the cusp of their teens, emigrate to Bombay, where she takes up a job as a construction worker. Her sons grow up homeless on the pavement under an arched bridge on the streets. Vijay takes up menial day jobs such as shoe-shining to support his younger brother, who goes to school and becomes educated. The adult brothers are eventually separated by education, class, and religious faith: Vijay becomes a blue-collar worker on the eastern docks in Bombay, while Ravi gets a job as a police sub-inspector; and Ravi visits the Hindu temple every day with his mother, while Vijay refuses to step inside the temple. Eventually, Vijay joins an organized crime syndicate to become a gold smuggler, operating out of a building that offers a panoramic view of Marine Drive.

As a smuggler, Vijay navigates spaces of high-end and low-end globalization in the city. He seamlessly brokers between rough waterfront locales such as docks and smuggling entry points, and the luxurious landscape of glitzy skyscrapers. Eventually Ravi, the policeman, is assigned the task of arresting his smuggler brother. Ravi faces an ethical dilemma—a choice between his allegiance to the state and his loyalty to his family. The film ends with fratricide when Ravi shoots Vijay in a chase scene on Ballard Estate. In this way, the film makes an effort at narrative closure around the defeat of lawlessness, the discrediting of illicit trade as a threat to the nation's economic prosperity, and the restoration of the state's prerogative to broker the common good.

Deewaar and the Docks

Scholars have noted how the plot of *Deewaar* hinges on the tensions between the nation-state and the family in the context of the 1970s social, political, and economic milieu in India.[24] This tension drives the narrative forward, and the film ends with a family that resolves the nation-state's failures.[25] In his analysis of *Deewaar*, Vinay Lal notes how "Vijay teeters between the skyscraper and the footpath," revealing extreme class stratification between pavement dwelling and skyscrapers and the tension between the allegiance to the nation-state and loyalty to the family. These tensions form the bedrock of *Deewaar*'s narrative.[26] However, Bombay's status as a city on the world stage, with its attendant spaces of globalization, have not been explored in depth in relation to the film. The waterfronts that form the film's *mis-en-scène* sit uneasily within Nehruvian political ideals and the unpredictable, uncontrollable effects of the global economy. In an anti-colonial economy of nationalization, in which the state controlled the flow of goods and capital at its borders, the smuggling of gold via Bombay constituted an illicit form of global trade. Nehruvian ideals had an unresolved relationship with globalization. On the one hand, Nehru's economic policies were geared at nationalization, but on the other hand his urban modernist ideals were ideologically grounded in globalization.[27]

Deewaar depicts the transformation of Vijay from a blue-collar dockworker into a smuggler entrenched in Bombay's crime world. As a coolie, Vijay unloads cargo from ships that enter Bombay legally. While working on the docks, he befriends an older Muslim mentor, Rahim *chacha* (Yunuz Parvez, *chacha* means paternal uncle), who informs Vijay that his *billa* (coolie identification metal badge tied on the forearm like an armlet) is numbered 786—a number that is auspicious to Muslims (Figure 26.2). Vijay, who is a non-practicing Hindu, treats the *billa* as a talisman after Rahim *chacha* assures him that Allah would protect him as long as he had his *billa* 786.

Deewaar depicts the port infrastructure as an historic site of both high-end and low-end globalization, and a waterfront of legal and illegal global trade. The harbor comprises planned infrastructure that knits together formal and informal spaces. The history of the port infrastructure represents high-end globalization through global flows of capital, technology, and expertise, and low-end globalization through the confluence of diverse émigré-labor cultural practices, which formed along the coastal seam between the Indian hinterland and Indian Ocean networks. Thus, Vijay's faith in *billa* 786 and his friendship with Rahim *Chacha* is not only emblematic of the dockyard's history as a site of low-end cultural mixing and exchange, but also an embodiment of existing Nehruvian secular ideas and Bombay's status as India's most cosmopolitan city. Rahim *Chacha* represents the pedigree of Bombay's Muslim émigré workforce from Konkan and Hyderabad, who not only constituted a significant portion of the dock labor from the 1870s to the 1910s, but were also part of an Indian oceanic religious economy.[28] In addition, the presence of Rahim *Chacha* on the docks embodies the spatial topography of the city, where key Muslim enclaves are situated close to the waterfront, including Bhendi Bazaar, Mohammed Ali Road, and Hazrat Abbas Road. By the 1970s, these locales had become home to a mercantile diaspora of Shi'a Isma'ili Bohras and Khojas, Sunni Memons, and Iranian émigrés from Shiraz and Yazd.[29] The key cultural attributes of these communities—religious devotion, architecture, street culture, and food—represent low-end global mercantile networks that linked Bombay to the Red Sea, the Persian Gulf, and the Swahili coast.

In the film, waterfront infrastructure is not just a site of restricted legal global trade, but a steppingstone for blue-collar workers and petty criminals into the world of organized crime. Vijay rebels against the *hafta* (the mafia's weekly extortion of dockworkers' wages), which elevates him to a cult hero at the docks and gains him entrance into a smuggling syndicate, which heralds his transition from an agent of legal to illegal globalization. The docks, as a site of low-end globalization, represent the dysfunctions and triumphs of the Nehruvian state vis-à-vis globalization. As a location of exploited labor, mafia

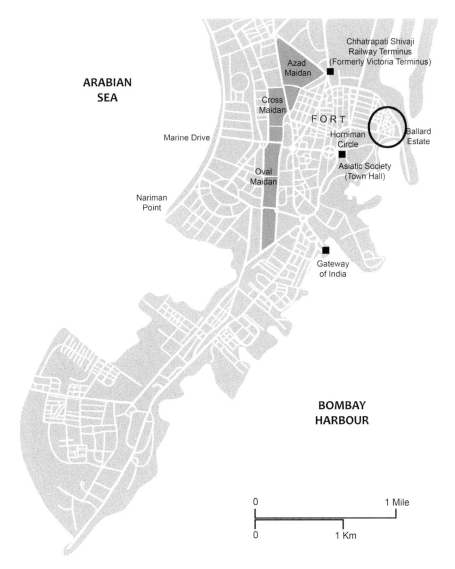

Figure 26.2 A map of South Bombay showing Nariman Point, Marine Drive, Maidans, Ballard Estate, and the Gateway of India.

Source: Map drawn by Vandana Baweja.

extortion, illicit global trade, and informal habitation, the docks are depicted as a site that failed the Nehruvian promise, but the friendship between Rahim *Chacha* and Vijay represents the success of secularism. The docks thus represent the tension between cultural and economic cosmopolitanism. As spaces that mark the border of the nation-state, the docks and their associated infrastructure are spaces that depict the limits of the Nehruvian project of a developmental state.

Deewaar: Marine Drive

The sequence of Vijay's induction into Davar's (Iftekhar) organized crime syndicate was shot in an upper-story room in the Oberoi Trident Hotel located at the end of Marine Drive. In the shot, Vijay gazes out of the window to admire the panoramic view of the seafront and reminisces about his homeless

Figure 26.3 Left: Vijay with *billa* 786. Right: Vijay and Rahim *Chacha* on the docks.

Source: Film still in possession of Vandana Baweja, from Yash Chopra, *Deewaar* (Trimurti Films Pvt. Ltd, 1975).

childhood with his mother and brother on the promenade (Figure 26.3). Marine Drive represents an urban space that he could formerly only access as a pedestrian. Now Vijay overlooks Marine Drive from the privileged vantage point of the elite who have access to interior spaces in the highly priced buildings. To cross the class barriers that the nation-state promised to erase, Vijay relinquishes the path of making an honest lawful living. As Vijay establishes himself as a successful gold smuggler, he invests his profits into a lavish bungalow and buys a skyscraper on the site where his mother was employed as a construction worker, which underscores how illicit global capital and black money drove the construction industry in Bombay. Along with the architecture, he has transformed his dress, mannerisms, and persona from a blue-collar worker to a suave elite buyer of global consumer products that were exorbitantly priced.

The film depicts Vijay navigating the world of glitzy waterfront skyscrapers. In a scene in the dining area around the rooftop swimming pool of the five-star Oberoi-Trident Hotel, Vijay meets with Davar's gang to plan smuggling operations (Figure 26.4). In these long shots, the characters are in the foreground with Malabar Hill and Marine Drive, and the skyscrapers of Nariman Point in the background (Figure 26.4). In the film, Marine Drive is presented as a key piece of infrastructure that connects spaces of high-end globalization. With its Art Deco architecture that in its interwar heyday represented the agency of semi-sovereign actors such as Maharajahs and Parsi entrepreneurs in India, Marine Drive depicts the kind of planned urban ensemble that would later become emblematic of Nehruvian modernity in the sphere of urbanism. On the one hand, then, these elite waterfronts are the products of large-scale land reclamation, engineering expertise, and architectural spectacle, making them icons of Bombay's cosmopolitanism. On the other hand, these very spaces have seduced Vijay into the murky world of illicit globalization, where lines between legal and illegal, national and international, right and wrong become blurred. The elite waterfront undermines the promise of a new Indian social order made righteous and just through commitments to democracy, equality, and the nation.

Deewaar: Versova Beach and Ballard Estate

In *Deewaar*, Versova Beach on the north-western coast of Bombay, is depicted as an entry point for maritime gold smuggling from Dubai. Merchants in Dubai would purchase bullion legally shipped from London, Zurich, and Beirut, and then arrange for the bullion to be shipped to Bombay via Indian *dhows* (wooden sailing ships) called *padaos*.[30] The *padaos* did not enter the Bombay port via the docks, which were the legal entry points for maritime trade, but often transferred their contraband to fishing

Figure 26.4 Top left: Vijay dominates the view of the coast with a long shot of Marine Drive, the Art Deco ensemble on the Back Bay in the Arabian Sea. Top right: Vijay reminisces about his homeless childhood with his mother and brother on the Marine Drive promenade. Bottom left: Vijay with Davar's gang by the swimming pool with a long shot of Malabar Hill. Bottom right: Vijay with Davar's gang by the swimming pool with a long shot of the Marine Drive coastline.

Source: Film stills in possession of Vandana Baweja, from Yash Chopra, *Deewaar* (Trimurti Films Pvt. Ltd, 1975).

boats, which then dropped it off on deserted beaches at night.[31] In *Deewaar*, when the gold is offloaded at Versova Beach, the two parties—the shipping and the receiving gangs—each would have one half of a Bank of England currency bill as verification of their identities. When the torn edges of the bill are perfectly aligned, the contraband is offloaded on the beach. The use of the Bank of England bill signifies the ongoing dominance of hard currency as a legacy of British colonialism, now linked to illicit trade.

The climax of the film is set at Ballard Estate, where Ravi chases Vijay and shoots him. George Wittet, the architect of Indo-Saracenic icons such as the Gateway of India and the Prince of Wales Museum, designed the business district of Ballard Estate during World War I as a Beaux Arts ensemble with elevation controls and height limits.[32] The key buildings in the Estate include Construction House, Darabshaw House, Neville House, Mahindra House, the Customs Building, and the Old Bombay Port Trust Building, characterized by features such as arcades, lower-level rusticated masonry, friezes, and ornate column capitals.[33] During the movie climax, Ravi chases Vijay through a rusticated masonry arcade in an area that is the epicenter of regulating global trade, with the offices of the Port Trust and the Customs House—the gatekeepers of the territorial borders of Bombay—in view. As an agent of the state, Ravi rejects his kinship-loyalty to uphold his allegiance to country. Vijay as an agent of illicit global trade is shot, and he eventually dies in the temple that he rejected all his life, which signifies a return to *dharma*, one's moral duty.

Thus, the movie ends with an effort to restore narrative equilibrium in which the seductive lure of globalization, skyscraper-lined glitzy waterfronts, and capitalistic consumerism is negated, and the nation-state triumphs as the agent for the enforcement of the public good. *Deewaar* depicts the urban socio-spatial nexus of white-collar, petty, and organized crime through the conflicting representations of waterfronts as liminal spaces of modern infrastructure that are sites of tension between cultural versus economic cosmopolitanism, informal versus formal urbanism, and high-end versus low-end globalization. Although the closure of the narrative restores the nation-state's control over its waterfronts that are spaces of infrastructure and constitute the state's borders, the film fails to resolve internal contradictions of the nation-state's foundational tenets—socialism, secularism, and urban modernity.

Notes

1 I would like to thank Joseph Heathcott for his editorial input, Adriana Dunlap for assisting me with making maps for this chapter, and the Quest One Program at the University of Florida for providing financial support for drawing maps.
2 Yash Chopra, *Deewaar* (Trimurti Films Pvt. Ltd, 1975).
3 Bhikhu Parekh, "Nehru and the National Philosophy of India," *Economic and Political Weekly* 26, no. 1/2 (1991): 35–48.
4 On issues of equity, see Jawaharlal Nehru, "Address at Columbia University, New York" (Speech, Columbia University, New York, October 17, 1949) where he declared that a democracy cannot survive amidst poverty and inequality. On how cities can promote a new social order, see National Institute of Urban Affairs, *Jawaharlal Nehru on Building a New India: A Construct of His Sayings on Art, Architecture, Heritage, Cities and City Planning* (New Delhi: National Institute of Urban Affairs, 1991), 93–122.
5 Norma Evenson, *The Indian Metropolis: A View Toward the West* (New Haven: Yale University Press, 1989), 1–46.
6 Ibid.
7 Ibid.
8 Meera Kosambi, "Three Colonial Port Cities in India," *Geographical Review* 78, no. 1 (1988): 32–47.
9 Special Planning Authority and Mumbai Port Trust, "Draft Report on Planning Proposals" (Mumbai: Mumbai Port Trust, December 2018), 1.
10 W.R.S. Sharpe and Bombay Port Trust, *The Port of Bombay* (Bombay: Bombay Port Trust, 1930), 22.
11 Sharada Dwivedi and Rahul Mehrotra, *Bombay: The Cities Within* (Bombay: India Book House, 1995), 85–160.
12 Special Planning Authority and Mumbai Port Trust, "Draft Report on Planning Proposals," 1.
13 Rajat Kanta Ray, "Asian Capital in the Age of European Domination: The Rise of the Bazaar, 1800–1914," *Modern Asian Studies* 29, no. 3 (1995): 449–554 and Tirthankar Roy, "Trading Firms in Colonial India," *The Business History Review* 88, no. 1 (2014): 9–42.
14 Dwivedi and Mehrotra, *Bombay*, 188.
15 Amar Farooqui, "Urban Development in a Colonial Situation: Early Nineteenth Century Bombay," *Economic and Political Weekly* 31, no. 40 (1996): 2746–2759.
16 Ibid.
17 Ibid.
18 Stanley A. Kochanek, "Briefcase Politics in India: The Congress Party and the Business Elite," *Asian Survey* 27, no. 12 (1987): 1278–1301. Subrata Ghatak and Jalal Uddin Siddiki, "Trade Distortions and Virtual Exchange Rates in India," in *The Indian Economy: Contemporary Issues*, ed. Nicholas Perdikis (Aldershot, UK: Ashgate, 2000), 11–36; and V. Venkata Rao, "Socialist Thought of Jawaharlal Nehru," *The Indian Journal of Political Science* 48, no. 2 (1987): 195–211.
19 See Kochanek, "Briefcase Politics in India," and M. Charles, "The Growth and Activities of Organised Crime in Bombay," *International Social Science Journal* 53, no. 169 (2001): 359–368.
20 Ibid.
21 Sanjay Swarnkar, "The Gold Control Act of 1965, Its Socio-Economic Implications," *Proceedings of the Indian History Congress* 70 (2009): 1181–1191.
22 Ajay Gandhi, "A Superlative Form: How Gold Mediates Personhood and Property in Mumbai," *Etnofoor* 25, no. 1 (2013): 91–110.
23 Chopra, *Deewaar*; Chandra Barot, *Don* (Nariman Films, 1978); and Ramesh Sippy, *Shaan (The Pride)* (NH Studioz, 1980).
24 Jyotika Virdi, "Deewar: The 'Fiction' of Film and 'Fact' of Politics," *Jump Cut* 38 (June 1993): 26–32; and Priya Joshi, *Bollywood's India* (New York: Columbia University Press, 2015), 63–90.

25 Joshi, *Bollywood's India* (New York: Columbia University Press, 2015), 63–90.
26 Vinay Lal, *Deewar: The Footpath, the City and the Angry Young Man* (New Delhi: Harper Collins, 2012), kindle edition 626 of 1982.
27 Jawaharlal Nehru, "Chandigarh: A Symbol of Planned Development," in *Selected Works of Jawaharlal Nehru*, ed. Sarvepalli Gopal, Vol. 28, II (New Delhi: Orient Longman, 1972), 25–28.
28 Nile Green, *Bombay Islam: The Religious Economy of the West Indian Ocean, 1840–1915* (Cambridge, UK; New York: Cambridge University Press, 2011), 170–208.
29 Ibid.
30 Esmond Bradley Martin, "The Geography of Present-Day Smuggling in the Western Indian Ocean: The Case of the Dhow," *The Great Circle* 1, no. 2 (1979): 18–35.
31 Ibid.
32 Urban Design Research Institute and Bombay First, *Ballard Estate: A Corporate District: A Proposal for Upgrading and Managing the Area* (Bombay: Urban Design Research Institute, 2000), 7–12.
33 Ibid.

INDEX

Note: Locators in *italics* represent figures.

2G phones with internet access 63

abarracamentos (shack concentrations) 78–79
ACA. *see* Automóvil Club Argentino
Adanson, Michel 48
adobe bricks 260, *261*, 265
AD + RG of Hong Kong 298
adventure 236–237; playgrounds 110–111
AESB. *see* Architects and Engineers Spanish Bases
Afghan Civil War 66
Afghan Hazara 64
Afghanistan: *burqa* 70; mandatory girls education 66; *purdah* 66–67, 70; Taliban, emergence of 70; television studio in Kabul 69; virtual forum for women 63; virtual media spaces 63; women's mobility and freedom 63
Afghanistan's Revolutionary Council 69
Afghan Ministry of Telecommunications and internet Technology 71
Afghan Trade Commission 65
Agrippa, Marcus Vipsanius 26–27
aguadores (water sellers) 286
Ahmed, Sheikh 200–201
Airport Express railway line 297
airports: access roads and rail lines 147–150; Atatürk Airport 143; Charles de Gaulle Airport, Paris 143, 145–146, *146*, 147–148; Chek Lap Kok International Airport 297; flat land, runways 143–144; Frankfurt Airport 143; Gimpo International Airport 143, 149; Hamad International Airport 205; Hong Kong International Airport 143–144, 147, 149; Incheon International Airport, Seoul 143–145, 149, *149*, 150; Istanbul Airport 143; Kai Tak Airport redevelopment 298–300; Kansai International Airport, Osaka 143–144; Kuala Lumpur International Airport 147; London's Stansted Airport 147; Madrid-Barajas Airport 143; Schiphol Airport 143, 145, 147; shopping 147; spectacles, protests, and politics 150–151; terminal building 144–147
air terminal: elevation 145; girders and skylights 145; London Heathrow 146; naturally lit and open-spaced 147; Paris Charles de Gaulle Airport 145–146, *146*; Schiphol 145; security concerns 144; terminal 2, Frankfurt Airport *144*; upper and lower roadways 145
Ajofrín, Francisco de 283, 288
Alagadiço Concentration Camp 79
Albano, Idelfonso 79
Albert Embankment 52
Al-Bidda 198
Alexander III of Macedon 25
Alexandra Dock 308
Alexandria 21, 23
Allom, Thomas 139
Al-Thani, Sheikh Hamad bin Khalifa 198–199
altimetry 272
aluminum 53
Amager Bakke waste-to-energy plant, Copenhagen *115*; hedonistic sustainability 114–115; recreation and play 115; ski slope and hiking trails 114
Amanullah, Emir 66
À margem da história (The Amazon: Land without History) 120
Amazon: agricultural and grazing plantation projects 118; cattle grazing *127*; demographic void 118, 123, 126; dictatorship and infrastructure 121–124; environmentalism 124–126; and nation-building 119–121; Operation Amazon 118, 123; Portuguese 119; sovereignty 118
"Amazônia Legal" 118
"Amenity Clause" of the Electricity Act of 1957 251–252, 255
American Exposition in Moscow 265
American University of Beirut (AUB) 265
America's urban bridge builder 168

Américo de Almeida, José 80
Anadolu Hisar 168
Anderson, Robert T. 111
Andreu, Paul 145–146, 148
Anglo–Afghan wars 64
Ankara 167
Anthropocene 53
Antony, Marc 20
Antwerp 187
Antwerp–Brussels–Charleroi (ABC) canal 98–99, *101*
Anwehr 66
AONB. *see* Area of Outstanding Natural Beauty
apartheid 154
Apollo Reclamation project 308
Arabian Gulf 198; pearl industry 199
Arab–Israeli conflict 55
Ara Pacis 26
"Arcadia," vision of 256
Arc-et-Senans. *see* Royal Saline at Arc-et-Senans
Arc-et-Senans Royal salt mine 34
Arc-et-Senans *saline* 33
architects 3, 13–14, 21, 24, 33, 37–38, 40, 51, 57, 98, 111–116, 142, 144–145, 147, 149, 151, 172, 174, 177, 181, 190, 194, 247–255, 284–285, 287, 292, 297–298; Architects and Engineers Spanish Bases (AESB) 276
architectural history 3
Architectural Review, The 250–251
architectural ruins 51
architectural symbolism 37
architecture, defined 3
Area of Outstanding Natural Beauty (AONB) 248, 253
Argolis, bridge 2
Arkitekten 114
Arup & Partners HK 298
asphalt: crude asphalt 219; hot-mix asphalt 217; natural (*see* natural asphalt); sheet asphalt 217–219; synthetic asphalt 220
Aswan granite 24–25
Atatürk Airport 143
Ataturk Bridge 168, 173
Atkinson, George 40
AUB. *see* American University of Beirut
Augustus (Octavian) 20, *25*; Egyptian granite 25; military presence in Egypt 21; ritual processions between Karnak and Luxor 26; sundial 26; transport of building materials 20
automobile caravans 234, 238, 240
Automóvil Club Argentino (ACA) 234, *241*; advocacy efforts 234; *Caracas Buenos Aires* 234, *235*, *241*; Gran Premio de la América del Sur *239*; international road races 236; travel 242
Automovilismo magazine 238, 240

Back Bay reclamation project 310
Baker, Newton 223
Ballard Estate 308, 314–316
Ballard Pier 308
ballast 211, 213
Ballent, Anahí 238

Baltimore, map of 228, *229*
bandeirantes 119
Bangalore-Mysore cloverleaf interchange 9
Barberá, Fernando Moreno 276
Barlindhaug Consult 58
Barroso, Benjamin 79
Barthelemy, Jean 103–106
Bartholomew, Harland 230
Battersea Power Station 250
Battle of Actium 20
BEA. *see* British Electrical Authority
Beard, Mary 19
bedouins (nomadic tribespeople) 258, 260, 265–266
Beery 111
Beijing Capital International Airport 150
Beijing Palace Museum 298
Belgian Congo 44
Bellville: city status 154; dystopic view 155; negative perception 155; Somali mall advertisement 154, *155*; Som City 156–158; VRCID 155; 'white' apartheid city 154
Belo Horizonte-Brasília Highway 180
Belt and Road Initiative, Afghanistan 73
benben 25–26
Benito Juarez International Airport, Mexico City 143
Benjamin, Walter 156
Benjamin Franklin Bridge in Philadelphia 168
Bentham, Jeremy 54
Benthem Crouwel Architects 145
Bertholletia excelsa tree 122
Bethlehem Steel 168
Beyan-ı Menazil-i Sefer-i Irakeyn-ı Sultan Süleyman 135, *135*, 137
Beylik Water Distribution Map 137
Bhakra Nangal dam 307
BIG and SLA landscape architects 114, *115*
big arch at At Pazarı 137, *137*
biodiversity 58
Black Lives Matter 72
Blondel, Jacques Francois 30
Blondel, Jean-François 31
Blue Circle Cement Ltd. 46
blue gum 216
Bolívar, Simón 235
Bombay Castle 307
Bombay Fort 307
Bombay/Mumbai waterfronts: from archipelago to city 307–308; *Bazaar* economy 308–309; *cottonopolis* of India 308; in *Deewaar* (*see Deewaar* [*The Wall*] (1975) (Hindi film)); economic and cultural cosmopolitanism, conflicts between 310; illegal "black money" economy 310–311; macroeconomic trade 308; OPEC crises 310; petty crime 311; secular cosmopolitanism 306; shifting economies 308–310; socialist and globalist economies 310; struggle to control 307; Western and Eastern Waterfronts *309*
Bombay Port Trust 308
bombers: B-47 heavy bombers 274; B52 long range bombers 277

Bonatz, Paul 172
Bonaventure Hotel 59
Bosanski Brod 187, *189*
Bosco, Dom Joao 177
Bosporus Bridge 165–166, *166*; historical precedents 166–167; ill-fated interwar project 167–170; proposal by Modjeski & Masters *169*; revision, controversy, and completion 172–174; revival of project 170–172
Bosporus silhouette 172
botanical imperialism 8
Bourgeois, Victor 98–100, 102, 104, 106
BPR. *see* Bureau of Public Roads
BR-364, diagonal interstate highway project 120
Branco, Humberto Castelo 118, 123
Brasilia, road construction 176–177; foundation of 177; highways linking 179; March of the Construction of Brasilia *182*; modern arcadia 181–185; national road system 176–177; position in Central Highlands *178*; project of modernity 177–179; sublime of infrastructure 179–181
Brazilian Revolution of 1930 80
Brazil's large infrastructural projects, labor mobilization 76–77; camp planning and development 80–82; consolidation of camps during the 1932 drought 79–80; droughts in *Nordeste* 77; migration and political order 77–78; modernizing Fortaleza 78–79; shift to migrant camps in 1915 79
Bredsdorff, Peter 111
brick: adobe bricks 260, *261*, 265; brick cathedrals 250; exposed brick 277; vitrified brick 211, 214
bridges: Ataturk Bridge 168, 173; Benjamin Franklin Bridge in Philadelphia 168; Bosporus Bridge 165–172; bridge of Valens Aqueduct 13; Galata Bridge 2, *2*; Golden Gate Bridge 168; Hamidiye Bridge 167; Loüe river bridge 32; San Francisco–Oakland Bay Bridge 168; suspension bridge 165; suspension bridge and connecting highway 173; of Valens Aqueduct 13
British Electrical Authority (BEA) 250
British Empire 307
British Royal Air Force 271
British textile mills 308
British War Office map of Afghanistan 65
broadcasting infrastructure 70
Brown, Capability 113, 248, 256
Brown-Raymond-Walsh 276
Brunhes, Jean 191
Bruxelles magazine 98
Buondelmonti, Christoforo 133, *134*, 139
Bureau of Public Roads (BPR), United States 224–225, *226*, 227–228, *228–229*
Buriti Camp 81
Burke, Edmund 179, 254
burqa 70. *see also* purdah

Cairo, necropolitan infrastructure 85; blurred boundaries 91–92; City of the Dead (Qarāfah) 85–90; death as agent in everyday living 90–91; everyday practices 88–90; historic necropolises 86; housing shortages 85; infrastructure of the dead 86–88; living with the dead 93
Calatrava, Juan 33
Calder Hall 248, 256
Camacho Bridge 290
camels 22–23
Campbell, Olive Dame 109
Campus Martius 26
cañadas (ravines) 287
Canal, Erie 11
canals: Antwerp–Brussels–Charleroi (ABC) canal 98–99, *101*; East Ghor Canal *259*, 264–265; Erie canal 11, 213; Greater Yarmouk project 264; great interoceanic canals 190; Panama Canal 237, 240; Suez Canal 308; West Ghor Canal 264; Xochimilco 4, 12
candangos 182–183
Canton-Kowloon railway 296
Caravanserai-i-Shah at Qazvin, Persia 6
CARE 261
Carr, E. Summerson 153
Carse, Ashley 278
cartography 269, 271; elements for mapmaking 272; of Western Europe 271
Casa del Real Ensaye 290
castles 255–256
CCC. *see* Civilian Conservation Corps
CEA. *see* Central Electricity Authority
Ceará 82–83
CEGB. *see* Central Electricity Generating Board
Cemaes Bay 254
cement in Africa 40–41; alternative genealogies (pre-1920s) 46–48; cement plants into meta-infrastructure 41; colonial project (1920s) 44–46; infrastructure of post-independence (After 1957) 41–44; materializing infrastructure 48–49; Nigeria 24; plants 40–42; production 41; wasteland 41
cement industry, Africa 41
central business district (CBD) 154
Central Electricity Authority (CEA), United Kingdom 250–251
Central Electricity Generating Board (CEGB), United Kingdom 247–249, 251–253, 256
Central Reclamation, Hong Kong *304*; contention over 300, 302–303; plan 303
Central Telegraph Office, Bombay 310
Cerdà, Ildefons 51
Cerfontaine village 102
Cerrado 179, 181
chadaari 64
Chamber of Architects 174
Chandigarh 307
Charleroi, terre d'urbanisme 100
Charles de Gaulle Airport, Paris 143, 145–148, *146*
Charles T. Main, Inc. 258–259, 264
Chattopadhyay, Swati 11
Chek Lap Kok International Airport 297
Chelsea Embankment, London 52
Chicago Mercantile Exchange 59
Chico, José Hernández 284
Chinese education and technology in Afghanistan 73

Chowpatty beach 308
Chrysler 227
Chrysler Plymouth car, 1941 model 236
CIAM conference *(Congrès internationaux d'architecture moderne)* 98, 194
Cimenterie Nationale in Kimpese 44
"City Beautiful" movement 223
"City Efficient" movement 223
City of Chaux 35
City of the Dead (Qarāfah) 85–93
"City of Tomorrow" *224*
civic associations 222
civil atomic program, United Kingdom 255
Civilian Conservation Corps (CCC), United States 265
Cleopatra 20
Cleveland Bridge and Engineering Co. 172
climate vulnerability 76
coal tar 217
cobblestones: Chinese 213, *214*; naturally rounded and irregular, use of 213; spread of 211, 213
Cohen, Elizabeth 264; "the consumer republic" 264
coivara 119, 125
Colbert, Jean-Baptiste 31
Cold War 14, 54–55, 57, 165, 170, 187, 190, 195–196, 231, 242, 254, 258, 260, 264–265, 269, 273–277
colonialism 122, 125; Belgian Congo 44; botanical imperialism 8; British Empire 307; bureaucracy 47; cordons sanitaires 11; East India Company 307–308; German East Africa 46–48; interior imperialism, Brazil 180; Portuguese, Amazon 119; settler colonialism 118
Colvin, Brenda 255
Comissão Rondon 118, 120, *121*, 123
commercial trade networks 213
Commission for a Strategic Telegraph Line from Mato Grosso to Amazonas (CLTEMTA) 120
communications: in Afghanistan 13; Afghan Ministry of Telecommunications and internet Technology 71; America's anti-Soviet broadcasting 69; broadcasting infrastructure 70; Central Telegraph Office, Bombay 310; fiber optic lines 59; intercontinental telegraph lines 190; microwave communication system 275, 278; mobile smartphones 73; Radio Afghanistan 69; Radio Kabul 69; radio signals 278; Radio Television Afghanistan 69; telegraph line, Rio Jamarí 120, *121*; telephones 53; television studio in Kabul 69; 2G phones with internet access 63
computational and photogrammetry techniques, development of 252
concrete 38, 40–41, 44, 51–53, 56, 93, 97, 103–105, 145, 148, 160, 172, 176, 199, 203, 213, 216, 253, 278, 310
Congo/Brazzaville cement plants 43
Congo Free State 47
Congrès Internationaux d'Architecture Moderne (CIAM) 194
Constantinople 131. *See also* Valens Aqueduct, Istanbul; map, *Beyan-ı menazil-i sefer-i Irakayn-i Sultan Süleyman 135*; map, Düsseldorf copy 133, *134*; map, *Kitab-ı Bahriye 136*
construction, economies of 250
Continho Caro & Co 43
conurbation 98, *101*
cooling towers 251, 256
Corbo, Stefano 13
cordons sanitaires 11
Costa, Lucio 179, 183
Coucill, Laura 14
Coup d'état, 1930s 80
Cross Bronx Expressway 5
cross-cultural transmission 24
Crowe, Sylvia 247; creation of Wylfa Power Station 247–248, 252–254
Cu-chi Tunnels, Vietnam 56
Cvijić, Jovan 191

da Costa e Silva, Artur 123
da Cunha, Euclides 120
Dadar beach 308
dams: Bhakra Nangal dam 307; Greater Yarmouk project 264; Los Pozuelos Dam 285, *286*; San Renovato Dam 285
Dangote Cement Plc 43
Danish Energy Model 109
Danish infrastructure: Amager Bakke waste-to-energy plant 114–115, *115*; "complex pastoralism" 108; experiential learning 108, 111, 116; The Finger Plan 111; folk schools 108–109, 111; Køge Waterworks *112*, 112–113; and popular education 109–111; recreational opportunities 116; soft infrastructure 108, 111; Sølrogård wastewater treatment 113–114, *114*
Danish infrastructure and popular education 109–111
Darién Gap 234, 242
Davis, Diana K. 261
Davis, Whitney 25
de Asís Cabrero, Francisco 276
de Calonne, Charles-Alexandre 31
de Castro, Luis Vazquez 276
de Castro Neves, Frederico 79
Deewaar [The Wall] (1975) (Hindi film) 306, *314–315*; Bombay/Mumbai waterfronts in 306, 310–311; and docks 312–313; Marine Drive 313–314; narrative 311–312; Versova Beach and Ballard Estate 314–316
DeGolyer Patent Improved Wood Pavement 216
Delano, Frederic 230
de Lequerica, José Félix 271
De Leuw, Cather & Co. of Chicago 171–172
de Mirabeau, Marquis 31
Demirağ, Nuri 168
demographic void 118, 123, 126, 179. *See also* Amazon
de Paula Andrade, Rômulo 180
depersonalization 69
DeSmedt, Edmund J. 217; hot-mix asphalt 217
de Sousa Rios, Kênia 79
Diário da Viagem Filosófica (Diary of a Philosophical Voyage) 119

dictatorship and infrastructure: agricultural colonization 122; domestic resource extraction 121–122; infrastructural links, Amazon 122; the Jari project 124; Operation Amazon 123; the Rodovia Transamazônica 123, *124*; SPVEA 123
Digital Silk Road initiative 73
dispositive 54
dispotif 54
Diwan-e Ayesha 64
Doha, Qatar, political tool of regime legitimization in 198; citizenship 201; controlling Doha 201–203; FIFA World Cup in 2022 206; modern capital 203–205; petroleum state 199–200; politics of growth 200–201; trading hub 198–199
Don (1978) (Hindi film) 311
donkeys 22–23
dot-com boom 70
Douglas fir 217
drought, Brazil: drought industry 76; drought refugees *(flagelados)* 76; droughts in *Nordeste* 77
Duintjer, Marius 145
Dupree, Louis 66
Dupree, Nancy 67
Durán, José Alejandro 286
Durrani, Ayesha 64
Durrani, Timur Shah 64
Dyckerhoff and Widmann 172

East Ghor Canal *259*, 264–265
East India Company 307–308
Eau d'Heure valley, Belgium: Charleroi, speculative plan 98–99, *103*; leisure and vacation sites 99; as pivotal site 98–100; postwar leisure landscape 102–103; postwar reconstruction to *Trente Glorieuses* 100–102
Egyptian granite 25, 27
Egyptian obelisks 20
Egyptian traders 24
Eisenhower, Dwight D. 223, 230, 258–259
electricity 6, 8, 11, 51, 53, 56–57, 93, 102, 108, 111, 114, 155, 199, 247–253, 260, 264–265
The Electricity Act (1957), United Kingdom 248, 251, 253
electricity supply system 250
Electronic News-Gathering units (ENGs) 69
elevators 53
El Kadi, Galila 86
Elliot, Charles 296
Elphinstone, Lord 309
Elphinstone Circle 310
embovedados (vaults) 287
Emdrup junk playground 109–110, *110*, 115
Emirs, Qatari 14
engineers 33; advanced engineering 248, *249*, 253; Architects and Engineers Spanish Bases (AESB) 276; Cleveland Bridge and Engineering Co. 172; U.S. Engineering and Exporting Infrastructure 262–264
Enquiry into Economy in the Construction of Power Stations 250

environmental imaginary 261; Arabian 262
environmentalism: *coivara* 125; deforestation, Amazon basin 125; Fazenda Cristalino fire 125–126; Marx, Burle 124–126; SEMA 126
Eski Kemerler (Old Arches) 136
esplanade or *Maidan* 307–308
Estado Novo recruitment 122, *122*
European *Belle Epoque* 77
excavation 51–53; command and control 54–56; hidden subterranean spaces 53–54; storage and retrieval 56–58; underworld 51–54
expeditions 234, 236–238, 240, 242
experiential learning 108, 111, 116
expert witness 252
exposed brick 277
express streets 227
express-traffic thoroughfares 227
extension-based farming 260

Fairbank, Herbert 230
Fallon Bill 231
Fant, J. Clayton 27
Farmer and Dark Architects 247, 250, 253
Fatih Mosque Complex 132–133, 135–137
fatwa 70
Favro, Diane 26
Fazenda Cristalino fire 125–126
"*fellah*" (farmer) 261, 265–266
female empowerment 64
fermiers (farmers) 32
Ferreira, Alexandre Rodrigues 118–120
Ferro, Sérgio 41
fiber optic lines 59
Ficek, Rosa E. 236
Finger Plan 111
Fink, Dan 109
First Brazilian Republic, 1889 118
Fisher, Carl 225
flagelados 76–77, 80; *sertanejos flagelados* 80
Flaminian obelisks 20
Flora Brasiliensis 119
Flora Fountain 310
folk schools 108–109, 111
Ford, Henry 122
Ford Foundation 265
Fordlândia project 124
"Forest Politics and the Destruction of Forests" 125
formalism 37
Forsyning, Hillerød 113
Fortaleza 76; bourgeoisie 77; concentration camp 80–82; modernizing 78–79; Pirambu Concentration Camp *81*; technological developments 79
Fort George 308
Forty, Adrian 41
Foster & Partners designs 297–298, 300
Foucault, Michel 54
Fourquet, François 53
France-Lanord, Albert 57
Franche-Comté 32–33
Frankfurt Airport 143

Frederic R. Harris, Inc. 276
Freeman, Carla 160
freguês 120
freight train lines 11
functionalist urbanism of the Athens Charter 196
Futurama: Highways and Horizons 223, 226

Galata Bridge 2, *2*
Galmés, Damian 276
Gateway of India 308
Gebel Fatireh 21
Geddes, Norman Bel 223
Gehl, Jan 111, 115
Geisel, Ernesto 123
General Motors 223, 227
Géographie Humaine (Brunhes) 191
German East Africa 46–48
German V-41 broadcasting transmitters 65
Gillem, Mark L. 272
Gillespie, William 213
Gimpo International Airport 143, 149
Giza plateau 24
glass 53
Global UNFCCC 109
Gmelina arborea (gamelina/gamhar) 124
Gold Control Act, India, 1965 311
Golden Gate Bridge 168
Golden Horn 166
González, Robert Alexander 236
Good Neighbors Policy: along "long tough trail" 236–237; and *Automovilistas* 238, 240; enduring imaginaries of travel 240, 242–243; travel as advocacy: *raides,* road races, and automobile caravans 238, 240
Good Roads Movement, United States 223, 225, 235
Goodyear 225
Gottlieb Paludan Architects 112–113
governmental institutions 222
G. Polysius 45–47
Graham, Stephen 10, 53
grain transport 20
granite. *see also specific granites*: durability of 24; from Egypt 24; monoliths 19; movement of 19; solar power and performative infrastructure 25–26; symbolic meaning 19; symbolic power of 24–25
granite Belgian blocks (or setts) 211
Gran Premio de las Americas 238, *239*
gravel 1, 211, 214, 217
Graves, Bibb 230
Great Depression 199–200, 238
Greater Yarmouk project 264
Great Fire, London 52
Great Indian Rebellion 307
great inter-oceanic canals 190
grey granite 21, 27; from Mons Claudianus 19
Grundtvig, N.F.S. 108–109, 111, 113, 115
Guanajuato: arrival of Velázquez 289; *cabildo* (town council) 284, 286, 291–292; dams at 286–287; description 283–284; difficulties in water and food supply 283; epilogue 291–292; hydraulic infrastructures 284–285; La Olla Dam or *Presa Grande* 284–285, *285*; Los Pozuelos Dam 285, *286*; major floods 287–289; masonry *atarjea* (canal) 284; Mexican Insurgency of 1810 291; new generation of local *maestros* 288; "Plano de la ciudad de Guanajuato" 290, *291*; prevention plans 287–288; recurrence of flash floods 284; San Renovato Dam 285; Socavón 290; supply of drinking water 284; topographic map 287, *288*; urbanized areas of Spanish America 283; water infrastructure and urban growth 289–291; water management 287–289; water-related infrastructures 283, 292; water supply 284–287
guerrilla warfar 55
gum wood 216
Guryev, V. P., hexagonal "Guryev Pavement" 215
Gutta purcha 8

haciendas de beneficio (refining mills) 289
Hagia Sophia Mosque 135
Halcón, Fátima 284
Halkalı Channels 132
Hamad International Airport 205
Hamad Medical Corporation 205
Hamidiye Bridge 167
Hammond Map of colonies and lines of communication and travel *8*
ḥarām 93
harbor of Kinshasa 47
harbors. *see also* ports: Ballard Pier 308
Hashemite Kingdom of Jordan 258, 260
Haussmann, Baron George-Eugène 51, 78
Hayes, Carlton J.H. 271
Hebblethwaite, Ronald 252
hedonistic sustainability 114–115
Heinsdijk, Dammis 125
Heliopolis 25
Hellmuth, Obata & Kassabaum (HOK) 203–204
Helper, Hinton Rowan 235; Three-Americas Railway 235
Herbert, John 252
Herbster, Adolfo 78
Hevea brasiliensis 120, 122
high-speed TGV trains 148
highways: Bangalore-Mysore cloverleaf interchange 9; Belt and Road Initiative, Afghanistan 73; BR-364, diagonal interstate highway project 120; congestion and efficiency 223; Cross Bronx Expressway 5; defense and territory 223–226; Federal-Aid Highway Act 1956 230–232; highways linking 179; Interregional Highway Report, 1944 230; Interstate Highway System, United States 222–223; Lincoln Highway 225; Long Island Parkway Motor Parkway 227; metropolitan expansion 226–227; national road system 176–177; Northern Marmara Highway system 174; North Lantau Highway 297; North–South Salang Pass highway 65; Pan-American highway 1, 234–235; Rodovia Transamazônica 123, *124*; superhighways 227; suspension bridge and connecting highway 173; Taguatinga Parkway

185; Toll and Free Roads, 1939 227–230; Trans European Motorway 165; Urban Expressway 232; West Kowloon Highway 297
Hindu Kush 64
Hinton, Christopher 248
historic monuments 256
Hochtief Co. 172
Hoehne, Frederico Carlos 120
Holford, William 252
Holston, James 182
Hong Kong: British colonists 294; Central Reclamation, contention over 300, 302–303; City of Victoria 295–296; collective memory 303, 305; Hong Kong Island 295–296; infrastructure-led "core programme" 297; Kai Tak Airport redevelopment 298–300; Kai Tak master plan and construction. *301*; on Kowloon Peninsula 295–296; land reclamation, ecological and social problems 294; Ocean Park and Disneyland 296; People's Republic of China 296; population in 296; "presumption against reclamation" principle 302; reclamation and urban development 294; transportation infrastructure 302; Victoria Harbor 294, *295*; waterfront architecture, historical evolution 294; West Kowloon Cultural District 297–298
Hong Kong Airport Core Programme 297
Hong Kong International Airport 143–144, 147, 149
Hong Kong Science Park and Cyberport 296
horse-drawn vehicles 212
House of Representatives 231
Hubregtse, Menno 142–151
hybrid landscape: construction, Eau d'Heure dams 103–105; modernism and regional space 98; postwar leisure landscape 102–103; postwar reconstruction to *Trente Glorieuses* 100–102
hydreumata 21
hydro-electric schemes 252
hydrological cycles 6

Ibn Khaldun 198
IDAB. see International Development Advisory Board
Ideal City of Chaux 30
Incheon International Airport, Seoul 143–145, 149, *149*, 150
Indian economy 307
Indian Ocean trade network 9
industrialization 31
Industrial Revolution 31, 53
inequality 5, 27, 176, 192, 253
infrastructure 1. *See also* airport infrastructure; Danish infrastructure; after WWII 272–274; beyond teleological narratives 9; as deeply implicated in spatial inequality and violence 11–12; definition 1–2, 273; design 3, 5; and dictatorship 121–124; as fragmentary and uneven 10–11; as nested in and connecting across scale 11; quality of 10; Spanish 274; as system 9–10
infrastructure in modernist urbanism, circulation machine 14, 187–190, 196; canals and skyscrapers in Antwerp 191–194; politics of infrastructure in

human geography 190–191; railways and highways in Brod 194–196
Ingels, Bjarke 108, 114–115
Institute of Landscape Architects 251–252
intendencias (provinces) 289
intercontinental ballistic missile (ICBM) 54, 277
intercontinental telegraph lines 190
interior imperialism, Brazil 180
international car races 234, 238, 240, 242
International Development Advisory Board (IDAB) 260–261, 265
Interregional Highway Report, United States, 1944 227, 230
Interstate Highway System, United States 222–223
inter-war Antwerp 189
intra-urban thoroughfares, role of 222
Ipi, Faqir 66
iron 36, 51, 53, 123, 167–168, 181, 195, 212
Israel Defensive Forces (IDF) 56
Istanbul: Bosporus Bridge (*see* Bosporus Bridge); Democrat Party (DP) 170; first Master Plan 168; geographical peculiarity 166; Istanbul Airport 143; suspension bridge and connecting highway 173
Istituto per le Opere di Religione (IOR) 57

jack pine 217
Jackson, Kenneth T. 226
Jameson, Fredric 59
Japanese International Cooperation Agency (JICA) 69
Jari project 123–124
Jarrah 216
João VI, Dom 119
Johnston, Eric 260
Jordan River Valley Authority (JVA) 258; displacement and translation 263; Unified Plan 264; water development projects 258
Josephus 21
JSK Architekten *144*, 145
Juhu beach 308
junk playground, Emdrup 109–111, *110*, 115
JVA. *see* Jordan River Valley Authority

Kabul 65; Kabul Polytechnic University 69; Kabul Skoda Works factory 66
Kai Tak Airport redevelopment 298–300
Kandahar 65
Kansai International Airport, Osaka 143–144
Karzai, Hamid 70
Kaspersen, Lars Bo 109
Kennedy, Donald 230
Khalifa, Sheikh 203–204
Khan, Daoud 69
Khan, Emir Amanullah 64
Khan, Muhammad Daoud 68–69
Khan, Sardar Muhammad Daoud 66
kiln of Lukala *45*
King Abdullah Canal 266
King Den's tomb in Abydos 24
Kingdom Tower in Jeddah 51, 53
Kitab-ı Bahriye 136, *136*, 138

Kırkçeşme water system 5
Klar Forsyning utility company 113
Kleis, Brigitte 114
Køge Waterworks *112*; glazed transparency 113; sloped roof 113; water filtration building 112–113
Köprülü map 137
Kowloon Peninsula 295; Kai Tak Airport redevelopment 297–300
Krushchev, Nikita 265
Kuala Lumpur International Airport 147
Kubitschek, Juscelino 177, 179, 180

labor: abolishment of slave labor 76; abuse of migrant Afghan workers in Iran 72; Brazil's large infrastructural projects, labor mobilization 76–77; depersonalization 69; drought refugees *(flagelados)* 76; *flagelados* 76–77, 80; Senegalese and Togolese immigrant laborers 44
Lacis, Asja 156
La Gileppe dam 101
Lallemand, Jean Baptiste 35
landscape architects 247–252, 254–255
Landscape of Industry, The 252
Langhorst, Frederick Lothian 276
Lanks, Herbert 237
Lantau Link, Route 3 297
La Olla Dam or *Presa Grande* 284–285, *285*, 291
Larkin, Brian 154
Larsen, Henning 113–114
Lash, Martha 111
late capitalism 53
Latour, Bruno 6
Le Corbusier 166, 187, 192
Ledoux, Claude-Nicolas 13, 30; approach to infrastructure planning 31–33
left-over spaces 51
leisure. *see* recreation
Lemaire, Raymond 105
Lempert, Michael 153
Libanius of Antioch 131
Lincoln Highway 225
Lispector, Clarice 181
London's Stansted Airport 147
Long Island Parkway Motor Parkway 227
Lons-le-Saunier 35
Lorich, Melchior 138
Los Pozuelos Dam 285, *286*
Lost Paradise 120
Loüe river bridge 32
Louis XIV 31
Louis XVI 31
Lourenço Marques 44
Louv, Richard 111
Loya Jirga 66
Ludwig, Daniel K. 124

macadam: layers of gravel 211; serviceable roadbeds, creation of 213; spread of 214, *215*; tar-macadam 217; water-bound macadam 217
MacArthur, Julie L. 109

MacDonald, Thomas 225, 229–230
Madrid-Barajas Airport 143
Madrid Pact 274; Defense Agreement 274; Economic Aid Agreement 274; Mutual Defense Assistance Agreement 274; Technical Agreement 275–276
MAGNOX program *249*, 250–252
Mahwash, Farida 68
Malabar Hill 306
Mamlūk period, 1250–1570 CE 86
Mamlūks 86
Manners, Ian R. 133
mapping 270–272; computational and photogrammetry techniques, development of 252
marble 20
Marcha para o Oeste (March to the West) 122
March of the Construction of Brasilia *182*
Maria I (Queen of Portugal) 119
Marine Drive 306, 310, 313–314
Marvin, Simon 10
Marx, Leo 108, 181
Marx, Roberto Burle 118, 124–126
Maschinenbau 66
Mass Transit Railway (MTR) 149
materials: adobe bricks 260, *261*, 265; asphalt 217–220; Aswan granite 24–25; blue gum 216; cement in Africa 40–41; coal tar 217; concrete 38, 40–41, 44, 51–53, 56, 93, 97, 103–105, 145, 148, 160, 172, 176, 199, 203, 213, 216, 253, 278, 310; Egyptian granite 25, 27; fiber optic lines 59; glass 53; granite (*see also specific granites*); gum wood 216; hardwoods, New South Wales 216; macadam 211, 213–214, 217; natural asphalt 217–219; oyster shells, use of 211; pine blocks 216; Portland cement 43; red granite from Aswan 19; red gum 216; rock asphalt 217; sheet asphalt 217–218; Swedish softwoods, importation of 216; synthetic asphalt 220; tar-based creosote 217; tar-macadam 217; transport of 20–23; vitrified brick 211, 214; white oak 216; white spruce 217
Mausoleum of Augustus 26
Mayan temples 9
McAdam, John Loudon: "macadamized" pavement technology 214; *Practical Essay on the Scientific Repair and Preservation of Roads* 214; *Remarks on the Present System of Road-Making* 214
Médici, Emílio Garrastazu 118, 123
Mehmed II 132–133
Menderes, Adnan 170
Merian, André 217
Merkel, Angela 150
Metcalf & Eddy 276
Meuse–Rhine delta 100
Meyers, Elizabeth 115
Michelle, Edna 111
microwave communication system 275, 278
migrant crisis 76, 77
migration: abuse of migrant Afghan workers in Iran 72; migration and political order 77–78; migration geography 81; shift to migrant camps in 1915 79; trans-Gulf migration 201

military: B-47 heavy bombers 274; B52 long range bombers 277; British Royal Air Force 271; Fort George 308; intercontinental ballistic missile (ICBM) 54, 277; North Atlantic Organization Treaty (NATO) 273; nuclear attack, threat of 231; planning U.S. Bases in Cold War Spain 274–277; submarine-launched ballistic missile systems 277; Titan I 55; Titan II ICBM *55*; Trench warfare 54; United States Strategic Air Command 274; USAF Strategic Air Command (SAC) 274; U.S. Air Transport Command 271; U.S. Army Map Service 271; U.S. Spanish Bases program 270, 278
mines 51
M+ Museum 298
mobile smartphones 73
mobility-oriented urbanism 179
Mobutu regime 44
modernism: CIAM conference *(Congrès internationaux d'architecture moderne)* 98, 194; and regional space 98
modernist urbanism 170, 306–307, 316; infrastructure in 14, 187–190, 196
modern streetcar 226
Modjeski & Masters 168, 172
Møller, C.F. 113
Mons Claudianus 21, *22–23*
Montecitorio Obelisks 20, 26
Montreux Treaty 168
Moqdishu trading, Cape Town: "Banadir One Coffee" 159; goods 158–159; interior, shop *158*; long operating hours 159; procurement method 159–160; Sara's shop 159
Morales, Lúcia Arrais 80
Mora wood 216
Morlaix Tobacco Factory 31
Moses, Robert 5, 170, 227, 240
Moza, Sheikha 198
Mujahid, Mullah Muhamad Omar 70
murallón (large masonry wall) 290
Muslim tomb in Egypt 86

Nariman Point 306–307, 310, *313*, 314
Nasser, Gamal Abdel 266
Nasuh, Matrakçi 135
National Grid, United Kingdom, introduction of 247, 250
National Integration Program, Brazil, 1970 118
National Parks, United Kingdom 248, 251
nation-building, Amazon: CLTEMTA 120; Comissão Rondon 120–121, *121*; rubber trade 120; telegraph line, Rio Jamarí 120, *121*
NATO. *see* North Atlantic Organization Treaty
natural asphalt: bitumen 217; crude asphalt 219; hot-mix asphalt 217; Pitch Lake deposit 218, *219*; sheet asphalt 217–219; spread of 211–212; Trinidad asphalt 217–218, *218*
Nead, Lynda 52
Near East Foundation (NEF) 265
NEF. *see* Near East Foundation
Nehru, Jawahar Lal 307; classless society, creation of 307; dams as new temples of India 307; secularism 310

Neidhardt, Juraj 187, 194–195
Neto, Paulo Nogueira 126
network archaeology 22
network of shipping lines 190
New Capital (NOVACAP) 181, 182
New Deal 227, 262; agricultural extension services 264; Civilian Conservation Corps 265; "portable knowledge" 262; Tennessee River Valley Authority 258–259
New Towns Act, United Kingdom, 1946 247
The New York Times 291
Nicolson, Samuel 216; Nicolson blocks, development of 216
Niemeyer, Oscar 179
Nigeria cement plants 43
Nile 23–24
Nixon, Richard 265
Noelle-Karimi, Christine 73
Nordenson, Catherine Seavitt 118–127
North Atlantic Organization Treaty (NATO) 273
Northern Marmara Highway system 174
North Lantau Highway 297
North–South Salang Pass highway 65
Notre Dame cathedral 193
nuclear attack, threat of 231
nuclear power stations in post-war Britain: advancements in engineering 248, *249*; changing aesthetics of power generation 248–249; economies of construction 250; economies of organization 251–252; economies of technology 250–251; Wylfa Power Station (case study) 252–254
Nye, David 174, 181, 183

Obata, Gyo 147–148
obelisks: Egyptian 20; Flaminian 20; Montecitorio 20; transport and erection 23; Vatican 23
Okpella/Ukpilla Cement plant *43*
Old Newgate prison in East Granby 54
Old Republic, Brazil 80
Olmsted, Frederick Law 214
OMA 298
Operation Amazon 118, 123
organization, economies of 251–252
Oslo Accords 56
Otlet, Paul 191–193
Ottoman cityscape: the Beylik Water Distribution Map 137; *Kitab-ı Bahriye* 136, *136*, 138; Köprülü map 137; miniature map, Matrakçi Nasuh 135, *135*; Süleymaniye water distribution maps 137, *137*; Valens Aqueduct 135–136; water supply maps 136–137, *137*
oyster shells, use of 211

Packard 225
padaos 314
Pakhtunwali 63
Palacios, Leopoldo Eugenio 284
Panama Canal 237, 240
Pan-American highway 1, 234; Caracas Buenos Aires tourist guide 234, *235*; Fifth Pan-American Conference 235

Pan-Americanism 234–235, 243
pan-Arab movement 266
Panopticon 54
Pantheon in Rome 19, *20*, 26; building 26–27; column shafts 19; Hadrian's design for porch 27; porch *20, 27*
Parcell, Stephen 4
Paris Agreement, 2015 109, 126
Paris Exhibition,1867 167
Paris Peace Conference 191
Parkpolitik I Sogn og Købstad (Park Policy in Parish and Market Town) 109
Pashtuns 66; code of conduct 63; guerrilla movement 66; society 63
Paul National Wood Paving 216
pavements: cut stone pavements 211; hexagonal "Guryev Pavement" 215; macadam 211, 213–214, 217; Nicolson blocks, development of 216; pine blocks 216; plank roads 215
Pedro I 119
Pedro II 120
Penck, Albrecht 190
People's Republic of China 296
Pereira and Luckman 276
Perronet, Jean-Rodolphe 32
Pershing, John 225; "Pershing Map" 225, *226*
Persian Gulf 308
Petroleum Development Qatar (PDQ) 199
Pharaonic mining 21
pharaonic unification 25
Phenomenal urban development 174
Philipp Holzmann AG 43
photographs 181
piers. *see* ports
Piglia, Melina 240
pine blocks 216
Pinus caribaea (Caribbean pine) 124
Pionen White Mountain 57
Plan de la Saline de Chaux 35
plan for Paris, 1853 78
planimetry 272
plank roads 215; "plank road boom" 215; spread of 211
plantation schemes 184
Plan Vert (green plan) 102
Plate-Taille lake *99*, 102, *104*, 105
playground movement 109
Pleiss, Paul 237
Pliny 23
Point Four program in Jordan 265; *Community Development Programs* 265; extension-based farming 260; PL480 grant 260, *261*, 265; Unified Plan 259; water development projects 258; water management 259
Political Agent (PA) 199
politics of infrastructure in human geography 190–191
Pongwe 46
pontos de trem 81
porous infrastructures. *See also* Somali malls: Bellville 154–156; Moqdishu trading 158–160; Som City 156–158

Portico access, Arc-et-Senans *saline 36*
Portland cement 43
ports: Bombay Port Trust 308; and docks 312–313; harbor of Kinshasa 47; To Lo Harbor 296; Rhenish port 194; Sassoon Dock 308; Thonis, Late Dynastic Port of 9; Victoria Harbor 294, *295*
Portuguese, Amazon 119
postwar leisure landscape 102–103
power generation: aesthetics of 247–249; nuclear program 256
power stations: Battersea Power Station 250; cooling towers 251, 256; MAGNOX program *249*, 250–252; Scott, Gilbert, treatment of Battersea Power Station 250; Wylfa Power Station 253–255
Premier Portland Cement Company, Bulawayo 46
Primeval Hill 25
"primitive technologies" 237
Prince's Dock 308
prison-mines 54
Pritzker, Jay 3
private automobile, adoption of 226
private capital 222
Program Acts, Belgium, 1955 100
Project Casey Jones 271
Prost, Henri 167
Ptolemaic mines and quarries 21
public-private-partnership 47
Purcell, Charles 230
purdah 66–67
purpose-built kitchen 88
pyramids 255

"*qaraweyoun*" or villagers 265
Qatari 201
Qatari heritage 206
Qatari population 205
Qatar's tribal system 198
Qing dynasty 213; reign of Emperor Jiaqing 213
quarries 19, 21, 99
Quddous, Ihsan Abdel 93
Queen's Necklace. *see* Marine Drive
Queen's Pier 302–303
Quesnay, François 31–32

racing. *see also* Automóvil Club Argentino (ACA): Caracas–Buenos Aires race 238, 240, *241*; *Gran Premio de las Américas* 238; international car races 234, 238, 240, 242; road races 238, 240, *241*; sports-car races 238; trans-continental automobile races 242
radar pulses 278
Radiant City model 192
Radio Afghanistan 69
Radio Kabul 69
radio signals 278
Radio Television Afghanistan 69
raides 238
rail: Airport Express railway line 297; Canton-Kowloon railway 296; freight train lines 11; high-speed TGV trains 148; Mass Transit Railway

(MTR) 149; modern streetcar 226; railways and highways in Brod 194–196; train station at Campo do Patu *82*; transcontinental railroads 190; Victoria Terminus, Mumbai 310
Rassmussen, Sten Eiler 111
Ratebzad, Anahita 69
Ratzel, Fridrich 190
Reclus, Élisée 190
recreation: recreational opportunities, Danish infrastructure 116; Snowdonia National Park 252; Tamar Park 302–303
red granite from Aswan 19
red gum 216
red pine. *see* "redwood (Pinus sylvestris)"
Red Sea 308
"redwood (Pinus sylvestris)" 216
"refeminization" of women 264
refugees from the droughts in Ceará State 76, *78*
Regional Plan for New York, 1929 230
Regional Planning Agency, Turkey 171
Reis, Thomaz 120
Repton, Humphry 248, 256
Rheinhausen, Friedrich Krupp 43
Rhenish port 194
Riaño, Juan Antonio 289–290
Richardson, Sullivan C. 236
Riquetti, Victor 31
roads: Belt and Road Initiative, Afghanistan 73; Brasilia, road construction 176–177; express streets 227; express-traffic thoroughfares 227; intra-urban thoroughfares, role of 222; Marine Drive 306, 310, 313–314; Roman roads 7; Toll and Free Roads, 1939 227–230
Rocco Design 298
rock asphalt 217; Seyssel deposit 217; Val de Travers deposit 217
Rodenbeck, Max 86
Rodovia Transamazônica 123, *124*
Roman roads 7
Rondon, Cândido Mariano da Silva 118, 120
Roosevelt, Franklin Delano 236, 262, 269; Interregional Highway Report 230; "Roosevelt Map" 227, *228*; Work Projects Administration 223
Rose, Mark 231
"Rose Garden Plan" 297
rose granite columns 19
Rossellino, Bernardo 56
Rostow, Walter 2
Rota Naval Station, 1960 277, *277*
Royal Institute of British Architects 251
Royal Museum of Ajuda, Portugal 119
Royal Museum of Natural History, Lisbon 119
Royal Ordinances of Intendancies, 1786 290
Royal *Saline* at Arc-et-Senans 30, 33; director's house and the chapel *38*; early industrialization and impact in architecture 31; introduction 30–31; Ledoux's approach to physiocracy 32; materialized urban project 34–36; physiocracy 31–32; water and progress 33; water and salt in Ledoux's route 33–34; wellbeing and control 36–37

rubber-tired automobiles 220
Rumeli Hisarı 168
"rural" typology 265

Saarinen, Eero 144
SAC. *see* USAF Strategic Air Command
Said, Edward 153
Salines de Salins 33
Salins-les-Bains 33–34, *34*
Salvatore, Ricardo 237
San Francisco–Oakland Bay Bridge 168
San Renovato Dam 285
Sassoon Dock 308
Sauer, Wolfgang 125
Saur Revolution, Soviet involvement in 69
Sayão, Bernardo 183
Scheldt–Rhine Treaty, 1963 100
Schiphol Airport 143, 145, 147
Schröder, Gerhard 150
Schwarzer, Mitchell 108
Scotch pine. *see* "redwood (Pinus sylvestris)"
Scott, Gilbert, treatment of Battersea Power Station 250
Second Schleswig War 109
Secretariat building 310
secularism 306–307, 310, 313, 316
sed festival 25
şehnames 135
Senegalese and Togolese immigrant laborers 44
Sennett, Richard 165
Serres, Michel 1
sertanejos (rural, back country people) 76–77, 80
settler colonialism 118
Shaan [Prestige] (1980) (Hindi film) 311
Shah, Muhammad Nadir 64, 66
Shaw, Metz & Dolio 276
sheet asphalt 217–218
Shepheard, Michael 252
Sherman, Forrest P. 273
Siemens Technologies 66
Silk Road 5
Simone, AbdouMaliq 11, 156, 160
Simonnet, Cyrille 41
Sinan, Mimar 5, 138
Sinoma International 43
Sisson, Jamie Huff 111
Slavonski Brod 187, *189*
Smith, Neil 271
Snowdonia National Park 252
Socavón 290
social control 54
socialism 306–307, 311, 316
Socialist Yugoslav government 187
Société des Ciments du Congo (CICO) 44
socio-technical systems 2, 25, 191; conditions 75; objects 28; relations 69
Søderman, Peter W. 58
soft infrastructure 108, 111
solar power and performative infrastructure 25–26
Solar worship 25

Sølrogård climate and energy park, Hillerød 114; future plans 113; recycling facility 113; wastewater treatment plant 113–114
Somali malls 153–154; Bellville 154–156; Eastleigh 158; Moqdishu trading 158–160; Som City 156–158
Sørensen, C.T. 108–113, 115–116
sovereignty 118
Spain: cartographic domination 269; mapping Spain 270–272; negotiating power, infrastructure after WWII 272–274; *Pactos de Madrid* 270; planning U.S. Bases in Cold War Spain 274–277; topographic map 271, *272*; Torrejón AFB in construction 275, *276*; Torrejón de Ardoz landscape 270, *270*; U.S. Spanish Bases program 270
Special Secretary for the Environment (SEMA) 126
Spence, Basil 252
Spirn, Anne Whiston 112, 115
Spry, James W. 274
Stafford Pavement 216
Standard Oil 227
Star Ferry Pier, Hong Kong 302
Starosielski, Nicole 22
steel 53
Steinmann, David B. 171–172
St. George, Katharine 269
stone: granite (*see also specific granites*); gravel 1, 211, 214, 217; marble 20
Stoner, Jill 90
Støvring, Søren 113
Stow's Foundation Pavement 216
street pavement materials and technology, spread of: cobblestones 213; macadam 213–214; natural asphalt 217–219; pavement types *212*; plank roads 215; wood blocks 215–217
Subías, Tiburcio Manuel 284
submarine-launched ballistic missile systems 277
Suez Canal 308
Suffrin, Sidney C. 274
Sufis 86
Süleyman I' 135
Süleymaniye water supply map 137, *137*
Sultan Mustafa 139
Sun god 25
Sunni Islam 198
superhighways 227
Superintendência do Plano de Valorizaçao Econômica da Amazônia (SPVEA) 123
surveillance 11, 37, 52, 54, 73; computational and photogrammetry techniques, development of 252
surveying 271
suspension bridge 165
Svalbard Global Seed Vault 58
Swahili coast 308
Swedish softwoods, importation of 216
symbolism 37
synthetic asphalt 220

Tableau Économique 32
Taguatinga Parkway *185*
Tai Po Industrial Park 296
Tajik communities 64
Taliban 70–71. *see also* Afghanistan
tallow wood 216
Tamar Park 302–303, *304*
Tangshan Earthquake of 1976 9
Taraki, Nur Muhammad 69
tar-based creosote 217
tar-macadam 217
Teamsters Union 231
Technical Agreement 275–276. *see also* Madrid Pact
technology, economies of 250–251
telecommunications infrastructure in Afghanistan 63–64; accelerated connection, 1939–1978 66–69; cell-phone towers 70–73; cellular data coverage *71*; internet 70; between Kandahar and Kabul 67, *68*; socialist connection, 1978–1987 69; strategic connection, 1912–1940 64–66; strategic disconnection, 1989–2001 69–70
Telefunken 65–66
telephones 53
television studio in Kabul 69
Telford, Thomas 213
temples 255; architecture 25; dams as new temples of India 307; Mayan temples 9; Temple of Trajan 23
Tennessee Valley Authority (TVA) 5; changing U.S. Tactics 266; constructing "Third World" 260–262; in desert 258; of environments and homes 264–266; exporting domesticity 264–266; in Jordan 258; rising Arab Sentiments 266; U.S. Engineering and Exporting Infrastructure 262–264
Termite hill lime kiln *48*
Terrible Years, Northeast Brazil 76
Thames Embankment project 51–52
Themistius 131, 139
Third Reich 66
"Third World": construction of 260–262, *262*; "Dear Farmer" Poster 261, *263*
Thonis, Late Dynastic Port of 9
Thracian Water Network 131–132, 139
Tiananmen Square Massacre 297
Titan I 55
Titan II ICBM *55*
To Lo Harbor 296
Toll and Free Roads, 1939 227–230
Tonkiss, Fran 7, 11
Torrione of Niccolò V 56
"tourism of destination" 242
Town and Country Planning Act, United Kingdom, 1947 252
Town Planning Institute 251
trade networks 211, 213, 216, 308
train station at Campo do Patu *82*
Trajan 27
Transacreana 120
Transcontinental Motor Convoy, 1919 223, 225, *225*, 230
transcontinental railroads 190
Trans European Motorway 165
trans-Gulf migration 201
transportation utopia 237, 242

travel: as advocacy 238, 240; automobile caravans 238, 240; enduring imaginaries of 240, 242–243; Good Neighbor Policy 240, 242; Good Roads movement 235; narratives 236–237, 240; Pan-American Highway system 234–235, 242; *raides* 238; road races 238, 240; "tourism of destination" 242
Trawsfynydd Power Station 252, *253*
Trench warfare 54
Trente Glorieuses 100–102
Trésaguet, Pierre-Marie-Jérôme 213; National Road, America 214
Trouard, Louis-François 30
Trucial Agreement 200
Trudaine de Montigny, Charles Philibert 32
Truman, Harry S. 258–260
Trump, Donald 206
Tsim Sha Tsui waterfront 297
Tugwell, Rexford 230
tunnels 54–56, 58–59, 166, 192, 234, 289–290, 303; Cu-chi Tunnels, Vietnam 56; West Cross Harbor Tunnel 297
Turgot, Anne Robert Jacques 31
Turismo Carretera 238
Turkish Chamber of Architects and Planners, 174
Turkmen Communist Party 69
turnkey contracts 250
TVA. *see* Tennessee Valley Authority
Tychaion 26

udeskole (outdoor classroom) 109
UKAEA. *see* United Kingdom Atomic Energy Authority
Ulloa, Antonio de 284
Underworld 53
UNDP. *see* United Nations Development Programme (UNDP)
UNICEF 261
"Unified Development of the Water Resources of the Jordan Valley Region" (Unified Plan) 258–259, 264, 266
Uniroyal 227
Unitede Kingdom Ministry of Fuel and Power 251
United Kingdom Atomic Energy Authority (UKAEA) *249*, 250
United Nations Development Programme (UNDP) 266
United Nations Framework Convention on Climate Change 126
United Nations Relief and Works Agency for Palestine Refugees in the Near East (UNRWA) 264
United States Agency for International Development (USAID) 266
United States Federal-Aid Highway Act: 1921 225; 1938 227; 1944 227, 230; 1956 222, 227, 230–232
United States Federal Aid Road Act 1916 225
United States Office of Road Inquiry 224
United States Strategic Air Command 274
University Library and Convocation Hall 310
urban agglomeration 98

Urban Expressway 232
urban infrastructures 51
urbanization 31, 98, 177–179, 181, 192, 194–195; of left bank of the scheldt in Antwerp *188*
"the urban," notion of 222, 226, 232
Ureña, Felipe de 284
Urrutia, Anastasio Miguel 285
USAF Strategic Air Command (SAC) 274
USAID. *see* United States Agency for International Development
U.S. Air Transport Command 271
U.S. Army Map Service 271
U.S. bases: in Cold War Spain 274–277; distribution of 274, *275*; U.S. Spanish Bases program 270, 278
U.S. cultural model 263
USDA. *see* U.S. Department of Agriculture
U.S. Department of Agriculture (USDA) 264
U.S. Spanish Bases program 270, 278
Ustadh 68

Valens Aqueduct, Istanbul 1, 13, *132*; Constantinopolitan life, role in 139; in early-modern depictions 133; environs 132; inclusion, Düsseldorf version 133, *134*; *Kitab-ı Bahriye* 136, *136*; as lasting edifice 138–139; Ottoman cityscape 135–138; water distribution 131–132
Vanaudenhove, Omer 100
Vanderbilt, William K., Long Island Parkway Motor Parkway 227
Vargas, Getúlio 80, 121–123, 180
Vatican obelisks 23
Vaux, Calvert 214
Velázquez de León, Joaquín 289
Venice Architecture Biennale 53
ventilation systems 53
Versova beach 306, 308, 314–316
vestries 216
Victoria Dock, Mumbai 308
Victoria Embankment, London 52
Victoria Harbor, Hong Kong 294, *295*, 300
Victoria Terminus, Mumbai 310
Vidal de la Blache, Paul 190–191
violence against the Shi'ite Hazara community 72
virtual forum for women 63
virtual media spaces 63
vitrified brick 211, 214
Vitruvius 20
Voice of Sharia 70
von Humboldt, Alexander 119, 125
von Martius, Carl Friedrich Phillip 119–120, 125
Von Ruppert, Carl 167
von Spix, Johann Baptist 119
Voortrekker Road City Improvement District (VRCID) 155
Vue perspective de la Ville de Chaux 37

Wagner, Martin 167
Waring, George 219
wastewater treatment plant, Sølrogård climate and energy park 113–114, *114*

water and waste management 5
water-bound macadam 217
water distribution maps: the Beylik Water Distribution Map 137; Köprülü map 137; Süleymaniye maps 137, *137*
Weizman, Eyal 55
West Cross Harbor Tunnel 297
West Ghor Canal 264
West Kowloon Cultural District 297–298, *300*, 303
West Kowloon Highway 297
West Kowloon reclamation area 297, *299*
Whitaker, Arthur 236
white oak 216
white spruce 217
Whitten, David O. 217
Willink, Harry 219
Wittet, George 308
women's mobility and freedom 63
wood blocks: hardwoods, New South Wales 216; hexagonal "Guryev Pavement" 215; in London 216; mercuric chloride 217; Nicolson blocks, development of 216; "redwood (Pinus sylvestris)" 216; softwoods, Swedish 216; spread of 211–212; tar-based creosote 217; vestries 216
World Bank 266, 271
World War II 230–231, 248, 250
Wylfa Power Station (case study) *255*; 1962 *Wylfa Landscape Report* 253; advanced engineering 253; reactors and steam generators 253; sketches of 253–254, *254*; vantage points 253, *254*

Xiqu (Chinese Opera) Center 298
Xochimilco in Mexico City 4, *4*, 12

Yugoslavia 194

zangarros (small metalworking factories) 289
Zayo Group Holdings 59
Zeiger, Dinah 73
"zero reclamation" scheme 299
Zerrato, Juan Esteban 284
Zhang Lin'an 213
ZTE 73
Zurich 198